Better Homes and Gardens
STEP·BY·STEP
Landscaping

Houghton Mifflin Harcourt
Boston   New York

INTRODUCTION

Do-it-yourself landscaping is not only possible, but also pleasurable, when you use *Step-by-Step Landscaping* as your guide. To make the book easy to use, we've focused each chapter on a common landscaping problem or area of the yard. Once you've determined your yard's need—which isn't hard, if you're the typical homeowner—simply look up the chapter that addresses that need. There you'll find text, illustrations, and photographs that compare and contrast various solutions, then show you in detail how to accomplish them. This handy organization, along with the book's 1,200 gorgeous and informative photographs, makes *Step-by-Step Landscaping* essential for every homeowner who wants to create a more beautiful and livable yard.

CONTENTS

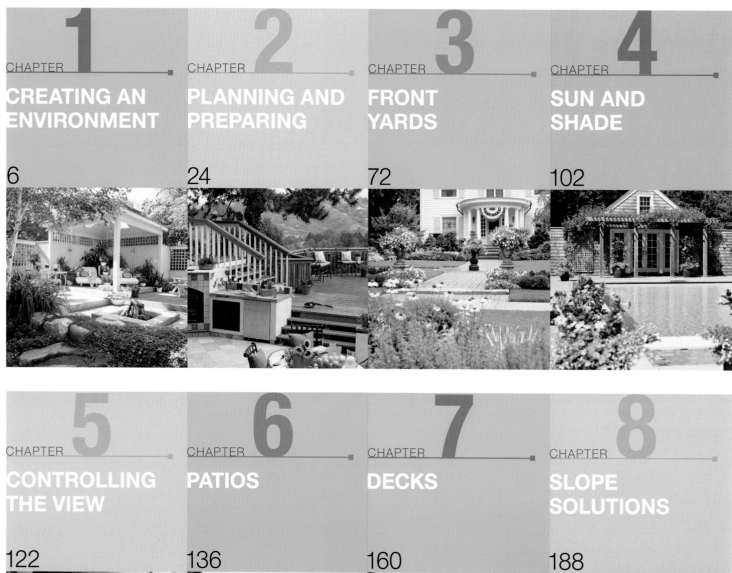

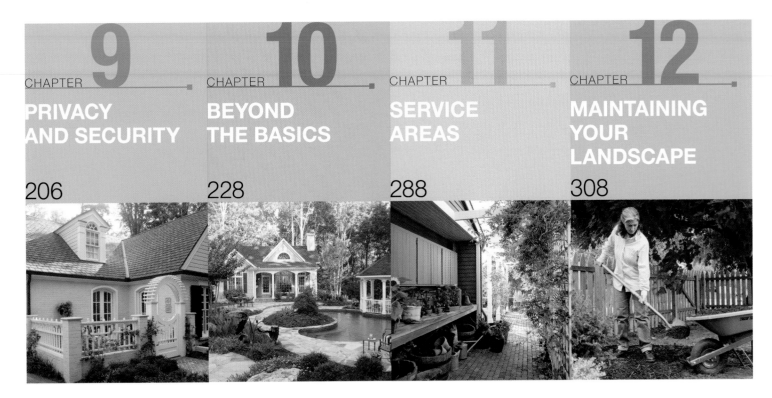

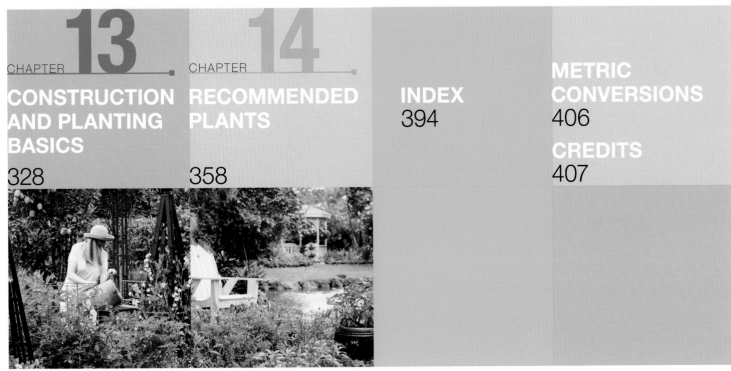

1

CREATING AN ENVIRONMENT

You are in control here. Whether you're completely redoing your front yard or turning the area behind your home into a kids' paradise, careful planning helps you landscape your way to a new world.

In that world, you're able to decree where the sun shines, shadows fall, and breezes blow. Your personal utopia can offer the openness of a park, the seclusion of a woodland, or the flavor of a foreign land.

You may want to begin with the backyard, as shown here. Let this special space set the mood for your time in the yard, offering a secluded place to relax with family and friends or on your own. Start by aiming for a landscaping scheme that complements the architecture of your home.

This setting proves it's possible to turn a small suburban backyard into a private oasis that serves multiple functions, whether you want to entertain a crowd, enjoy some solitary quiet time, or hang out with the family.

With its ceiling fan, soft futons, and privacy fence, the gazebo-sheltered getaway zone makes room for relaxing with family and friends. The skylight allows for stargazing.

For convenience, when this outdoor living area was created, concrete was poured for the fire pit and the gazebo's footings at the same time.

FRONT YARDS

Curb appeal ... curb appeal. How many times are you reminded how important that first impression is? It certainly underscores the value of designing an inviting landscape out front for everyone to enjoy. And that should include your own family. When you return home from a long day, you want to be greeted by an eyecatching landscape that beckons to you and fills you with pride.

Match landscaping and architecture

If your home has formal lines, so should your landscaping—with such features as symmetrical planting areas, square or rectangular layouts, straight walkways, traditional fencing and gates, and a manicured look throughout. On the other hand, informal architecture calls for curved walkways, greater use of rock and weathered wood, and a variety of other rustic touches. Regardless of the exterior styling of your home, you're free to add features of interest; simply make sure their designs complement the lines of your

home. And as your tastes evolve through the years, your design treatments may evolve as well. Keep this in mind as you plan the first stage of the process.

Stretch your imagination

There's no unwritten rule requiring all front yards to consist of a walkway, some grass, and maybe a few shrubs or flowers. On the other hand, you may have to deal with overbearing and outdated building codes or restrictive neighborhood covenants, so be sure to check them out before proceeding. But if the coast is relatively clear, jump out of the box as quickly as you can and plan some features that not only will breathe new life into your front yard, but will also add some excitement and fun for your family.

Consider, for example, building an intimate seating area, shielded from the street and neighbors by vine-covered trellises. Then find a spot near it for a small pond surrounded with ornamental grasses. Or create a series of small floral attractions connected by stylish passageways. You also may want to consider buying or building your own yard art to add even more personality. Or make a big change with a ground-hugging deck or patio. And if your front yard is the only sunny location on your property, why not incorporate a well-maintained vegetable or flower garden? There's no reason that your front yard can't be as functional, attractive, and pleasurable as your backyard.

Make a good circulation plan

Give serious thought to the subject of foot traffic. Once you've created clear and direct avenues between your entry and the driveway and sidewalk, expand your plan to include all secondary travel—walkways to take you and others to those special attractions you want to add, as well as help direct visitors to the side or rear yards. Then make sure all paths are well illuminated at night.

For more detailed information and examples of successful front yard transformations, see Chapter 3, "Front Yards," pages 72–101.

The semiformal design of a square front yard gains balance and strength from its focal points: neat bluestone edging, a centralized bed of roses, and a sheltered seating area.

Gracefully flowing between beds of groundcovers and shrubs, a flagstone walkway helps create a welcoming entrance to this cottage-style home. A purple and white planting scheme adds subtle charm.

BACKYARDS

Unless you choose to use tall plantings and fencing to close in the space between the curb and your home's entry, your front yard typically will be fairly public. But your backyard can be much more personal and private. The idea of the backyard as a place to play and to discover ever-changing wonders and terrific new hiding places does not have to pass with childhood. Instead the enchantment of the backyard should intensify with time.

It's your backyard

Each family's lifestyle, needs, and preferences will influence how a backyard is used. One family may want formal beds of show-quality roses; another, abundant fruits and vegetables. Some families design for a woodland or desert or Asian atmosphere, for the easiest possible maintenance or for constant experimenting and puttering. Others need sandboxes and room for riding toys, or want pools or hammocks.

Even the smallest backyard can become an additional and special outdoor living room during warm days and a peaceful place to view year-round. Add a birdbath and feeding area to serve as a focal point while attracting the garden's best helpers.

Plan first

However you will use your backyard, start with a plan. For every backyard need or problem, several landscaping possibilities exist to increase beauty, use, and enjoyment, as well as boost property value. By making a list of what you want in your backyard, you start with objectives that will help you achieve your goal with a minimum of time, expense, and work. Without such guidelines, you can work forever and are likely to make more mistakes than improvements.

Keep in mind, though, that a backyard is for living, and your needs—and plans—will change as years go by. Sandboxes can give way to basketball courts as children grow. And gardens can revert to lawn or to trees with mulch beneath as times, growth, and interests change.

Allow access

No matter what evolutionary stage your plan is in, allow for easy access between its separate outdoor living areas. You won't use spots that are hard to get to, so include paths to assist the walking and enhance the mystery of each area. And if you anticipate larger projects that will require heavy equipment, be sure to reserve enough space to reach the site with that equipment.

A well-designed patio in a tight space offers plenty of room for outdoor entertaining. The flooring— aggregate paving with brick inserts—gives the area the look and feel of a finished room.

Compact and airy, a backyard gazebo provides an ideal place to rest between gardening chores. As an architectural element, it contrasts with the cutting garden and the evergreen backdrop.

PATIOS

Patios—in the form of courtyards—go back thousands of years to the gardens of ancient Egypt. When lawn mowers came along, yards went largely to grass. But patios, roofed or not, provide a cleaner, drier, and lower-maintenance area for sitting and walking. Patios also make better use of space and resources than do unbroken lawns.

In the front yard a patio can be an extension of the driveway or the open area around the entrance. It can help direct traffic from the sidewalk to the door without muddying feet, or it can serve as a spot for sitting.

A patio can turn wasted space along the side of a house into additional outdoor living space, or it can designate an area of the backyard for outdoor cooking, eating, sunning, reading, playing, or resting.

In any area of the yard, a patio makes an outstanding focal point. It can also help keep garden areas condensed and unified. In a large yard, lawn usually lies beyond. But in a small yard, a patio and its surrounding plantings can eliminate the need for a mower altogether.

Location influences

Privacy, protection from the sun and wind, and access to the kitchen and family room are all important influences when determining your patio's location. You may want more than one patio for a choice of settings: shady or sun-warmed, secluded or convenient, small for intimacy or large for entertaining.

Because a patio is a substantial and permanent home improvement, check local building codes and zoning ordinances first. Then plan the location and design on paper before beginning construction.

The shape, size, and material of your patio should complement the house and the garden style. And your plan should include working around existing trees and beneath their limbs for immediate shade. Design surrounding plantings to provide interest in every season—color, fragrance, form, and texture—while adding shade and seclusion. Choose plants that will stay in proportion nicely without constant pruning.

For help in selecting patio surfaces and plantings, and for detailed building instructions, see Chapter 6, "Patios," pages 136–159.

Stamped and stained concrete pads create a patio walkway with the look of stone at a fraction of its cost. The walkway is set at ground level and allows for mowing around and between the pads.

Spacious concrete squares cut into the lawn form an even path to the patio and ensure smooth footing.

Concrete is also used for the entryway and the patio, echoing the tone of nearby pillars, fireplace, and walls.

DECKS

The porches and verandas of our past have given way to the wooden deck. As links between the home and the garden, decks combine the comfort and low maintenance of the indoors with the openness of nature more subtly and completely than was possible with porches and verandas. Often decks continue the level of indoor rooms, permitting easier access to the outside than patios do, an especially important point to the very young or old, or those carrying food and drinks.

A well-built deck sheds rain efficiently, and they lend a whole new point of view to both a yard and its surroundings. You can enclose them with tall attachments such as screens or trellises, or open them to the scenery beyond with low railings.

Bring decks alive, too, with containers of flowers or vegetables. Plants in containers need more frequent watering than those in the ground, but the advantages of having beauty nearby far outweigh any hassle.

Where a slope presents problems, a deck offers solutions. A multilevel deck can follow the landscape's contours and provide spectacular views. Decks also can be built around existing trees. Where shade is lacking, plant a potentially large tree nearby, or build a shade structure such as a pergola over the deck.

Steps, edges, built-in benches, and wide-sided raised planters can provide seating for a crowd or sit-down gardening.

But decks need not be complex. You can build a deck so simple that it can be dismantled for winter or moved from the sunniest spot for spring and fall to the shady east side of the house for relief from the summer sun.

It's important to establish visual harmony between a new deck and an existing house. Compatibility should include the size and shape of the house, the types of materials used in the deck, and the scale and placement of stairs, railings, arbors, screens, and other elements. The best designs integrate key features with the size of the yard and existing plantings.

Since most decks are permanent structures, check building codes first. Also be careful to provide safe railings. (See Chapter 7, "Decks," pages 160–187.)

There's room for a relaxing getaway zone in even the smallest of yards. This raised deck features a built-in spa, planter, and benches as well as a privacy fence.

This wraparound deck provides an easygoing transition between house and garden. It includes a step-up lounge, partly shaded by a pergola and vines, as well as places for container plantings.

OUTDOOR ROOMS

You and your neighbors likely share the same desire: to feel a sense of excitement and anticipation when you step into your private world outdoors. This thrill doesn't come easily, but it doesn't have to drive you into debt either. The key is plenty of careful planning. You and your family will be spending endless hours gathered around sketch pads, tracing paper, and lot plans. You'll be designing and redesigning. It's important to write down every idea that comes up.

As you plan each square foot, think of your surroundings as a series of rooms, based somewhat on your indoor spaces. For example you might want to plan individual places to entertain, participate in a hobby, dine, play, and relax. Of course much depends on the size of your lot. If it's smallish, you may be limited to, say, a kids' play area and maybe a sunken barbecue pit. On the other hand, a large lot gives you the opportunity to build and create until your money, time, or muscles give out.

• Start with the entry. Why not make it as gorgeous and inviting as the entry to your home? Begin with a splash of color, a stylish walkway, maybe a gate, and possibly an archway. Then lay out a system of pathways that lead to the main rooms.

• Play spaces for the kids, of course, are necessarily age-related. Sandboxes lead to play structures that lead to a basketball hoop that leads to a skateboard facility that leads to a volleyball court, etc. Consider reserving a general area just for the young ones and their friends.

• Entertainment areas can be as fancy as a pavilion or courtyard, or as simple as a seating unit on a small patio or deck. Tall plantings, lattice dividers, or other types of screening devices help separate you and your guests from the rest of the landscape. And if the budget stretches far enough, a spa or pond adds extra fun.

• Some families prefer to include a dining spot within their entertainment areas, while others opt for a separate location.

• Is there an outdoor hobby more popular than gardening? If anyone in the family is an avid dig-in-the-dirt kind of person, by all means make room for a potting shed and enough storage for garden tools and equipment. And, of course, stake out some sunny planting areas for vegetables and flowers.

• A special room for relaxation needs privacy, so try to reserve the most isolated location for it. Plan some type of shade structure, as well as a wind barricade, if needed. Add a hammock and maybe a relaxing fountain or soothing waterfall to mask any ambient noise pollution. If you have any self-indulgence in you, this is the place to satisfy it.

Don't let a steeply sloping lot get you down. Terraces not only overcome that problem but also do an attractive job of separating one area from the next. If you expect a lot of foot traffic, plan steps and pathways carefully to avoid accidents.

One remaining thought: Think ahead. Because interests and tastes may change over the years, try to keep the design of your outdoor home flexible enough that you can make future alterations without endangering your pocketbook or sanity.

Built into a garage wall, this French-inspired fireplace provides the backdrop for relaxed outdoor living. An arched trellis frames a built-in banquette and caps a corner made for intimate gatherings.

An outdoor kitchen, comfortable seating, a stereo system, and a cozy fireplace make this 27×25-foot deck perfect for socializing with friends or hanging out with the kids.

OUTDOOR LIVING

In a classic novel or movie, pulses quicken the moment the gentleman says, "Let's go out for a breath of air." After all, even the largest and most elegant house is but a prelude to the appeal of the simplest garden by moonlight. Yet, this "simple garden" can be much more than an intimate entertainment area for fancy parties or family cookouts. The challenge for you is to design your landscape so all of your outdoor rooms will blend together in a tasteful setting that charms visitors and family alike. As you work on your layout, here are some guidelines to help you get the most living possible from your new outdoor world:

• Privacy for parties and consideration for neighbors are critical. Shrubs will not block all noise or light but will help considerably.

An outdoor kitchen and dining area, reminiscent of an old Mediterranean cafe, reflect the character of the house and extend its living space. The custom fireplace adds to the room's livability.

• For large gatherings, a well-thought-out garden plan becomes vital. Allow for open places, then strategically place some refreshments in those areas to encourage people to spread out and mingle.

• If much of your entertaining is at night, plan your gardens with plenty of white blooms for a shimmering setting. Fragrance intensifies at nightfall too.

• Locate your rest-and-relaxation rooms as far as possible from the entertainment rooms and kids' playrooms. Frame areas with noise-abatement devices, such as dense shrubs and screening covered with vines. To maximize privacy surround the space with a wall or fence. And if the budget permits, consider a flowing water feature of some kind.

• In your quest to create privacy, remember that you also are supplying a topnotch hiding place for an itinerant thief. However, some well-placed motion-sensor lights should send potential burglars packing.

• Avoid planting trees or flowers where children will want to play or people might gather for sports such as volleyball. Also making outdoor rooms such as patios or decks too large is a common mistake. They need to be small enough for ease of maintenance and a feeling of intimacy.

• In general, garden lighting adds both safety and atmosphere. For constant use, consider permanent lights in strategic places or a series of lamps along the footpath. For decorative and romantic effects, string up twinkle lights or lanterns, or stake torches.

• A fire pit or space heater will warm your garden on cool evenings to stretch both spring and fall use. On the hottest days, overhead fans make porches more enjoyable.

• Don't give up on land that appears too steep to be of any value. Visualize cutting into the slope, retaining the soil with an attractive wall, then building an intimate patio in your newly claimed space.

An outdoor kitchen and eating area can expand your dining options. This brick-floor back porch includes complete kitchen facilities (sink, grill, refrigerator, and storage) and ample room to sit back and enjoy the view.

SWIMMING POOLS

Nothing provides more fun or a more dramatic focal point in a yard than a swimming pool. On the other hand, nothing is more expensive to install and maintain—or more potentially dangerous. Careful planning is vital. Begin with the counsel of professionals and knowledge of legal regulations.

If you value relaxation and conversation more than exercise, consider a spa or hot tub. It requires less space and costs less than a swimming pool. Easier to seclude, a spa also offers a longer season of use.

Whether you prefer a pool or spa, also consider design features for the surrounding deck, which should be nonskid, well drained, fenced, and planted for privacy and attractiveness. If your plan calls for a pool in the future, leave access now for the heavy equipment to come.

Choose the site, size, and materials for your pool keeping in mind sun and wind patterns as well as access to bathrooms and changing rooms. Avoid siting a pool or spa under deciduous trees that drop their leaves annually. Select poolside plantings that can withstand chlorinated splashing.

See Chapter 10, "Beyond the Basics," especially pages 248–259, for further details.

Retaining a shallow ledge for poolside sitting, a rock wall provides enough elevation for a waterfall. The combination of massive rocks and lush plants enhances the pool's scale and natural appearance.

A tile stair-step waterfall flows from a spa and follows one wall of the 10×40-foot lap pool. Where stairs descend into the pool, one step extends along the full length of it, providing access from end to end and to the spa area.

GARDEN PONDS

Water in the garden creates new dimensions of beauty, tranquillity, and interest—and with fewer maintenance demands than most people imagine.

Your garden water feature can be as simple as a half barrel with water lilies or as complex as a multilevel pond with waterfalls. Between these extremes is an array of possibilities.

Since water in any form tends to dominate the landscape, forethought and careful choice are the secrets of success. Do you want a pond for viewing, for reflecting surrounding beauty, for attracting birds, for growing water plants, for stocking with fish, or a combination of these?

Will a formal or informal pond fit best with your landscape? Formal ponds are marked by geometric shapes and straight lines. These shapes and lines must agree with other landscape elements to make the formal pond an integral part of the whole. Informal ponds, on the other hand, are defined by smooth, flowing lines. These lines must remain uncomplicated. The informal pond looks best when it appears as a natural part of the garden, with an abundance of plants.

A fountain suits a formal pond, while a gentle waterfall splashing over boulders is more fitting for an informal pond. In either case your pond should be designed to be attractive year-round.

Location is the most important design decision. Ideally a waterscape should be easily seen from both inside the house and various locations in the yard. At least four to six hours of sunlight a day are necessary for water plants to thrive. Nearby trees can pose a problem if they shed their leaves or other litter regularly.

Place your pond where you'll have easy access to a water spigot, drainage, and perhaps electricity (for a pump and lights). A spot that's naturally wet usually isn't the best site for a garden pond because it may be prone to flooding. Avoid windy spots if you plan to have a fountain. Provide a walkway to your pond for curious visitors.

Despite their shallowness, garden ponds can be hazardous to small children. Be sure to check all codes when designing your water feature.

Pond ecology

The water in a garden pond will not be as clear as that in a swimming pool. A slightly green cast is natural and indicates a balance of life within. The balance is delicate and will likely need assistance from a filtration system (pump and filter).

Water features are magnets for wildlife, especially birds and amphibians. Fish, birds, and other insects will eat almost all of the mosquito and other harmful larvae that attempt to thrive.

A pond brings a new appreciation of gardening beyond growing plants in beds and borders. The palette of plants suited to life alongside, in, or on water is evergrowing. For more details about ponds, see pages 238–247 in Chapter 10, "Beyond the Basics."

A shady patio beneath a second-story deck offers a cool place to sit and enjoy the pond on hot days. There's enough room for a bar-height table and chairs as well as comfy seating. The buffet cabinet to the far right shelters the pond filter.

A beautiful water feature beckons, drawing you and visitors to gather nearby and enjoy the scene. An adjacent patio, set up with cushioned furniture, provides the ideal place to sit, watch, and listen contentedly.

2

PLANNING AND PREPARING

Turning your yard into your own personal environment means dipping into the broad palette of landscaping possibilities. In this chapter you'll find an overview of those potential options, plus a guide for creating an overall plan. The secret to ultimate success is to first work back and forth from mind to paper; in doing this, ideas can flow while expenses stay on hold. Once done, your plan becomes the blueprint for the best possible outdoor world for you and your family.

The slate patio, a few steps down from the redwood deck, offers a somewhat sheltered area for the kitchen, fireplace, and dining table.

Different levels and flooring materials separate areas where the family can play, relax, dine, and entertain—all while enjoying the outdoors and being together.

Details go a long way toward making a multipurpose outdoor living area work as well as this one does. Built-in planters, lighting, and appliances add to its success.

ASSESSING YOUR LANDSCAPING NEEDS

Good use of existing trees provides excellent framing and background for this traditional home on a typical lot. Small accent trees and low, neat planting beds give the setting a well-planned appearance.

Some landscaping ideas are born fully grown. New homeowners have been known to put in a pool before they unpack their boxes. But most plans take longer to gain shape. And so they should, because the process of assessing the needs of your family and your yard—and figuring out the best solutions to those needs—is essential to creating an effective landscape.

The present

Begin by looking critically at what you've got. As you live in your house through the next cycle of seasons, compile a list of little and large blessings already in place: the shade, blooms, or fruit of a special tree, or the view at sunset or when the winter trees are bare. At the end of 12 months, you may be pleasantly surprised at just how long your list is.

A year of surmising your situation may seem excessively long, but taking your time has a built-in advantage: If you move too fast, you could destroy one of your yard's present pluses before you are even aware of it.

During the year also compile a list of dislikes about your setting: lack of privacy or outdoor living space, for instance, or too much wind or too little light. Good landscaping can solve most, if not all, of your yard's shortcomings.

Purpose

Next weigh your family's needs. All landscape improvements—from the planting of a single shrub to the building of a deck and patio system—should add to the ease, comfort, and delight of your everyday living. And this can be true for all members of the family, from grandparents who spend a lot of time indoors and appreciate easy entrances and grand views of the grandkids, to children who play in every inch of yard from the sandbox to the treetops, for example.

Add nothing to your landscape without having a specific purpose in mind—whether it's to solve one of your yard's problems or to accent one of its best features.

The ready-made, detailed plans throughout the book are designed to address your landscaping needs. But the combination of site, climate, and family desires makes each yard one of a kind. And even the best-planned yard will change slightly from season to season and year to year as family wants and hobbies change over time.

No one knows as well as you what your family might require or enjoy. And you will know that much more clearly and completely after considering the many possibilities that are available to you.

Ideas

Start gathering ideas by observing the good and bad points of other yards. Drive slowly and carefully; or better yet, ride a bike or walk. You soon will notice details: colors and textures of flowers and foliage, moods of promise and mystery evoked by a winding path or a charming gate, or the way an entrance planting distinguishes one house from all the similar houses around it.

RETHINKING THE TYPICAL LOT

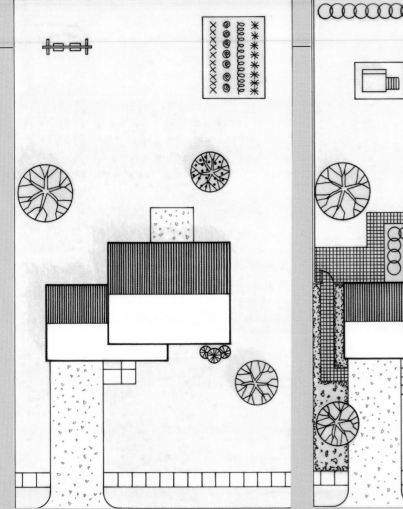

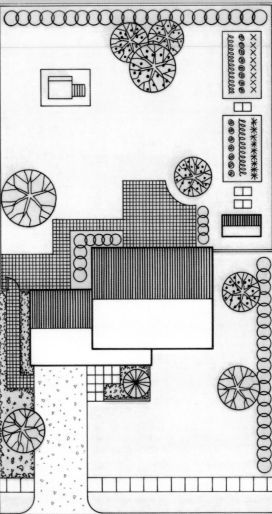

A tall fence around the backyard transforms public space to private grounds. The play area is in full view from the house for supervision but far enough away to give parents peace and children freedom.

With the garage a good hike away, a small shed near the gardens saves steps while offering super storage for tools. Shrubs screen it from the patio. The backyard now offers two service areas (the second one is near the paved side yard), an outdoor living area, an outdoor playroom, and gardens, all neatly divided into zones.

The front yard extends a warm greeting, and a side walkway makes the transition from front to back a pleasant journey.

BEFORE

Many homes sit on a rectangular lot with the drive and entrance in front and a larger area in back, like the one above. Landscaping problems for these typical lots include lack of privacy from the sides and rear, relatively unusable side yards, and lack of access from front yard to backyard. Also such lots often offer only a small open area for outdoor living. Plantings generally include a few foundation shrubs and one or two trees in the front as streetscape. Lucky is the homeowner who has older trees.

AFTER

To create a more pleasant and individual personality for such a home—and increase curb appeal—add plantings to one or both sides of the drive, along part of the property line, and around the front door. Construct a distinctive entryway that complements your home's architecture. Use structures or plants to divide the backyard into activity zones. Finally, to make sure the yard doesn't end up with a split personality, join the front to the back with a side walkway or other connecting feature.

ASSESSING YOUR LANDSCAPING NEEDS *(continued)*

A front porch and enhanced entry pack the most interest and best use of space into this small, shallow lot. Carefully combined features include stone retaining walls, stone and brick steps, and architectural details on the house.

Move your search for landscaping ideas indoors by browsing through this book. Regard pages 34–41 as your landscaping palette and select the colors with which you want to paint your private world. Check out later chapters for specific advice on each of the options.

From magazines and other books, gather photographs, plans, and anything else that might prove useful. Skim over the pictures and plans the way a clever clothing designer looks at a pattern book, ruling out the completed look of many outfits as unfit but choosing a collar here, a sleeve there.

Similarly you can combine a front entry from one plan with a back patio from another; add a certain curve or zigzag border or walk from yet another; and choose a grouping of trees for spring bloom, fall fruit, or a woodland feeling from another.

You will do much of your initial landscape planning in your head. But to put all that power to work most efficiently, write down your observations, ideas, and expectations as they come to you. This can be done in any form and is mostly for your own use, so don't let formality stop the flow of ideas.

Dare to dream
Check building codes, deed restrictions, and setback and easement regulations early in your planning so that you can keep them in mind.

Otherwise don't worry if your landscaping ideas seem muddled at first. The details will come in time. Don't let worries about expense and labor stifle your dreams either. Planning often makes the impossible possible.

Perhaps you won't wind up with a forest, but you can have a corner where a path and some trees, shrubs, groundcovers, and wildflowers make you feel as if you do. And though you can't stretch a small lot into a wide plain, a section of fence along the rim of a slope can visually extend your backyard.

The whole site
As the details develop, think of your yard as a whole. Everything should blend harmoniously. You don't have to be an artist or know much about the aesthetic principles of line, scale, texture, and balance. These elements of good design are largely common sense. Your inner eye will tell you whether they are present or missing.

Visualize the changes you plan as they will look tomorrow, in 5 years, in 20 years. Remember that plans are flat on paper but three-dimensional in reality. Trees and shrubs grow up as well as out. Look up and be sure that no electric or phone wires already are in the space where you envision oak branches.

RETHINKING THE NARROW LOT

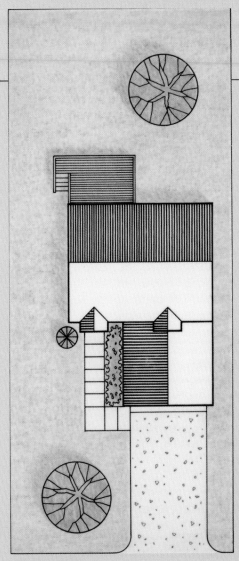

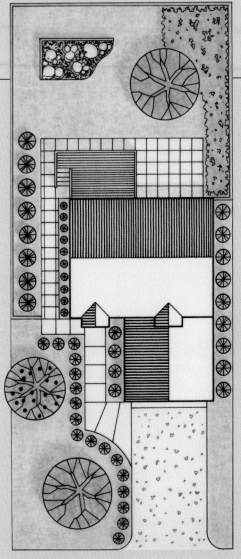

The smaller the space the more important it is to define zones within the site. Here a streetscaping zone and an outdoor-living zone are developed with a concern for detail that brings as much beauty and usefulness as many large yards offer.

The rock garden, with a low fence in front, is a fine focal point and makes the small space seem larger. A taller fence behind it screens an area where equipment can be stored.

Along the property lines, low-maintenance plants that will not grow out of bounds solve the problem of mowing in narrow places as well as add to a sense of seclusion.

BEFORE

Rising land costs make narrow lots the norm in many locations these days. Unfortunately landscaping problems tend to increase in intensity with such closeness. One wall of the house may rest nearly on the lot line, leaving a narrow, hard-to-plant space on the opposite side. Privacy, though harder to achieve, is more essential than ever. Access and traffic flow within the yard are concerns too. Every inch of yard on the narrow lot must be used wisely.

AFTER

To create the illusion of more space, try some visual trickery. Expand the entry as it adjoins the drive to make the space feel larger. Set low-level plantings along the drive and walk to lead the eye to the front door and soften the harshness of one house on top of another. For outdoor living, build a patio or deck, or a combination. You'll gain a needed sanctuary while retaining an open feel. To provide privacy in the backyard and help absorb neighbors' noise, plant trees and shrubs and build a fence.

ASSESSING YOUR LANDSCAPING NEEDS *(continued)*

Small trees and shrubs, along with flowery borders, transform this largely exposed corner yard into a showplace. Framed by low boxwood hedges, even the lawn becomes an outstanding part of the scene.

One of the most common landscaping mistakes is misjudging the growing room that plants require. If you want to avoid the empty look for the present, fill in with temporary annual flowers, or vegetables that can be replaced with choice trees and shrubs, for instance. Always keep scale in mind. Also maintain the same theme throughout the entire yard, whether it is natural, formal, English cottage, Japanese, modern, or any other desired look.

Record the heights, colors, and times of bloom or season of interest of all plants, and be sure that they complement one another and the structures. If your house is white or gray, you can plant any nice combination. Other colors may entail more careful planning to achieve a harmonious look.

Do the same analysis for all structural materials you consider using in your landscape. Wood, concrete, brick, stone, and natural materials all have characteristics that make them fit better in some situations than in others.

Consider, too, as much as you can, your future needs. You won't be able to do this with crystal-ball clarity, but having the forethought to leave your options open helps ensure rewards later on. Adding on to the back of the house in the future could be more challenging, let alone wasteful, if you must tear out the deck and shrubs that you installed when you acquired the place.

Don't worry if you're having trouble visualizing your entire yard. When you put your plans on paper, as mentioned below and described on pages 42–53, you'll be better able to see and rearrange the parts for the most convenient and beautiful whole.

Drawing a plan

Because some decisions will firm up more quickly than others, the sooner you move from your lists and dreams to the actual planning, the better. The day you buy the house, you can begin planting flowers, cover crops, vegetables, small shrubs, and trees that you could remove or move if necessary. These activities, in fact, will help you form and appreciate your plans. But you may not want to pay for the substantial expense of a permanent installation until you have an overall landscaping plan.

So while all of the ideas are settling, get busy and measure and sketch your yard. Then draw a map to scale on graph paper. Over this, lay tracing paper and sketch various arrangements. Try options on the tracing paper just as you would try on clothes to see what is right for you.

If putting an idea on paper shows that it won't work, the process may bring to mind another idea that will. Then select the ideas that will best fit your plan and your family's way of life.

The pages that follow walk you through this process until you have your own custom-made landscape plan.

RETHINKING THE CORNER LOT

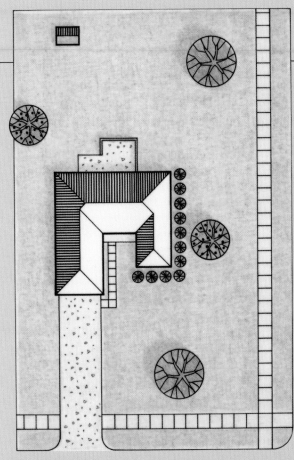

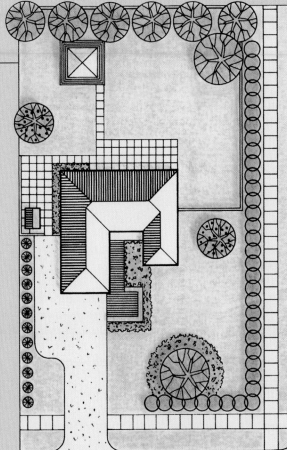

A hedge now frames much of the landscape, shielding the home from view. Trees across the back of the lot plus a section of fencing enhance privacy.

Plants circling the tree near the corner shape a focal point for the front yard. A wide front-entry walk helps tie the house to the site.

Off-street parking for an extra car uses otherwise wasted side yard space. The back portion of that side yard has become a service area.

A pavilion and a larger patio yield better outdoor living facilities, especially now that they are much more hidden from passersby.

BEFORE

The corner house, bordered on two sides by car and pedestrian traffic, needs careful landscaping to keep it from looking like an island in a sea of lawn. Privacy is a major concern, too, with the exposure in all directions making usable outdoor living space hard to define and more difficult to privatize without appearing standoffish.

If left open, the front lawn on a corner lot all too often becomes a shortcut from one sidewalk to the other. Such layouts may pose great dangers, too: Balls and children are much more apt to go into the street. Moreover, the open expanse behind the house offers no place to hunker down and relax after a long day of work.

AFTER

To solve many of the problems associated with a corner lot, plant a hedge along the entire side street and the largest part of the front yard. Such a hedge screens the house from the view of passing traffic. It also absorbs noise, blocks headlights at night, and provides a barrier for children playing in the yard or passing by. Planting the hedge near the sidewalk instead of against the house helps break up the expanse of lawn.

Absorb noise and visually separate the house from the street—as well as stop people from taking a shortcut—by establishing a front yard focal point in the corner where the two streets intersect. An ornamental tree surrounded by shrubs and flowers often works well. To help expand the house into the site, widen the front-entry walk.

31

ASSESSING YOUR LANDSCAPING NEEDS *(continued)*

At some point, of course, you'll have to start worrying about what your various landscaping ideas might cost you (see page 54 for more about costs). Estimates are easy to obtain and are vital before your plans become definite.

Because landscaping can be expensive, it's often done in stages. A driveway and a few trees probably will be needed right away. But you can just as well work on and pay for the entryway one year, the back patio or deck the next, the side yard another.

Also as you sift through ideas, you'll want to keep in mind your own willingness to work in your yard. Although installation is done only once, maintenance goes on forever.

Until they take on the task as a homeowner, few people understand that a lawn takes more time, expense, and natural resources such as water than any other landscaping option. Cut down on your lawn with areas of groundcovers and mulches around trees and shrubs.

Put in a rose garden, a vegetable patch, or an orchard if you enjoy gardening. But avoid such features if you don't have time to spend on them.

Patios, decks, walks, and permanent plantings require little work and expense after the initial construction. In return they give plenty of outdoor living enjoyment for each dollar spent.

Professional help

Throughout the process, consider whether you want to consult a landscape professional for help. Such help can come from three types of individuals: landscape architects, landscape designers, and landscape contractors.

The landscape architect is the planning expert and is comparable to a building architect in training and in the time frame when he or she can most help you: while the property is being designed. Although landscape architects do mostly commercial work, many will consult with homeowners on an hourly basis, and some will oversee entire residential jobs. Because of their expertise, landscape architects tend to be the most expensive landscaping professionals.

Landscape designers often do much the same work as landscape architects, but they have less training and usually are more plant oriented. The fees of landscape designers employed by nurseries often are absorbed if you buy enough plants from the nurseries.

Landscape contractors do or hire done the actual work. If you deal with a landscape contractor, be sure to discuss what materials you must provide, and ask for samples of materials the contractor will supply. As with any contractor, ask for a written estimate of costs and a schedule.

Finding good help

Before choosing a landscaping professional, ask the owners of yards you admire for recommendations. Or go to the phone book, call four or five landscapers listed, and ask for addresses that show their work. Then go out for a look. Keep doing this until you've found at least three professionals who do high-quality work, then ask them for bids on your job.

Depending on your own time and expertise, and on your site's complexity, you may not need a professional. But the money spent to consult an expert—especially concerning such problems as difficult grading, eroding hillsides, high walls, or high decks—is often saved many times over in the final satisfying and safe result.

No professional can know your needs and dreams like you do. That's why good planning becomes even more important when you are putting the results into the hands of a highly paid person.

Trees and topsoil

A final note: Be careful with existing trees and topsoil when planning and working on your landscape. Both, once lost, take many years to replace. During construction, protect your trees from machinery, soil compaction, and changes in soil level. Transplant choice small shrubs and trees from a construction area to a temporary, out-of-the-way place. If topsoil will be moved during construction, save it for making grade changes or replace it before replanting.

SOLVING THE JUNGLE LOOK

In the early stages of planting an empty yard, some homeowners yearn for the look of mature plantings. Others see anything other than near-bareness as too much, and resort to overzealous pruning.

And then there is the overplanted or overgrown situation. Because they grow quickly to maturity, shrubs and vines are the most likely contributors to the jungle look. Beware of this when you plant them—particularly when you plan their spacing and siting. Little potted bushes and seeds of honeysuckle, for example, grow so well that they can take over an area.

Chances are, your biggest task will be to carve out of your existing greenery some spaces for entertaining and playing—an art described by one pro as "landscaping by the judicial removal of plantings." Moreover, when shrubs or vines obscure the best lines of the house or shut out views and light, these are also signals that it's time for rescaling, by either pruning the plants or tearing them out.

Trees need thinning less often, but they, too, can become overgrown, particularly in warm and wet climates. Careful pruning for a higher canopy of leaves opens the area beneath the tree to more sunlight and air circulation while preserving the tree's irreplaceable form, silhouette, and shade.

If ripping out plants seems ruthless and extreme, do it in stages. As the advantages of openness appear and you see that new plantings will quickly replace the emptiness, you will gain the needed assurance to press on with the transformation.

Similarly, you don't have to endure walks, drives, or patios that are overgrown, cracked, or outdated, or that were out of place to begin with. Yards, like houses, can be remodeled. Just make a to-do list so that when time and money become available, you're ready.

Shrubbery had overgrown this house's foundation and overpowered even the front entry.

Although a cracked and worn concrete sidewalk had been replaced with a warmer brick walkway, it was rarely being used by the homeowners or visitors. The result was an unwelcoming entry that had become little used.

BEFORE

New French doors greatly improve the light level in the adjacent indoor living room. The trimmed shrubbery appears neater and no longer blocks the view from indoors. The shrubs enhance rather than hide the new door. What's more, the front walk is easier to see and access from the driveway. Best of all, the house no longer hides behind the shrubs and it presents a more welcoming face.

AFTER

33

WEIGHING YOUR LANDSCAPING OPTIONS

STRUCTURES

DECKS
(pages 14–15, 160–187)
Type: Raised, grade-level, multilevel, freestanding, or portable; used at an entrance, adjoining a house or pool, with a patio, surrounding a spa, or as part of play area; usually wooden.

Uses: Decks are an ideal way to gain outdoor living space on level, sloping, or hilly lots. They work best when connected to a kitchen, family room, or dining room. They can be built around existing trees without changing the ground level. With various railings and trellises, decks can be made to fit into either natural or formal settings. Avoid creating a boxy deck by rounding or angling at least one corner, by varying the pattern or the levels, or by surrounding the deck with interesting planters or plantings.

PATIOS
(pages 12–13, 136–159)
Type: Brick, tile, flagstone, wood blocks, paver blocks, or cobblestones—all usually set in sand, solid concrete, or exposed aggregate, pebbles, or the like.

Uses: Patios provide a solid surface for outdoor living rooms. Connected to a kitchen, family room, or dining room, they work well as eating or entertaining areas. They set off the scene around a pool and are great for sunbathing. In the front yard they serve as a porch or courtyard. They can also reclaim narrow side-yard spaces. Locate patios for sun, shade, or wind protection; be sure drainage is good; use plants or railings for privacy, arbors or roofs for shade.

FENCES
(pages 210–211, 216–217, 220)
Type: Styles and materials vary widely. Can be transparent or semitransparent for ample air circulation, opaque for windbreaks and complete privacy, or a combination.

Uses: Fences frame, accent, and provide background to set off plantings. The many styles, colors, and forms unify the yard and tie various areas of it to the house with formal or natural beauty. Fences keep children or pets in, unwanted visitors out. Mix opaque and open styles to cover unsightly views but frame and accent pleasant vistas. Fences can be tall for privacy or short for accent. Cover with vines or espaliers for vertical gardening.

SCREENS
(pages 210, 218–219, 221)
Type: Can be made of sections of fence or lattice; connected or not. They can be head-high or taller and set at different angles.

Uses: Screens provide privacy without the cost and enclosure of a fence. They give focus, emphasis, and vertical interest to the landscape while blocking unpleasant views or accenting desirable aspects within the yard. By breaking up the open space, they add a feeling of separation to outdoor rooms. They can make a small space seem larger and a large space more intimate. Screens enhance patios and decks as well as service or storage areas.

WALKS

(pages 82–101)

Type: Can be made of any of the materials used for patios or decks. Loose mulching materials such as pine needles, wood chips, and gravel also work well for walkways.

Uses: Walks allow people to move around your yard with comfort and safety. In entry and service areas, they should be solid and definite. Farther from the house they can be more casual. Let them flow with the natural route of traffic, curving around special plantings or leading to hidden nooks. Materials should complement the house and yard. Make walks at least 3 feet wide (wider at curves and ends if possible). Plan low plantings along walkways to avoid crowding.

STEPS

(pages 73, 76, 88–89)

Type: Made of wood, concrete, or rustic materials such as split logs, landscape timbers, or long stones. Ramp steps are a series of single steps alternating with sloping surfaces.

Uses: Steps make a safe and pleasant transition from one grade level to another. Materials should be in harmony with the surrounding area; if chosen well, they can greatly add interest. Make steps as broad as the path that leads to them and less steep than interior stairs. For slight grade changes, leave the slope rather than building a single step. Angle treads downward for drainage. A railing on at least one side is recommended (some building codes may require it). If the total rise exceeds 6 feet, include a landing along the way.

RETAINING WALLS

(pages 198–201)

Type: Can be made of reinforced concrete, timber, or stone laid dry or with masonry. Dry walls are less expensive and can be planted. Mortar makes stronger walls.

Uses: Retaining walls turn difficult slopes into interesting architectural features that also serve to unite the garden with the house. Walls combine well with plants, creating level planting beds above and charming backgrounds below for flowers, foliage, and espaliered trees and shrubs. Retaining walls must be strong enough to hold back the weight of the earth behind them. Be sure to provide for adequate drainage.

ARBORS

(pages 112–115, 130, 134–135)

Type: Often wooden; metal and resin available. Sides can be open, latticed, or patterned. Arbors can adjoin a house, roof a swing, or frame a gate.

Uses: Arbors provide support for vines or espaliered fruit and increase garden space vertically. They provide shade in much less time and space than do trees and are ideal places to hang plants, lights, or hammocks. Used to roof part of a patio or deck, they give the ideal choice of shady or sunny space. With vined or latticed sides, they increase privacy yet let air circulate. Sides also can have louvers or panels.

WEIGHING YOUR LANDSCAPING OPTIONS *(continued)*

STRUCTURES *(continued)*

OVERHEAD SUNSHADES
(pages 104–111)

Type: Can be freestanding or attached to the house; usually wood but can be combined with canvas or other shading materials. Varying styles; can drastically alter a house's look.

Uses: Overhead sunshades give instant and permanent shade that can greatly improve the comfort and usefulness of both outdoor rooms and adjoining indoor ones, especially where glass doors connect the two. Adding deciduous vines increases the summer shade and still lets plenty of sun warm the house in winter. Like arbors, these can give yards the advantages of some sunny and some shady areas.

SCREENED ROOMS
(pages 276–281)

Type: Parts of porches, patios, or decks connected to the house; freestanding summer houses or gazebos. Screening can combine with almost any style of architecture.

Uses: Screened rooms offer the ultimate in protection from insects. They also provide a measure of privacy and protection from the elements that makes them almost like additional indoor rooms. But they have all the advantages of open air, cool breezes, and nearness to the garden. Combine with gentle vines such as Virginia creeper or clematis to give additional shade and summer interest.

GAZEBOS
(pages 230–237)

Type: Usually freestanding and wooden; can combine with bridges, fences, decks, or other structures. Colors, shapes, railings, floors, and ceilings can be chosen to fit any yard.

Uses: A gazebo is a definite garden accent and focal point, and as such should be in scale and harmony with the rest of the yard. It provides a separate outdoor room that's ideal for relaxing, entertaining, dining, or quiet seclusion. To avoid having the gazebo look out of place, tie it to the rest of the yard with walkways and architectural elements, such as fencing or an arbor that repeats the structure's details. Fabric and portable gazebos are now available.

SWIMMING POOLS
(pages 20–21, 248–259)

Type: In-ground pools: Gunite, concrete, fiberglass, or vinyl lined; almost any size or shape. Aboveground pools: Less costly and permanent, fewer shapes, usually smaller.

Uses: Swimming pools offer the ultimate in outdoor recreation, relaxation, and exercise. They usually are the focal point of the yard and often of indoor rooms as well, so surrounding decking and plantings require as much planning, care, and expense as the pool itself. Study soil type and sun and wind patterns, and consult experts as you plan. Screening the area around and above will keep a pool cleaner, especially with trees nearby.

GARDEN PONDS
(pages 22–23, 238–247)

Type: Clear reflecting pools, fishponds, and water gardens. Can be made of poured concrete, PVC liner, or preformed fiberglass.

Uses: A pond opens new dimensions of fish, foliage, and flowers to your garden. And you can add the music of trickling water simply by outfitting your pond with any form of fountain or falls. Always delightful and dramatic, garden ponds can be used as either accents or focal points. They require less upkeep than most people think, seldom need emptying, and can be heated in the winter. A sunny location is best. Water plants include submersible, surface, and pondside types.

LIGHTING
(pages 224–225, 260–267, 344–347)

Type: Porch, door, post, and floodlights. Low-voltage flood, accent, mushroom, path lights, or spot lights also available.

Uses: Exterior lights allow people to come or go at night with sure steps and little fear of intruders. Additional garden lighting can effectively extend outdoor living and enjoyment into the evening hours and create striking views. Choose the fixture types and positions that best fit your purpose: providing security, lighting recreational space, accenting plantings, or dramatizing architectural features.

STORAGE UNITS
(pages 294–299)

Type: Tool or potting shed, separate or adjoining the house or tucked into a portion of the garage, under a bench or deck, or in a handy corner.

Uses: Proper and convenient storage can save time and frustration for the gardener, rust and wear on tools, and, by providing a secure place for chemicals, even the life of a child or pet. Ideal storage area is about 60 to 100 square feet and includes racks and hanging space; shelves; compartments for soil and compost; a potting bench; and floor space for a wheelbarrow, lawn mower, and a couple of garbage cans. If designed to harmonize with the house and landscape, a shed can be an attractive garden feature.

DRIVES, PARKING AREAS
(pages 304–307)

Type: Concrete, flagstone, tile, brick, asphalt, or aggregates. Circular is good for large or formal yards; straight, L, or T shapes can double as play areas or entryways.

Uses: Driveways must be clearly visible and easy to turn into and negotiate in any weather. Gentle curves may add visual interest but also cost and time. Where needed, curves reduce the steepness of a slope and add to the formality of the house. Space for parking is a great convenience. A place to turn around so motorists can enter traffic head-on is a good safety feature; it's a necessity in areas of heavy traffic or limited visibility. Plantings can screen parking areas from the street.

WEIGHING YOUR LANDSCAPING OPTIONS *(continued)*

PLANTS

SHADE TREES
(pages 116–118, 359–367)
Examples: Amur cork tree, ash, edibles (such as cherry, cherry laurel, crabapple, nuts, persimmon, plum), ginkgo, goldenraintree, honeylocust, magnolia, maple, oak, tulip tree.

Uses: Shade trees add more to the landscape than any other plants. Besides filtering or blocking the summer sun for cooling comfort, shade trees give needed framing, privacy, and interest to the landscape. Shade trees tie a house to its site, convey a sense of oneness with nature, and provide protection from the elements. Deciduous trees let in the winter sun to brighten and warm the scene. Plant one or two of the largest trees you can afford.

ACCENT TREES
(pages 78–79, 359–367)
Examples: Apple, birch, cherry, cherry laurel, crabapple, dogwood, hawthorn, holly, Japanese maple, magnolia, pear, persimmon, plum, redbud, serviceberry.

Uses: Accent or ornamental trees are ideal for perking up a front yard or creating a focal point in a backyard. Place them in center-stage locations for the most dramatic results. Spring-blooming trees work well where they can be clearly seen from indoors, the street, or the entrance. Position fruit trees away from the driveway or patio. Accent trees work well against a house, fence, or evergreen background. Consider the mature size and scale of trees with your house and any other structures in mind.

SCREEN SHRUBS
(pages 124–125, 368–377)
Examples: Clipped: barberry, hazelnut, juniper, privet, yew. Unclipped: arborvitae, azalea, blueberry, boxwood, bush cherry or plum, currant, elderberry, quince, rose.

Uses: Shrubs make fine screens because they quickly grow into place. You can choose them by height; for open, dense, or thorny growth; or for their flowers, fruit, or foliage color. Some places, such as side windows or front doors, will gain enough privacy from a single specimen. Other areas will need a group of plants. For maximum effect, make the grouping all the same; for maximum interest, judiciously mix the selections. Choose sizes that will not overgrow their sites.

ACCENT SHRUBS
(pages 128–129, 154–155, 368–377)
Examples: Cornus, cotoneaster, fringe tree, holly, honeysuckle, mahonia, roses, rhododendron, viburnum; all tree-form, weeping, or espaliered shrubs.

Uses: Accent or specimen shrubs are so lovely they often steal the garden show. Use them as focal points in the yard, at the entrance, or at a corner of the house. Many shrubs offer something striking for at least two seasons: flowers and fruit; summer or autumn foliage color; general form; and winter twig, bark, or foliage. Make your selections according to the seasons in which you'll see the shrubs most often. Accent shrubs also can serve as privacy, screening, or foundation plantings.

VINES
(pages 114–115, 154–155, 186, 377–381)

Examples: Bougainvillea, clematis, passionflower, and wisteria for flowers; bittersweet, grape, kiwi for fruits; Boston ivy and Virginia creeper for fall foliage; evergreen English ivy.

Uses: Vines are wonderful for giving shade and privacy in a short time and in a narrow space. You can choose vines that have fragrant or outstanding flowers, bountiful fruit, or open or dense growth. You also can choose according to tolerance for dry or wet conditions. Some are annual, others perennial. Some are softwood, some hard. Many grow easily from seeds or cuttings. Choose plants carefully to minimize pruning, maximize seasonal interest, and fit the structure on which they are to grow.

GROUNDCOVERS
(pages 154–155, 195, 382–386)

Examples: Ajuga, artemisia, barberry, bellflower, bishop's weed, cotoneaster, English ivy, juniper, lily-of-the-valley, mint, pachysandra, phlox, strawberry, thyme, yarrow, yew.

Uses: Grow low-maintenance groundcovers in narrow areas or on steep slopes where mowing is difficult or dangerous; also grow them under trees where it is too shady for grass. Save mowing time and watering expense—and add interesting textures, colors, and blooms—by using groundcovers to reduce the size of a large lawn. You can choose among groundcovers that are a few inches to a few feet tall, annual or perennial, evergreen or deciduous, edible or ornamental, and for shade or sun, wet or dry soil.

LAWN GRASSES
(pages 312–313)

Examples: Cool-season grasses include bentgrass, bluegrass, fescue, and ryegrass. Warm-season grasses include bahia, bermuda, centipede, st. augustine, and zoysia.

Uses: Lawns give a clean, attractive look to the yard and provide a living surface that will withstand more walking and playing traffic than any other plant. Lawn grasses hold the soil and are the most common outdoor carpets. Few yards would be complete without at least some areas of green grass. But grass takes much time, water, and work—more so than other plants—so seed or sod only as much as you want to mow or irrigate.

ORNAMENTAL GRASSES

Examples: Blue fescue, cloud grass, fountain grass, foxtail millet, job's-tears, liriope, maiden grass, mondo grass, plume or pampas grass, quaking grass, squirreltail grass.

Uses: Low-maintenance ornamental grasses make dramatic edgings or accents. When dried, they work well in winter bouquets. They come in a wide variety of colors, forms, and heights. Research how each will grow before you plant, because some are extremely hard to remove once established, and others will self-sow. Use clumps of different types at intervals for balance, blooms, and interesting textures.

WEIGHING YOUR LANDSCAPING OPTIONS *(continued)*

PLANTS *(continued)*

PERENNIALS
(pages 106, 387–389)
Examples: Aster, bleeding-heart, candytuft, columbine, coral bells, coreopsis, delphinium, iris, lily, peony, phlox, poppy, Shasta daisy, speedwell, violet.

Uses: Perennials make fine focal points when combined with shrubs or groundcovers. They form the backbone of most flower borders because they come up year after year. After planting, they take minimal care. Some can be divided every few years. Others will stay happy for decades. Some like shade, some like sun, and some thrive in both. For greatest appeal, combine them with height, color, and time of bloom in mind. Many will bloom again if cut back. Use in bouquets.

ANNUALS
(pages 106, 390–392)
Examples: Alyssum, amaranth, bachelor's button, calendula, coleus, cosmos, dahlia, geranium, impatiens, larkspur, marigold, petunia, portulaca, salvia, snapdragon, spider flower, zinnia.

Uses: No other flowers bloom as abundantly and continually as do annuals, so they are ideal for color accents. Use them in massed plantings, as edges and hedges, for cutting, or in containers. Buy started plants for earliest use. Start seeds indoors or out if you need a large quantity. Keep color and height in mind when choosing annuals. Mix spike and round flowers for balance and drama. If you remove dead blooms, many plants will flower until frost.

BULBS
(page 393)
Examples: Caladium, canna, crocus, daffodil, dahlia, Dutch iris, gladiolus, grape hyacinth, hyacinth, lily, snowdrop, squill, tuberous begonia, tulip.

Uses: Bulbs, a loose grouping that includes corms and tubers, give generously of their striking, often fragrant, flowers. The early bloomers increase rapidly; daffodils, snowdrops, squill, and grape hyacinths will spread for carpets of bloom. Bulbs make fine accents in flower or shrub borders. Cut off dead blooms; allow the foliage to die down naturally. Let annuals, grass, or groundcovers spread and cover fading leaves. Tender bulbs must be dug up and stored inside over winter.

HERBS
Examples: Basil, catnip, chamomile, chives, cress, dill, fennel, garlic, lemon balm, lemongrass, marjoram, mint, nasturtium, oregano, parsley, rosemary, sage, tarragon, thyme.

Uses: Herbs can be used in special gardens, as shown at left, or be planted in containers or among other flowers and shrubs. Plant herbs used for flavoring near the kitchen for easy access. Choose others for their textures, foliage and flower colors, interesting forms, and wonderful fragrance. Put aromatic ones such as lemon balm and rosemary where you will brush against them. Use chamomile and mint underfoot, but beware of mint. Plant it where mowing or barriers will control it.

FERNS
(pages 245, 383)

Examples: Asparagus, climbing, common, hay-scented, maidenhair, mountain wood, narrow beech, New York, ostrich, resurrection, royal, sensitive, staghorn.

Uses: Ferns grace many garden settings, especially those in the shade, though some will take a little sun as well. Ferns thrive as groundcovers and accent plants, in rock gardens and woodland shade, on the banks of streams and the edges of water gardens, or in boggy sites. Many are so easy to grow that they flourish in such unlikely places as beneath decks. They offer a variety of textures and colors as well as fine foliage for indoor arrangements.

HOSTAS
(page 245, 388)

Examples: Many hybrids and cultivars with such names as 'Blue Skies,' 'Daybreak,' 'Gold Standard,' 'Lemon Lime,' 'Shade Master,' 'Sum and Substance.'

Uses: Hostas lend a sense of serenity to a summer setting that few other plants can match. Most require some shade. They are excellent for entire gardens or as accents, as groundcovers in shady areas, or as plantings at woodland edges. Many sizes, colors, and textures are available. Some also have showy or fragrant spikes of white or lavender blooms. They are easy to grow.

CONTAINER PLANTS
(page 184–185, 390–392)

Examples: Annuals such as begonia, geranium, petunia, verbena, vinca; bulbs; herbs; roses; vegetables; dwarf and tender trees; strawberries; fruits; houseplants.

Uses: Containers are the best way to add color to patios, decks, poolsides, and entryways. Annuals give the most and longest-blooming flowers, but ferns, fruits, herbs, and vegetables work well too. Move containers (put casters on large ones and light soil or soilless mixtures in all) from sun to shade and vice versa to distribute color where you want it and to transfer plants past their prime to places they prefer. Move tender plants indoors for the winter. Check moisture needs daily.

FRUITS
(pages 359, 361)

Examples: Apple, apricot, blueberry, cherry, citrus, fig, gooseberry, grape, kiwi, mulberry, nectarine, peach, pear, persimmon, plum, quince, strawberry.

Uses: Fruits—whether in tree, shrub, vine, or groundcover form—can be used with or instead of ornamental plants for an edible landscape that has all the color, bloom, interest, texture, fragrance, and beauty any plan needs. They take no more space than similar nonfruiting plants and require comparable feeding and watering in most climates. Plan for a varied harvest that stretches over a long period of time to balance fresh eating with winter-preservation needs.

MEASURING YOUR EXISTING SITE

Transforming a bare or bedraggled yard into a private paradise is more than a willy-nilly process. It's a step-by-step operation that involves measuring and drawing a map of your site, sketching the new landscape possibilities, choosing a final plan, and, lastly, staging the work according to personal priorities, logical work order, and budget.

Taking measurements

A map of your lot may already exist. Consult the builder or architect of your house, local Federal Housing Administration (FHA), U.S. Department of Veterans Affairs (VA), or mortgage office, or check the deed. Your town or county building department may have a property survey on file too. Check any plan for accuracy, especially if it is old. If you find plans, ask also for any topographical data that may show grade changes and drainage.

If no plans exist, don't worry. Just follow the directions below, and in less than an hour you can do the measuring. Or hire a surveyor (especially if property lines are in question). Most people, however, can measure their yards themselves.

Grab a notebook, the largest measuring tape you have, and a pen or pencil, and head for the outdoors. Someone to hold your tape and double-check your measurements will help immensely, but you can do it alone if necessary. Just use an ice pick, a skewer, or a large rock to hold your tape.

If your yard is large, pace off the measurements. To be most accurate, measure a strip 50 or 100 feet long. Walk this and count your steps. Then convert paces into feet (for example, 50 feet at 20 steps equals 2½ feet per step).

First make a rough sketch of your house and property. Next accurately measure property lines, then locate the house by measuring from each corner to the two nearest property lines. Finally measure and mark all other structures and all trees, shrubs, and planting areas you plan to keep. Put the figures on your rough sketch as you go.

Now or later you will want to mark the eaves of your house, first-floor doors and windows, downspouts, meter locations, relevant utility and water lines, and anything else that may affect your plans.

To pinpoint a tree on your sketch, measure a right triangle, beginning at the corner of a nearby structure (such as the house) and positioning the tree at the apex. To make sure the angle is square, use a carpenter's square and heavy string.

Measure and record the distances from one landmark to another. Sight from post to corners of both structures, if possible, to make sure you are standing square.

Record your measurements as you go. Accuracy counts more than neatness at this point. Be sure to locate all structures, trees, walks, drives, overhead and underground utilities, and other major elements.

To measure the grade of a slope, mark a board in feet, then butt it against a stake at the top of the slope. Level the board, then measure from board bottom to ground. This grade is approximately 2.5—comparable to 2 feet of vertical drop to 5 feet of horizontal distance.

DRAWING A MAP OF YOUR EXISTING SITE

With the rough sketch of your property drawn and accurate figures gathered (see pages 42–43), you are well on the way to redesigning your yard's landscape. Now go back inside and turn the rough sketch of your yard into a detailed, drawn-to-scale map. This base plan will give you a good picture of your yard as a whole. The sooner you do this step, the fewer trips you'll have to make back outside to recheck any measurements.

A drawing board and T-square will make the job easier, but they aren't essential. All you really need are any flat surface (a breadboard or large piece of cardboard makes a fine portable one) and a piece of paper large enough to draw your yard plan. Most yards up to a half acre can be drawn on graph paper 18 to 24 inches square or vellum 17 to 22 inches square.

Use a scale of 1:4 (1 inch equals 4 feet or ¼ inch equals 1 foot) for a small yard, down to 1:20 (1 inch equals 20 feet) for a half-acre lot. The larger the second number of the scale, the smaller everything will appear on paper.

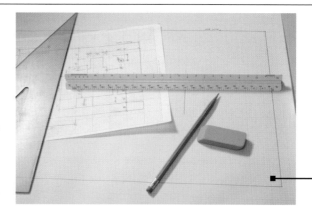

To make your base map, you must have a large piece of paper, pencils, an eraser, and a ruler. You may want to visit an art or drafting store to get large sheets of graph paper or vellum, an architect's or engineer's scale like the one shown, a compass, and a triangle or two.

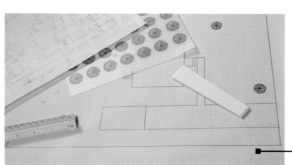

Draw the property lines first, structures next, then existing walks, drives, trees, shrubs, and plantings. Use the symbols shown below or buy press-on stickers, which you apply with a burnishing tool (both shown at left).

LANDSCAPE SYMBOLS

Deciduous tree or shrub	Evergreen tree or shrub	Wall or fence	Wood (Deck or walk)	Tile	Brick
Concrete	Mulch	Gate	Hedge	Flagstone	Groundcover

Graph paper and vellum come with 4, 8, or 10 squares per inch. These will not reproduce on a blueprint but will be helpful prior to that stage.

If your yard is very large, you may want to make one map of the whole yard at a small scale first, then later make separate plans of individual areas at a larger scale.

You can use a professional scale as an aid (see photo, opposite, top). An architect's scale is calibrated in eighths of an inch, an engineer's in tenths. You can buy one scale that combines both. Or you can simply use a ruler.

Tape your paper to your surface with a sturdy but removable tape, such as masking tape.

Draw an arrow pointing north. You can, of course, fill this in later, but it is best to have the north point at the top or side of your paper for quick reference. It will tell you much about the sun and shade patterns that, in turn, will help you determine many plant and placement decisions.

Then, using pencil, draw your map, starting with the property lines. Fill in the lines of the house and other structures. Measure with your scale, compass, or ruler and make dots on the plan.

Join the dots to make lines. Mark the trunk positions of the trees and shrubs you plan to keep. You also may want to sketch in the present branch lines with thin but solid lines and keep the possible future spread lines in mind.

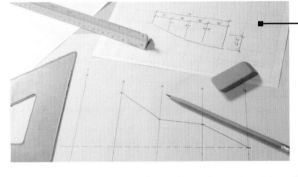

A scale or ruler and triangle allow you to transfer any slope measurements to a formal drawing like this for help in deciding about grades. You can use the same methods to make elevation sketches (see page 49).

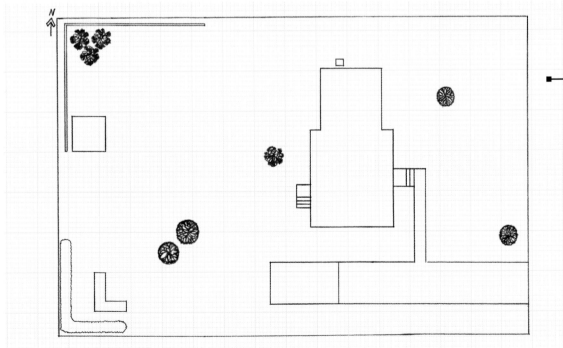

Here is the formal base map drawn from measurements you've recorded. Once you complete your plan, make several photocopies or blueprint copies for you and any contractors to work with. Put the original in a safe place.

45

DRAWING A MAP OF YOUR EXISTING SITE *(continued)*

Having drawn your base map, you now have done more professional landscaping preparation than most people ever accomplish. The next step is to tape a piece of tracing paper over your base plan and go outside again.

This time, on the tracing paper, make notes about your yard, similar to those shown below. Indicate any feature that may affect your landscape decisions: sun, wind, good and bad views, privacy needs, soil, topography, and any other problems or special features your yard presents. Add arrows to indicate directions or intensity.

Also include on the paper any notes about adjoining properties that may be relevant to your plan: nearby trees, for example, or noise, erosion, or drainage problems.

Next, to make sure you fully analyze your lot, go back indoors. Check the views from the windows in the rooms where you spend the most time, and from

your entryways, noting all the pluses and minuses of each view.

Get out any lists of likes and dislikes you've noted about your yard over the years. Write everything of importance to your plan on the piece of tracing paper.

If you are drawing up this plan after studying your yard for a full cycle of seasons, you are ready to proceed. If not, the plan will help you notice more keenly how such features as sun, shadows, wind, and views change with the time of day and time of year. Put your plan in a handy spot so that you can add to it as needed.

Only after creating such a plan can you apply the information supplied in the rest of this book to the climate and other characteristics of your yard. Combine the possibilities with your own realities and you will make decisions that will enhance the best—and change the worst—landscape features.

This tracing page puts the sample original base plan into the context of the lot's unique climate and surroundings. Pin your own "problem plan" on a wall or some other place where you can refer to it easily.

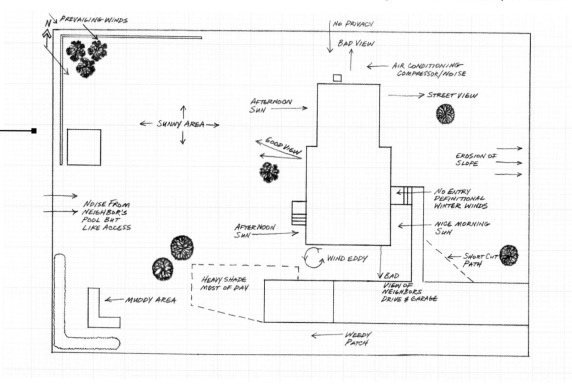

DESIGNING YOUR NEW LANDSCAPE

The initial design stage is the most important, creative, exciting, and forgiving of all the landscaping steps. Let it be the most fun as well.

The process is a simple one: Lay tracing paper over your base plan, sketch all sorts of ideas, then select or change ideas based on how they fit together, and how they solve the problems or accent the features you highlighted on your problem plan.

Ideas

Be sure to give your plan time to evolve. You may find that ideas come slowly at first but possibilities multiply as you play with them. (See pages 26 and 28 for hints on generating ideas.)

You'll want to decide early on if there's a single landscape style—formal, natural, English cottage, and such—that you'd like to adopt. To help you with this decision, check to see whether your ideas seem to be leaning toward a specific look. Once you've selected a style, you can choose and reject ideas more readily. This saves you time and helps you develop a more unified design.

Bubble tracings

At the start, instead of sketching specific ideas on the tracing paper, draw bubbles representing the possible general-use areas you see for the yard: entry, outdoor living, service, and play, for example. (See illustration below.) Most of the front and perhaps some of the side, for example, could be entry area. Most of the back and perhaps part of a side yard could be reserved for outdoor living and entertaining. Drawing such bubbles keeps you from getting too specific too early in the process.

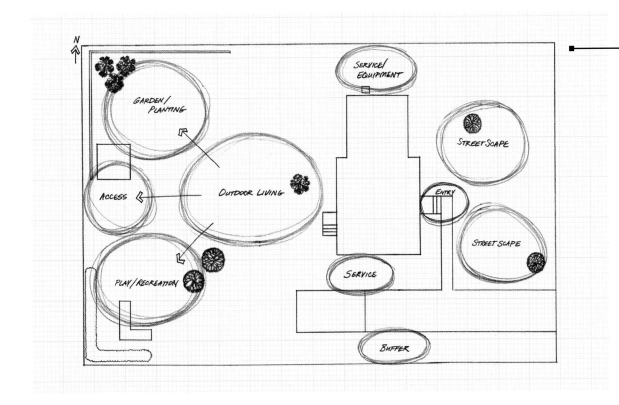

Still looking at your yard as a whole, begin to consider the separate uses you'd like your landscape to serve. Draw bubbles representing general-use areas—and erase and redraw them—until you find the locations that work best in terms of function and looks.

DESIGNING YOUR NEW LANDSCAPE *(continued)*

Continue to trace over the base map, trying new options and erasing or tossing rejected solutions until you come up with several feasible combinations.

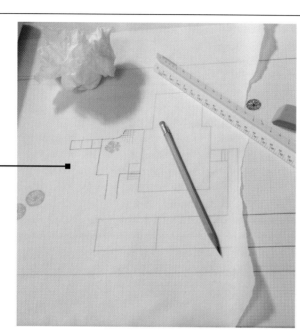

Here's a handy way to visualize your plans: Lay tracing paper over an enlarged photo of your house or other yard site and draw sketches of proposed additions.

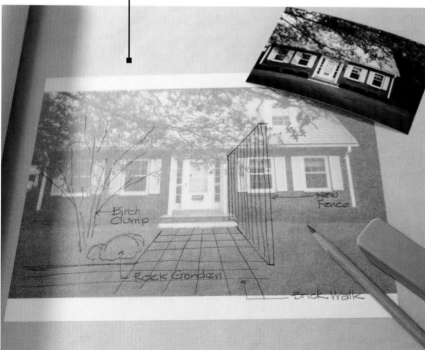

As you do your bubble tracings of general-use areas, you may also want to cut out some smaller bubbles—from any kind of slightly thicker paper—to represent areas that will have a specific use, say a patio, deck, or pool. You can move these patterns around easily, trying different arrangements within the broader space you've allotted to that general use.

Be sure when you're considering the general uses for your yard that you set aside space for a service area or two (see Chapter 11, pages 288–307). These are the areas in your landscape that will accommodate everything from trash cans, recycling bins, and drying clothes to pets and fireplace wood. Put these service areas in the least conspicuous but most convenient spots possible.

As you sketch the bubbles and as you begin to draw more specific ideas on your tracing paper, be sure to refer to your problem plan (see page 46). Double-check all dimensions to make certain the pieces you're considering still fit in the whole. Refer, too, to any lists you made of your family's outdoor needs. Ask often what the rest of the family thinks about the plan. Considering everyone's ideas and desires will help in assessing and implementing the plan and in the ultimate success of your landscape.

Concentrate on problems and solutions at this stage, not fine detail. Think of the plants as architectural forms: background or specimen trees, high or low screens. Save the decisions about varieties for later.

Three-dimensional thinking

Remember that your scale plan is accurate but flat. Expand on it by walking around the yard and pacing off proposed changes, then by sitting on a step and visualizing the finished scene.

Use some props too. Lay out hoses to indicate the edges of patios. Put up bed sheets to mark the height of fences. Go out after dark and shine a flashlight to give the effect of night lighting.

Draw some simple elevation sketches. They don't have to be as accurate as those shown at right, although you can implement the same tools and methods you used for your base plan to make your elevation sketches every bit as detailed; and the greater the detail, the easier it will be for you to picture the results.

Or, for a quick elevation view, enlarge a photo of your house, lay tracing paper over it, then sketch in possible changes (see bottom photo, opposite).

This may be a good time to make separate, large-scale plans of various sections of the yard. At some point, you also may want to draw specific plans indicating lighting, drainage, or other special construction needs. These detailed plans will greatly help those doing the work.

Long-term thinking

When testing the pros and cons of ideas, think of how things will look not only at the time the work is completed but also in 5 years, in 10 years, in 25 years. Consider, too, how your landscaping needs may change over time. After all, landscaping is an evolutionary art form that's never really finished.

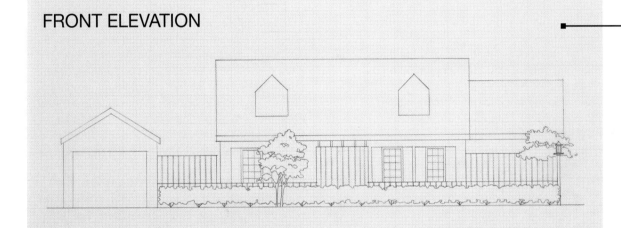

FRONT ELEVATION

Simple elevation drawings such as these can help you make decisions and better visualize the results of your plans. Note how the height and spread of planting materials relate to the size of the house.

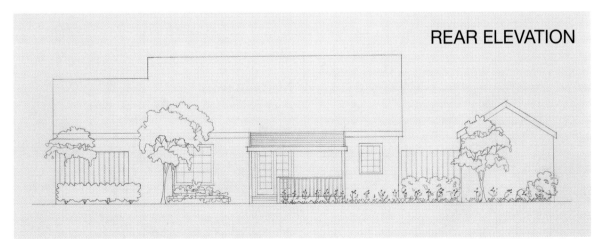

REAR ELEVATION

CHOOSING YOUR FINAL PLAN

If you diligently dream up different solutions to your site problems and ways to achieve the functions that your family wants to include, you're bound to come up with several possible landscape plans.

Your alternative plans probably won't be as definitively drawn as those shown opposite and on the two pages following, since you will have been automatically condensing and eliminating along the way. These plan options were drawn so that you could see three approaches to the same problem plan.

You may say, "If it were my house, I'd definitely choose Plan B." Or you may eliminate it as "Nice, but not for us" and prefer the first or the third or a combination.

The main point is that each of these plans accommodates all the notes presented on the problem plan. Be sure that the options you finally choose do the same for your problem plan.

Further study

While you are moving from concept to final plan, you will want to carefully read the relevant parts of the rest of this book.

Interesting homes and yards that you quickly drove by earlier will demand more detailed study now. You may find yourself driving by certain homes slowly—and often—but the time will be well spent.

In fact you may want to park and make sketches—or take photos—of concepts you like. Or get out and ask the homeowners about certain features that particularly interest you. Most people will be flattered and more than willing to expand on how and why they did what they did.

Go to the library and take another look at books and plans. Check prices at home-supply stores and in catalogs. Seek estimates from contractors as you approach the final decisions.

Keep drawing

By drawing through your ideas, you will keep the concept developing toward its final stage. No one can say for sure when you reach that point. When you think you're getting close, ask yourself these questions:

● Does the plan meet all building codes or deed, setback, or easement restrictions?
● Have I solved all of the problems presented on my problem plan?
● Are my choices realistic in view of the cost, work, and time involved to implement them?
● Will the yard I've planned provide for all of the functions my family wants, or at least the most important ones?
● Is the plan in keeping with our lifestyle? Does it fit my family? Will my family fit it?
● Can we safely move cars (or trucks and other necessary equipment) onto and off the property and park them where needed?
● Are there usable and pleasing sequences: easy access from car to kitchen or front door, from indoor rooms to outdoor living areas, from garden to shed?
● Will the yard be pleasant to the eye, ear, nose, sole, and soul in every season? From indoors looking out? From the street looking in? From the outdoors looking around?

No plan is perfect. It doesn't have to be. It only has to be the best that you can come up with at the moment for your site, your climate, and your family.

Nor is any plan ever completely finished. As you, your family, and your trees grow and mature, you will no doubt have to make some minor changes. Maybe you'll even decide to make major changes. That's OK, too. This is paper, not stone; a guide, not a law.

The final plan

When you're ready, place a new piece of tracing paper over the base plan and draw your final plan. Try to make your plan neat and concise now. Make sketches and notations bold enough to read easily.

You can still indicate plants by general type. Remain vague about structure design and materials, too, if you like. Workers at your local nursery and building-supply center can help you make decisions about specific plants and structural details after looking at your final plan.

PLAN A

The fence across the back and around to the garage provides the utmost in privacy for the backyard. The gate saves good-neighbor relations. Trees buffer noise and stop prevailing winds.

This clump of trees adds interest to the new deck, making it more usable and enjoyable. Walkways and surrounding plantings tie the deck to the site. The walks provide access to the yard.

In this logical and problem-solving scheme, the backyard includes well-defined play/storage and lawn/visual zones. In front, the inviting streetscape gives the house distinction.

This short bit of fence gives privacy from the house next door. Trees soften it and buffer noise from neighbors. Shrubs around the air conditioner soften sound and improve the view.

The deck itself is on the same level as important rooms inside. The vined arbor shades the deck, softens the summer shadows indoors, and lets in full sun in the winter, when it's needed.

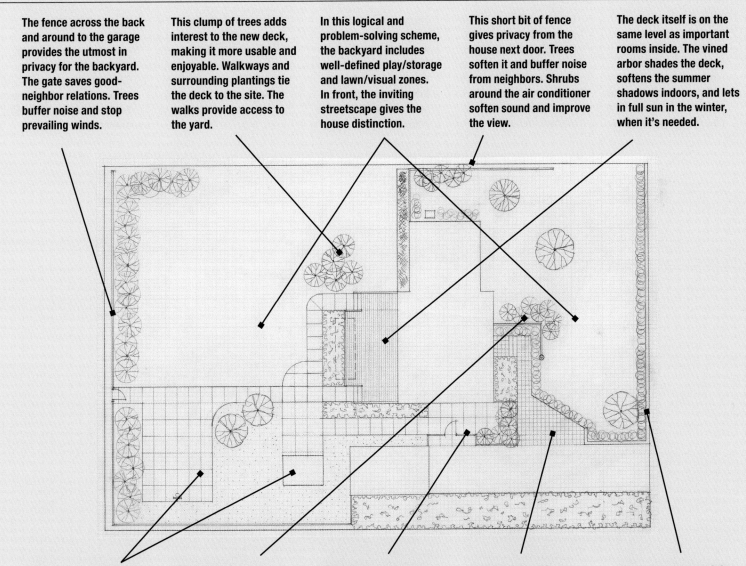

Shady and muddy areas where few plants would grow are ideal for a storage shed and play court. The existing trees make the walkway system seem natural and keep the court from looking bare.

This clump of trees gives scale, beauty, and distinction to the front of the house. It keeps the winter wind from whipping the front storm door out of hand on blustery days.

This high fence screens the view of the neighbors' drive and blocks the wind eddy where groceries are unloaded. The gate adds interest and access. Flowering trees create a pleasant view for those inside the house.

A wider entry takes in the shortcut path. Low flowers and groundcover and a low fence separate the yard from the entry without blocking the morning sun. They also add color and elegance.

A new concrete retaining wall solves erosion worries, eliminates the need to mow the slope, and adds visually to the streetscape. Topped with a low hedge, it turns at the drive.

CHOOSING YOUR FINAL PLAN (continued)

PLAN B

This plan uses many of the same elements as Plan A (page 51) but is more formal. Here the outdoor living, service, and streetscape zones are defined more clearly. The play area is out of sight.

A gazebo provides a focal point and also serves as a windbreak. A pool and rock garden separate the main deck and gazebo for two outdoor rooms yet provide visual and audio interest for both.

This angular deck and walkway also are more formal and elaborate. Notice the symmetry and balance. As on Plan A, the deck adjoins and is on the same level as the important rooms indoors.

A fence and clumps of trees give privacy and quiet to the bedroom end of the house, create a pleasant view from the inside, separate front yard and back, and make the house seem longer.

A retaining wall again solves the erosion and mowing problems on the slope. Of brick instead of concrete, it blends with the tone and style of this plan. Turf replaces the shrubbery of Plan A.

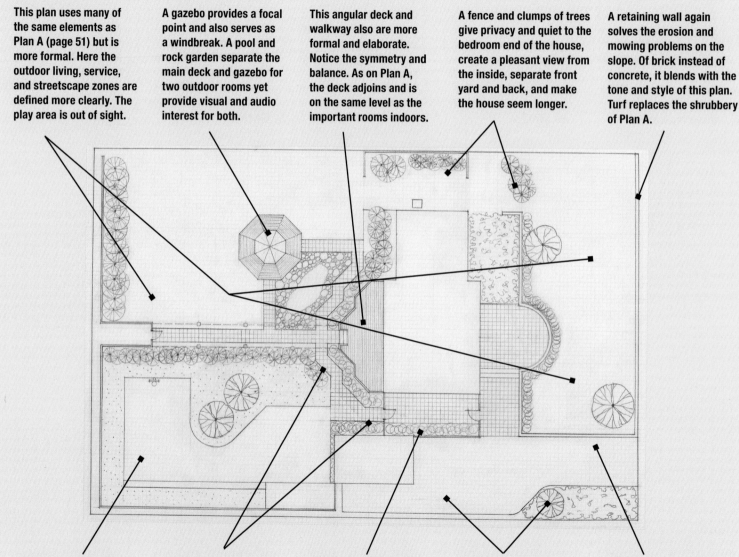

The game court is more elaborate and is separated from the passive lawn area with a hedge and arbor. Existing trees are used and protected. The plan still resolves mud and shade problems.

A patterned and formal walkway system of brick unites the entire yard. From the deck to the back gate, it is covered by an arbor that gives visual interest, shade, and separation.

A hedge at the retaining wall in Plan A is at the entry patio wall here to give a look and feel of substance. Flowers and groundcover at the far end eliminate mowing and look lovely from bedroom windows.

Additional parking space covers a weedy patch. The tree at its approach helps to screen, soften, and shade the greater expanse of paving. The tree is back from the street so as not to block an exiting motorist's view of traffic.

The wall continues along the driveway and entry for continuity of the streetscape and to block the shortcut. This and the simplicity of the front lawn help bring the house visually closer to the street.

PLAN C

This plan gives more informal, natural, and open solutions. Areas of lawn, the unifying elements throughout, are broken only by walkways and trees or tree clumps.

This deck has a spacious shape and feel. A sunshade on the west side of the house cools the deck and the indoors on summer days. The deck continues around to the south side of the house.

A fence and ornamental trees give privacy and provide a sound buffer. Here mulch instead of plantings makes maintenance easier. A bench here would turn this into a secluded nook.

The front lawn is more expansive, with the entry walk and house more of a unit. This version gives the front yard a trimmer, more cottagelike appearance. A fence blocks the old shortcut.

A timber retaining wall along the front lends a more natural-looking solution to the mowing and erosion problem on the slope. Grass grows up to the edge of the wall.

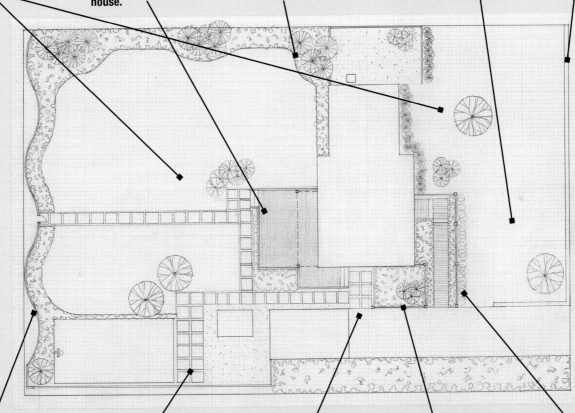

For special interest and a more free-form, informal feeling—in addition to privacy—the back fence undulates across the yard in this plan. Groundcovers and flower borders match the pattern.

Again a series of walkways, expanded in the play and service areas and at the foot of the deck steps, connects and unifies the entire yard. Mulch around the storage shed eases maintenance.

In this plan the service area is not completely enclosed, yet it still is screened by plants and structures for privacy. This gives easy access and a feeling of freer flow from drive to house to yard beyond.

This fence flanks the walk and returns to the house. It screens the view of the drive, as well as the neighbor's drive beyond. It also softens the house corner and sets the tone for more natural landscaping.

The house base seems longer because of this hedge, which extends from the drive to the upper lot line. Though it appears continuous to passersby, breaks make it more interesting and maintainable.

SCHEDULING THE WORK

Now you are ready to get down to the work. The beauty of having a plan is that you know where you are going. Even if it takes years to accomplish, all of your work and expense will be taking you in the right direction. Relax and enjoy the process.

Where to start

Common sense will dictate the work schedule you now should add to your notebook. Most work in most climates will be seasonal, with major planting in spring and fall. Here are some guidelines:
• If landscape destruction is involved, do that first. Clear the site. Be sure to have underground cables, lines, and pipes (TV, telephone, natural or propane gas, water, electricity, drains, etc.) marked by the utility companies to avoid dangerous accidents.
• Visit local building authorities and ask them to explain the procedures and fees for obtaining proper permits. You probably will need to supply scale drawings for decks and other structures, along with distances between them and house and lot lines.
• Do rough grading and the installation of a swimming pool, drainage system, and all underground utilities next. Prepare any large areas of soil while you have the equipment there.
• If possible build structures next. If they are on the waiting list, keep their areas and equipment needs in mind as you plant.

Trees take time

All the money in the world cannot buy the years it takes to grow a large tree, so protect any choice trees you have as if they were gold. You may want to keep even less-choice trees because of the privacy and shade they contribute. Also try to salvage and relocate existing plants that are small enough to withstand transplanting (you can circle the fingers of one hand around their trunks).

When buying trees, get the largest ones you can afford, and plant them as soon as possible. Protect new and existing trees during construction, shielding them within rings of snow fencing.

Consider costs

You probably have been gauging costs instinctively during the planning stages. Now it is time to work up specific figures.

Real estate agents consider it reasonable to spend 10 to 15 percent of the cost of the house and lot on landscaping, not including such large improvements as pools and patio roofs.

If you keep your landscaping costs in this range, most of the expense is likely to boost the value of your property. Some of the work, too, will immediately or eventually reduce the costs of heating and cooling. And all will make an appreciable difference in your quality of life, comfort, and health.

Most plans call for some work that is beyond your capability, time, or desire to do personally. See page 32 for available help. Then check your local Yellow Pages. Begin talking to contractors or doing some comparison shopping for materials.

To get a realistic picture of costs, double any number you come up with initially. You can save about half of the hired cost if you do a job yourself. Skimping on such things as erosion control, walls, utilities, and such could cost you more in the long run or jeopardize your family's safety.

Work in stages

Whether you do your landscaping work over weekends or years, breaking large jobs into small segments makes goals more attainable. Ask yourself:
• What existing conditions can I live with longest? In a new home, a lawn will reduce glare, summer temperatures, erosion, and tracking into the house. An old lawn, however weedy, may do for an older home until the patio and walks are in place.
• Which improvements will contribute most to my use and enjoyment of my yard?
• Will a new entryway that visitors and passersby see every day mean more, or should I build the deck that will expand my house and outdoor living? The most satisfaction and success usually comes from concentrating on one area at a time.

PLAN D

Only you can decide whether to landscape the backyard or front yard first. The front will add to lot value sooner. You—and others—see it every day. How will backyard use compare?

Plant tree clumps for privacy, windbreak, and shading the deck as soon as possible; plant more mature trees where the need is most urgent. Preserve existing trees at all costs.

How severe is the noise and privacy problem? A fence can be put up and make a big difference in a day. Add vines until the trees grow large. Do your own planting and mulching.

The hedge is another project that almost anyone can do almost anytime. The ratio of improvement to time and cost is high here, and shrubs grow to maturity in only a few seasons.

If the erosion is serious or mowing dangerous, this retaining wall should be a high-priority project. Otherwise it could wait. It will take considerable work, skill, and cost to build this wall.

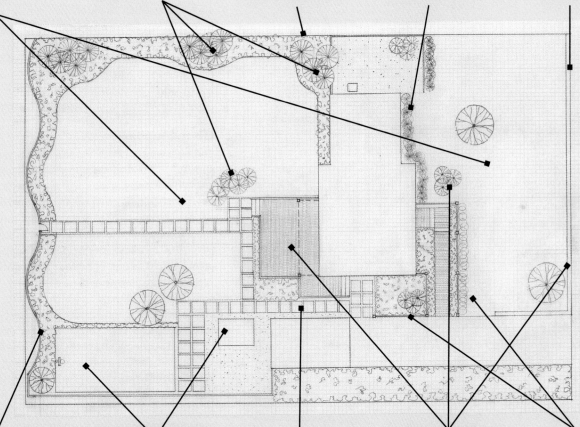

How soon can you afford this fence? It will be costly but make a major difference. Put in trees right away; leave smaller plants until after the fence has been installed.

Play yards for big people might wait; for little people, play areas—and mud solutions—are necessary at once. How long can the garage serve your storage needs?

Walkways can wait or be done in mulch now; pave them when you get the money and time. Start around the house and play court first and work out to the back gate as time, money, and energy are available.

The deck, front wall, and fences are the major structures on this lot. Which does your family want or need the most? Save surrounding deck planting until after construction. A sunshade could come a year later.

The privacy fence at the house corner might be the first to go in. It will make the most difference. The low fence by the walk could be put in after planting. Start groundcovers here; then divide and spread them.

SOLVING DRAINAGE PROBLEMS

Retaining walls need weep holes or other drainage systems so groundwater doesn't back up behind them. To learn about proper drainage for retaining walls, see page 198.

Patios and other paved surfaces should slope away from the house at a rate of at least 1 inch for every 4 linear feet. Earth under decks should slope, too, so water doesn't puddle.

Swales across a site—or from front to back—serve as channels that intercept runoff and direct it to storm sewers or natural drainage areas. For more about swales, see page 58.

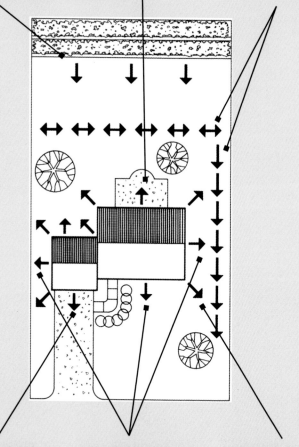

A driveway should slope away from garage doors at a rate of 1 inch per 4 linear feet. If this is impossible, install a drain near the doors.

Water that collects around a foundation can seep into your basement and eventually damage foundation walls. To improve foundation drainage, refer to the instructions on page 57.

Water from downspouts also can threaten basements and foundations. Downspout extenders and splash blocks can solve drainage problems here.

Faulty drainage can play havoc with the best-laid landscaping plan, so pay close attention to where water on your property is originating and where it's going. Correct any drainage difficulties before you begin a project and consider how the project will affect existing drainage patterns when it's completed.

Where you live determines, in part, your approach to drainage. In dry regions, you'll probably want your site to retain as much rainfall as possible; in temperate climates you may need to get rid of excess runoff.

Though water may be water to most of us, to landscapers it falls into two categories: surface water, which flows on top of the ground, and subsurface water, which seeps through the soil.

On the surface

The best way to check out the surface-water situation at your house is to wait for a heavy rain, then go out and get your feet wet. The illustration at left identifies the points where you might find water either puddling or running off. Follow runoff to see if it's coursing into a natural drainage system (such as a stream), invading your neighbor's property, ending up in a storm sewer, or turning a low spot in your yard into a swampy pond.

Sculpting the terrain so that it diverts the flow or installing drainage pipe, as explained opposite and on page 58, will correct most surface-water problems, especially around the foundation. For solutions to more severe drainage situations, see page 59. And to learn how to check erosion caused by surface water, see pages 194–197.

Snow, driven by prevailing winds, also can create drainage problems. Tramp around after a winter storm and note whether drifts and ice are building up at points around the outside of your house. Consider buffering these with fencing, plantings, or both.

Going underground

Surface water that doesn't run off soon percolates through the soil to become subsurface water.

Even though you can't see it, subsurface drainage still affects your landscaping scheme.

One way to assess subsurface drainage is to test your soil's porosity. To do this, dig a hole about 2 feet deep and fill it with water. After the water drains out, fill the hole again. If all the water disappears within 24 hours, the soil is too porous. If water remains after 48 hours, the soil is too dense. If the water level gradually rises, the water table is too high.

Some subsurface drainage problems can be cured by improving surface drainage—directing runoff to parched areas, for example, or away from low spots. Other subsurface problems call for below-the-surface solutions, such as correcting soil that drains too poorly or too quickly, or installing underground drain lines, as shown at lower right, which carry water away from the foundation.

Wet basement

If the floor or walls of your basement are chronically wet, improving surface or subsurface drainage—or a combination of the two—could dry them out. The box at right shows the steps to take. But first, here's how to evaluate which steps are appropriate for your situation:

• Water seeping through a basement wall at or near grade level is probably the result of a grade or downspout problem, both easily corrected, as shown at right.

• Leaks farther down the wall or at floor level usually indicate that subsurface water is building up around the foundation and forcing its way through cracks. Dig down to the level of the leaks—to the footings for floor-level leaks—and install perforated drain lines to carry the excess water away.

• Subterranean water starts out as a thin, barely visible film of moisture on the basement floor. A spring or high water table is forcing water up from below under high pressure, turning your basement into a well. Drain lines around the footings may help reduce subterranean water, but you also may need to install a sump pump.

IMPROVING FOUNDATION DRAINAGE

Use fill to create a gentle slope away from foundation walls. The grade should fall a minimum of ¼ inch per foot for a distance of at least 4 feet from the wall. Use topsoil if you intend to plant here. For more about correcting a grade, see pages 62–63.

Splash blocks may not carry downspout water far enough away from your foundation. If this is the case, dig a trench that will lead from the house to a remote, well-drained exit point that doesn't encroach on your neighbor's property.

Extend the adapter and connect it to a solid, corrugated drainpipe that will carry water away. Connect a special adapter to the downspout outlet. Fill the trench with earth, then cover with sod or mulch.

In some cases, however, even these remedies may not sufficiently reduce the amount of water that collects in the soil next to your foundation. If this is your predicament, proceed to a more involved plan, which is sometimes described by the fancy name "French drain." See page 59 for complete details.

SOLVING DRAINAGE PROBLEMS *(continued)*

Pages 56–57 help identify areas where good landscaping can improve surface or subsurface drainage. Here let's look at specific ways in which you can recontour the terrain or siphon off underground water.

Reshaping slopes

Plan carefully before you cut into a slope. Aim to either slow runoff or redirect it; attempting to dam up water only causes flooding. If you're redirecting runoff, make sure you don't discharge it onto a neighbor's property, which may be a code violation

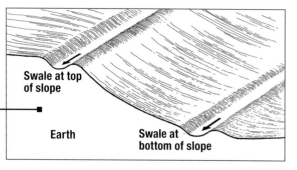

Swale at top of slope

Earth

Swale at bottom of slope

Swales divert water coursing down a hillside. Dig shallow trenches pitched in the direction you want water to go. Mound and compact earth on the downhill side of each trench, then lay sod or plant with groundcover.

Baffles slow runoff. Dig zigzag trenches across the hillside. Make the trenches slightly shallower than the thickness of landscape timbers. Set the timbers so that their tops tilt back into the slope.

and could cause ill feelings. Most codes permit dumping rainwater into a storm sewer but not a sanitary sewer.

Locate swales at the top and bottom of a slope, as shown at left. Make trenches about as wide as a spade, using the earth you excavate to create berms along the swales' lower edges. If swales will cause a mowing problem, plant them with a hardy groundcover.

Baffles impede water's descent, giving it more time to soak into the slope. Baffles also can control erosion, as can bevels and contours.

Installing drain lines

Years ago the most popular material used for drainage was clay tile. Then homeowners latched onto rigid, 4-inch-diameter PVC pipe that typically comes in 10-foot-long sections—either perforated or nonperforated—and can be interconnected using couplings and PVC cement. Today most homeowners and professional landscapers prefer to work with corrugated drainage tubing. You can usually find it in 3-, 4-, and 6-inch diameters, although in most installations you'll see the 4-inch size being used. This handy tubing makes turns easily, comes in slotted (same concept as perforated) or solid versions, and is typically available in 10-, 100-, and 250-foot rolls.

If the purpose of your project is to collect water, you'll want to use the perforated product. On the other hand, if all you need to do is to haul away the water you've already collected, stick to the solid tubing. For either installation, dig a trench about 4 inches wider than the tube's diameter and about 12 to 18 inches deep.

For solid tubing, simply position it at the bottom of the trench and cover it with soil and sod. To collect the water using slotted tubing, see the French drain installation, opposite.

INSTALLING A FRENCH DRAIN

To capture or absorb water where it has collected—or, as in this example, to intercept subsurface water oozing toward your foundation wall—the French drain is your best bet. Begin by digging a drainage trench alongside the entire wall. When you come to the end of the wall, start angling your trench toward the nearest storm-sewer collection point or to a piece of well-drained ground. Both portions of your continual trench—the collection run that follows alongside your foundation wall and the exit run that wends its way to the nearest outlet point—should have a slope of about ¼ inch per foot of horizontal run.

For the collection portion of your system, you'll want to use slotted corrugated drainage tubing. After you've finished the 12- to 18-inch-deep trench, line the bottom and both sides of the trench with landscape fabric, leaving plenty of excess fabric on each side so that you can fold it over the pipe later. Then add a couple of inches of gravel in the bottom.

Position the slotted tubing on top of the gravel, cover the tubing with another 2- or 3-inch layer of gravel, and carefully fold the landscaping fabric over the tubing and gravel—first one side, then the other. (Be sure to fold fabric over the open end of the pipe as well, then cover with more gravel.) After you've worked your way along the entire length of the foundation wall and are ready to channel the water to an exit point, use a coupling piece to connect the end of a roll of solid corrugated tubing to the end of the slotted tubing. From that point onward you won't need either gravel or landscape fabric. Now cover your entire trench with soil and sod or mulch.

1 Dig a 12- to 18-inch-deep trench through the overly saturated area, then angle it toward the nearest piece of well-drained ground.

2 Line both sides and bottom of the trench with landscape fabric, then shovel a couple inches of gravel into the bottom.

3 Unroll slotted corrugated tubing on top of the gravel throughout the saturated area, then shovel a layer of gravel on top.

4 Fold the fabric over the tubing and gravel, add gravel, then cover with soil and sod. Connect to solid tubing for the exit run.

Note:

An increasingly popular alternative to landscape fabric is a product made especially for corrugated tubing called a drain sock. It's made of filtration-barrier fabric and pulls onto the tubing just as a sock pulls onto your foot. You can purchase tubing that already has the drain sock installed or buy tubing and sock separately. If you use this system, you simply pour gravel into the bottom of the trench, place the sock-covered tubing on top of the gravel, then cover the whole works with more gravel. (Tie a knot in the sock at the uphill end of the tubing and screw a special louvered piece onto the exit end.) Using a preformed drain sock eliminates the need to fold and position long sheets of the landscape fabric.

SOLVING DRAINAGE PROBLEMS *(continued)*

Even if you've sloped the soil away from your foundation and installed a drainage system, you still might have one additional source of foundation seepage— an overabundance of evergreens or deciduous shrubs planted right next to the wall. Whenever you give the plants a generous drink of water, there's a good chance excess moisture will saturate the soil and run down the wall, seeking an opening into your basement. If you have this problem, one solution entails moving all plantings at least 4 feet away from the house.

In order to improve drainage around the house, sometimes it's necessary to remove shrubbery planted too close to the structure. If located under eaves, plants often require supplemental watering, which can complicate the issue.

Ideally, foundation landscaping slopes slightly away from the house. In this case, the front walk also has enough of a slant to drain readily in all kinds of wet weather. The well-designed plantings work together to enhance, rather than obscure, the house.

DEALING WITH SPECIAL DRAINAGE PROBLEMS

Contouring, redirecting the flow of surface water, and installing simple below-the-surface systems such as the French drain help remedy most drainage problems, but some situations require more extensive measures.

What do you do, for example, about a larger-than-typical low spot where water chronically collects? What if your yard has compacted, poorly draining soil, or a discharge from drain lines that can't reach a disposal area? Is your soil too dry to support plants?

Each of these systems calls for one of the special approaches listed below.

Catch basins

Drain an expansive, swampy area with a catch basin, illustrated at right. Water falls through a grate at ground level and collects until a sloping (⅛ inch per foot of run) drainpipe can carry it off to a proper discharge area. A sediment trap snags leaves and other debris that also wash through the grate.

You can buy a ready-made catch basin or you can make your own basin and drainage system. Choose the basin's location and the location of the drainpipe carefully, as well as the discharge point.

Because sediment piles up in catch basins, they need periodic cleaning.

Drainage chimneys

Improve the absorbency of dense, slow-draining soil with drainage chimneys. Dig 8- to 12-inch-diameter holes, spaced 2 to 4 feet apart. Make each hole deep enough to penetrate the hard surface soil but don't go down to the water table. Fill the holes with gravel or crushed rock. To hide the chimneys from view and give your yard a finished look, top off the holes with sod or other plants.

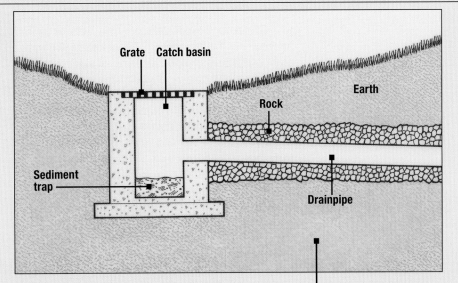

Dry wells

What can you do with drain lines—from downspouts, for instance, or along a foundation—that can't be emptied into a storm sewer or natural drainage area? Answer: Connect them to a dry well, which is simply a large hole filled with rock and covered with a concrete slab or other impervious material.

Local codes, pegged to regional rainfall data, dictate the size of dry wells, but 2 to 4 feet wide by 3 feet deep is typical.

Irrigation

Contouring and underground drain lines can bring water to dry areas of your lot, but if there's simply not enough rainfall to keep your lawn and gardens green, you'll need to irrigate them. One good way to do this is with an underground sprinkler system that automatically supplies moisture at optimum times of day. To learn about installing an underground sprinkler system, see pages 318–321.

In a particularly troublesome low spot that's prone to heavy flooding, install a catch basin. Cover it with a grate or fill the basin all the way to the top with crushed rock. Extensive low-lying areas may need several catch basins for satisfactory results.

CORRECTING THE GRADE

Improving surface-water drainage, adding contours to a flat site, and excavating for a new walk or patio all require some remodeling of your lot's topography. Making changes in grade is the necessary—and sometimes arduous—first step in any number of landscaping projects.

Work out a complete grading plan, from lot line to lot line, before you begin excavating. This way you can conserve soil and effort by moving earth from high spots to low ones. A comprehensive grading plan also can save money if you must order additional soil or have excess amounts hauled away; many suppliers and truckers add a surcharge for quantities of fewer than 5 cubic yards (for more about purchasing soil, see the opposite page).

For safety's sake, mark the locations of all underground telephone, gas, sewer, water, and other utility lines before digging. Many utility companies will come out and mark their lines for you, usually at no charge. Also file with your building department for any permits you might need.

Moving earth

All but very major regrading can be accomplished with a pick, shovel, rake, wheelbarrow, and other simple hand tools. To make the job easier, consider renting equipment such as a power tiller to break up the soil and a front-end-loading garden tractor or even a skid loader to push soil around.

If you decide to do the job the old-fashioned way (and give your body a modern-day workout), plan short sessions of digging and hauling. Spread them out over several weekends, if need be. Dig when soil is slightly moist, neither heavily laden with water nor rock hard and unyielding. To conserve your strength, don't overload the shovel or wheelbarrow, and lay a path of planks from excavation to fill sites.

Professional excavators can move a surprising amount of earth in a few days. Be warned, however, that heavy machinery can do a lot of damage to landscaping around the area to be excavated—not a problem for jobs with easy street

Here a slope adjacent to a foundation is being corrected by laying out the new grade level with string, as explained opposite. Measure to determine how much fill you will need.

Shift soil from a spot higher than the final grade to build up lower areas, a process known as cutting and filling. If you can't cut and fill, you'll have to haul soil from another area in your yard that needs lowering—or buy it.

After you've moved soil and compacted it, rake to shape the final grade. Here fill comes to slightly below the chalk line because a layer of crushed rock will go on top. If you plan to lay sod, allow for its thickness as well.

access, such as a driveway, but you wouldn't want a heavy tractor crunching across an established lawn or planting beds.

Laying out a slope

To drain properly, any grading you do must slope away from the house or other structure at a rate of no less than ¼ inch per foot. With rough recontouring projects, you can visually estimate the fall, making sure that it doesn't drain toward areas where water would puddle.

For greater precision, use stakes, string, and a level, as shown opposite and on page 65. Drive stakes at the top and bottom of the new slope, stretch string between the stakes, and level it. Measure the string's length. Finally, slide the string down the lower stake at least ¼ inch for every foot of length. Bear in mind that even a nearly level project, such as a patio, must have some pitch to it.

Making the grade

After you've determined the slope, grading proceeds in three phases. First you strip away the sod, if any, shovel up topsoil, and set the two aside for reuse. Next you establish the rough grade by removing or adding subsoil. Finally you replace the topsoil, smooth it, then lay sod or plant.

In a small area, skim sod by slicing into it with a sharp spade held almost parallel to the ground. Separate sod from the soil underneath with short, jabbing strokes, rolling it up as you go. If you have a lot of sod to deal with, rent a power-driven sod cutter. As you remove topsoil under the sod, chop it up to destroy any grass roots.

Attack subsoil next, digging into the earth at about a 45-degree angle. Push the handle downward, then lift and pitch the soil into a wheelbarrow or low spot. After moving the subsoil, break it into chunks measuring an inch or less. If you encounter rocks, split them with a sledge or use them as fill. Mound the fill slightly, then compact it until it's even with surrounding undisturbed soil.

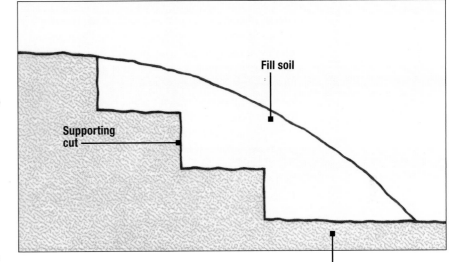

Fill soil

Supporting cut

To make a steep slope more gradual, dig a series of stair-stepped supporting cuts first, then add fill. The supporting cuts help hold the fill, protecting against erosion until grass or groundcover establishes itself.

After you're satisfied with the rough grade, spread out the topsoil you've saved and smooth it with a steel rake.

Purchasing soil

If your grading project will require extensive filling, you may need to buy additional earth. First determine how many cubic yards to order; 1 cubic yard will cover 300 square feet to a depth of 1 inch.

Look for soil that approximates the texture of the existing soil. Differing textures can cause drainage problems because water does not move easily from one soil texture to another. Soil quality and prices vary widely, so check with several suppliers and be sure to take a look at the merchandise.

Test soil by crumbling it in your hand. Soil that breaks down easily into uniform particles works best. Avoid compacted, sandy, or poor-quality earth, which could be contaminated by weed seeds and other soil problems.

Before the soil is delivered, plan a route for the truck so that you can dump the load as near as possible to the work site. If a truck can back into the site, the driver can spread out the earth, saving you a lot of hard work.

63

LAYING OUT PROJECT SITES

Now—after you've assessed your landscaping needs, developed a plan, and solved any drainage problems your lot might have—comes the moment when you begin to get your ideas off the ground. The chapters that follow proceed step-by-step through dozens of landscaping projects—everything from rustic paths to raised decks. But all start in the same way: You mark the site, then square and stake corners. Let's take a look at how to lay the groundwork for a successful project.

Siting basics

To lay out the site for a landscaping project, arm yourself with two 50-foot tape measures, a chalk line, line level, mason's level, plumb bob, carpenter's square, sledge, and pointed wooden stakes. You'll also need a helper and chalk, lime, or sand. The job doesn't take long, but take your time: A measurement that's off by just an inch at the outset can compound itself into feet down the line.

Begin by marking an approximate outline of the project's boundaries with stakes and string. Use rope or garden hose to mark curves. This outline gives you your first full-scale look at how a new fence, patio, or other improvement will affect its surroundings. If you don't like what you see, making changes at this point is as easy as pulling up stakes and erasing a line on your landscape plan.

Once you're ready to formally measure and mark the layout, consider using batter boards (crosspieces nailed to stakes) to locate any corners, as shown opposite, bottom right. Batter boards make good sense for decks, fences, and other projects where height or slope is a factor. Batter boards also come in handy for inground projects such as patios if you prefer to remove the strings before digging, then put them up again to see if edges have strayed.

Just run string from batter board to batter board, and—if you're building an attached structure—from batter boards to the house.

If your terrain and your project are level, you can dispense with batter boards and lay out the project with strings and stakes. In fact, if your design has a curve or two, this is about the only way to go. For straight edges, simply stretch strings from stakes at each end. For curves, stake a garden hose in position. For precise curves, use a stake and string as a compass. Locate the stake equidistant from the beginning and end of the curve, then swing the string in an arc, driving stakes at 1-foot intervals.

(Note: When putting up strings for concrete patios and walks and other projects that require forms, be sure to mark a perimeter several inches outside the actual planned slab to allow room for form boards and stakes.)

Checking corners

Whether you lay out your project with simple stakes or use batter boards, you'll want to be sure that any corners are exactly square before proceeding. Use a simple geometric formula.

As you probably recall learning in school, the square of the hypotenuse in a right triangle equals the sum of the squares of the two shorter sides. This means that if one leg of a triangle measures 3 feet (3 squared = 9) and the other 4 feet (4 squared = 16), the diagonal hypotenuse must be exactly 5 feet (square root of 9 + 16).

To mark the perimeter of a project, stretch string between stakes a few inches above ground level, square any corners, then use a hose to lay out the perimeter. Next pour powdered chalk, white sand, or lime along the hose. This tactic works best on level land.

One way to position posts on a slope: Mark 1-foot intervals on a 2×4. Butt this against the starting stake at the slope top. Level the board, drop a plumb bob, then drive a stake at that point.

Use the principle of the 3-4-5 triangle to square a corner. Use the largest multiple practical. Here, the reference points along the string are 6 and 8 feet from the corner. A diagonal measurement of 10 feet indicates a square corner.

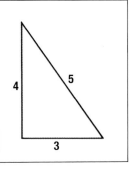

The sides of a triangle with a square corner always relate to one another in the same way. You also can use multiples of 3-4-5 (6-8-10; 9-12-15).

Use the principle of the 3-4-5 triangle to assure that a corner is square. First mark a spot 3 feet over from the corner. Extend a tape measure 4 feet along the string line. The diagonal between these points must be 5 feet. Use multiples of 3-4-5 for larger layouts.

After you turn a second corner and plot locations for a third run of posts, as you would with a square or rectangular structure such as a deck, measure diagonally from both sets of opposite corners; these measurements must be equal for the layout to be a rectangle or a square.

Marking for digging

For patios and other projects requiring excavation, once you know the corners are at right angles, sprinkle powdered chalk, lime, or sand along the strings, as shown opposite. These marks will guide you as you dig. Also adjust the string to the proper grade so you can use it as a reference when determining how deep to dig.

For projects that require posts, measure along the strings, drop a plumb bob, and drive stakes.

Make batter boards by nailing crosspieces to stakes. You'll need two assemblies for each corner, situated one foot or so beyond the corner. Stretch strings, square them, and drop a plumb bob to position each corner stake.

ERECTING POSTS

After the site is laid out, the next step in the construction of many projects is erecting posts.

Posts for a deck, fence, or other structure must be absolutely plumb and firmly rooted in the earth or bolted to a concrete footing. To ward off rot, posts should be of heartwood cedar, pressure-treated lumber, or the newer PVC versions, and steps should be taken to ensure that water drains away from posts made of wood. To prevent posts from heaving, postholes must extend below the local frost line.

Step by step

Begin by digging holes at the points you've staked. Choose your digging equipment based partly on how hard or rocky your soil is and partly on how deep you must go to reach your area's frost line. For shallow holes in soft earth, use a clamshell digger; for hard soil or holes deeper than about 30 inches, you'll need a hand- or motor-powered auger. Most rental outlets offer all three of these tools.

Next you'll need to determine whether you want to set the posts in the ground, as shown here, or on top of separate footings (see page 108). Separate footings require more concrete because you must completely fill the postholes. You'll also need to insert anchors into the tops of the wet footings. Local codes may dictate one method or the other.

To set posts in the ground, first soak the holes, then drop in 2 to 3 inches of gravel. Put tubular forms in the holes, if you like, so you can extend the concrete above ground, which helps keep surface water away from the posts.

After you set each post in place, adjust until it is plumb in two directions, then secure the post with two diagonal braces nailed to the post. If necessary, use string tied to end posts to check the alignment of intermediate posts.

Recheck that the posts are plumb, then pour concrete into the holes, poking with a rod to remove air pockets. At the top of the hole or form, round off the concrete. Let the concrete cure 24 hours before doing any other work.

To ensure that posts are an even height, you can dig holes to a uniform depth or cut posts after the concrete cures. To check depths, make a square as shown at left and stake a level string. Cut the square's longer arm to reflect desired depth; the shorter one rests on string when you reach that depth.

Once posts are braced in position, backfill around any forms, then pack holes or forms with concrete. After the concrete has set for about 20 minutes, check the posts for plumb again and adjust if necessary. Leave the braces in place for at least 24 hours.

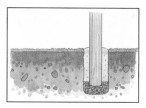

Good drainage begins at the bottom of each posthole you dig. Wet down the hole, then pour in 2 to 3 inches of gravel. This prevents groundwater from collecting at the base of the post.

DEALING WITH EXISTING PLANTS

Most large-scale landscaping projects demand that you first tear out a considerable amount of existing landscaping. Aim to reuse what you can and decide in advance what you're going to do with the debris you don't need. If more than a few cubic yards of branches, bushes, earth, or other materials must go to a landfill, consider renting a refuse container.

Leave large or dangerous jobs, such as major grading and removing trees, to professionals with equipment and know-how. Consider renting a power-driven sod cutter, mulcher, small tractor, or other machinery to make clearing jobs easier.

Clear weedy and overgrown areas by carefully applying an herbicide and removing all plant remains. Alternatively, dig out plants, including roots. The best time to do this is in early spring.

Transplanting

Want to relocate choice shrubs and trees? You may need help lifting them out of the ground and setting them in again, but shrubs of medium size and trees no taller than 6 feet, with trunks no larger than 1 inch in diameter, lend themselves to amateur transplanting. Of course, with professional help, you can safely transplant trees many feet taller.

Spring and fall are the best times to move shrubs and trees, but if you keep the roots moist, you can shift plants in the summer too.

Dig carefully around the root zone—shaping a mass of roots and soil—and gently free the root ball from the ground. When the root ball can be rocked from side to side, wrap it in burlap, then fasten with twine.

After you've set the plant in its new home, remove the twine and burlap. Replant at the same depth as the plant's former location. Water thoroughly. Water weekly, if it doesn't rain, through the first season.

To move a deep-rooted shrub to a new home, dig around and under the plant, severing as few roots as possible. Roll the root ball onto a heavy-duty tarp and slide the plant to the place where it will be transplanted.

If young shrubs can't be planted or transplanted right away, tuck them into a temporary bed in a shaded place, covering the root balls with soil and a 2-inch layer of mulch.

GALLERY OF BERM IDEAS

Defining berms

Berms are little more than pretty bumps in the landscape. But their sizes and shapes can vary almost infinitely. Berms can be just a foot tall or can rise a dozen or more feet above the ground. Make a berm 4 to 40 feet wide, depending on the site. Whatever their ultimate design becomes, berms can contribute significantly to a gracefully rolling landscape. Depending on the space you have available, you can build your own versions of these eyecatching features and top them with everything from sod to a rock garden to trees and shrubs—or whatever else your imagination envisions.

Regardless of their sizes or shapes, berms contribute much more than sheer beauty. They can define areas, direct traffic, reduce street noise, buffer winds, create privacy, divert runoff, and serve you in a host of other ways.

Consider their impact

If you decide to add one or more of these landscape-changing features, be sure to consider their potential effect on two important issues—surface-water movement and proportion.

• **Water movement.** Depending on where you put it, a berm can either help or hinder water flow. So when you sketch it in on your plan be sure to walk the landscape and make certain that this new element will direct water to a natural exit point rather than cause it to pool up.

• **Proportion.** Obviously a massive mound has no place on a tiny lot. As you size and locate your berms, keep this caution in mind. You want your new landscaping features to blend well with their surroundings rather than dominate them.

Visualize the mowing process

You've probably had the experience of running your lawn mower over a bump in the grass and, much to your chagrin, creating a bald spot. The same thing can happen if you make the bottom edge of your berm too steep. You can avoid this problem by creating a very gradual incline all around the base.

The same concept applies at the crown—that is, if you lay sod over the entire mound. Make the transition between sides and top very gradual, and form a level surface at the top before proceeding down the other side. This way you'll prevent another scalping job.

Build your own berm

Don't underestimate the amount of back-challenging work ahead of you. If you intend to create a very large berm or a series of good-sized undulations, you may be wise to rent a skid loader or hire a pro to bring one in to do the hauling and piling. One of these powerful machines can get a lot of work done in a day.

On the other hand, if your plans call for a smaller project—say, a berm with a maximum height of 4 feet—you can handle it yourself with a little help. Begin by having loads of two materials delivered: clay and topsoil. The outer foot of your berm should be topsoil, the rest clay. However, if you are building a much larger mound, consider using rubble for the bottom layer, followed by the clay and, finally, the topsoil. Rubble—small chunks of rock, bricks, and concrete—is usually less expensive than clay. In fact, check around. You might be lucky enough to come across a neighbor who's tearing out an old sidewalk; you could put those surplus pieces to good use and the neighbor most likely would be thrilled to see them disappear from his/her property.

If the area where you're installing the berm is now covered with lawn, remove and re-lay the turf or give it to someone who can use it. Then loosen up the soil where the lawn used to be.

Now's the time to organize a wheelbarrow party for family and friends. Lay out some large boards—2×10s or 2×12s are great—for wheelbarrow paths and start hauling. After your berm reaches a couple of feet high, it's time to shovel and throw, shovel and throw. And when you get to the topsoil stage, have someone continually tamp the dirt as you go. As soon as you are finished, cover the entire surface with sod or plantings to control erosion.

Once the trees mature, it will be difficult to tell that there's a busy street on the other side of this front yard berm. Built to block the sight and sound of traffic, it already adds privacy and a pretty view.

On a spacious site, a massive berm and adjacent walkway will create privacy and direct foot traffic.

Soft contouring makes this bermed area of lawn appear to be a natural part of the landscape. While creating visual interest, it's also easy to mow.

In this tricky situation the house sits at the top of a slope. The front-yard landscaping eliminates drainage issues and creates a flat front terrace. Boulders help hold the bermed area between the house and the sidewalk.

BUILDING RAISED BEDS

Ground-level planting areas are an essential part of any good landscaping plan. Spread them throughout your property so that you can enjoy a sprinkling of color and beauty in every direction. But what do you do if your soil is too hard to work, doesn't drain properly, or won't support heralthy, vigorous plants? One solution entails building and installing a raised planting bed—or a series of them—filled with just the right mixture of soil and amendments.

You'll find raised beds made of everything from landscape timbers to rock, rustic logs to vertical posts (standing tightly together), bricks to 1½-inch-thick lumber. (Boards that are ¾ inch thick, such as 1×12s, are too weak to stand up to the pressure from the soil inside.) Depths can range from about 10 inches up to 2 feet or higher. However, the typical bed is about 10 to 12 inches deep, and its frame is usually made from ground-contact, pressure-treated 2×10s or 2×12s. A practical width is 4 feet, which allows you to reach all plants from one side or the other. Choose whatever length your plan can accommodate but be sure to brace the unit at least every 2 feet of length. Use galvanized fasteners throughout the project for lasting quality.

Size and shape is up to you, but the same process applies. Let's take a look at the basic steps involved to duplicate the project shown here:

A raised bed offers many advantages. It provides an easy-to-manage garden where soil is poor, improving drainage and accessibility.

1 Locate your raised beds where the ground is fairly level. Outline each area with temporary stakes and some string. Remove any sod and reuse it somewhere else if possible. Then use a shovel and/or garden rake to smooth out the area and level it.

2 This frame assembly, a 4-foot square, features 4×4 corner posts that establish the bed's height (11 inches, in this case). For the first pair of walls, attach two 48-inch lengths of 2×6 lumber to the posts as shown, using 2½-inch deck screws.

3 Cut 2×6 lumber for the remaining two walls to a length of 58 inches. Clamp the lower course to the posts, ends flush with the outside of each post as shown. Check for level, then use more deck screws to attach these side wall boards to the posts. Repeat for the remaining side wall, then measure diagonals across the top of the frame and adjust the corners until the diagonals measure the same.

4 To reinforce the side walls and help prevent them from bowing outward, drive at least one 2×2 stake at the midpoint outside of each wall. The stakes should penetrate the ground at least a foot or more in order to provide adequate support. Fasten the stakes to the side walls using deck screws. For a larger frame, place support stakes approximately every 2 feet along each wall.

5 Fill your completed bed with good topsoil and the proper amendments, mix the soil well with a fork or shovel, and level out the surface to within an inch of the top. The soil mix encourages plant roots to reach beyond the depth of the bed and into the ground. Deep-rooted plants draw on subsoil moisture and are thus better able to tolerate and even thrive in dry weather. Water throughly after planting.

3

FRONT YARDS

The importance of the front yard to your landscape design cannot be overstated. Each day it welcomes you home and makes that all-important first impression on passersby. Its design should fit the neighborhood yet be distinctive. It should enhance your house, tie it to the landscape, and indicate to the visitor where to park and knock. Some front yards boast the welcoming arms of mature trees. Newer landscapes offer a blank slate and room to grow. No matter what you have to start with, get ready to put your home's best face forward.

Extra-large jardinieres, placed atop pedestals to be appreciated at eye level, hold showy petunias and verbena. These annuals stand up to a range of weather conditions from spring to fall.

Passersby will stop to admire this front-yard masterpiece. A wide brick walk, accentuated by raised containers, leads to a grand portico.

Planting pockets are responsible for some of this front yard's appeal. Eyecatching clusters of annuals and perennials decorate the lawn's perimeter.

ASSESSING FRONT YARD OPTIONS

The front yard is the place most people fix first—and for good reason. Often, it's the only part of the yard that others see, and it's the part your family sees most often. The patch of lawn, two trees, and a few foundation shrubs initially provided by the builder fall far short of the exciting possibilities.

Streetscaping is an excellent investment in both present enjoyment and future value. A pleasant view from the street gives a sense of individual pride and accomplishment. And it adds greatly to the value of your property by setting your yard apart and making it beautiful.

How to begin
The first thing to do when planning a new front yard is to recognize your bias. The mere satisfaction of returning home and the fact that you most often look at your front yard from inside the house can skew your feelings about the face your yard presents to the public.

For a more honest assessment, walk down the street, then turn back. Do the same from the other direction. Also, get in your car and approach your house slowly from each direction.

Does your house blend with those nearby? Is it appealing? Distinctive? Does it sit well on the site or look out of place? Does it need stronger horizontal or vertical lines? Does it nestle among trees? List all virtues and shortcomings.

When you go to other houses, take note of the convenience of their entryways. Can you easily see where to turn into the drive? Is the drive wide enough for you to open your car door and get out without stepping on plants or grass? Can you quickly tell which door to approach? Is it easy to negotiate the walks and steps?

Take what you learn during these studies and weigh carefully your front yard's planting needs—street trees, trees and shrubs for framing and accent, flowers, lawn, and groundcovers—and its structural needs—walks, steps, drive, stoop, edgings, and fences.

Plants and structures
The architectural features of your yard will be the most expensive and the most permanent. You may want to plan them in stages: Make good walks and steps first, a porch or fence next, and a driveway the following year. Select materials that will add to your landscape's design and its sense of harmony.

Plantings are easier to install and change, but you'll want to be sure to put them in the right places so that they can play a role as soon as possible.

Trees, shrubs, and groundcovers are permanent purchases that increase in size and value and need little maintenance. You can even use many edible plants in place of—or along with—ornamentals. They present little extra work except for harvesting.

Flowers take more care and often require replanting, but they can fill in the gaps until your woody plants gain enough size to stand alone. Annuals—such as four-o'clock, strawflower, impatiens, datura, and angel's trumpet—and perennials—such as peony, bee balm, and hosta—can substitute for shrubs the first year or two.

Lawns take the most resources, work, and equipment of any aspect of landscaping. To conserve both fossil fuels and human energy, consider alternatives to lawn, especially in regions where rainfall is inadequate.

If your front yard is too large for constant mowing and watering, use mulch or groundcovers for islands around trees and shrubs. Fence or mark off an area for turf and use the rest for meadow, pasture, or woodland. Don't let your front yard make you a slave to more work than you enjoy.

Planting under a tree can pose a landscaping dilemma. But a slightly raised planting bed allows for perennial color under this mature canopy without smothering the tree's roots or risking its health.

ASSESSING FRONT YARD OPTIONS *(continued)*

Entries

When planning your front yard, pay particular attention to making your home's entrance clearly discernable and inviting. Use plants and structures to lead people to the place where you can greet them most gracefully. Dramatize the front door with a lamppost, an accent shrub, a trellis to block the rain or wind, or pots of vibrantly colored geraniums or comparably bright flowers.

Be sure a door knocker or bell is visible. The best stoops are large enough for two people to stand on with some cover from the elements and for doors to swing open. A bench here is a great help as well.

Driveways, too, should be readily visible. A simple, low planting can mark the turn. If trees or shrubs obstruct the view, trim them for safety's sake. Where curves or slopes are involved, the placement of the driveway on one side of the yard or another can provide a marked increase in visibility.

For nighttime arrivals, lighting should mark the turn from the road to the drive and from the drive to the walk. Add lighting at any curves or steps as well as the front door.

Walks

Follow natural access patterns when laying out walks. If you don't, children or dogs will carve their own paths right through your prize petunias. A straight path, though less charming, is the shortest and least expensive, and sometimes the most sensible.

Use curves, jogs, or steps only when there is a reason, not just to meander. Combine practicality with visual appeal by making walks at least 36 inches wide. If scale permits, 42 to 54 inches is better so that two people can walk side by side. For an illusion of greater or lesser distance, widen one end. Extra width at curves is pleasant too.

Ideally walks should slope 1 to 5 percent, never more than 10 percent. If the entry is steeper, use curves, jogs, steps, or ramps. Let plants make the journey interesting and colorful.

Install walls, fences, or hedges no taller than 2 feet near walks so people can swing their arms or carry packages without feeling crowded. Between the walk and taller verticals, a buffer zone of groundcover, lawn, flowers, or mulch that is at least 2 feet wide allows more room for movement.

To add interest to walks, choose brick patterns or exposed-aggregate textures. If you have plain concrete walks, cover them with brick pavers, slate, or tile. Loose materials such as tanbark or wood chips are fine for natural garden paths farther away from the house, but they end up being tracked into the house if used in the front yard.

Steps

Make steps as wide as the walks they connect. Steps should be emphatic and noticeable. A plant accent can help. So can a change of texture underfoot. Avoid using a single step. If the slope is that slight, use a ramp. Three steps are the ideal minimum although two are acceptable. Check regularly that your steps are safe and skidproof in snow or rain. As an alternative to steps, consider terracing a sloped area. This can make stepping up or down more gradual.

Edgings

Edgings neaten the appearance of your yard and add contrasts of form, texture, and color. For permanent neatness, build in small concrete curbs; set bricks on edge, end, or diagonally; lay landscape timbers; stand flagstones or tiles on edge; or install one of the ready-made edgings available at garden centers. Metal or rubber strips are less attractive, but they are inexpensive and serviceable.

Borders of flowers, bulbs, or groundcovers can be used with—or instead of—other edgings. Use plants such as ajuga, alyssum, impatiens, or lily-of-the-valley, or similar ones with the proper ultimate spread and pleasing year-round appearance. Set plants where they won't overgrow the walk.

Inventive planting and clever placement create privacy without fences in this front garden. Small trees, ornamental grasses, annuals, and expanses of paving make it an easy-care landscape.

CREATING AN ATTRACTIVE FRONT

Every house exterior and site has visual assets and liabilities. With luck, your front yard highlights the pleasing points and masks the poor ones.

All the elements of good design come into play as you arrange the components for your ideal front yard. But don't be put off by the aesthetic terms—balance, scale, unity, and the like—used by many designers. All are largely a matter of common sense. If a scene pleases your eye, then it's probably well-designed.

If your house needs—or will adapt to—your desire for a special theme garden such as colonial, cottage, Asian, or Spanish, the look must begin in the front yard. Themes are successful only if you carefully unify all of the garden aspects.

You'll also need to determine whether your preference is for—and your site demands—a formal or informal landscape. Formal settings include strong geometric lines and architectural features, clipped hedges, and uniformly shaped plants and beds. Informal designs are marked by freeflowing, natural-looking elements. Generally, informal home styles and sloping land require less rigid landscapes. Formal houses and flat land can be treated either way.

To achieve balance in a landscape, try to position elements so that they give equal weight—through size, color, texture, or other aspects—to any side of a scene. How formal this weighting should be is again dictated by style of house and personal preference. Symmetrical houses often look best when each feature and plant is duplicated on the opposite side of a front walk (as long as the walk isn't too long or too narrow). Most houses, though, are asymmetrical, since they have only one garage or drive. In this case balance is more subtle. Perhaps a tall tree belongs on the side opposite the driveway.

Achieving pleasant scale—or keeping elements in proportion to one another—also is subtle because plants must grow before you can be sure of size and balance. Choose plants that will complement your home's size at maturity, along with some other plants that will grow fast enough to make a mark. Your ultimate goal is to avoid planting anything that eventually will dwarf your house.

Several plants of the same color and kind have more effect and give greater pleasure in a landscape than one each of several types. Use only enough variety for sustaining bloom and adding visual interest. If you want more types of plants, say for continual harvests of many kinds of fruit, try combining plants with similar or at least compatible shapes, textures, and foliage or bloom colors.

Trees for impact

Trees (and larger shrubs) are the first components to consider in front yard design.

Because a framed view often is more attractive than a view that's completely revealed, give serious thought to planting taller trees on either side of your house and at least one in the backyard if possible. Trees in these spots give the yard and house a feeling of permanence and soften the look of the second story or roofline against the sky. If you can afford only one or two mature trees, these are the places for them.

Besides providing framing, trees and larger shrubs, along with the buildings, make up the masses in the landscape. Trees and shrubs are good for marking boundaries and separating functional areas. Also choose and place them for interest of outline, texture, and color in all seasons and for shade and energy control. Harmonize the shapes of the plants—round, pyramidal, weeping—with one another and the structures. Give visual relief by judiciously varying the leaf size and shape and the textures of structural materials.

Accent trees

To add beauty and perhaps additional shade to a front yard, carefully situate a choice shade or accent tree between the street and the house. Accent trees make such a lasting impression that you may find yourself identifying certain houses by the dogwood or Japanese maple in the front yard. When selecting accent—also called specimen or ornamental—trees, use reliable native types with few disease and pest problems.

Charm and character
result when landscape
and home are carefully
matched, as they are
here. Trees and fencing
frame, soften, and
highlight the view. When
planted next to a front
entry, small trees or
shrubs, such as holly or
boxwood, won't outgrow
their welcome. Framing
the entryway, they add
statuesque shelter
without blocking views
of the house.

CREATING AN ATTRACTIVE FRONT *(continued)*

If you'd like a pair or row of trees to line the street in front of your house, choose carefully. Check with your city for any ordinances on street plantings. These regulations might govern both the kinds of plantings and planting distances. Find out who will be responsible for maintaining the trees.

Determine the location of water and sewer lines. If there are any plans for widening the street, plant far enough back. Look up to check for overhead wires, and plant only small trees beneath them.

In the inner city only a few trees—including maple, ash, hawthorn, ginkgo, smoketree, amur oak, Austrian or Scotch pine, littleleaf linden, and plane tree—survive the pollution and limited soil surface.

In the suburbs, growing conditions are better, making plant selection easier, but you still need to avoid trees that might drop staining fruit or petals on nearby cars.

Trees should be planted at least 3½ feet away from the curb in most municipalities. It usually is better to plant a tree that will be small at maturity. Smaller plants adapt more easily to adverse conditions and are less expensive to maintain later. Streetside is not the place to crowd trees, particularly large ones.

Foundation plantings
In the past, plants were set where house met ground to hide foundations and first-floor basements. Today these so-called foundation plantings often are inappropriate and widely abused—and often they invite water seepage into the foundation due to overzealous watering. Builders typically put in plants with enough size but little character, and they can soon outgrow their usefulness. Many houses come with a surrounding cloud or border of stiff evergreens that does nothing but destroy a house's style.

Plants near the house are essential only to soften its angles and help it blend with its surroundings. Concentrate on the complete setting, not just the foundation line. Your plantings here should be simple and dignified—and at least 3 to 4 feet from

PLAIN

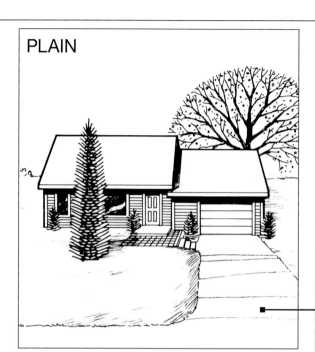

Standard plantings for a one-story house often lack design. Here the few shrubs make the house look drab and out of place. The tall evergreen blocks the view and offers no shade. The scene is broken into discordant thirds.

BETTER

Here, shorter shrubs, a planter, and better-placed trees frame the facade, soften its lines, and wed the house to the site. Decorative railings set off the entryway, and a run of groundcover defines the driveway and controls the slope.

the foundation. They should be in scale so that they enhance rather than hide the house. You won't see these plants from inside except, perhaps, a little by the windowsill, so don't waste your beauties here.

Planters

Raised planting beds often are used instead of— or together with—foundation plantings. Build them deep enough to provide ample soil for root growth and bottomless so that the bedding soil mixes with the soil below.

Because soil in raised beds dries out more quickly than it does in the ground (and because few plants can withstand full sun plus the heat reflected from house walls), place beds a few feet away from the foundation and in spots that receive shade for part of the day.

Plants here have star billing. Be sure they are hardy, are of appropriate ultimate size, and have a potentially neat appearance all season. Choose dwarf evergreens, flowering shrubs, fruit trees, perennials, or bulbs. For the most profusion and longest season of bloom, rely on annuals. Mounding petunias, impatiens, or petite marigolds can beautifully soften a bed's edges.

Front yard gardens

The old rule that the front yard is for the public and the backyard is for fun and family is sometimes better broken. Is your front yard the sunniest in a cool climate? The coolest in summer? On the south side where tender plants and fruit can best survive the cold? The largest part of your yard? Then reclaim some or all of it for private family use. A wall, fence, or sometimes only a small screen can give you the privacy you need. (See Chapter 9, "Privacy and Security," pages 206–227.)

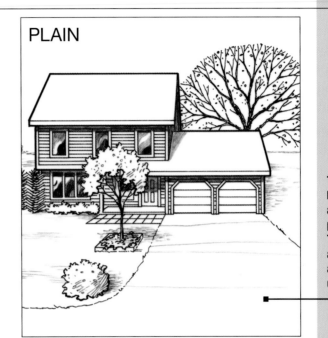

PLAIN

This typical two-story house has the usual shrubs and tree. The entry is too plain, the front too busy. The landscape lacks unity and makes the house appear lopsided and uninteresting.

BETTER

Here the tree in front frames rather than interrupts the scene, is in better scale, and makes the house seem farther from the street. The fence and vines define the driveway, protect the entryway, and help tie together the house and site.

BUILDING WALKWAYS AND PATHS

Constructing a walk or path offers you some excellent do-it-yourself experience that gives you confidence to take on bigger projects as you proceed with your landscaping plan. Unlike the bigger job of pouring a patio, you needn't move a lot of earth, prepare extensive footings, or wrestle with large volumes of tricky materials. Best of all—even for a project as rigorous as the exposed-aggregate walk shown at right—you can work at your own pace, completing several sections one weekend, more the next.

Note that only two of the myriad possibilities for walkway paving materials are shown here. And if you already have a concrete walk that's sound but drab, consider veneering it with tile, flagstones, brick, or other materials, as detailed on pages 150–153.

Exposing aggregate

To achieve the rustic, skidproof texture of exposed aggregate, use one of two methods. You can either pour concrete with the aggregate mixed in it, then, after the concrete begins to set, scrub some of it away. Or you can seed aggregate on top of a just-poured slab, screed the stone into the concrete, and then scrub.

Masonry dealers offer a variety of aggregates that vary by region. Pea gravel is usually used, but you might prefer the look of river pebbles, granite chips, or another option.

As with any concrete project, timing plays a critical role in the outcome of an exposed-aggregate finish. Don't try to abrade away the concrete until the aggregate holds firm. If weather conditions are right, this stage should occur in about 1 hour, but it could take up to 3 hours. To test, lay a board on the surface and kneel on the board; if the board leaves marks, allow more time. If any aggregate dislodges when you start brushing, stop and let the concrete set some more.

Slow curing enhances concrete strength and helps prevent cracks, so cover with plastic sheeting for up to one week, if possible.

EXPOSED-AGGREGATE WALKWAY

1 Excavate, build 2×4 forms, pour sand, and lay reinforcing mesh. If you plan to leave the forms as decorative dividers, apply sealer, then cover them with duct tape when the sealer is tacky so that they won't be damaged during the pour. Pour concrete with aggregate mixed into it (or, if seeding, pour plain concrete) in only a few form frames at a time. Strike off the concrete.

2 If seeding, after striking off concrete, evenly sprinkle wet aggregate onto the surface; carefully push it into the concrete with a trowel until it is thinly covered. For either method, after the concrete firms up, scrape with a brush or broom to expose aggregate. Spray water over the surface; brush again. Repeat spraying and brushing until exposure is uniform and water runs clear.

3

In case a module hardens too quickly, scrub concrete from aggregate with a 1:10 solution of muriatic acid and water. Wear goggles and other protective clothing. Once the aggregate is sufficiently exposed, rinse well with water.

4

To seal the concrete, wait at least a week for the concrete to thoroughly cure, then brush on concrete sealer. Apply a waterproofing solution, if you prefer. Remove tape strips from the decorative forms.

CUSTOM FINISHES

MAKING A BRICK PATTERN

Set a brick form—just right for small jobs and available at home centers—on top of the base and scoop concrete into it, to the top but no higher. After the water has evaporated from the concrete surface, carefully wiggle the form out, so clean-looking lines remain. Flick away crumbs and gently give the surface a trowel finish. Continue this process of moving, filling, and removing the form until you've completed the walkway.

CARVING A FLAGSTONE PATTERN

To make your surface look like flagstones or geometric shapes, score the fresh, finished concrete after the water has evaporated from the surface. A concave jointer works well for this technique. Go over the marks with a trowel to produce a uniformly smooth surface.

CREATING A TRAVERTINE FINISH

This finish should be used only in areas that stay above freezing. Begin by pouring, screeding, and floating the concrete. As soon as the water evaporates from the surface, use a brush to spatter on pigmented mortar the consistency of very thick paint. After the mortar has stiffened slightly, use a steel trowel to smooth the high spots and make a distinctive travertine pattern.

LAYING BRICK WALKWAYS

Bricks provide an easy way to dress up your landscape, and the good news is that you can create attractive brick patio and walkway projects without ever touching concrete or mortar.

Brick pavers come in a multitude of sizes and colors that add texture to your outdoor living spaces and encourage eyecatching patterns. Unlike house bricks, paving bricks don't have the holes that make building walls easier. You can buy paving bricks with a worn, antique look or with beveled edges. Some brick pavers also have a 1/16-inch nib on each side to maintain uniform spacing. Check with a brick distributor or manufacturer for the best selection.

A brick patio offers low maintenance and classic good looks, and you can parlay these same advantages into a patchwork of brick walkways that steer visitors to your favorite areas of the yard.

Consider the following tips before you begin your brick project:

• **Drainage.** Grade the area to be bricked with a pitch of about 1 inch per 4 feet, sloping away from any adjacent building.

• **Edging.** Pressure-treated wood works well for simple projects with straight edges. For curves, use plastic or aluminum brick-edging products; they also offer greater longevity. It's usually easiest to install edging along one or two sides, lay brick, then finish the edging.

• **Cutting.** For minimal cutting, a type of chisel called a brick set might be all you need. But saws produce a cleaner cut and are easier to use, so they're recommended for projects that require a lot of cutting. You can buy appropriate blades for your circular saw, or—preferably—rent a wet saw fitted with a diamond blade.

• **Base material.** You can choose from several types of materials for brick projects. Road base is as good as any, and you can purchase it in bulk from most materials suppliers. You can also buy it by the bag at your home center, but it will cost more in this quantity. (A 1-inch layer of sand will cover the base.)

Walkways vary, of course, depending on the material you choose. In the project pictured, reclaimed bricks create the appeal of age. The pavers in the photo above have sharper edges and achieve a tighter fit, resulting in a more contemporary look.

Outline the area to be paved with chalking or landscapers' paint. Excavate at least 6 inches beyond the edges of the area. The thickness of the brick, added to 4 inches of base material plus 1 inch of sand equals about 8 inches (10 inches in northern states), so you'll need to excavate about 7 (or 9) inches deep. (You want the top surface of the bricks to be about an inch above grade for drainage.) Dig only as deep as necessary; backfilling with loose soil may lead to settling. After excavation the ground should be firm, fairly smooth, and slightly pitched for drainage.

2

Get your wheelbarrow warmed up and start adding the road base, which is usually a mixture of crushed stone with some finer particles. Extend the material about 6 inches past the ultimate edge of your project. Spread out the material as uniformly as you can, using a level from time to time to check your work. Now—unless yours is a small project like the one shown here—install the edging. Then either use a hand tamper, as pictured here, or—for larger areas—rent a power vibrating tamper to create a very firm and stable base.

3

Add a 1-inch layer of sand on top of the base and screed the sand to create a level bed for the brick. A notched 1×4, as shown here, makes an effective screed if a single board can span from one edge to the other. For larger areas, lay lengths of 1-inch pipe on the base before adding sand. Then drag the screed board over the pipes to level the sand (remember to remove the pipes and carefully smooth out the sand again).

4

Start laying bricks in one corner or along one edge and work your way across. Place the bricks onto the sand and gently tap each with a rubber mallet to make minor adjustments. A slight gap (about ⅛ inch) between bricks is beneficial, so don't worry about entirely eliminating the gaps. If necessary, work from on top of the bricks you've already laid but avoid standing on the leveled sand. When finished, install the remaining edging according to the product instructions.

5

Finish by spreading a light layer of sand over the brick and sweeping it into the seams with a broom. Move the sand back and forth across the bricks until the seams are filled; this helps lock the bricks together. Sweep off excess sand but do not wash or blow it off. You may have to repeat this procedure two or three times until the sand completely fills the cracks.

LAYING FLAGSTONE

The simplest method of installing a flagstone patio or walkway is to place the stones on well-tamped soil. Such a surface is quick to install; however, you'll need to readjust settled stones every year. A better solution is to add 2 to 3 inches of sand to the tamped soil and tamp the sand just as firmly. This way you won't have to deal with the yearly routine of stone adjustment.

Consider these bits of advice before you begin the job:
• Choose flagstones that are at least 1 inch thick; thinner slabs likely will crack over time. Pick stones that are fairly uniform in thickness so that they'll form an even and consistent surface.
• Work with a combination of small, medium, and large stones, making separate piles of each. As you proceed with the laying process, select from the piles alternately; this way you won't end up with a lot of small stones in one corner and big ones in another.
• The trick to a professional-looking flagstone surface is to keep the gaps between the stones reasonably consistent. Test gaps with a piece of wood, such as a scrap of ½-inch plywood.
• Keep trying; there's no shortcut to making a pleasing pattern given the variations in flagstones' shapes. You'll have to test different configurations and occasionally cut a stone or two to maintain goodlooking gaps.

1 Whether you're making a walkway or a patio like this one, flagstone projects look best if they don't have sharp edges. One way to create graceful curves is with a water hose. Charge the hose by closing the nozzle and turning on the water; this helps the hose hold its shape. Lay out the hose in the shape you choose and pour flour or sand all along its length. When you remove the hose, you'll have a clear line marking the excavation area.

2 Dig up the sod and, if possible, use it elsewhere to fill bare spots. Remove enough extra soil to accommodate the total depth of the sand and stones; smooth out the soil and tamp it well. Then add the sand, raking it out as you go. Firm up the sand with a hand tamper—or use a rented power vibrating tamper, if the area is large. Then install any edging you have chosen.

3 Begin your stone-laying process with the large stones around the perimeter. If a stone sits too high, pick it up and dig out some sand; if it's too low, add some sand beneath it. Test each stone to make sure it doesn't rock. Work slowly and take breaks; this kind of labor can harm your back even if you do not feel any strain at the time.

4 Wherever possible it's easiest to use uncut stones. But eventually you'll be faced with the chore of cutting one to size. When you get to that point, lay the stone over the stone it will adjoin and trace the outline with chalk, a pencil, or a scratching tool.

5

Use a brick set and small sledgehammer to score the line, making a groove about ⅛ inch deep. Set the stone on top of a scrap piece of wood. For large stones have someone stand on the other end (as shown above). Split the stone with a single blow from the sledgehammer. If the scrap piece is large enough to use elsewhere, protect it with a lumber scrap. Make more than one split if you need a curved edge.

6

Fill the joints either with sand or soil. Wet the patio surface with a fine spray, cleaning the stones while thoroughly wetting the soil. Fill in low spots, spray again, and repeat until you have level-looking joints that are about ⅛ inch below the surface of the stones. Plant the gaps with moss or a low-growing groundcover to discourage weeds and to create an established look.

LAYING A STEPPING-STONE PATH

For a quick stone walkway that is easier to create than a flagstone path, consider this alternative. It involves only cutting special openings in the sod and setting in place a series of stepping-stones that lead you safely along your way.

Choose stones—either flagstones or look-alikes made of concrete—that are at least 2 inches thick; thinner slabs likely will crack over time. Pick stones that are fairly uniform in thickness so that they'll form an even and consistent surface.

1

Place the stones or pavers in the pattern you've selected onto the grass and cut the sod around each stone with a long knife.

2

Use a flat shovel to dig out the chunks of sod and enough soil below the sod to create a depth equal to about 5 inches plus the thickness of the stone.

3

Pour into each hole a 4-inch base of gravel and tamp it firmly in place. Cover it with a sheet of landscape fabric to block weeds and serve as a foundation for a 1-inch layer of sand that you put on top. Now drop the stone in place and tamp it down firmly with your feet or a mallet.

BUILDING STEPS

Properly constructed garden steps take a walkway into another dimension. They also serve as a retaining wall, holding back soil erosion. Plan carefully and securely anchor them into the slope they ascend.

Select materials to coordinate with adjoining walks. Besides the brick and timber versions shown here, you can build steps entirely of concrete, set bricks or concrete slabs into a sand base, mix stone or concrete treads with brick risers, or terrace the slope with timber risers and surface the treads with gravel, wood chips, or other loose fill.

Whatever materials you choose, first decide how many steps you will need, how deep each horizontal tread will be, and how high to make each vertical riser. Here's a useful rule: The tread dimension plus the riser dimension should equal about 18 inches. Try to make your riser dimension no more than 7 inches and no less than 4 inches. No matter how you juggle the figures, be sure all treads and risers will be exactly the same depth and height: Step variations—particularly in the height—break a person's stride and cause stumbles. Also take into account the depth of tread-finishing materials and mortar, if any, when you're planning a concrete foundation.

Use stakes and a level string to determine the total rise your steps will ascend and the total run they will traverse. To determine how many steps you will need, divide these measurements by combinations of tread and riser sizes until you come out with equal-size steps.

A caution: Building codes often limit tread and riser sizes and other stairway dimensions, so check with local authorities before finalizing your plans. Codes also mandate handrails in some situations.

TIMBER-AND-BRICK STEPS

Steps such as these take about the same time to build as do concrete steps. The result, however, is more stylish and inviting. If the timbers are fastened firmly with steel rebar and spikes, and the sand bed is well tamped, the steps will be nearly as solid as concrete and much easier to repair.

Choose timbers that will withstand the climate in your region. Pressure-treated varieties are readily available; choose from 4×6s, 6×6s, and 6×8s. Pave the steps with severe weathering (SW) brick (see your local materials supplier.)

Here are some background tips to help you get off to the right start:
● A safe and practical width for a set of steps leading up to a main or side entrance is 36 inches; 48 inches is even better if space permits.
● The rise of each step is determined by the size of timber you choose to work with. For example, a 6×8 placed so that its narrow side is up creates a stair rise of 7½ inches—a comfortable step up or down for most adults. But if a lot of kids or elderly persons will be using these stairs, 6×6 timbers and their resulting 5½-inch rise will create a shallower step for them.
● The total depth or run of each step added to the total rise or height of each step should have a sum of about 18 inches. So if the rise is 5½ inches, the run should be about 12½ inches. And for a 7½-inch rise, the corresponding run needs to be in the neighborhood of 10½ inches.
● Before you proceed you'll need to determine overall rise and overall run of your completed step project. Pound a stake in the ground at the point where the bottom stair will end. Then hang a line level on a line and attach the line to the house at the point where the top stair will adjoin it—usually just under the door threshold.

This finished timber-and-brick inlay is suitable for an informal or formal entryway to your home, deck, or patio. Consider using older bricks for a more rustic look or laying the bricks in a more sophisticated pattern for a formal design.

● Pull the line tightly to the stake and mark on the stake the point indicating a level line. Measure the distance from the mark to the bottom of the bottom step; that's your overall rise. If this figure isn't divisible exactly by the timber's thickness, you'll need to fudge a little bit by making up the difference at the door sill and at the lowest step. Just try to avoid making the bottom step more than 1 inch higher than the others.
● When you get to the point where you're drilling pilot holes in the timbers for the long spikes and rebar, be sure to use a heavy-duty electric drill. You'll be working typically with long, auger-type drill bits— probably ¼ inch and ½ inch in diameter—and they create a lot of torque. Avoid working with short bits fastened to extensions; these tend to come loose frequently.
● Cut off the ends of the timbers by sawing all four sides with a circular saw, then finishing off the middle with a handsaw. Or rent an oversize saw that can make the cut in one pass.

1 Excavate the site according to your plan layout. But when you dig, allow an extra 6 inches of working space on each side. Lay a 2-inch bed of well-tamped gravel for the bottom timbers. Make sure the steps slope away from the house $\frac{1}{4}$ inch per running foot. Where the tops of the timbers will not show, drill $\frac{3}{8}$-inch holes about every 2 feet and drive 3-foot pieces of rebar through the timbers and into the ground to anchor the steps. Where the tops will show, drill long pilot holes with a $\frac{3}{16}$-inch bit and fasten the timbers together with 12-inch spikes.

2 Starting with the bottom step, tamp the gravel firm, then spread 2 to 3 inches of sand. Notch a screed board the thickness of the bricks or pavers and screed the sand to that level. Tamp, add more sand if needed, then screed again. Once you install the bricks, move to the next step up and prepare it in the same way.

3 Cut the pavers or bricks with a brick set and small sledgehammer or use a masonry saw or a circular saw with a masonry blade. Use a rubber mallet to pound in hard-to-fit bricks. Once each section is finished, spread fine sand on the surface and sweep it into the joints. Gently spray with water, add more sand, and repeat the process until the joints are filled. Screed and tamp.

TIMBER STEPS

Rather than digging out a large area and then installing a complex supporting system of timbers that serve as underpinnings for the steps, why not just use the stable soil to support at least part of each successive stair?

1 Cut carefully into the slope, making room for the desired tread and riser dimensions. Steps of two 8-inch timbers work well if they overlap by 2 inches. Lay the timbers, pound into place with a sledge, and check for level.

2 Using an electrician's extension bit, bore holes at the front edge of each timber into the one below it, then pound in rebar to tie them together. Also bore horizontal holes to secure each timber to the one behind it.

BUILDING RAMPS

A ramp makes a gentle transition from one level to another, smoothing the path for everything from tricycles to wheelbarrows to—most especially—wheelchairs. If your family includes someone who relies on a wheelchair for mobility, you'll need a ramp to one or more of your home's entrances, and maybe to outdoor living areas as well.

Poured concrete was used for the ramp at right, but you can use a variety of other materials, including wood, or even earth topped with fine gravel. Whatever material you use, make sure the surface the chair will ride on is nonskid. Textured rubber toppings and textured concrete (see opposite) work well.

Ramp basics

Safety and ease of use are the prime considerations for any ramp. Appearance plays a part too, especially for a ramp visible from the street.

Regardless of the design you come up with, certain norms apply. Slope a wheelchair ramp at a rise of no more than 1 foot per 12 feet of run. This standard can make for some incredibly long ramps—a total rise of 2 feet, for example, requires a total length of at least 24 feet. But a gentle grade is essential for a ramp to be useful to the people who need it most.

Even if your ramp won't be used by anyone in a wheelchair, slope it no more than about 1 foot for every 7 feet of run.

For wheelchair use, include handrails on both sides of your ramp (see opposite) and make the ramp wide enough so that the distance between the handrails is at least 36 inches. Also, any incline longer than 30 feet needs a landing where a wheelchair user can maneuver the chair. Whether your plan calls for an L-shape, switchback, or broken straight-run ramp, all landings must measure at least 5×5 feet. Where doors open outward, the adjacent landing must be at least 5×6½ feet; this gives wheelchair users room to move back when the door is opened.

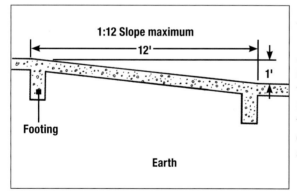

1:12 Slope maximum

12'

1'

Footing

Earth

For wheelchair use, plan a ramp that slopes no more than 1 foot in 12, with 5-foot-square landings at top and bottom. A concrete ramp must tie into the slope with footings on either side of each landing. Dig the footings to the frost line in your area (check local codes). Make your concrete ramp at least 4 inches thick.

1 This ramp extends down from an existing slab, which was fitted with a piece of expansion strip. Cut and fill with earth as necessary. Construct forms with 2×4 lumber and stabilize them with stakes every 2 to 3 feet. Double-check that the forms do not slope more than desired. Add gravel and reinforcing wire mesh. Tie in each footing with horizontal and vertical rebar.

2 Pour the concrete next, using a slightly stiffer mix than you would for a level slab so the concrete won't slide down the incline. Strike off and screed, then smooth with a float (see page 147 for more details). Define edges with an edging trowel and tool in some control joints every few feet.

3 To make your ramp skidproof, pull a damp broom across the surface of the just-troweled concrete. For a fine texture, use a soft-bristled broom; for a coarser one, use a stiffer bristle.

INSTALLING HANDRAILS

If you're building a ramp, outfit both sides of it with handrails to allow wheelchair users to pull themselves up the ramp and control their speed going down. For steps, put a rail on one side.

Handrails for ramps should be about 32 inches high. If people in wheelchairs will use your ramp, install rails that have a grip width of about 1½ inches. Along stairways, set handrails about 30 inches high; at stairway landings, 34 inches high.

At right, a metal railing is shown being attached to a concrete curb that runs alongside a ramp. To attach wooden railings to a wooden ramp, see the

instructions for deck railings on page 175. Particularly important is that balusters be securely attached to a wood ramp's structure, rather than its surface.

Similarly, for concrete steps, attach rail brackets to the treads. But for wood steps, attach the balusters to the structure.

For metal railing brackets, drill holes into the ramp's surface (or into an adjacent curb, as shown here). Install brackets with lead masonry anchors and screws. Slip vertical balusters into the brackets; tighten set screws. Install rails top and bottom and assemble intermediate balusters.

INSTALLING WALKWAY EDGINGS

Looking for a way to dress up an ordinary path, provide crisp lines between paving and landscaping materials, or hold masonry units in line?

Edging can do all these jobs—and more— for only a modest investment of time and money. In most cases, you simply decide on the material you'd like that puts a lip at each side of a walk or path. A mowing strip installs flush with the walk so that you can run one wheel of a mower along it.

Make mowing strips 6 to 12 inches wide and set at ground level. That way, mower wheels roll over the strip, while the blade cuts freely without nicking any edging. Concrete, brick, tile, and other smooth-surface masonry materials form the best mowing strips.

Raised edgings

A raised edging stops an aggressive groundcover from overgrowing a walk, channels water runoff, and makes a clean break between differing surfaces. If you're planning a path of gravel, mulch, or other loose-fill material, a raised edging is the only way to go.

Keep a raised edging low, ½ inch or so, or make it 3 or more inches high. Anything in between poses a tripping hazard. The photos at right and opposite show how to install two popular types of raised edgings; pages 96–97 show several alternatives.

Give thought, too, to the type of plantings you select to go alongside a walk or path. See page 93 for four good choices that are easy to keep in bounds.

Loose paving materials

Walkways made of loose paving materials are easy to install and comfortable to walk on. Pressure-treated 4×4s make an attractive edging, but you also can use brick soldiers, metal or plastic edging, or concrete. One drawback to this type of walkway is that some loose material, such as pea gravel or river rock, is kicked up easily onto neighboring lawn areas, which makes mowing difficult or even dangerous. Also, loose material can compact or degrade over time and may need to be replenished.

TIMBER EDGING

1 After laying out the pathway, dig deeply enough so that your edging protrudes 1 or 2 inches above ground level. Be sure to remove organic material, especially tree roots. To construct a border of pressure-treated 4×4s, pour about 1 inch of gravel or sand in the excavation to provide drainage away from the wood. Cut the timbers with a circular saw. Position the 4×4s, making sure they are at the correct height and are stable. Level them or, where there's a slope, position them at a consistent incline. To secure the timbers, drill ⅜- or ½-inch holes through them every 2 or 3 feet and drive 2-foot-long pieces of rebar (many home centers sell these precut) through the timbers and into the ground.

2 Spread landscaping fabric between the 4×4s to inhibit weed growth throughout the path. Add 1 inch of coarse sand and tamp it level. Follow with a layer of the loose material of your choice. For fine material, lay only 1 inch at a time, tamp or roll it firm, then add more layers until the material is 1 to 2 inches below the top of the edging. Backfill behind the edging and lay sod or reseed the grass.

INTEGRAL CONCRETE EDGING

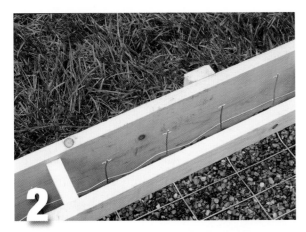

Construct wooden forms at the edge of your planned walk. For a 3½-inch-thick walk, leave a 3½-inch gap between the gravel bed and inside board. Temporarily nail short pieces of wood between the inside and outside boards. Stake forms every few feet.

Lay reinforcing mesh, bending it so that its tips stick up into the curb forms. These tie the walk and edging into an integral unit that will ride out settlement and frost heave. When you pour the concrete, pull up the mesh into the middle of the slab and curb with a claw hammer or rake.

Pour concrete; strike off and trowel. Pull wood spacers and inside board after concrete sets up; patch voids. Let the concrete cure for a week, then remove stakes and outer forms.

WALKWAY PLANTINGS

AJUGA is a perennial groundcover with low rosettes of beautifully colored foliage and, in spring, blue blooms. It tolerates sun or shade. Divide crowns for quick spreading.

ALYSSUM is a low annual with clouds of dainty white or pink blooms. It needs to be sheared back whenever it becomes seedy. It prefers cool weather and full sun or partial shade.

IMPATIENS vary in height and color of flower and foliage. Most need some shade; a few take full sun. All bloom neatly from summer to frost. Start impatiens easily from seeds or cuttings.

LADY'S MANTLE is a low-maintenance perennial with superb flowers and foliage. It thrives in sun if the soil if rich, but prefers some afternoon shade.

Other good perennials for edgings include pachysandra, thyme, and lamium. Spring bulbs and summer annuals also make good edge plants.

CHOOSING WALKWAY MATERIALS

BRICK

Description: Styles include common brick, paving brick, used or salvaged brick, and clinker bricks.

Effect: Due to the variety of colors available and the many patterns you can create with brick (see below), this product can be the star of a whole host of design styles—from very rustic to extremely formal.

Cost: The common bricks most frequently used are relatively affordable.

Comments: Exterior brick comes in many grades and styles. The most common are MW (moderate weathering) and SW (severe weathering). The MW is more porous, absorbs water, and will crack and chip over time due to the freeze-thaw cycle. Conversely, the SW is less porous, so it withstands the freeze-thaw cycle quite well; it's also more resistant to stains. Salvaged bricks, though attractive because of their worn look, have uneven surfaces that limit their use. Clinker bricks result from improper firing, giving them irregular shapes, scorching, and pits. They're used mainly as borders for walkways and other projects.

COBBLES

Description: Often salvaged from streets in historic areas, cobbles are small round-edge stones, about 2 to 12 inches wide. Contemporary alternatives include cast-concrete and cut-stone cobbles.

Effect: Cobbles conjure visions of romantic faraway lands, and if small enough, can transport that same feeling to your yard. Combine cobbles with pavers, as shown, to create attractive, patchwork-style patterns.

Cost: Genuine historic cobbles can be costly. New cobblestones present an economical option.

Comments: Cobbles contribute a sense of lasting strength, character, and beauty to a setting. Set in sand, they create a permeable surface.

CONCRETE PAVERS

Description: Most pavers are made from dense, pressure-formed concrete cast in molds. Today's manufacturing techniques produce a variety of interlocking shapes and sizes.

Effect: Pavers offer aesthetic appeal, with a range of colors and styles. Some have exposed aggregate surfaces. They make popular additions to a variety of landscaping styles.

Cost: Affordable and widely available.

Comments: Easy to install, pavers' ability to withstand the freeze-and-thaw cycles of many regions makes them one of the most durable materials available. They're suitable for formal and geometric designs.

LOOSE FILL

Description: Crushed stone, river rock, lava rock, pea gravel, and seashells are used to cover paths or patio areas.

Effect: Available in a wide variety of colors, loose fill adds a rustic look and interesting texture to a variety of settings; informal or formal design schemes.

Cost: Among the most economical walkway and border materials, gravel is durable but may need to be replenished periodically.

Comments: Easy to install, loose fill drains well and conforms to contours. Once tamped down, these materials form a stable surface. They may be hard on bare feet however.

MULCH

Description: Wood chips, bark, straw, pine needles.

Effect: Suitable for creating a path-less-traveled feeling, mulch is more rustic than other materials.

Cost: It is less expensive than most materials, especially if you can use locally available mulch.

Comments: Durability depends on the material. Some mulches, such as pine straw, readily break down, but others, such as some types of bark, take longer to decompose. One maintenance drawback is that you will need to replenish the mulch periodically. The feel underfoot varies greatly; some types, such as coarse bark, can be uncomfortable to walk on, especially with bare feet.

STONE

Description: Flagstone, stone tile, fieldstone normally used to build large, long-lasting walkways and other extensive surfaces.

Effect: Earthy stone introduces a rugged element to your landscape. It also works well as an added detail on adjoining structures such as fireplaces or walls.

Cost: Stone is sold by the ton or square yard. For large projects, buy stone in bulk to cut costs. Select less-costly indigenous stone commonly available in your region.

Comments: Stone tile (which is cut as precisely as other tile) and flagstone are the most commonly used stones for patio surfaces and are nearly as popular for walkways.

BRICK AND PAVER PATTERNS

Many brick patterns have been developed over the years by installers, always trying to come up with exciting new designs for their clients. The modular shape of bricks lends itself to creating a variety of interesting designs. Most layouts are usually fairly simple. On the other hand, some patterns, such as the pinwheel, do require special planning and thought. (Curved and irregular-shape bricks and pavers can be purchased at extra cost.) The walkway and patio patterns shown here work well for bricks or pavers that are twice as long as they are wide. The diagonal herringbone pattern requires you to cut a large number of bricks at a 45-degree angle. Try using one pattern for a border and another for the main surface.

Diagonal herringbone

Straight herringbone

Pinwheel

Stagger step

Half-square

Straight bond

Running bond

Basket weave

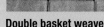
Double basket weave

95

CHOOSING EDGING MATERIALS

Edging materials usually are sunk lower into the ground than the rest of the walkway or patio to provide a stable framework. When a landscaping material such as concrete pavers are set on a drainable base, the edging should withstand the rigors of freeze-and-thaw cycles in cold climates and resist the tendency to heave out of the ground.

For the best border appearance, use the same material as the patio surface or choose a material that creates a pleasant contrast between the patio and yard. If your patio is made of loose material such as crushed stone be sure the edging seals it in and is high enough to keep stones from scattering into the grass. If grass comes right up to the patio, you may want to choose an edging that is lawn mower friendly, such as one with a smooth, raised edge.

Consider, too, how well the border material complements the materal used in the walkway. For example, a poured concrete edging marries nicely with river rock to create a contemporary appearance, while flagstone edging alongside bark mulch produces a more rustic look.

Plastic edging, upright timbers, tilted brick soldiers, and upright soldiers are less substantial than concrete, heavy timbers, and edgings that are staked strongly.

The accompanying photos shows you nine popular options to consider while you're planning your walkway or patio edging. Before you make any big decisions, take note of the amount of labor each material requires. And be sure to shop around and compare prices; costs vary considerably.

CONCRETE PAVERS:
For a neat and durable edging, start by digging a 6-inch-deep trench, tamp, add 2 to 3 inches of gravel. Lay concrete pavers end to end, set at ground level.

Concrete pavers set on end

UPRIGHT (SOLDIER) BRICKS OR PAVERS:
Edging or pavers should rest on a porous base. Excavate to 8 inches, add 2 inches of road base (gravel and sand). Stand pavers in place.

Bricks or pavers set on end

TILTED SOLDIERS:
To install a tilted edging of bricks or pavers, dig a trench 8 inches deep, tamp, add 2 to 3 inches of sand, and set the bricks. Backfill and tamp firmly.

Bricks or pavers set diagonally

FLAGSTONE EDGING: Flagstones can be set in well-tamped ground. Make adjustments as you go, digging or adding soil to keep the top edges of the stones even.

LUMBER: Choose pressure-treated, composite, or cedar lumber. Set 2×4s in a shallow trench and brace them with metal stakes.

Flagstone

Metal stake

Weather-resistant 2x4 lumber

LANDSCAPING TIMBERS OR RAILROAD TIES: This strong edging is quick to construct. Dig a trench, tamp, and add 2 inches of sand. Place the timber, drill holes, and drive in 16-inch spikes or rebar.

STEEL RIBBON: This works well for curves. Mark a curved line on the ground and tap the metal into the ground. Pound retaining stakes through premade slots in the edging.

Landscaping timber or railroad tie

Steel edging and stakes

PRESSURE-TREATED TIMBERS:

Cut timbers into sections, using a power miter saw. Brush cut ends with sealant. Dig a trench, add sand, and install logs (embedding at least half their length).

Half-round logs on end

PLASTIC EDGING:

Plastic is cheap and easy but may crack and lose its shape over time. Slice a line in the ground with a shovel and push the edging into it. Reinforce with stakes.

Plastic edging and stakes

GALLERY OF FRONT YARD IDEAS

A savvy selection of brick for the all-important front walk demonstrates how landscaping materials should complement the house. The Japanese maple, dwarf conifers, and groundcovers suit the rustic scheme.

An outdoor room need not be confined to the backyard. Tucked into a corner outside the front of the house, a charming 12×14-foot terrace offers alfresco dining and adds to the home's curb appeal.

Setting a gently curving sidewalk against the porch angles creates visual interest. The curves (and brick) are repeated around the planting beds.

Faced with dust and hot sun—as well as salt and sand in some areas—a streetside garden requires tough plantings that will withstand the elements. Low-growing, drought-tolerant perennials do the trick here.

A stone retaining wall skirts the curvaceous perimeter of this home, including its attached deck and gazebo. The wall forms planting pockets for colorful perennials.

A white-and-green scheme dresses up this classic, symmetrical entry, where planters flank the front door. A vine-covered arbor and low plantings frame the walkway.

GALLERY OF FRONT YARD IDEAS *(continued)*

The contemporary architecture of this home merits a creative approach to landscaping. A small collection of unusual dwarf trees and shrubs bolsters the front walk and gives the place a sense of rootedness.

Right angles and clean lines frame a stylishly architectural garden highlighted by white blooms. A gravel patio with a splashy fountain welcomes visitors.

A gravel path cuts gracefully across the yard and leads to the house. Along the way, colorful blooms of azalea and dogwood decree the season in this naturalistic setting. A pond entertains year-round.

Where a gravel walk encircles the garden island and pond, visitors can pause to admire the view on their way to the porch. The shaded garden's formal layout is reinforced by potted boxwood accents and mondo grass edging.

An open-air front porch gives this cottage an easygoing feel, fitting its beach community setting. The structure's curves add dramatic architecture to the house.

This Tudor-style home called for a cottage garden, with a backbone of lush shrubs and a long season of colorful perennials. Islands of lawn allow strolling.

4

SUN AND SHADE

The glimmering, shifting patterns of sun and shade in the landscape add interest and drama to your everyday world. The effects of light and dark stimulate your natural human response to day and night; seasons of nature and life. In addition to their profound effect on your state of mind, the pleasing mixture of sun and shade should also determine the placement of every plant and landscaping feature on your property.

Yet that pattern changes subtly with time of day, season of year, growth of plants, and addition or removal of structures. So the ultimate enjoyment of your surroundings depends to a great deal on how well you use the sun and shade. Too much of either throws your environment—and you—out of harmony.

A vine-covered pergola brings cooling shade to the poolside retreat. Flower-filled pots soften the hardscape that surrounds the pool. Lattice gives plants a foothold on the exterior walls of the poolhouse.

Family activities often revolve around the sun-drenched swimming pool. Nearby, a badminton court and strolling garden offer shaded areas to play or unwind.

A poolside cottage offers comfortable living space, no matter the weather. During swimming season, it provides a place to escape from sun and heat but remain near the hub of activities. On rainy days, it's a perfect place to play cards or board games.

ASSESSING SUN AND SHADE SOLUTIONS

A yard needs both sun and shade to modify otherwise uncomfortable weather. Sitting outdoors in the sun on a crisp autumn afternoon is uplifting and invigorating. But if, instead, you're shrouded in shade on that same nippy day, you'd probably head for the warmth of your home. On a hot summer day the opposite is true.

A full year

If you've just moved to a new home, study the sun and shade patterns in your yard for a full year before you make any landscaping decisions.

If you consider only the uncomfortable heat of the high summer sun, you may miss an opportunity to take advantage of the low, warmth-giving winter sun. Conversely, if you think only about the effects of winter sun, you may not give a thought to the possible excess-heat problems you might face in the summer. Besides, knowing the sun and shade patterns on a yard (from spring to fall, at least) is essential to knowing what plants will grow where.

First orient yourself to the north and other compass points of your yard. Then note patterns of sun and shade in different parts of the yard at different times of the day and year.

In the meantime, if you have spots where shade is essential, plant fast-growing vines or even some of the tallest annual flowers, such as sunflowers. These plants provide shade within a single summer. Many vines can be trained on makeshift stakes or wires until you're certain about the placement of more elaborate trellises and arbors.

Many shrubs are fast growing. To avoid constant pruning, select shrubs with the mature height and width you want and set them far enough from walls, walks, patios, and property lines. Most deciduous shrubs will reach mature height within three growing seasons; evergreens take a little longer.

Trees, of course, take much longer. But as a stopgap measure, you can plant fast-growing species such as poplar, silver maple, willow, and Chinese elm. Unfortunately most of these quick-maturing trees are weak-wooded, short-lived, and inferior in quality, so plan on planting them among slower-growing trees, then cutting them out as the stronger trees grow tall. (To prevent clogged pipes, keep willows and poplars away from water pipes or septic fields.)

Options

Once armed with the knowledge of year-round sun and shade patterns, start considering your options.

If your problem is too much shade, careful pruning can work wonders. Consider removing the lower branches from trees or hire a pro to do it. This simple step can open new vistas and increase the light and air circulation that reaches your living areas, indoors and out. By raising the canopy of leaves, you preserve the shade you need and the health and shape of the trees.

If your problem is too little shade, consider creating more of it with either structures, plants, or a combination of both.

To create shade, build an overhead sunshade, arbor, or trellis. Such structures are particularly appropriate if you have only a small area to shield or if you don't plan to stay in your house long enough for a tree to grow to maturity. Build structures over patios, decks, paths, or at a corner of the garden.

A well-designed, well-positioned sun structure screens out the summer sun yet lets the winter rays stream through. Match the material, size, and shape of any structure to your house, lot, and other landscape features. As with most projects, the simpler the design, the better.

If you build an overhead structure, choose a canopy that fits your sun or shade needs. Loosely spaced boards let in more sun; tightly spaced boards do the opposite. Or, for even more sun protection, select a solid material such as canvas or fiberglass. Use vines to soften a structure's lines and obtain additional shade.

A simple pergola visually extends the home's roof and draws visitors to the rosy room. What a pleasant way to welcome people to your home.

5836

ASSESSING SUN AND SHADE SOLUTIONS *(continued)*

Trees

A tree or large shrub provides the most natural source of shade in a landscape.

If you're building a new house on a lot with existing trees, decide which ones are keepers and spare no expense to protect them. Money cannot buy their years of growth.

If you're faced with an empty yard, resist the temptation to plant a lot of young trees and shrubs close to walls and one another. Unless you think about the mature sizes of plants, your bare yard can become a jungle.

When choosing shade plants, consider how their shapes, textures, and colors will blend with the rest of the landscape. Make sure their mature sizes will be in scale. Weigh maintenance needs as well.

Decide whether the plants you're considering provide the type of shade you want: Large-leaf species such as maple and sycamore may shade so much that little else will grow near them; fine-leaf trees such as honeylocust or mountain ash, on the other hand, provide filtered shade. A deciduous tree on a house's south side blocks summer sun, then sheds its leaves and admits winter light. An evergreen shields light year-round.

Also give prime consideration to the growing conditions in your area. Seek the advice of local nursery workers and extension service personnel. Use reliable native trees for best results.

Position

When positioning shade trees, keep in mind they will spread their branches about as wide as their height and send their roots much farther. So, in general, for ideal growth, allow as much as 65 feet between spreading trees, 35 feet between nonspreaders.

A walk in any woodland, however, will show you how nature adapts. With careful pruning and control, and planned crowding, you can plant more trees or smaller trees in a yard. Plan on thinning some of them out as they grow. (Avoid crowding weeping trees so you can showcase their special beauty.)

When placing shrubs or trees near the house and its foundation, plant them where their roots can readily receive rainfall, but will not compromise the structure as they grow. Plant shrubs at least 3 to 4 feet from the house, making sure to check the drip line. Within it, you will have to water the plant more often. Right under it, the plant could drown if no gutter catches the runoff from the roof.

Care

Your woody plants will grow faster and claim their space sooner if surrounded by mulch. Cultivated plants are the next-best choice for beds around the trunks. They will remind you to feed and water their woody neighbor, and they'll soften the emptiness of the new landscape at the same time.

Tree care is more important than most homeowners realize. Don't hesitate to have a trained and well-recommended tree expert treat pests, diseases, and wounds. Seek a second opinion if an expert suggests removal too quickly. The loss of a mature tree can devastate the best-planned landscape and take decades to replace. Take care when mowing around young trees and shrubs to avoid damaging the plants' trunks.

Plants in sun and shade

As your landscape plan develops and the woody plants grow, you will have to adjust your gardening below and around them. Every plant has its own sun and shade needs. Some thrive in a wide range of light conditions; others perish in the wrong exposure. Some survive in shade but need sun to bloom and bear fruit.

Take maximum advantage of the conditions at any given time. Put shade-loving plants, such as hostas and woodland wildflowers, in the darkest spots. Place adaptable plants—daylilies, for example—in partial-shade areas. Save the bright spots for vegetables and sun-loving flowers. If need be, plant the sun lovers in containers and move them around.

A tiered deck and an airy pergola transform an ordinary backyard into an expansive outdoor living area. The deck's curved edge and the pergola's trusses were custom-made by the homeowner.

BUILDING OVERHEAD STRUCTURES

ATTACHING A SUNSHADE TO A HOUSE

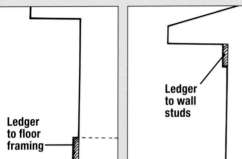

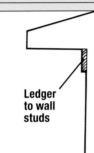

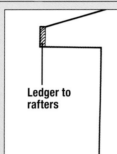

TWO-STORY HOUSE:
Lag-screw the ledger to second-floor framing, as you would a deck to the first floor. To locate joists, measure up from a window, both inside and out. Add the thickness of ceiling materials.

ONE-STORY HOUSE:
Screw the ledger to wall studs. This will put the sunshade several inches below roof level. If your home has lap siding, remove one course so the ledger will lie flat. In brick or stone, drill with a masonry bit.

ONE-STORY HOUSE:
Remove the fascia board that covers the ends of the rafters and attach the ledger to them. Protect the ledger from water by covering its top edge with metal flashing tucked up under the roofing.

ATTACHING TO AN EXISTING DECK

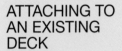

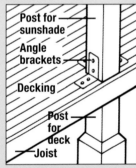

Locate sunshade posts directly above those that support the deck. Secure the new posts with angle brackets or post anchors. Use posts that are several inches longer than the plan calls for, then trim their tops later.

ATTACHING TO A NEW PATIO

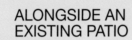

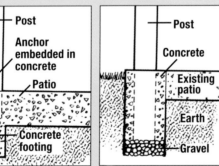

Pour a concrete footing along with the patio and embed a post anchor in it. Don't rest posts on a patio that has no footings underneath; the concrete could crack. Let concrete cure a week before erecting posts.

ALONGSIDE AN EXISTING PATIO

Rather than break into an existing patio to pour footings, position the posts just outside the patio. Dig to below the frost line; put gravel in the holes for drainage. Set the posts in concrete (see page 66).

ANATOMY OF A SUNSHADE

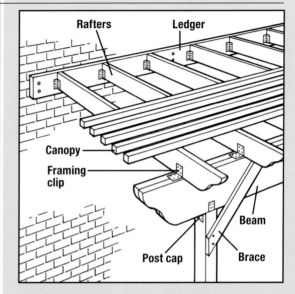

With an attached sunshade, 2×6 rafters fasten to a 2×8 or 2×10 ledger at one end and rest atop a beam of doubled 2×12s at the other. Diagonal braces strengthen the post-beam connections. The canopy consists of 2×2s fastened to the rafters.

CANOPY ALTERNATIVES

LATTICE: Crisscrossed slats of wood or vinyl—in panels or individual laths offer a lacy effect. Paint or stain/seal the strips (if wood) or use inexpensive grape-stake lattice, which has a rough, furry texture.
REED OR BAMBOO: These inexpensive materials have a limited lifespan. Prolong their use by rolling them up and storing them inside during winter.
SHADE CLOTH: Meshed fabric coverings provide filtered shade from sunlight but let air and moisture through.
CANVAS: Heavy cotton duck provides some protection against rain but must be stretched taut so water won't collect.
FIBERGLASS: Corrugated plastic panels are easy to cut and nail. Slope the canopy so water will run off.

BUILDING A PERGOLA

The best time to think about an overhead sun structure is while planning a new patio or deck. Then you can provide footings for its posts or simply extend a deck's posts 8 feet or so to carry the load.

If you need to shade an existing patio or deck, refer to the drawings opposite for post basics, then assemble the framing. Framing for a sunshade needn't be as strong as the underpinnings for a deck. It must be sturdy enough, though, to withstand strong winds and avert a potentially dangerous collapse, especially in snowy areas.

Two ways to go

Like decks, sunshades can either be joined to your house with a ledger or be freestanding. Where you attach the ledger depends, in part, on whether your house is one or two stories high. The project shows how to build a freestanding pergola (with beams at either end); for an attached version, substitute a ledger for a beam and posts.

Shades of difference

Give thought, too, to the sort of canopy material you'd like to top your sunshade with. There are at least a dozen types—ranging from an eggcrate layout to angled louvers. Aesthetics will play a big role in your choice, of course, but also ask yourself how much shade is needed.

A deck or patio on a treeless southern exposure could require protection all day long; a deck on an east or west side can get by with only partial shade.

A freestanding pergola frames a garden room, shading the sitting area and allowing cooling breezes to improve the comfort level there. To build the project shown, see pages 110–111.

BUILDING A PERGOLA *(continued)*

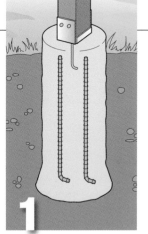

1

After marking the site layout and preparing a posthole for the concrete footing, set and plumb the first post. Clamp a temporary brace, staked to the ground at the opposite end, to hold the post until the concrete sets. Repeat for the remaining posts, and allow at least three days for the concrete to cure before proceeding.

2

Determine the desired post height, then use a line level to transfer that mark from one post to the next. Use a square to mark the cut line on all four sides of the post. If you are using 2×8 post caps as in the project shown here, deduct 1½ inches to allow for the thickness of the cap.

3

With most portable circular saws, you'll have to make cuts into all four faces of a 6×6 post, then finish the cut with a handsaw to sever the very center portion. Clamp an angle square or similar tool in place to guide each cut and be sure to wear ear and eye protection.

4

Check beam layout and connections on the ground before installation, then place the first long beam on top of the posts, with its half-lap notch facing up. Check for correct extension and centering, then drive timber screws through the beam and into the posts. Counterbore for the screw heads so they nest below the face of the notch. Also fasten the other beam end to the top of its supporting post, driving the screw through the post cap.

5

The second long beam features a corresponding (down-facing) notch that nests into the first beam. Fit the joint together and align the beam's opposite end on its corner post, then drive timber screws through the beam at both ends to secure it to the posts.

6

At the remaining corners and the front posts of the pergola, the beams butt together rather than overlap. Secure these connections by driving 6-inch timber screws through the face of the crossing beam and into the end of the beam that abuts it.

7

Fitting and cutting the joists is easier if the layout marking and bracket installation are done when the beams are test-fitted together on the ground. Number the joists and remove them, then simply refit them after the beams are secured to the posts. Attach the joists with screws and, if desired, paint the hardware to match the wood stain color.

8

Notching the posts during the early stages of construction provides a strong connection for the 2×8 rails that will support the benches. The rails themselves are also notched to receive support cleats; align the notches on the inside and outside rails when you attach them to the posts.

9

Bench slats, made from durable hardwood, are treated with a clear sealer to bring out their rich color and accent the pergola's larger timbers. Sand the edges and corners to remove roughness. Fasten the slats using stainless-steel screws, which won't rust and stain clothing.

BUILDING ARBORS

If you're looking for a leafy way to create shade for part of your yard, install an arbor and drape it with a canopy of vining plants. The job requires little effort, but the rewards will last for years.

Typically, you can build a start-from-scratch arbor in a couple of days—several days apart. Spend one day digging postholes and setting the posts; on the other day, cut and assemble the remaining components. Although some arbors are made from metal or heavy plastic, most use pressure-treated 2×4s—or preferably 4×4s—for the posts and treated or sealed wood for the rest of the structure.

If you like, choose one of the many kits on the market. They come complete with lumber, hardware, and assembly instructions, and are available in a variety of designs and materials.

Design considerations

Choose a metal arbor with delicate proportions for a small garden. On the other hand, a rustic wooden structure looks more appropriate in a cottage or country garden. For a more traditional or formal scheme, incorporate brick or stone into the arbor base and in the paths leading to and from it.

Placement tips

At the beginning of a walkway or the entry of a garden, an arbor forms a doorway and an instantly welcoming garden feature. In a large garden, install it partway down a path to invite strollers to explore what's ahead. In a small space, use it to create an impression that the garden extends beyond it.

Follow these steps to install the arbor: Dig four postholes 8 inches deep, pour heavy gravel into the bottom of the holes, and partially fill the remainder of each hole with concrete. When the concrete has just begun to set, carefully lift the arbor and set the stakes into the concrete. Then mound more concrete around the tops of the holes to encourage rainwater to drain away from the legs.

This arbor was built from a kit that included metal spikes for anchoring the posts in concrete. When building a similar version from scratch, you'll most likely be sinking the posts in concrete in the tried-and-true way.

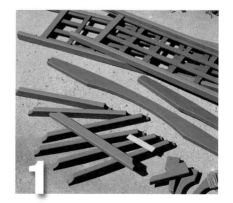

1

Apply exterior-grade stain or paint to the arbor pieces before assembly. Red cedar, redwood, and cypress possess natural weather resistance and do not require finishing. However, a waterseal finish helps protect the wood over time; a semitransparent stain in the same tone as the wood helps maintain its natural color. Work on a clean, flat surface such as a driveway, deck, or yard.

2

Most kits come with predrilled pieces; using a power screwdriver simplifies construction. Assembly usually begins by attaching curved brackets to the top inside edges of the upright side frames. Drive a screw into the lower end of the bracket first to hold the bracket flush. The brackets connect the upright posts to the overhead timbers to stabilize them and to add support to the structure. Curved detailing adds to the stylized design of this arbor.

3

Connect side frames to the header by laying the header on the work surface with two pilot screw holes facing up. Set one side frame on top of the header, with the bracket facing in toward the arbor opening. Align screw holes in the bracket and the side post with pilot holes in the header. Drive a screw through the top of the side post hole and into the header. Repeat the process on the other side frame.

4

Square the two posts to the first header. Measure the distance between the side posts at the top and at the bottom of the structure, adjusting until the arbor opening is parallel. Drive screws through each side post into the header board, and through each bracket into the header. Carefully lift the structure, turn it over, and align the screw holes in the side posts and brackets with the pilot holes in the header. Repeat step 3 to attach the side posts to the header; measure carefully to ensure the structure is square.

5

Prepare to attach cap boards to the top of the header by driving nails into predrilled holes in the ends of each cap board. Drive each nail until its tip protrudes through the bottom of the cap board.

6

Prop the arbor up off the ground by sliding a wood block or similar support under each side frame. Center one cap board atop the two header boards. Position nail points in the middle of each header board and drive the nails into each board.

7

Use a lath spacer to guide placement of the remaining cap boards, centering the nail ends in each header board. Finish nailing. Carefully stand the arbor and check it for stability. Tighten screws. Carry it to the site and complete installation.

ARBOR AND TRELLIS PLANTINGS

The vine-covered arbor or trellis makes a cool garden wall, curtained in green and decorated with dappled sunlight and fragrant flowers. The privacy and shade it offers rival those of a tree, but in a half season instead of a decade and in a planting-area width as narrow as a single foot.

The secret to enjoying vines is to understand their individual traits then match the right vines to your needs—whether that be spring bloom, fall color, fruit production, or to frame a view or screen it—and to the support you want them to climb. Keep in mind a vine's soil preference, hardiness, and sun or shade requirements too.

Matching vines to the right supports

Vines can be divided into four basic groups, depending on how they climb.

Twining vines need a pole or at least a finger-thin means of vertical support to climb. Arbors and trellises provide good support for such smaller twining vines as morning glory and trumpet honeysuckle. Substantial columns and pergolas are needed to support the heavier twining trunks of wisteria and silver lace vine.

Some vines climb by winding tendrils or modified leaf stalks around whatever they can. Clematis, grape, melon, pea, passionflower, and creepers all climb this way, and good supports for them include narrow lattice on trellises and arbors, chain link fencing, and string or wire netting. Small, light-weight vines such as large-flowered clematis, are good for growing up and through shrubs such as roses.

Vines such as Boston ivy, climbing hydrangea, English ivy, and wintercreeper cling by adhering small rootlike grips to a surface, usually to a wall. While ideal for brick and stone, these vines should not be planted on frame houses because the holdfasts may penetrate and damage the siding.

Some climbers are not vines at all, but long-stemmed shrubs that lean. Some, such as roses, use thorns to help them grab. This kind of shrub needs to be trained to climb by tying or winding its stems around a column or trellis.

Vines that climb by twining wind their stems around a vertical object. They grow on bamboo poles and stakes, lattice, chain-link fences, posts, timbers, and columns, and other plants. Examples include morning glory, mandevilla, wisteria, and honeysuckle. Avoid growing twiners on trees.

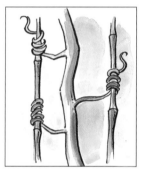

Vines that climb by tendrils or leaves modified into tendrils wind these specialized structures around narrow cylindrical supports. They grow on strings, netting, chain-link fences, narrow lattice, and other plants. Examples include clematis, sweet pea, and passionflower.

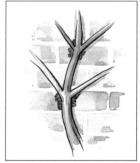

Vines that climb by clinging use specialized structures called "holdfasts" to adhere stems against a surface. They are good for growing on masonry as long as it is in good condition, and most are good choices for growing up into large, mature trees. Avoid growing these vines on wood such as siding as they will damage it, or on trees not large enough to support their sometimes massive growth. Examples of clinging vines include Boston ivy, English ivy, climbing hydrangea, creeping fig, and wintercreeper.

SUPPORTING CLIMBING ROSES ON A BRICK WALL

1 Determine where each bracket is going to be set and mark holes. Use a plumb bob to ensure each bracket is exactly below the one above so that the cables will be vertical. Drill holes with a masonry bit large enough go nearly brick to brick. We used a 5/16" double-barreled expansion fastener which required a 5/8" hole.

2 Attach both fasteners to the bracket by threading the bolts partway into the fasteners. Do not thread the bolts all the way at this point in order to allow the fasteners to insert completely into the holes. Push the fasteners into their holes as far as they will go, until the bracket is flush against the brick.

This custom system for training climbing roses against a brick wall is designed to be long-lasting and safe for masonry, unobtrusive to the eye, and provide plenty of sturdy support for plants that can grow quite large and heavy. To grow roses fifteen feet up a wall takes five vertical cables spaced four feet apart and supported 12" out from the wall to allow for good air circulation behind the roses.

A blacksmith was commissioned to fabricate fifteen brackets out of 1/2"×1/2" square steel stock with 1/8"× 2"×6" stock welded on as a base. Holes in the base were drilled to match the brick wall's mortar spacing and the fastener size.

In the five top and five bottom brackets a 90° bend was made 12" out from the base, and 1/4"-20 threads tapped 1 1/2" deep into the bent end. Two 1/4"-20 holes were tapped into the side of the 1 1/2" hole for two 5/16" set screws used to grip the cable.

The five middle brackets do not have a bend or threads, but simply a 1/4" hole set 12" from the base to stabilize the cable and keep it from swaying.

The fasteners are 5/16" double-shell expansion anchors inserted in 5/8" holes drilled into the mortar joints with a mortar bit. Bolts and washers are 2 1/4"×5/16". The cable used is 3/16" vinyl coated cable. The brackets were coated with a rust-resistant paint.

Twine roses around cables and tie them loosely with twine. The rose variety used here is 'New Dawn'.

3 Tighten the bolts into the fasteners. As you do this the fasteners will expand and grip onto the bricks above and below it. It is important that the expansion anchors grip onto the bricks rather than just the mortar. Repeat steps 2 and 3 for the rest of the brackets.

4 Bare the end of a cable by stripping off the vinyl, insert it into the hole in the top bracket and tighten the set screws firmly with an allen wrench. Thread the cable through the hole in the middle bracket, and then measure and cut the cable to the appropriate length at the bottom bracket. Strip the vinyl off the end, insert it in the bracket, and tighten the set screws.

CHOOSING PLANTS TO PROVIDE DENSE SHADE

TREES

CRABAPPLE

Malus spp. and hybrids

Type: Deciduous
Height: 15–25 feet
Zones: 3–8
Soil: Rich, well drained; tolerant
Light: Full sun

Comments: Crabapples, with their profusion of fragrant spring flowers and fall fruit, are among the best of trees. Much fruit stays on the trees throughout winter, providing food for birds and a nice decoration when crowned with snow. Some is good for jams and jellies. 'Transcendent' and 'Dolgo' are best for eating.

DOGWOOD

Cornus spp.

Type: Deciduous
Height: 15–30 feet
Zones: 5–9
Soil: Rich, slightly acid, moist
Light: Prefers some shade

Comments: One of the most beautiful and useful flowering trees, dogwood offers spring bloom, good summer foliage, dark red autumn color, berries, and, with its horizontal branches and crownlike buds, winter interest. Red and pink varieties are available. Kousa dogwood (*Cornus kousa*) blooms later with pointed bracts. The other dogwoods all are good ornamentals with attractive foliage and berries but inconspicuous flowers.

MAPLE

Acer spp.

Type: Deciduous
Height: To 80 feet and more
Zones: 3–8
Soil: Average, moist
Light: Full sun or light shade

Comments: Ninety species of maple vary in habit, rate of growth, and leaf size and color. Spring and summer foliage can be red or many shades of green with white, yellow, or pink markings or silver undersides. The fiery autumn color of New England is largely from maples in brilliant red, yellow, and orange. Maples are easy to grow and have few serious pest or disease problems. Sugar maple and several others produce sap used in making syrup.

OAK

Quercus spp.

Type: Mostly deciduous
Height: 50 feet to much taller
Zones: 4–9
Soil: Acid, moist, well drained
Light: Sun or light shade

Comments: Oaks make excellent shade and specimen trees, especially where they have plenty of room. The many species vary greatly in leaves, color, and acorns, which are good for wildlife. Valued for their sturdy growth and wide-spreading branches at maturity, some have brilliant autumn color and some are evergreen. Many keep their leaves long into winter. Difficult to transplant.

Most trees will develop as much width as height if given room. You can get columnar varieties of maple, oak, and plane trees for narrow spaces. Low trees—such as hawthorn and amur maples—will give shade and still stay in bounds under electric wires. Other excellent shade trees include evergreen hemlock, some pines, arborvitae, and deciduous trees such as katsura tree, sweet gum, and linden. For quick-growing temporary trees, use silver maple, catalpa, silk oak, and willow. See pages 359-367 for more tree suggestions.

SPRUCE
Picea spp.
Type: Evergreen
Height: 50–100 feet
Zones: 3–8
Soil: Rich, well drained
Light: Full or partial sun

Comments: Spruces are stiff, formal trees with cones that hang down. They eventually grow to great heights and can grow out of scale. Blue spruces are greatly prized for their color. Older spruces often lose their lower branches, changing their shape but opening up the yard to traffic, views, and more air circulation. Red and black spruces are less choice, as they are subject to spruce gall and aphids.

TULIP TREE
Liriodendron tulipifera
Type: Deciduous
Height: 75 feet or more
Zones: 5–9
Soil: Deep, rich, acid, moist
Light: Full sun or light shade

Comments: Tulip trees are fast growing. They have a pyramidal shape, green leaves like squared-off maple leaves, yellow autumn color, and tulip-shape green flowers with a band of yellow and orange in late spring. The flowers hide among the foliage but are beautiful when viewed from a second-story deck or upstairs window. Seedpods dry in tulip shape for winter. Tulip trees can develop sooty mold or honeydew from aphids; use away from patios or driveways.

SHRUB

JAPANESE PIERIS
Pieris japonica
Type: Broadleaved evergreen
Height: 2–9 feet
Zones: 4–8
Soil: Sandy, acid, moist
Light: Sun to partial shade

Comments: An excellent shrub, Japanese pieris has lustrous dark green foliage with much bronze in the new leaves. Buds are showy all winter. Nodding clusters of lily-of-the-valleylike flowers, white to pinkish, cover the shrub in the spring. *P. floribunda* is hardier than *japonica*. Plant both in more sheltered spots in the North. These fine entrance or accent plants have few problems, and will produce more flowers in sun than in shade.

Other dense shrubs include summersweet, privet, deciduous viburnums, and evergreens such as juniper, yew, and mountain laurel.

VINE

SILVER LACE VINE
Polygonum aubertii
Type: Woody perennial
Length: 25 feet
Zones: 4–8
Soil: Average; tolerates dry
Light: Full sun best

Comments: Rapid-growing silver lace vine has fragrant greenish white flowers in long erect or drooping clusters in late summer and early fall when few woody plants are blooming. It produces dense bright green foliage. A member of the knotweed family, it climbs by twining. Prune severely in late winter to control vigorous growth. Silver lace vine is easy to grow from seeds, root divisions, or ripe wood cuttings. Also called fleece vine.

Other dense vines include grape, bittersweet, trumpet vine, climbing hydrangea, and wisteria.

CHOOSING PLANTS TO PROVIDE LIGHT SHADE

TREES

BIRCH
Betula spp.
Type: Deciduous
Height: 25–90 feet
Zones: 2–10
Soil: Moist
Light: Full sun to light shade

Comments: Birches are widely planted, often in clumps, for their interesting gray, white, black, or reddish-brown bark that splits and hangs like wrapping paper. The weeping birch is valued for its shape. All have early catkin blooms that herald spring and leaves that turn yellow in autumn. All are short lived and subject to many pests. River birch needs more moisture but resists problems better. 'Heritage' is an improved cultivar. Plant a variety native to your region.

CHERRY, PLUM, PEACH
Prunus spp.
Type: Deciduous
Height: Mostly 20–25 feet
Zones: Variable
Soil: Well drained
Light: Full sun

Comments: The *Prunus* group, with more than 400 species, includes all the stone fruits, from chokecherry to cherry laurel. Many of these are excellent choices for edible landscaping. Select an ornamental variety if fruit is not your priority. Most are low growing and decorative, with clouds of spring flowers, single or double, in white, pink, or rose. Some have bronze foliage or glossy red bark; a few are evergreen. Shade density varies.

GINKGO
Ginkgo biloba
Type: Deciduous
Height: 50–80 feet
Zones: 5–10
Soil: Deep, loose
Light: Full sun to part shade

Comments: Hardy and slow growing, ginkgo trees are among the oldest plants in cultivation. They are ideal as lawn or street trees because they're pest free, widely adaptable, and tolerant of smoke and pollution. Provide extra watering after planting. The male tree is neater; berries have a rancid odor when crushed. Fan-shape leaves turn golden yellow in autumn, and all fall at once, making raking a one-time affair.

HONEYLOCUST
Gleditsia triacanthos
Type: Deciduous
Height: 60 feet
Zones: 4–9
Soil: Any
Light: Sun

Comments: Thornless honeylocust provides fine-textured, filtered shade and permits shade-tolerant turfgrass and perennials to grow under it. For best results, plant honeylocust in spring. The trees prefer moist, deep soil in full sun but are adaptable to adverse conditions. Mulch young trees and protect the thin bark from damage with a loose collar of hardware cloth. Yellow-leaved varieties are available.

MOUNTAIN ASH
Sorbus spp.
Type: Deciduous
Height: 20–40 feet
Zones: 3–7
Soil: Well drained
Light: Sun to part shade

Comments: European mountain ash grows best in cooler climates. It prefers moist, slightly acid, well-drained soils and full sun. It is short lived in alkaline or dry soils and full sun. Place it where you can enjoy the light shade, spring flowers, and bright orange fruits of summer.

SHRUBS

FORSYTHIA
Forsythia ×intermedia
Type: Deciduous
Height: 2–12 feet
Zones: 4–8
Soil: Well drained
Light: Full sun

Comments: Forsythia's golden showers in early spring on arching or upright branches make it hard to resist. The plant is much hardier than the buds. Give it plenty of room; plant 8 to 10 feet from walk or patio. Never prune until after bloom; then remove unwanted canes at the ground. Forsythia can claim more room than its limited season merits. Extra hardy varieties are 'Northern Sun' and 'Ottawa.'

JAPANESE MAPLE
Acer palmatum
Type: Deciduous
Height: 15–25 feet
Zones: 5–8
Soil: Rich, well drained, acid
Light: Sun to part shade

Comments: Japanese maple prefers morning sun and filtered shade in the afternoon. With its sculptural form and striking leaf color, Japanese maple is an excellent accent plant. Its preference for moist soil makes it a good choice next to a water feature. Protect plants from winds and late spring frosts. Choose a fine-leaf variety for the light shade it will cast.

SERVICEBERRY
Amelanchier ×grandiflora
Type: Deciduous
Height: 15–25 feet
Zones: 3–8
Soil: Well drained, acid
Light: Sun to shade

Comments: Serviceberry is useful in windbreaks and in naturalized plantings, where it will attract birds and other wildlife. Its delicate white flowers, purplish red fruits, and silvery gray bark make it worthy of a mixed border. With pruning and shaping, it will develop into a fine specimen tree. It makes a good courtyard or patio tree. Some varieties sucker at the base, forming multiple stems.

Other good shrubs for filtered shade include tall cotoneasters, smokebush, red-vein enkianthus, mock orange, and rhododendron. Pruning dense-foliaged shrubs can let in more light.

VINE

CLEMATIS
Clematis spp. and hybrids
Type: Perennial
Length: 5–30 feet
Zones: 4–9
Soil: Well-drained
Light: Full sun to light shade

Comments: Beautiful plants, clematis species and hybrids vary widely in bloom type, color, fragrance, and season. The large, star-shaped flowers of the hybrids are spectacular in early summer. Pair plantings with other vines with a different bloom time, such as roses, for a longer flowering season. Plant in humus-rich soil with a little lime and mulch

Many vines have dense, vigorous growth that requires pruning to achieve a filtered-shade effect. Other vines desirable for light shade include Carolina jessamine, silver lace vine, and dutchman's pipe.

GALLERY OF SUN AND SHADE IDEAS

When lattice is used to enclose an outdoor area, such as this deck, it creates privacy while filtering sun and allowing air circulation.

Grapevines make an excellent sunscreen and furnish tasty edible fruit as well. Two varieties of grapes form a green roof over this arbor.

A study in light and shade, this poolside pavilion adds romance to the secluded oasis. Adjacent sago and Mexican fan palms bolster the shade and seclusion with tropical flair.

Designed as a place to sit and view the garden or relax and read, a sturdy pergola holds a comfortable garden swing.

This classic freestanding pergola serves as an elegant transition from one part of the yard to another, and adds shade to the seating area beneath it.

Linked arbors transform a former alley of baked sand into a pleasant walkway. The structures cast some shade and connect outdoor living areas.

CHAPTER

5

CONTROLLING THE VIEW

The scenery you enjoy is yours to choose when you plan your landscape carefully. You can open and accent a distant horizon, be it city lights or mountain peaks. Or you can create a nearby focal point of beauty and interest: a blooming tree or winding walk. Or perhaps your need is to minimize less-than-lovely sights: the trash cans in your yard; the busy driveway in your neighbor's. Carefully and deliberately, you want to spotlight the beautiful and desired; hide the unsightly and unwanted.

Matching arbors frame a formal garden where the focal point is a potted water garden and its resident lotus. The substantial arbors, with classic detailing, uphold clematis vines and a shade-tolerant climbing rose, 'Zépherine Drouhin.'

As a passageway from the historical home to its lushly planted backyard, this formal garden offers a sense of calm and order.

Dwarf boxwood shrubs encircle the bubbling water feature as well as the rustic pathway of bricks.

SCREENING UNWANTED VIEWS WITH PLANTINGS

Planting carefully selected trees and shrubs is the most natural, inexpensive, and subtle way to maximize or minimize the scenery in your yard. A neighbor who might resent a fence can hardly object to an evergreen or flowering shrub. A single planting, well situated, can make the old car next door all but vanish as far as you're concerned.

To wall out even more, plant a hedge or group of shrubs and small trees. You can buy quite mature plants for the price of fencing. Do not stint here. You are buying instant relief. But choose plants that will not grow too big or need more pruning than you are willing to do.

Deciduous shrubs grow tall in just a few seasons. Plant them around areas you don't use in winter such as decks. Plant evergreens for year-round screening of unpleasant views from your most-used windows and walks. A bonus: Since most summer breezes blow opposite to winter winds, evergreens can save on heating bills and won't block cool winds in summer.

Small and large deciduous trees will hide tall neighboring buildings eventually and soften their effect in the meantime. Choose or prune for open or dense seclusion. And be sure that plants do not grow over important views such as the stop for the school bus, the mailbox flag, or the swing set.

Vines on arbors, fences, or trellises offer screening in very little time or space. Annuals take until late summer to make a good screen; combine grapes or kiwi with morning glories for a lacy curtain from early spring.

Picket fencing forms a pretty backdrop for a garden, though its open pattern proves more decorative than functional. Backed by a forsythia hedge, however, it increases the home's privacy.

A wire and rebar fence, planted with flowering vines, will form a 6-foot-tall living wall within a few years and provide maximum privacy for this front yard.

Looking into the yard or windows of a nearby house can take the relaxation right out of a hot tub soak.

Tall, lacy foliage here feels open and airy but quite effectively screens soakers from the outside world.

SCREENING UNWANTED VIEWS WITH STRUCTURES

This cozy deck boasts a balance of sun and shade, thanks to its pergola and screen. Crafted of cedar, the low-maintenance structures are also weather resistant.

Sights and sounds of nearby traffic disappear as you step into this tranquil side yard. The 8-foot-wide garden and screens do an excellent job insulating the house from street noise.

There is no quicker or more definite way to reduce a view than to block it with a fence, screen, wall, gate, or building. Nor are there many landscaping options that offer as much room for creativity.

Some structures may be built specifically for screening views. Others may serve several purposes. If you are going to build a playhouse or potting shed in any case, situate it to obstruct an unpleasant view rather than shut off a view you cherish. Make the side that shows enchanting, the side that serves convenient.

Because structures are permanent, evaluate your needs and plan carefully before you build. First check building codes and any restrictions written into your deed. Be sure to verify property lines; even then, it is best to stay slightly within in case of error.

If a pool or spa is in your plans, consider fencing regulations, as well as access to the area. Be sure that what you build now will not be wasted or destroyed by future landscaping endeavors.

Choose materials that will complement existing structures, the house, and the mood of the garden, as well as the budget. Hiring a pro to complete a project typically doubles the cost of doing it yourself. Keep future maintenance in mind. Painting or staining can be costly and time consuming.

Simple solutions

Often a simple screen, series of panels, or arbor well within the property can make an amazing difference when blocking views. Work these into pleasing patterns that fit into the complete landscaping plan. Don't let them look like isolated attempts to correct existing eyesores.

A combination of open and solid fencing will save money and let you select your outside views. You may want a solid section to block the next yard but an open one to accent a panoramic view of meadows, rooftops, or hills beyond.

Where slopes are involved, it is better for fences or walls to definitely jog or slope at the top than to slant slightly.

The privacy screen blocks views from next door but lets light pass through keyhole cutouts inspired by a similar design in the home's entry. Limestone accents on the brick columns add structural support and visual appeal.

CREATING DESIRABLE VIEWS WITH PLANTINGS

Once you have enclosed your yard, the real delight comes from filling it with your favorite forms, fragrances, flowers, and fruits. Plan just one wide garden area or connect several separate outdoor areas with shrubbery and pathways.

Your view can be serene and peaceful with minimal maintenance or bold and exciting with bright flowers. Combine ornamentals with edible plants for delightful blooms and tasty meals.

Plan carefully for maximum seasonal interest. Lilacs perfume the air for a few precious days in the spring. Dogwoods offer spring flowers and excellent autumn color, as well as interesting winter shape. Viburnums and crabapples have showy flowers and fruit that attracts birds. Smoketrees bloom for months.

Flowering shrubs, trees, and groundcovers give form, color, and interest for decades with very little work. Yet many gardeners find that flowers, herbs, and vegetables are always worth the extra effort.

Plan your plantings so that colors will combine harmoniously and continue at every season of the year. Perennials and spring bulbs can be the backbone of such plantings, but annuals are the color champions that will bloom from spring until frost. Keep heights, colors, and times of bloom in mind for a view that tantalizes onlookers all season. Large drifts of the same flower and clumps of three or more of the same small shrub will make a more definite statement than too much of a mixture.

Some plants, such as spring's first crocus and early magnolia, should be near the house and entryways so you can see them up close. Others—such as butterfly-attracting Mexican sunflower—are better seen from afar, where their coarseness is obscured by their other virtues.

Remember that blues, purples, and dark colors fade in the distance. White accents stand out. Bright colors light up dark corners and bring them into focus.

One purpose of good landscape design is to control a view using an object or a series of objects that you choose and place. It's as much about what you don't see as what you see.

Using the natural arching growth habit of trees and shrubs, you can direct the view. Columnar crabapple trees draw you into this garden by framing the bench and the structure beyond it.

A path made with reclaimed materials leads from the house to an arbor and the yard beyond. Mulched planting beds line the path and give strollers a verdant view along the way.

129

CREATING DESIRABLE VIEWS WITH STRUCTURES

Potted topiaries flank the entry to a front yard garden. The arbor, fence, and gate give this streetside sanctuary a certain appeal that is welcoming and mysterious.

Picture this view of your backyard: through a lattice porthole. This situation happens to be a creative solution, where an exterior staircase framed a view of the garden from indoors. The lattice, attached to the staircase, turns the problem into an asset.

While plants create subtle views that change with the seasons, structures bring decisive design, framing, or focus to the picture. These structures include anything you may build or add to the garden: arches, arbors, gates, walkways, steps, birdbaths, benches, and raised beds, as well as decks, patios, pools, screened rooms, walls, and fences.

Plantings can soften and enhance structures, but the structure's size, materials, and location determine the style of a garden setting. Even your choice of edgings—wood, brick, or stone—makes an important contribution to the overall picture.

As you select larger investments, balance family needs and desires with the garden vista you're trying to achieve. If your children want a playhouse, for example, do you want to create an elaborate structure that will turn heads, or keep it simple to downplay its presence? Do you need a place to keep the lawn mower? A handsome shed can be the center of attention. A homely structure, however, may require relegation to a spot behind the garage.

Also consider a structure's purpose when determining its importance in your garden scene. A bench or garden swing can become a focal point, or it can be a hideaway that you want to keep isolated from the house.

The route of your garden paths will influence garden design and its structures, and vice versa. Let your natural footsteps serve as a guide but add surprises, too. Grass pathways limit your garden walks to dry days. More functional paths can have a hard surface (flagstones, for example), a soft surface (such as pea gravel), or a combination of the two.

What could be a more charming way to welcome guests to your yard than a classic gated entry?

CREATING DESIRABLE VIEWS FROM WITHIN

You don't have to be out in your yard to appreciate its many charms and changes. More often than not, most of us view our gardens from indoors, looking out through windows, particularly when the weather turns bad. Because of this, the best landscape designs take into account potential views from inside the house.

Begin by marking on your landscape plan the location of every window. Note the windows you look out most often and the angle from which you usually look out of them. When planning your landscape and determining priorities, improving views should be at the top of your list.

Arrange plants, structures, or a combination of the two to create scenes that, when framed by the windows, resemble well-composed photographs, with a background, middle ground, foreground, and focal point. Important paths and structures should be in view from indoors whenever possible.

Be sure to put special plants where you can see them from inside. This is especially true for plants that bloom in spring, when the weather often is too chilly for venturing outdoors. You may miss the crocus altogether if they are under a window instead of visible through it.

Aligning the rows in the vegetable garden to follow the line of sight instead of crossing it will let you watch the details of growth much more closely.

Parts of most yards cannot be seen from indoors at all. Locate the compost pile in one of those concealed, out-of-the-way spots.

A bird's-eye view of a backyard proves delightful, especially when planned for viewing from indoors. Even in late winter, this landscape pleases with its textures and hints of color.

When your backyard holds spectacular scenery, French doors are essential to savoring the drama from indoors, rain or shine.

Trim trees and shrubs,
along with a privacy
wall, frame views of this
semiformal terrace.

GALLERY OF CONTROLLED VIEWS

An arbor defines the sight line to an herb garden or any favored place in the landscape. Arbors are entryways and passages that make visual connections between parts of the landscape. Place them where you would locate a doorway or a gate.

Plan ahead to take advantage of the best views your landscape can offer. When laying out the planting areas or picturesque vistas, stand in the house and look out at the area you're planning and imagine the prospective view.

Screens serve various purposes in blocking, framing, or creating views. This custom-made structure works well with surrounding plants to create an eyecatching feature. Without it, the setting would be bland.

Place a focal point, such as a covered bench or sculpture, at the end of a path as a destination. Lay the path on a diagonal to make the stroll more interesting.

A curving path creates a sense of allure and surprise, especially when the destination is unseen. Here boxwood hedges echo the curve of the path, while a lofty rhododendron masks the view of what's to come.

134

The view from the street is all-important if you want to put your home's best face forward. In communities where streetside planting is allowed, a few bright flowers go a long way toward civic pride.

CHAPTER 6

PATIOS

One of the best ways to civilize your yard is to add a patio. Whether you snug it against the house or hide it in the back reaches of your yard, you'll soon be escaping to the great outdoors at every possible chance. As a bonus, you'll find that a patio enriches life within your home too. The new inside-looking-out views of a nearby sanctuary will visually expand crowded indoor rooms, as well as help assuage fits of cabin fever by stirring memories of many pleasant moments spent outside.

The lower landing—a brick rug—makes a graceful transition between the bottom of the dramatic stairway and the entertainment patio at ground level.

The staircase leads visitors down one flight to a nesting spot just off the first landing, then continues the journey to the level below.

A series of separate entertainment areas begins with a deck situated off the home's main level. Here a group can gather near the grill.

This lower-level stone and brick patio—punctuated by a planting area behind a sturdy retaining wall—serves as yet another pleasant gathering place.

ASSESSING PATIO OPTIONS

A house needs more than four walls, a floor, and a ceiling to make it a livable space. Outdoors, then, why settle for lawn, trees, and lot lines? Yards, like indoor rooms, should offer an irresistible invitation to wander, rest, gather, and enjoy.

One way to bring this about is with a patio. It'll cost much less to build than a room addition and barely disrupt the household during the construction process. You can build the simpler ones yourself.

Start by thinking about your family's needs and your landscape style, then imagine which of the many options shown in this chapter might work best.

At the start

Check local building codes, regulations, and zoning restrictions first. It may be that overhead sunshades need approval or that overhead power lines present obstacles. Property lines and easements will reduce your options too. So will any deed restrictions and the location of a septic tank.

Where you place your patio is most important. Access to kitchen, living room, or family room will make a big difference to outdoor use and indoor appreciation. Entry from more than one room or a pass-through at the kitchen window will make a patio more useful as well.

Patios on the north and east will receive less sun and more cooling breezes in warm climates and warm weather. Those on the south and west will receive much-appreciated extra sun in cooler climates and seasons. Take time to study wind and rain directions in your yard, as well as sun and shadow patterns. See how they vary with the seasons before choosing a site.

Remember that cool air moves downward over land. If your patio is on the uphill side of your house, you'll be more comfortable on chilly evenings.

Depending on your climate, you may want to make provisions for rain protection, either overhead or from the direction summer rains usually blow.

If space or privacy dictate that you build where climate is less favorable, overhead sunshades, screens, or well-placed trees can make your outdoor room much more comfortable. Remember that deciduous trees will cool the scene in summer yet allow the winter sun to shine through.

Patio pluses

Patios have a permanent look and feel. Because of the wide variety of paving materials available, patios can complement any style of house and landscape. They do require level ground, though. If your yard is completely flat, you might consider excavating for a sunken patio. Such a patio will be cooler in summer, give a different view of the surroundings, and provide privacy. It also will cost more because of the need to remove soil, build walls to retain the surrounding area, and install tubing to drain off excess water.

A patio's reflected heat can feel pleasant in spring. At the peak of summer's heat, the surface can become uncomfortable under bare feet. You can enjoy your patio into colder weather if you add a firepit or chimenea to warm the area.

For an attached patio, 15×25 feet is probably a good minimum size. It provides ample room for furniture, a grill, and some storage. A few smaller patios, perhaps connected by steps or paved walks, are often more satisfactory than one large one; each unit can serve as a separate room and offer its own unique view and function.

Since you may choose your location because of the shade and beauty of surrounding trees, you'll want to take every measure to preserve them. The major root systems of most trees extend to the drip line. If you wish to lay a masonry surface over this area, consider loose gravel or bricks set on sand, which will allow air and water to reach the roots. Concrete won't.

Before you proceed, stake off the area and connect the stakes with string. Hang sheets to simulate privacy screens. Mentally or actually put your patio furniture in place, and then consider it in terms of scale and unity.

The quiet, subtle design of the brick patio and the minimal silhouettes of the furniture create a restful backyard retreat that barely intrudes on the beautiful plantings that make this place so inviting.

139

CREATING THE ULTIMATE PATIO

Build the perfect patio and your summers will be filled with breezy afternoons, outdoor suppers, and gentle evenings with children chasing fireflies while adults relax and watch.

This ideal patio is visible indoors from doorways and windows, quietly inviting you to go outside, if only for stolen moments. It's so easily reached from the kitchen and family room that it becomes an extension of both.

It has enough privacy and comfortable, practical furniture to make it as cozy as the den. Yet it also has space for a breath of fresh air and for entertaining a crowd with flair.

The surface drains and dries quickly after a rain. (Certain flagstones, when wet, give off a lovely reflection that amplifies the garden's appeal.) Most important, the surface is safe, nonskidding, and comfortable underfoot. Softer materials will do for paths, but more-solid surfaces are better for feet mostly at rest.

The perfect patio is a focal point of beauty for both house and garden. The choicest plants grow around it, so you can pull weeds, plant seeds, or pull off spent flowers from your chair if you wish. You are close enough to notice the butterflies on the marigolds and to water plants easily at the first sign of wilting.

While you have the hose out, you can whisk away any dirt or debris. Patio maintenance should be mostly pleasant puttering.

The ultimate patio blends the beauty of the garden with the comfort of the house. Container plantings prove ideal, whether you prefer to grow annuals, herbs, vegetables, or more permanent selections. Blooming flowers and visiting birds at feeders or birdbaths entice even the most indoor person to venture out.

The ideal patio has a natural feeling of being part of a magnificent landscape, as if it grew there, and the owners were wise enough to make the most of such a pleasurable site.

This all-masonry outdoor area—more intricate and expensive than most—elegantly enhances the home. A majestic fireplace commands the view, while rafters and vines overhead bring vital shade to this magnetic setting.

BUILDING PAVER PATIOS

Concrete pavers come in a variety of shapes, sizes, and colors. Stronger and denser than ordinary concrete blocks, they resist moisture absorption and damage from repeated freeze-and-thaw cycles. New styles of pavers interlock in a variety of geometric patterns. Your design can be casual or formal.

Take measurements with you when you're ready to purchase pavers. Most retailers will assist you in estimating the number of pavers, amount of gravel, and volume of sand you will need. Buy extra pavers to compensate for breakage and incorrect cuts, and to keep on hand for future repairs.

To create a patio with a uniform appearance, use same-color pavers from the same bundle or pallet. Conversely, to create interest, mix colors.

Some pavers benefit from a sealant that can help prevent staining in areas with heavy foot traffic or frequent cooking. A sealant may also accentuate the pavers' color. Repeated applications may be required.

Before you begin any work, have the local utility company or locating service check for underground pipes and wires. They will mark the location and depth of utilities.

Before you begin the excavation process, lay out the site. Measure and then mark the perimeter of the patio by driving stakes into the ground or using a garden hose and flour to create curves (see pages 144–145).

1 To excavate the site, remove the sod and soil. Dig deep enough to allow for a 4- to 6-inch base of gravel or crushed-stone, plus a 2-inch sand bed, as well as the thickness of the pavers. Slide a 2×4 across the surface to level it.

2 Ensure a firm, stable base. Use a tamper on loose clay soil; a vibrating plate on sandy soil. Lay the crushed-rock or road-grade base, spreading it evenly, and compact it firmly.

3 Cover the base with a layer of landscaping fabric. It will act as a permeable weed barrier, allowing moisture to drain, but preventing weeds from developing.

4 Install border or edge restraints to keep the edge blocks from drifting and creating gaps. Edging options include plastic trim. Lay out the trim and use a small sledgehammer to drive oversize stakes to secure it in place.

5 Add a 1- or 2-inch layer of sand to the base. Smooth and level the sand, using a 2×4 and sliding it over the surface. Fill in any depressions. Dampen the sand; tamp it.

6 Pavers vary in size and shape, so there is no single starting point or method for placing them. Lay pavers using a carpenter's level to check the surface as you complete sections. Fill low spots. Tap raised pavers using a rubber mallet.

7 If necessary, cut pavers to fit voids along edges. Break pavers using a masonry chisel and hammer or make precise cuts using a circular saw with a masonry blade.

8 Spread clean sand on the surface and sweep it into the joints to help hold pavers in place. Use a garden hose to mist the surface and settle the sand. Repeat until the gaps are filled. If necessary, apply sealant according to product directions.

9 If you choose to include an attached walkway as part of your patio design, use the same or a complementary material. Make walkways at least 4 feet wide to accommodate two people walking side by side.

BUILDING CONCRETE SLAB PATIOS

Although concrete is very strong in many respects, it has limited tensile (bending) strength. This means that a slab without a firm, uniform base almost certainly will crack and heave unevenly, leaving you with a difficult repair job.

If possible, place your slab on a gravel bed over undisturbed soil—soil that has never been dug up. In many areas, this means digging down until you reach clay. When removing the topsoil, spread it over other parts of the yard or stockpile it for use around the patio.

If you must pour a slab on top of recently dug soil (for example, backfill from a foundation), pack the soil by watering it for several days, giving it time to settle. Then compact the earth using a hand tamper for small areas or a rented vibrating tamper for larger expanses.

Locate your slab away from large trees whose roots may crack the concrete. You may need to remove roots as you grade the excavation and before you add the gravel and sand base. If you live in an area with periods of heavy rain or winters with below-freezing temperatures, the patio should rest on a bed of crushed gravel (4 to 6 inches deep) plus a 1- to 2-inch layer of sand. In dry climates with soil that has a heavy clay, sand, or rock content, a sand base alone—6 inches deep—may be sufficient.

Slabs collect a lot of precipitation, so slope the slab away from the house. It should be no closer than 1 inch below a doorsill or threshold. The slab surface should also be set at 1 inch above ground level. Use a flat spade or square shovel to dig the final inch of soil from the bottom and sides of the excavation. Excavate a small area by hand; rent a skid loader or hire an excavating contractor for a larger job.

Because concrete that cracks can separate, you'll need to add reinforcing mesh. Control joints are also important because they allow the slab to flex without creating unsightly cracks. In addition, expansion joints provide a buffer between the house foundation and the slab. Plan on having an experienced concrete finisher on hand.

1 Check for square. Drive in a stake at one corner of the foundation, for example, and attach a mason's line to it. Working from that fixed point, check for square as you drive stakes for the corners of the slab. Follow the 3-4-5 method of measurement (see page 65).

2 Verify the accuracy of your 3-4-5 work by measuring from corner to corner in each direction. Make sure you line up the same edge of the tape measure when you do this. The two measurements should be the same. Don't use this process in place of the 3-4-5 method, only to verify accuracy.

3

If your slab plan calls for a curve, lay a charged garden hose (turn on the water with the nozzle shut) in position to mark the slab perimeter. Take into account the width of the stakes and forms. Pour flour or sand over the hose. Lift the hose and you'll have an easy-to-follow curved line.

4

Before you trench the perimeter, mark the location of the slab edges by sprinkling flour or sand over the mason's lines. Remove the line, leaving the stakes in place. Use the marks as a guide for digging a shallow trench about 1 foot wide and about 3 inches beyond the outside edge of the slab.

5

Mark one of the corner stakes to indicate the top of the slab. Reset the lines at this height and install stakes for the forms. Drive the stakes approximately 1½ inches (the actual thickness of a 2×4) outside the line and 3 to 4 feet apart. When you drive the stakes, leave their tops a bit below the line level.

6

Remove the sod and topsoil to the desired depth. If you plan to place sand or gravel beneath the slab, excavate at least 6 inches deep. Lay a 4-inch-deep base of tamped gravel and then a 2-inch-deep layer of tamped sand.

BUILDING CONCRETE SLAB PATIOS (continued)

A few additional notes: Don't skimp on bracing your forms. Pay attention to places where two forms meet. If the forms butt end to end, drive in stakes to lap the joint. At corners, drive stakes near the end of each form. To strengthen curved forms, drive stakes every 1 to 2 feet along the outside radius.

Mix your materials as near to the job site as you can. Or have the ready-mix truck park as close as is safe. (A concrete truck is very heavy and may crack sidewalks or driveways.) Wet concrete weighs 150 pounds per cubic foot. When wheeling it, keep loads small enough to handle. To cross soft soil or lawns, lay a walkway of 2×10 or 2×12 planks. Build ramps over the forms so you don't disturb them. Use two or more wheelbarrows to keep the job moving; the ready-mix company may charge you for waiting time.

7 Use smooth, straight 2×4s for forms. Anchor the forms, using nails or screws to fasten the 2×4s to the stakes. Be sure the forms are straight and level, and the tops of the stakes are set below the top edge of the forms to ease the screeding process (see step 13).

8 To form a curve, use 3½-inch-wide strips of ¼-inch hardboard. For strength use two or three plies of hardboard. Don't try to measure the length of the pieces to be bent. Instead tack one end temporarily through the thin material and into the stake. Spring the material into the shape you want, mark the point where you'll cut it, and make the cut. Then nail the piece in place.

9 Add a level layer of sand or gravel. Now unroll and place your reinforcing mesh with its curve facing down to help keep it from rolling back into its original shape. Position the wire so that its edges reach within 1 to 2 inches of the edge of the finished slab. Optional: Place small concrete blocks 2 or 3 feet apart under the mesh so the wire is supported about halfway up the depth of the slab-to-be.

10 If your new concrete will butt up against an existing structure, separate the two with an expansion joint to prevent cracking. Temporarily hold the expansion strip with bricks or blocks; remove them when pouring the concrete. Sprinkle the compacted base and the forms with water to prevent the concrete mix from losing moisture too rapidly. This is especially important on a warm and windy day.

11 Start placing fresh concrete in the farthest corner of the form. Dump it in mounds that reach ½ inch or so above the top of the form. It helps to have one person working a shovel while two or more others run the wheelbarrows. The shoveler directs the wheelbarrow handlers and tells them where to dump the concrete.

12 While pouring the concrete use a hoe, rake, or shovel to pull the wire mesh up into the concrete. For the greatest strength keep the mesh positioned halfway between the bottom of the excavation and the finished surface of the slab. Watch that the mesh doesn't get pushed against the form at any point. Keep it 1 to 2 inches away from all forms.

13 Begin screeding (leveling) as soon as you've filled the first 3 or 4 feet of the length of the form. Keep both ends of the screed—a straight 2×4—pressed down on the top of the form while moving it back and forth in a sawing motion and drawing it toward the unleveled concrete. If depressions occur in the screeded surface, throw on a shovel or two of new material, then go back and screed the area again.

14 Floating pushes the large aggregate (pebbles) deeper into the concrete, smooths the surface, and consolidates the wet mixture of fine sand and cement at the top, making further finishing possible. Move the float in long, back-and-forth motions, slightly raising its leading edge so that it doesn't dig into the concrete.

FINISHING CONCRETE

Finishing concrete is a skill that takes practice to master. If your project is large or highly visible, ask an experienced finisher to do the job. If you're a beginner, work on smaller, less prominent projects in advance to develop your skills.

Timing is critical. If you start too soon, you'll weaken the surface. Start too late and the concrete will be unworkable. The waiting period depends on the weather and type of concrete. Start when the water sheen is gone from the surface and the concrete will carry foot pressure without sinking more than ¼ inch.

1 Use an edging tool to minimize damage from chipping and add a finished look to your patio. This process also compacts and hardens the concrete along the form. Hold the edger against the form, flat on the concrete surface. Tilting the front edge up slightly, push it forward; raising the rear slightly, draw the edger backward. Use short, back-and-forth strokes to shape the edge. Repeat the edging process after each finishing task.

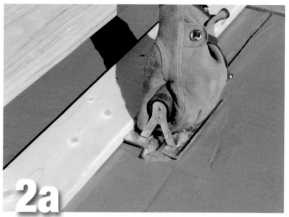

2a Make control joints or a series of grooves that prevent concrete slabs from cracking randomly. To be effective, a control joint should be one-fourth as deep as the thickness of the slab. Prepare for this process by nailing or screwing straight 1×4s to the tops of the forms to serve as guides for the hand groover you'll be using. Position the guides at distances equal to the slab's width. For patios wider than 10 feet, also run a joint down the center.

2b Some pros prefer to saw the grooves for the control joint after the concrete has hardened—usually between 12 and 24 hours after the final troweling and/or brooming. To cut the concrete, use a circular saw, fitted with a diamond-edge masonry cutting blade. As with the hand groover, always use guide boards.

3a Use a wooden float to smooth the marks left by edging and jointing and to create a rough, skidproof surface throughout. Hold the float nearly flat and sweep it in wide arcs. If water comes to the surface when you begin this step, stop and wait awhile before working again. Make two complete passes.

3b

Stop with a floated surface (see step 3a) or make a smoother, more dense finish using a steel trowel. Hold the trowel blade nearly flat against the surface, with the leading edge raised slightly. Overlap each pass by one-half of the tool's length, troweling all the surface twice in the first pass. For an even smoother finish, trowel the surface a second or third time.

3c

Another surface option is the broom finish; it's attractive and provides slip resistance. To create this type of finish, pull a damp broom across the just-troweled concrete. The stiffer the bristles, the coarser the texture will be. Pull the broom only; don't push it. And have a brick or piece of 2×4 handy and occasionally knock the broom against it to keep the bristles clear of concrete buildup.

CURING CONCRETE

Proper curing can make or break a concrete project. Hydration, the chemical process that hardens cement, stops after the concrete first sets, unless you keep it moist and fairly warm. Without adequate hydration, the concrete will never reach its maximum potential strength.

Your goal is to keep the concrete damp or wet for several days after pouring it. One method is to set up a fine-mist sprinkler next to the site and direct a continuous spray onto the concrete. Before starting the sprinkler, make sure the concrete is set hard enough so the spray won't damage the surface. (If you apply too much water before the concrete is set, it could cause spalling or chipping at a later date.) Avoid cycles of wetting and drying.

One effective curing method, however, is to cover the concrete surface with burlap or old blankets and keep them wet with frequent waterings. Be sure the fabric is clean so it doesn't stain the concrete. Place the covering on the concrete as soon as it's hard enough to resist surface damage. Weigh down the covering with scraps of lumber.

If a sprinkler won't reach the entire area or if you can't wet the surface often enough, cover it with plastic sheeting to trap the moisture.

And if the nighttime temperatures might drop below freezing, insulate the concrete during curing: Spread 6 to 12 inches of straw or hay over the top of it, and cover the straw with canvas or plastic sheeting. Carefully cover the edges and corners of the slab, because these are the areas most likely to freeze.

SURFACING EXISTING CONCRETE PATIOS

Amortared stone-veneer surface is beautiful, long-lasting, and needs almost no maintenance. By adding such a surface to the top of a lightly cracked or otherwise ugly old patio slab, you can dramatically improve its appearance at a relatively low cost. Any stone-veneer that's ¾ inch thick—or thinner—must be installed on a solid concrete surface. If the slab isn't smooth, you'll need to level it with concrete patch first because it's difficult to level a veneer surface as you install it.

One caution: This type of project is most successful in warmer climates and will eventually result in some cracking and heaving in the northern states.

INSTALLING STONE ON A SLAB

1 The existing concrete patio must be solid. If it shifts or buckles, the veneer will crack. The old slab also should consist of at least 2 inches of concrete over a 4- to 6-inch sand base. Make sure it's level. Fill in any low spots with patching concrete and knock off any high spots with a hammer and masonry chisel.

2 If you're using irregular-shape stones, dry-lay the pieces on the surface in the pattern you want before you mix the mortar. Maintain consistent joint spacing and avoid placing small pieces along the edges. Once you've laid out about a 16-square-foot section, set aside the pieces, being careful to preserve the pattern.

3 Cut an irregular piece of stone by holding it on top of the adjacent piece to mark it. Score the line using a brick set. (For large stones, have someone stand on the other end to hold it down.) Then place a small lumber scrap on the waste portion you'll be tossing (or keeping if it's large enough) and pound sharply on the scrap with the sledge.

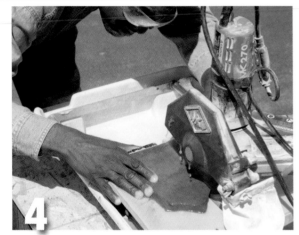

4 For thicker stone or to cut inside corners accurately, rent a wet saw. The saw continuously pumps water from the tray onto the blade to cool it and reduce wear. It cleanly slices through the hardest of materials, even granite.

5 Mix the mortar, allow it to set for about 10 minutes, then mix it again. Now apply the mortar in two steps: Trowel on a smooth base coating about ½ inch thick. Then go over the surface with a large-notched trowel, taking care that the notches don't penetrate through to the concrete base. Use long, sweeping strokes as you apply a second coat.

6 Carefully lay the stone pieces, one by one, in the pattern you dry-laid. Use spacers or eyeball the joints to ensure they're even. Use a rubber mallet to gently tap pieces into alignment.

7 Let the mortar set for 2 days. Mix the grout, using a latex additive to help prevent cracking later. Push the grout into the joints with a grout float, moving the float in at least two directions at all points. Fully pack the joints. Clean the grout from the veneer surface using a damp sponge. Rinse the sponge often in a bucket of clean water. Repeat until the last of the grout haze vanishes.

SURFACING EXISTING CONCRETE PATIOS *(continued)*

As an alternative to the stone-veneer applied in the project pictured on pages 150–151, a mortared tile surface is also recommended only for warmer climates.

Tile is just as long lasting and low maintenance as stone but creates a more precise finish. It's a relatively low-cost way to improve a standard, though worn, concrete slab. Study the other materials used in your landscape and consider whether tile will coordinate with the look of your home and yard.

Select tiles with a nonslip surface for patios, as well as for porches and walkways. Vitreous and impervious tiles absorb the least amount of water, making them better able to withstand freezing weather. In regions with a varied climate, all of the setting materials must be labeled as freeze-thaw stable for installations in cold climates.

Any tile ¾ inch thick or less must be installed on a solid concrete surface. If the slab isn't smooth, you'll need to level it out first with concrete patch because—as with stone veneer—you'll find it difficult to level a tile surface as you apply it.

INSTALLING TILE ON A SLAB

1 The existing concrete slab should be at least 2 inches thick, on a sand base, and generally solid. Otherwise, shifting or buckling will crack the tile. Use a straightedge to locate any defects in the surface. Fill in any low spots with patching concrete, and knock off any high spots with a hammer and masonry chisel.

2 Dry-lay the tiles on the surface in the pattern you want before you mix the mortar. Maintain consistent joint spacing and avoid ending up with small pieces along the edges. Once you've laid out about a 16-square-foot section, set aside the pieces, being careful to preserve the pattern you've created.

3 When you need to cut a tile for a clean fit, mark the cut line on the tile by holding it on top of the adjacent piece. An inexpensive tile cutter works well for straight cuts on most types of tile. It has a guide that can be screwed in place to cut a series of tiles, one after the other.

4 On a patio slab of typical size, you will be time and neck strain ahead if you rent a wet saw. It will also make cleaner, more accurate cuts.

5 Use thinset mortar with a latex additive, available both in liquid and powder form. Mix the mortar, allow it to set for 10 minutes, then mix it again. Apply the mortar following the same two steps recommended for the stone veneer. Trowel on a base coat, notch the surface, and then apply a second coat.

6 Set each tile in place without sliding it into position. Use spacers to make even joints. If tiles aren't flush, place a flat piece of scrap wood wrapped in carpet on the uneven area and gently tap the scrap with a rubber mallet to nudge the tiles into alignment.

7 Allow two days for the mortar to set. Then mix the grout with a latex additive. Push the grout into the joints by moving the float repeatedly across the tiles in various directions. When the joints are filled, scrape off any excess grout. Let the grout set for a few minutes. Clean the tiles using a damp sponge, rinsing it often in clean water.

PATIO PLANTINGS

Patios offer ideal conditions for plants. Typically these areas are protected from winter winds and summer sun, and nearby structures often reflect springtime warmth and sunshine.

Still you'll want to choose carefully what you grow near your patio because nowhere are plants more the focus of attention.

Select only tidy, long-blooming plants that grow to size quickly, then stay in scale without regular pruning. Relegate to more distant parts of the yard all plants that have a short season of interest, a season of excess seediness, or a coarse appearance.

The principles of design seem more important near a patio. Color clashes that you could live with in a border at the back of your yard will dizzy you if they appear at the edge of your patio. Form and texture, too, are accentuated, especially when the plants are brought closer to your eye level in raised beds.

Fragrances, which often go undetected away from the house, are easily enjoyed around the patio. Especially good choices are the fragrant plants— such as moonflower, evening primrose, and angel's trumpet—that open widest in the evening, when you're most likely to be using your patio.

To add a dramatic accent to your patio, select a spot nearby to espalier a small tree, arrange a vine in tracery shape, or grow a rose or shrub in standard form. For a delightful evening show, surround your patio with white-blooming plants.

The nitty-gritty

Lawns and planting beds around patios should be an inch or more below the level of the paving to allow for digging and adding soil amendments without having soil wash onto the paving. Planting beds above the patio level need to be held back with some sort of retaining wall. Good drainage in either case is vital.

Set plantings far enough from patios so that their growth won't encroach on the paved space. To avoid cracked concrete later on, select trees with small root systems.

PATIO PLEASERS

Spiff up your patio with small plants between paving sections or cascading plants surrounding them. Choose fast-growing vines and partner them with upright structures for quick shade and privacy.

Between pavings	Cascading plants	Fast-growing vines
Ajuga or bugleweed	Asparagus fern	Clematis
Corsican mint	Cotoneaster	Grape
Corsican sandwort	Cucumber	Hydrangea, climbing
Pearlwort	Geranium, ivy-leaved	Ivy, English
Sedum, creeping	Pachysandra	Kiwi
Sempervivum, creeping	Petunia	Morning glory
Speedwell, creeping	Strawberry	Nasturtium, climbing
Thyme, creeping	Vinca	Rose
		Wintercreeper

A grass-and-paver patio adds creative flair to a backyard where the homeowners have carved out rooms for dining, strolling, and having a private soak in the spa.

This sectioned patio gets its appeal from the fence and gate at one end, the pergola at right, and a combination of daylilies, azaleas, and creeping thyme at the edges.

A metal gate and stone walkway leading to an inviting seating area combine with a handsome stone patio to create a relaxing setting in a limited space.

A window box—tastefully designed to match the architecture of the house—is home to geraniums, bacopa, and other bright annuals that show off their color and texture for those dining indoors or on the patio.

Low retaining walls add depth and angles to a once-flat patio, contribute privacy, and create a second level to display phlox and other perennials that complement the annuals in the main-level containers.

155

GALLERY OF PATIO IDEAS

A pergola, situated at the back of the yard, creates an attractive view from the patio and a balancing counterpoint to it. Frames of lavender and evergreens also work together.

This bluestone patio complements a native stone retaining wall, while a planting pocket softens the overall look. This savvy design carved valuable patio space out of a steep slope.

From the sweeping arc of the steps to the meandering lines of the retaining wall, graceful curves give this small, ground-level patio its personality. Lush foliage and green grass abound.

A white pergola with sturdy columns serves as an effective transition between the house and this cheery dining spot. The brick patio, with its matching step up to the double doors, lends a feeling of continuity.

Bordered by an evergreen hedge and a raised bed filled with annuals, this sideline seating area beckons you to pause for a while and contemplate the important things in life.

Where a large lot posed a what-to-do-with-it challenge, a patio became the solution. The floor was formed using concrete-aggregate pavers and framed by a low wall of dry-stacked reclaimed stone.

157

GALLERY OF PATIO IDEAS *(continued)*

This patio and its adjoining walkways step up to an inviting dining area. The pergola pulls the setting together and holds a relaxing place for swingers.

The symmetry of this design enhances an otherwise ordinary and small brick patio. The limestone-slab path, set in swaths of creeping thyme, draws visitors into the setting.

A steep slope and deep shade from mature trees didn't stop the creation of a flagstone patio on this site. There's plenty of room for outdoor dining and entertaining. The stone-capped tree ring provides added seating as well as space for the tree to mature.

Artful and contemporary, this serene scene gets much of its appeal from the stone wall fountain. Between the water music and the cushioned furniture, it's as comfortable as any living room.

A beautiful water feature proves more enjoyable when there's a place nearby to sit and view it. Carefully placed stone creates planting pockets for iris, azaleas, Japanese maple, and dwarf conifers. A bamboo screen and tall foliage contribute privacy.

159

7

DECKS

A well-designed deck serves as a natural extension of your home, providing an inviting transition to the surrounding landscape. You might be surprised how quickly it also becomes a special place of tranquillity and rest for every member of your family as they join there to commune with nature.

When planning a deck, ensure its complete success by collecting ideas from the whole family. Identify features that everyone wants as part of the plan. As a result, you'll build a deck that everyone will enjoy to the fullest.

This deck offers three dimensions of interest. Arbors, contemporary railings, and plants with strong vertical lines help create a structure that rises above the ordinary.

A recessed central staircase helps define either side of the deck while leaving the area closest to the house more open. The steps allow extra seating.

Arbors over the opposite ends of a west-facing deck supply afternoon shade, while stainless-steel cabling provides necessary railing without blocking views from the seating areas.

The deck was designed to provide individual but connected spaces for relaxing and entertaining.

ASSESSING DECK OPTIONS

Freestanding decks may not get as much use as those attached to the house. But a small freestanding deck stationed at the edge of the yard or among trees and shrubs can be an ideal hideaway. Add a gazebo or a pergola and the freestanding deck can become a focal point for the yard, particularly when inviting paths or steps direct visitors.

Deck pluses

The wood of decks blends well with hot tubs, and the structure itself is easily expandable to include them as well as sandboxes and play structures. Moreover, decks often have a soft look and are more in accord with a wooden house or a rustic setting. They don't reflect unwanted heat and light.

One of the greatest advantages of decks is that they don't require level land and thereby can make a terrible terrain lovely and useful. You can also put decks over old, cracked concrete without having to tear it out.

A good combination is a deck at floor level of the house, with steps leading down to a garden patio.

Renters or those who want an instant outdoor room should consider building a portable deck. These units can be built in a day, moved from sun to shade with the season, and stored away for the winter. Later, you can place them permanently.

Modular deck walkways can be useful, especially in a new yard. When final plans are made, move the units or arrange them into a deck.

Perhaps best of all, decks are a do-it-yourselfer's dream. If you're an amateur builder, or even if you're completely new to carpentry, you can design and build a deck that will give you years of enjoyment. You need only a modest set of tools, a few basic skills, and the patience to work one step at a time.

At the start

Check local building codes, regulations, and zoning restrictions first—especially when you're planning footings, spans, railings, and steps—and verify details for permits. Make sure that you anchor your deck against wind blasts and that your structure is strong enough to support the weight of expected snowfalls.

You may want to build some sort of overhead sunshade to frame the view, create shade, or shelter the area from the elements—extending the deck's utility and enjoyability. While still in the planning stage, remember to include needed lighting and electrical outlets. Consider your storage needs too, because decks, benches, and raised planters are perfect places for built-in hideaways.

Decide on size

Keep all aspects of your deck in scale as you plan. Outdoor rooms need to be about the same size as the largest indoor rooms. Measure your deck furniture and add enough room for pulling out chairs and walking around.

A minimum of 5×6 feet allows two people to sit and relax beside a table, but it's cramped if anyone else comes along. Put such small decks away from the house for solitude. Or start small and add on as family size, time, energy, and budget dictate.

Before you begin building

As your outdoor room progresses from dream to reality, you'll need to weigh choices such as railings and benches, all of which are discussed in the next few pages.

If you grade or fill more than 3 to 6 inches within a tree's drip line, serious damage to the roots could cause the eventual death of the tree. Here, a deck has the advantage over a patio. You need only build around the trunk, and the tree lives happily ever after. But that means it grows, so make the hole's framework large enough that you can cut off board edges as needed.

If you decide on more drastic grade changes, check with a tree specialist for details about building a raised bed or a dry well.

This platform deck makes room among the trees for visitors to sit and savor the fire pit. The post-and-beam railing features see-through acrylic panels.

163

CREATING THE ULTIMATE DECK

The best decks make outdoor living so much like indoor comfort that they become extra rooms, with the added advantages of easy care and the wonderful sights, sounds, and scents of nature.

The well-designed deck begins at the floor level of the adjacent indoor room, enabling you to step out without stepping up or down. And because we tend to look up and away—rather than down and around—when we move from the indoors out, a well-placed deck takes maximum advantage of any treetop views or distant vistas you might have.

In addition you can enjoy the function and feeling of separate rooms by creating two or more levels only a few steps up or down from the main room outside your house. And you can even build a dramatic stairway to serve as an entry to all of your yard's attractions.

Privacy is crucial (few people are comfortable on stage), but some well-placed screens can provide the sanctuary you prefer. If made of lattice—and perhaps entwined with vines of fragrant flowers or clusters of grapes—they add a romantic effect to your outdoor experience.

Design counts

Although decks seem simple, their design is important. Unimaginative planning can result in a deck that looks like a large box. To avoid this and to add interest, alter the square or rectangle—even the slightest bit—by cutting off a corner diagonally or adding a point or a half circle. Repeat architectural elements from your house.

Railings or surrounding planters or benches (see pages 178 and 179 for an easy-to-build seating project) can set the mood of this outdoor room, too, while adding comfort, storage, and safety. Be sure that relaxing adults or rambunctious children won't have to worry about falling over the edge, even if this would be only a foot or two.

Gardening on a deck proves easy when you make bright blooming containers a necessary accessory. Built-in planters and railing-mounted containers typically place plantings at an easily accessible level. Where arbors, screens, or overhanging tree branches offer anchorage, hanging pots are appropriate. Use groundcovers, flowers, and shrubs, too, to tie your deck to its site.

For do-it-yourselfers, on-grade decks are easy to build. The higher your raised deck, the more complex the project, but you are still capable of pulling off the task with little or no professional help.

Do your homework first

When checking with your building department about securing a permit, ask for code particulars regarding decks in your area. And while you have an official's ear, find out the setback requirements—distances between your lot lines and the edges of your deck. Then contact your local utilities and inquire about determining the locations of any possible underground lines—telephone, cable, plumbing, electricity, gas, etc. They might be willing to mark the lines at no cost.

Now you're ready to make three scale drawings of the entire deck—a plan version (looking at it from above) and two elevations (one from the side and one from the end). As you draw each component, refer to a span chart (see page 181) to make sure you're using the right sizes of posts, beams, and joists.

Then take your completed drawings to local building officials for approval. Find out which stages they will want to inspect before you proceed. Once you get the go-ahead to begin, order lumber and line up some talented friends to help you now and then.

Step out into a two-level dreamland where recreational pleasures abound. A deck and matching gazebo invite you to dine with nature, while a few steps down the deck lead you to a relaxing spa and a nifty built-in grill.

BUILDING BASIC DECKS

A grade-level deck, which stands on its own only a few inches above the ground, is considerably easier to build than its elevated cousin, the raised deck. The simple design of a grade-level deck spares you the intricacies of constructing the stairs, railings, and structural bracing required for even the most basic raised deck. And with a freestanding, ground-level deck, you needn't worry about securely attaching the structure to your house.

You can situate this type of deck just about anywhere, including adjacent to the house or, if you'd rather, in a shady corner of the yard. Build one over an existing too-small patio, or stair-step two or three of them down a gentle slope.

Though more formidable than a grade-level deck, a raised version is still doable. Unlike its ground-level relative, a raised deck is almost always attached to the house. In this scenario, one of the deck's most critical points is the ledger that anchors the deck to the house and serves as its starting point.

POSITIONING POSTS

1 Drive two temporary stakes near the house at about the point where the two corners of the deck will meet the siding. Then measure and stake the other two corners. Run a mason's line between the stakes a couple of inches above the ground. Measure the diagonals and adjust the stakes until the diagonals are equal. Tighten the lines and use spray paint or chalk to mark the footprint on the grass. (You'll finetune this perimeter outline later.)

2 Use batterboards and mason's lines to finalize positioning of corner posts. Tie a mason's line—perpendicular to the house—between the center of each house stake and its corresponding corner batterboard, passing over the center of the corner post. (The post will move later—after you've squared the layout—to accommodate the deck overhang.) Tie a third line between the two corner batterboards.

3 To locate the centers of the corner posts, first confirm that the layout is perfectly square, using the triangulation method. Then go to each corner footing and hold a plumb line barely touching the intersection of the two mason's lines. Drive a spike to mark the spot directly below the plumb bob. This locates the corner of the finished decking but not the center of the post. Adjust both corner posts toward each other accordingly.

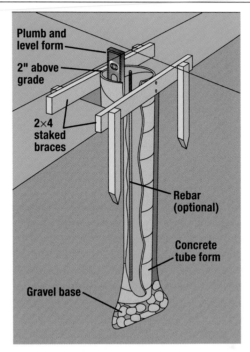

Plumb and level form

2" above grade

2×4 staked braces

Rebar (optional)

Concrete tube form

Gravel base

1 Now you're ready to install and backfill the forms for the concrete. Dig each hole deep enough to satisfy your local codes. Then pour in 4 inches of crushed gravel and tamp it solidly. Cut a tube form to reach from the gravel to 2 inches above ground level. Screw a 2×2 brace to each side of the form. Drive 2×2 stakes into the ground—one at each end of the horizontal braces. Then raise or lower the braces to level the top of the tube and screw the braces to the stakes. Finally, backfill the area outside of the form, tamping the soil lightly as you go.

Study this typical footing installation so you'll know what's ahead. The footing consists of a tube form set in a hole and plumbed with braced stakes. The hole will be a little larger than the form, so be sure to center the form before you stake the braces. If codes require rebar, place it slightly off-center so it doesn't interfere with the installation of the anchor bolt.

2 Mix and pour concrete into each form. Have a helper guide the flow with a round-nosed shovel. Stop pouring when the hole is half full and work a 2×2 up and down in the concrete to remove air pockets. Continue pouring, overfilling the form by about 2 inches, then screed off (scrape off and level) the excess with a short length of scrap 2×4. Seesaw the screed back and forth to level the concrete.

3 You'll be installing a J-shape anchor bolt in each footing. When the concrete begins to set (it will resist finger pressure), push a bolt into the center of the form, leaving about an inch of bolt exposed. Center the bolt with a tape measure. Square the threads to the footing with a layout square. Repack any loose concrete with a pointed trowel, adding a little more if necessary.

BUILDING BASIC DECKS *(continued)*

INSTALLING A LEDGER

1 Begin your project with the ledger, if you prefer. When you positioned the house posts, you marked on the house siding the locations of both ends of the ledger; you need one additional line to position the top of the ledger. The top surface of your finished deck should sit from 1 to 3 inches below the bottom of the threshold of your access door. Add this space to the thickness of the decking and make two marks on the siding—one at each end of the threshold. Using a mason's line longer than the ledger—and a line level—hold the line so that it touches both marks and make two additional marks—one at each end of the ledger site. Snap a chalk line between these latter two marks, then use a level to double-check for accuracy. Set a circular saw to the thickness of the siding and cut along the ledger outline. (You may have to use a chisel to touch up the corners of wood siding—or metal snips if the siding is vinyl or metal.) Then cut flashing to length and slide it at least 1 inch under the siding above the cutout. Overlap flashing joints by 3 inches and notch out for the doorway. Attach the ledger in place using a few screws; level it as you go. (You'll fasten it permanently later.)

2 Make marks for all joist hangers; space them according to your plan (typically 16-inch intervals). Then mark the locations of your fasteners—probably lag screws. Beginning about 3 inches from one end, mark fastener locations at 18- to 24-inch intervals. Don't worry if a fastener is at a joist-hanger location; in those instances, counterbore for the lag screws. Drill pilot holes for all screws through the ledger and about one inch into the band joist or studs. Then, install the lag screws with washers, using a socket wrench.

3 In those rare cases when you have access from inside your house to the area directly behind the ledger, you can use bolts and nuts, as in this example. If not, however, lag screws work well; just slip a washer onto each screw and drive it with a socket wrench. Let the ledger settle overnight, then tighten the lag screws again, stopping when the washer begins to dent the wood. Seal the counterbores, if any, as well as the top of the flashing and the bottom of the ledger with exterior silicone caulk.

INSTALLING POSTS

1 Prepare the area under the deck-to-be by removing and reusing the sod, excavating the site to a 2-inch depth, laying landscape fabric, and pouring in crushed gravel. Attach an adjustable post anchor to each anchor bolt, using a washer and nut. Tighten each anchor enough so that you can move it only slightly. On the footings parallel to the house, set a long, straight 2×4 across the front edges of the anchors (as pictured) to line up the anchors. Then tighten each anchor with a socket wrench.

2 Set each post—whether you're building a grade-level or raised deck—in its anchor and tack it there temporarily. Have a helper hold the post as plumb as possible while you plumb and anchor it with braces. Tack and brace the remaining posts. Move the mason's lines (tied to the crosspieces) outside the center line by half the width of the post. Restring the lines and clamp a second 1×4 staked brace to the post. While the post's outside face touches the mason's line, drive the remaining fasteners into the anchors.

3 Rest one end of a long, straight 2×4 on top of the ledger. Hold the other end against the nearest post and level the 2×4. Mark the post where the bottom of the 2×4 intersects it. This line is the reference for the next lines you'll draw. Hold a piece of joist scrap on the reference line and mark the post at the bottom of the scrap; this locates the top of the beam. You'll cut the posts along this line if you use a beam system. Extend this cut line to the other posts.

BEAM OPTIONS

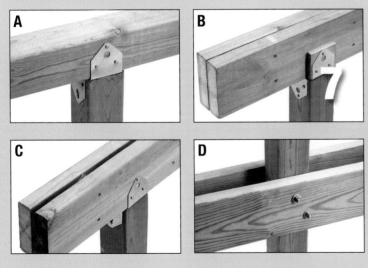

In the deck pictured above, the ledger fastened to the house supports one end of the deck joists, and a beam parallel to the ledger supports the opposite end. There are several ways to construct a beam, including:

(A) For short spans, 4×4 or larger timber sometimes suffices. Rectangular timber (4×6) set on edge performs better than square timber (6×6).

(B) Build a beam on site by nailing 2× together, allowing you to use wide stock to create a taller, stronger beam. Note the spacer required to fill the gap at the metal connector.

(C) To build a full-width, 4-inch beam (when lumber is actually 3½-inches) that will rest flush with the post on both sides, insert spacers cut from ½-inch pressure treated plywood, then nail the beam together.

(D) Where a post will extend upward through the deck surface, create a split beam by bolting two lengths of 2× stock to the post, as shown. Although this concentrates the load on a pair of ½-inch bolts, it's usually plenty strong to support the deck's weight. Attach blocks to the posts for additional support to the beams, if needed. Different deck designs may require you to use a particular method, but local codes will be the last word.

BUILDING BASIC DECKS *(continued)*

INSTALLING BEAMS

1 If you choose to work with a solid beam or doubled-up 2× material resting on top of the posts, install post/beam connectors on the posts, orienting all in the same direction. (Also cut the posts shorter by the depth of the beam.) Haul the beam assembly to the site, and lower it into the connectors, placing it carefully.

2 Use 2×4 bracing to stabilize the solid beam. Attach it to the connectors. (Make a sandwiched beam by clamping a piece of 2× stock on each side of the post and inserting spacer blocks between the two members every 24 inches.) Level both sides of the beam, tighten the clamps, predrill holes, and insert carriage bolts.

CROWNS UP

When you're working with beams and joists, be aware that dimension lumber often has a slightly bowed edge called a crown. You can see this crowning, if it exists, by sighting down the edge of each board. If there is a crown, mark it, and make sure you install this beam or joist with the crown edge up.

HANGING JOISTS

1 Build a box, using the ledger as one end. The first and last joists (rim joists) are perpendicular to the ledger and represent the two sides. Another perimeter (outer rim) joist runs parallel to the beam and fastens to the ends of the rim joists. Rest one end of a rim joist on the beam (as pictured); fasten the other end flush with the ledger using screws and a corner bracket.

2 Set a framing square inside the corner at the ledger and again at the intersection of the beam and adjust each of the two rim joists and the beam position until the assembly is square to the house. The outer faces of the rim joists should be flush with the ends of the beam. For now, tack the rim joists to the top of the beam with a toe nail or screw.

3 If you have someone to help, one of you should hold the outer rim joist while the other screws it to the ends of the rim joists. Square the frame and check it with the triangulation method. If necessary, remove the toe nails at the beam, square the rim joists to the ledger, and drive the fasteners in again. Attach angle brackets in the two beam corners for extra stability.

HANGING JOISTS *(continued)*

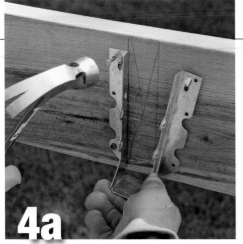

4a

Mark joist locations on the header, making sure the joists are spaced as specified on your dimensioned plan. You can fasten the hangers at the marks, as shown here, or use the method described in the next step. Stabilize the frame on the beam with framing connectors called seismic ties—one at each of the two points where the rim joists cross the beam.

4b

An alternative way to attach joist hangers is to screw a 2× flange to the top of each joist, as pictured, extending the flange 1½ inches past the end. The flange keeps the top of the joist flush with the top of the ledger and header. Set the joist on the marks and slide a joist hanger tight against the bottom of it. Fasten the hanger to the ledger and header.

5

Continue fastening hangers, nailing or screwing each joist to the hanger as you go. If the header is bowed away from the end of the joist, have a helper push the header back toward the joist while you drive the hanger fasteners. (The two members in the lower-right portion of the photo are the components of the support beam.)

BLOCKING JOISTS

1

Blocking adds lateral stability to a deck frame and provides additional nailing surfaces for special decking patterns. Mark the midpoint of the deck (half the distance from the house to the beam) on both rim joists and snap a chalk line between the marks across the tops of the joists.

2

Temporarily screw a 1×4 on top of all joists near the chalkline to hold the joists straight and parallel to one another. If necessary, pull the joists into proper alignment before you drive the screws. Use a framing square to mark the locations of the blocking.

3

Measure the spaces between joists and cut 2× blocking to fit. Don't cut all the blocks the same size because the thickness of the joists may vary. Install the blocking with nails or screws on alternate sides of your chalk line. Then fasten seismic ties between the joists and the beam.

171

BUILDING BASIC DECKS *(continued)*

INSTALLING DECKING

1 Measure from the house to the point where you want the inside edge of the starter board to fall; mark both rim joists at this distance. Snap a chalk line at the marks. Remember that the position of the first board will depend on whether you will overhang the decking.

2 Lay out the decking boards loosely on the deck. Cut the starter board to the exact length you want, then align it with the chalkline and drive in two screws centered on each joist. If you have joints, offset them randomly and install cleats, as described in step 4.

3 If the wood has moisture in it, butt the boards right next to one another; if kiln dried, space them slightly apart. To do this, use a jig made from a 1×4 and 10d nails. Space the nails so that one falls at each joist and drive the nails an inch through the 1×4.

4 Make sure all joints are centered on the joists and strengthened with 2×4 cleats fastened to both sides of the joist under the joint. Predrill the decking (especially near the ends) to minimize splits. Angle the screws slightly toward the joist to strengthen the connection.

5 When you get within three boards of the last one, lay them loosely with ⅛-inch spacing. If the last board fits, you're home free. If not, either install one and slim down the others with a tablesaw, or rip the excess width evenly from all three. Fasten all but the last one to the joists.

6 Cut the last board to length before you screw it in place because you won't be able to trim off the ends with your circular saw after it's installed. Snap a line between the cut edge of this last board and the identical edge of the first board. Using a guide, cut off the wild ends.

172

BUILDING STAIRS

1 Stair specifications must comply with local code requirements, so be sure your plan passes muster. The total rise (vertical distance from bottom of stairs to top of deck) should combine with the total run (horizontal distance the stairway travels) to give you a safe and gradual ascent. This translates into short risers (height of each step—called unit rise) and deep treads (horizontal distance of each stair tread from front to back—called unit run). The typical deck stairway is three feet wide with three stringers (long diagonal framing members, usually 2×12s, that support stairs). It also has risers about 7 inches high and treads about 11 inches from front to back. Measure your deck's rise and run so that you can determine how to mark and cut your stringers, as well as where to locate your landing pad, as explained at right. Now's the time to pour your concrete pad. Refer to pages 82–83 for instructions.

2 Using your calculations for the treads and risers, mark the cut lines on one of the 2×12s. Cut the top and bottom of the stringer and test its fit between the deck and landing. Then use a circular saw to cut the outline, stopping the blade just short of the intersection of the lines. Finish the cuts with a jigsaw or handsaw. Set the cut stringer on top of the second 2×12, clamp the boards together tightly, and mark the second one. Repeat the process for the third stringer. Then notch the bottoms of all three stringers for a toe-kick (See step 4 on page 174).

3 Depending on your design, you will either attach the stringers to one of the outer joists or to a crossbrace fastened below one of them. Mark the framing for both outside stringers and snap a chalkline between the marks. This line shows the top of the stringers. Square all three stringers to the deck frame and attach them with angle brackets.

CALCULATING RISE AND RUN

Divide the total rise—58 inches—by the unit rise you prefer—7 inches. For this example, the result is 8.2. Round that to the nearest whole number—8. This is the number of steps you'll have. Then divide the total rise—58—by the number of steps—8—to find the exact unit rise—7 1/4 inches. Each of your steps will be a very comfortable 7 1/4 inches tall. Now multiply the unit run you prefer—11—by the number of steps minus one—7—(because the last step is the deck surface). So the stairway will end 77 inches away from the deck. This is where you will pour the landing pad.

BUILDING BASIC DECKS *(continued)*

BUILDING STAIRS *(continued)*

4 The toe-kick is a 2×4 fastened to the concrete pad. (Note notches in stringer ends to accommodate a toe-kick.) Predrill holes in the toe-kick for lag screws, then position it and mark the pad for anchor holes. Remove the toe-kick and drill the pad with a masonry bit to fit the lag-screw shields. Attach the toe-kick to the landing with the lag screws, and screw the stringers to the toe-kick.

5 Cut the treads with a 1½-inch overhang on both sides. Predrill holes for the screws—three per joint for a 2×12 or 2×10 tread, two for narrower boards. Screw the treads to the stringers. (If you prefer to fill in the riser spaces, be sure to allow extra overhang at the front edges of the treads to accommodate the riser boards—typically cut from 1× material.)

Stairs provide access to and from the surrounding landscape. They can also increase the seating area of your deck and provide an important element in its overall style. Once you get the knack of it, you may want to add another stairway on another side of the deck to handle high-traffic occasions. Of course all steps require railings. See the following pages for details on rail construction.

CALCULATING BALUSTER SPACING

Building codes specify the maximum distance between balusters (upright railing supports). Here's how to calculate uniform baluster spacing. Add the width of one baluster (here, 1½ inches) and the maximum spacing (4 inches). Divide this total (5½ inches) into the space between posts to find the number of balusters: (60 inches÷5½ inches =10.9). Round up to 11 balusters. To calculate the actual spacing, multiply the number of balusters by the width: (11×1½ inches =16½ inches). Subtract that from the post spacing (60 inches–16½ inches =43½ inches). Divide this by the number of spaces, which is always one more than the number of balusters, to determine the final spacing between balusters (43½ inches÷12=3.625 or 3⅝ inches).

BUILDING RAILINGS

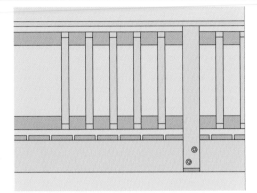

As in the case of the stairway portion of your project, the design of your railing will be strongly affected by your local building codes. Still you have many options—from wood balusters, like those shown in this example, to wrought-iron configurations to a freeform array of tree branches to welded sun symbols connected to posts and rails by metal rods.

1 Measure each post, add ⅛ inch, mark a notch on the decking, then cut it with a jigsaw. Predrill two holes in each post to accommodate ⁷⁄₁₆-inch carriage bolts. Hold each post in position and have a helper plumb it while you clamp it to the joist. Drill holes through the joist, insert carriage bolts, and tighten washered nuts from behind.

2 Notch the posts so you can attach the two rails flush with the inside faces of the posts. When you get to the junction of deck and house, instead of fastening a post to the joist, cut a 2×4 to the height of the railing and fasten it to the siding with 5-inch lag screws and washers. This connection is far sturdier than a post fastened to the joists and will add stability to the railing.

3 Cut several balusters at a time, angle-cutting the ends or leaving them square. When you're ready to install the balusters, use a jig like the one pictured to plumb them and space them uniformly. Check every fourth or fifth baluster to make sure it's plumb. (Baluster stock is not always consistent; you may have to adjust the spacing to make everything come out right.)

4 Cut the cap rail (usually a 2×6) to length and miter-cut one end for the corner. Make sure caps meet each other at the center of a post. (For more attractive junctions, make 45-degree cuts on the ends that meet.) Attach the cap rail with screws at each post and into the top rail every 2 feet between posts. Delay driving screws at the mitered corner until after step 5.

5 Miter joints add style to the corners of a deck, but they're difficult to fit accurately, and they often develop gaps from weathering. At each corner, drive #8 screws, as pictured, to draw the sides of the joint together. First you may have to clamp a board to the tops of both cap rails to pull their top surfaces flush. Then drive longer screws down into the top rail.

DECKING STYLES

Diamond patterns—whether used for the entire deck or built in small sections that are scattered throughout an especially large expanse—require more work and produce extra waste. But the beautiful results are worth the trouble.

Basket weave (also called parquet, modular, or grid) requires a support system in the form of squares and uses doubled-up joists at key locations. Dividers between grids in the above example slightly modify the typical look.

Decorative insets in a variety of shapes and sizes effectively break up the monotonous lines of standard parallel decking. Depending on the shape you choose, you may need to add a few extra joists or blocking pieces.

Curved decking is perhaps the biggest challenge of all and usually requires a professional builder who specializes in this technique. Though this example involves steps, you can make rounded edges on the deck itself using a simpler process.

Constructed with spacers on top of a joist system, this built-in mat allows dirt to fall through. The mat's frame was tinted with an oil-base stain, giving it a realistically finished look.

The combination of wide and narrow tread boards make these steps more interesting than the typical design. The wider boards, used as edging, give the steps a strong appearance and allow you to create the necessary overhang.

RAILING STYLES

Simple horizontal crosspieces centered in each railing section are a simple way to break up the typical look of vertical balusters. Check with your local building officials to find out if this stair-step addition satisfies their safety codes.

Ornate posts, rounded caps, and specially milled balusters combine to add a formal, traditional look to this otherwise standard wood deck. This example demonstrates the compatibility of a white-painted railing and natural decking.

Vertical dividers, a third rail located almost midway between top and bottom, and fore-shortened balusters produce a distinctive design reflective of the Arts and Crafts era. Trim at the tops and bottoms of the posts completes the look.

Coated metal rods produce a clean look in this contemporary railing. One installation method is to drill the holes for the rods, insert the rods in the bottom rail, then lift the rail—and rods—into place and attach the rail to the posts.

For maximum visibility, use infill panels of plastic glazing or tempered glass. Some carpenters cut slots in the posts and rails, insert the panels, then install the top rail last. Others prefer to use stops on each side of the panel.

There's no reason why you can't combine looks. Here bright, airy panels of lattice team with sections of vertical balusters and double top rails to create a cheery, contemporary design. Use this treatment on any style of deck.

BUILDING DECK SEATING

Provide your deck with one or more comfortable benches and you might end up with some of the best seats in—or out of—the house.

Orient benches so that sitters take in an attractive view or turn their backs on one that's not. Define the edge of a grade-level deck without blocking your line of sight by building a backless bench. Or on a higher deck, integrate the bench and railing.

Think of any deck seating as more than just a place to sit down. It not only can define the perimeter of your deck but can also suggest boundaries for different areas of use.

Benches should be between 15 and 18 inches high, with seats at least 15 inches deep. Allow 30 inches of width per person. Make the backs slightly lower if you want an unimpeded view, slightly higher for privacy. Open, slatted construction lets air circulate and also drains water more effectively.

As with railings, you can attach benches to the same posts that support the deck or fasten uprights to joists. For safety's sake, be sure to use bolts, not nails, at all critical structural points.

Built-in perimeter seating—the example pictured here—not only can handle large numbers of people but also leaves the rest of the deck area open for parties with lots of mingling. This type of project must be designed to carry a heavy load, and nothing can provide better support than the railing posts. A perimeter bench is easy to build, and because the railing posts support it, it doesn't require much extra lumber.

If possible, place your posts no more than 4 feet apart for proper strength. Support bench spans wider than that with a 2×4 rail centered on the span and supported by short legs cut from 4×4s.

Although this example is 8 feet long, this kind of seating can line one entire side of a deck or the complete perimeter.

Cut bench posts to the same dimensions as your other railing posts; just space them closer together where you're building the bench. Predrill for carriage bolts and either notch the decking or the post to match the railing posts.

Mark the location of the front post. (See drawing opposite.) Cut the post from 4×4 stock and toenail the base of it to the decking. Clamp the 2×6 seat rails to both the front and rear posts, drill them, then fasten them together with carriage bolts.

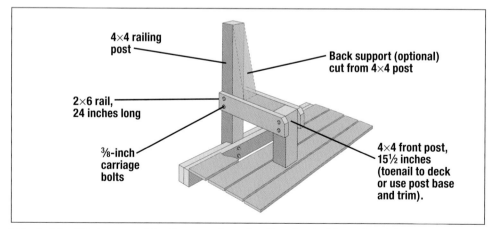

4×4 railing post

Back support (optional) cut from 4×4 post

2×6 rail, 24 inches long

⅜-inch carriage bolts

4×4 front post, 15½ inches (toenail to deck or use post base and trim).

This sketch will help you envision the general construction plan. Build your bench from the same stock as your railing, using the ballpark dimensions shown above. If you modify this design, be sure the bench remains strong.

3 Cut seat slats to length from 2×2, 2×3, 2×4, or 2×6 stock, allowing at least a 1½-inch overhang at the ends. Fasten the slats to the rails with either one or two screws at each rail, depending on the slat width.

4 Cut angled back supports from 4×4 posts and screw them to the rear posts. Then cut and install the back slats the same way you handled the seat pieces. Finish up by cutting and installing the 2×6 cap rail.

Mounted perpendicular to joists: This project takes place before you install the decking boards. Mark the joists for the 2×10 legs, placing them the same distance from the header. Fasten them with three machine bolts. (Make sure the top two bolts are low enough to leave room for 2×4 cleats to support the decking.) Insert vertical blocking between the joists to keep the bench from rocking side to side. Cut seat rails to match the depth of the bench seat and screw them to the legs. Add 2×4 cleats to the outsides of both legs so the decking will have a nailing surface beneath it.

Mounted parallel to joists: This project, too, takes place while you still have access to the open joists. Mark the joists to space the 2×10 legs at about half the total width of the seat slats. Machine-bolt the legs to the joists and block the joists to keep the seat from rocking. Cut the seat rails to about 16 inches for a 19-inch bench seat and screw them to the legs. Then cleat both sides of both legs to give the decking a nailer. You can install the seat slats before or after you apply the decking, but if you mount the slats first, you may find them to be a hindrance when you put down the decking.

Mounted at the perimeter: Cut the 4×6 post 15 to 17 inches long and cut the 2×6 support piece the same length as the post plus the depth of the rim joist. Screw the 2×6 to the post, keeping the tops flush. Notch out the decking, if necessary, clamp the 2×6 to the joist, and join the two with carriage bolts. Repeat this process for another post 3 feet away. Sandwich two 2×6 seat rails to each post, using lag screws. Cut 2×2 seat slats long enough to overhang the rails by 1½ inches at each end. Using a 2×2 as a jig, drive one screw through each end of each slat.

CHOOSING DECK MATERIALS

LUMBER SELECTOR

CEDAR
Description: Naturally rot-resistant wood noted for its strength, light weight, and good weathering properties. Use common-grade cedar above ground; use heartwood for ledgers, posts, and near-ground members.
Appearance: Light-red cedar weathers from tan to silvery gray; some finishes will reverse or retard this weathering.

Cost: About 10–20 percent less than redwood, depending on local availability. A good alternative to redwood, especially in regions far from the South and West Coast.
Comments: Cedar is lightweight but a good performer for decking and railings. Stains or sealers improve its appearance and prolong its life.

CYPRESS
Description: Naturally rot-resistant lumber that is logged in the Southeast, where cypress is a popular alternative to cedar. As with redwood and cedar, use common-grade above ground and heartwood for elements where rot could set in.
Appearance: Slightly lighter than cedar; has a strong grain pattern. Weathers to a pale gray.

Cost: Slightly less than cedar in the South, slightly more elsewhere. Not distributed in every region.
Comments: Lightweight, soft, and easily worked. As with redwood, consider using cypress for appearance items and pressure-treated wood where strength counts.

PRESSURE-TREATED LUMBER
Description: Southern yellow pine, saturated with chemical preservatives that are safer than the previous preservative—arsenic, which is no longer used. Above ground, use wood treated to .25 pounds per cubic foot (pcf). Posts and other ground-level members need .40 pcf wood.
Appearance: Most has a greenish cast that weathers to a silvery gray.

Cost: About 30 percent less than redwood— and, in fact, your lowest-cost alternative.
Comments: Heavier and stronger than most other deck lumber. Pressure-treated lumber poses no danger to plants or groundwater, but it still contains chemicals, so cut it outdoors, wear a mask over your nose and mouth, and do not burn scraps.

REDWOOD
Description: Handsome and naturally rot resistant. Use common-grade redwood for framing members, decking, and railings; use construction- or clear-heartwood for posts and for near-ground structural members.
Appearance: Redwood's distinctive red hue weathers to a brown-gray. Preserve original color by applying sealer every other year.

Cost: This premium-grade exterior wood is one of the most expensive ways to go. To save money you might want to use redwood only for parts that show, particularly the decking.
Comments: Redwood exhibits good stability and resistance to cupping, and because it contains little or no pitch or resin, it is easier to saw, drill, and shape than treated lumber.

SYNTHETICS

Description: Manufactured, usually a combination of recycled wood fiber and resins or plastic. Highly resistant to decay, rot, and insects; most varieties need no weather preservative.

Appearance: Various colors and appearances, including some with wood-grain patterns and others with an embossed finish on one side and a combed finish on the other.

Cost: Higher cost to build, but savings in long run.

Comments: May require special fasteners. Many offer matching railing materials. Be careful when moving heavy furniture on these surfaces; dragging a metal leg across synthetic decking will most likely scratch or otherwise mar the finish.

FASTENERS

Decks seem to eat nails. For every 40 square feet of deck, you'll need 1 pound of 16d common nails (for joists) and 2 pounds of 12d common nails (for decking). Use only galvanized or stainless-steel nails; ordinary steel rusts and stains the lumber.

Galvanized nails cost less and are the most popular type used. Stainless-steel versions are quite pricey but resist rust best. Spiral-shank or coated nails grip better than smooth-shank common nails.

For a variety of reasons, more and more deck-builders are using screws to install decking boards. If you are one of them, be aware that pressure-treated lumber requires stainless-steel or triple-coated screws (or other fasteners that meet a minimum ASTM standard).

Depending on the manufacturer, synthetic decking may require its own screws or a completely different attachment system involving hidden fasteners made for a particular decking.

All bolts, nuts, washers, and hangers should be galvanized. Bolts should be as long as the total thickness of the materials being joined, plus ¾ inch. Screws should be long enough so that two-thirds of their length goes into the member to which they're being fastened.

JOIST AND BEAM SPANS

Joist size	Distance between joists		
	16 in.	24 in.	32 in.
2×6	8 ft.	6 ft.	5 ft.
2×8	10 ft.	8 ft.	7 ft.
2×10	13 ft.	10 ft.	8 ft.

Beam size	Maximum distance between posts
4×6	6 ft.
4×8	8 ft.
4×10	10 ft.
4×12	12 ft.

These spans will carry 40 pounds per square foot, a typical code requirement. Use 4×4s for posts up to 8 feet high, 6×6s above that.

DECK PLANTINGS

Deck plantings, like their patio counterparts, assume great importance in a landscaping scheme. The trees, shrubs, and flowers immediately surrounding a deck should offer the greatest interest for the longest season while having the fewest faults possible. Although maintenance is convenient in an area close to a water source, give low-maintenance deck plantings prime consideration. After all, you shouldn't feel obliged to toil when you are working hard at relaxing.

What to consider

Before choosing plantings for your deck area, keep in mind the landscaping role they'll play. Edging plants, for example, are especially important to tie a deck to its surroundings. Around a grade-level deck, plant neat groundcovers or low flowers or shrubs. Use ground-hugging evergreens for textural variety. Around a raised deck, take advantage of the bird's-eye-view and plant flowers, shrubs, and small trees that will look good from above.

The underside of your deck may need shrubs of appropriate height to screen from view the void or storage space below. For a low deck, try dwarf winged euonymus, barberry, viburnum, floribunda rose, dwarf juniper, spreading yew, or azalea. For a high deck, try upright juniper and yew, or rhododendron. Where the ground slopes steeply, the plants also must check erosion.

Container plants such as those listed above bring needed color to decks. Use soil substitutes that have more water retention and less weight so that you can move the containers as desired. Remember, too, that the smaller a pot is or the brighter the sunshine it receives, the more often you will need to water the plant. Containers in full sun may need to be checked twice a day and watered if dry on hot days. Large pots in shade may need checking only twice a week. Herbs are ideal on decks. Many release lovely aromas when you barely brush against them and they will be handy for grilling and cooking.

CONTAINER PLANTS FOR DECKS

Container plants are likely to play an integral part in your deck's landscaping. Try some of these in your baskets and pots.

Hanging baskets	Potted flowers
Achimenes	Begonia
Browallia	Browallia
Campanula	Caladium
Dianthus	Calendula
Fuchsia	Celosia
Geranium	Chrysanthemum
Herbs	Geranium
Lantana	Impatiens
Nasturtium	Marigold
Petunia	Nicotiana
Portulaca	Sea lavender
Snapdragon	Spring bulbs
Torenia	Tuberose

Low evergreen shrubs skirt this deck and spa, serving as a soft edge that helps blend the structures with the surrounding landscape.

Adjacent decks would seem at odds without the plantings that link them. The planting pockets at ground level work with the containers on both decks to create visual unity.

A curved planter, built into the back of a graceful bench, adds an essential counterpoint of green to the mass of decking. Additional spacious planters serve as step-ends at another level.

GALLERY OF DECK IDEAS

An ornate gazebo adds to this deck. Note how the dramatic sunburst section of railing adds even more style to the overall setting.

This deck consists of three giant steps—the top one serving as a dining area. The beauty of this design is that it allows easy traversing.

From indoors, the homeowners can look out onto a low-lying platform deck that subtly gives way to a pond and wild habitat. Because the deck is low, a railing hasn't been added, but it would be essential for safety where children live.

Among the design highlights of this project are the wide composite decking and gently curved steps. The bricks give it a stable, finished look and are more attractive than concrete steps would be. Built-in seating on an extended area accommodates large gatherings.

Here's an example that shows what a visual difference a good deck can make. There's a lot going on here in a relatively small space—a planter railing, curved seating, two dining areas, and a built-in grill.

185

GALLERY OF DECK IDEAS *(continued)*

Sometimes a deck serves family and visitors without dominating the scene. In this case, a vine-covered arbor shades a freestanding deck and offers a secluded haven.

This cantilevered deck serves as a lookout for all to enjoy. Combined with a ground-level patio, it provides outdoor living areas for different activities at once.

A platform deck, nestled in the landscape, offers a shaded spot for conversation or solitude, away from the house.

Where the existing site includes a steep slope and mature trees, a deck serves as a smooth and graceful transition from house to surroundings.

More difficult to design and build than a single-level deck, this example features sloping sections that lead gently down several levels—with nary a step in sight. A series of 2×4s outlines the edges and pathway.

CHAPTER 8

SLOPE SOLUTIONS

Tilt your world a bit and you get a whole new landscaping perspective that's invigorating and challenging. The first rule of designing new surroundings is to study and work with site conditions. If your land includes slopes, your design begins and ends with a more interesting scene. Sometimes the result of an update or a small improvement can be dramatic where the land has highs and lows. Take full advantage of the sometimes superlative views or the feeling of enclosure. Let initial problems push you to creative solutions.

This beautiful hillside required a substantial investment in time, money, and heavy labor. A slope this steep requires sturdy terraces with deep setbacks.

It takes a massive amount of stacked stone slabs to retain a steep hillside. The job is accomplished beautifully here, in terraces that overflow with cascading plants.

As a bonus, bench seating is perched here and there, making the slope enjoyable as more than a view.

Terraces—linked with mortared-rock steps and topped with plant-edged walkways—make it possible to traverse and cultivate the steep terrain.

ASSESSING SLOPE SOLUTIONS

Slopes pose landscaping challenges, but they also offer opportunities. Properly used, slopes boost your landscaping plan. They screen views, buffer noise, and add to the overall design appeal. They even create illusions: A rail fence along the top of a gentle slope makes the yard within seem to extend to the edge of the world.

Sloping terrain can be desirable. Some flat lots could use artificially created mounds and terraces to generate more interest, for instance. A sloping yard also gives you more planting ground in the same lateral space, and slopes sometimes create microclimates, such as sunny south-facing slopes or shady northward ones, which enable you to grow a wider variety of plants.

Slopes, though, can be limiting. For instance, if your site slopes so much that you'd use the word "hillside" to describe it, you'll want to choose a natural, flowing landscape design instead of a symmetrical, formal plan.

And slopes, if left untreated, can create erosion problems, limit outdoor living space, and hinder plant growth. But these potential downsides are treatable if you anticipate them and adjust your planning accordingly.

Controlling erosion

Ideally, your lot slopes away from your house at least 4 inches every 10 feet, assuring that water doesn't seep into the building. If your concern is slowing water to prevent erosion, rather than diverting water to improve drainage, consider adding plantings, baffles, terraces, or retaining walls to your slopes.

Plantings, at least those with root structures that bind banks, usually are the easiest—and least expensive—erosion-control measure to install. Groundcovers and low-growing shrubs are usually the best choices.

On slopes where plantings may not stem erosion, install rows of stones called riprap, or plastic or wood baffles. The baffles or riprap act as small dams, slowing the water and encouraging soil to build up.

To hold the soil on medium-grade slopes, put in contours or bevels—two types of miniterraces. For sharply sloping land, retaining walls are the best option, despite their expense and engineering demands. They take less room than a bank and are easier to maintain. They also yield level areas for kids' play or plantings. Keep in mind, though, that you need to take special care when you build your retaining walls so that they'll withstand the tremendous pressure coming from the soil they hold back.

When planning retaining walls, strive to disrupt the site as little as possible. Be sure the walls you build are in scale and harmony with your house and the rest of your garden. Brick or stucco walls work well in formal gardens or near houses of the same materials. Rock walls fit into more natural plans. Wood blends with either. Generally, the simpler its construction, the better a wall looks.

Select materials for strength, too, in addition to appearance. Wood walls can't be as big as masonry walls because they can't hold back as much earth. Uncut stones work without mortar or footings unless the wall is taller than a couple of feet. Poured concrete yields the strongest walls.

Because low walls are cheaper to build and their design is less crucial (they retain less soil), you're better off building a series of step-down versions rather than one high wall.

Outdoor living

If slopes limit your outdoor play space, consider decks, paved or unpaved terraces (basically, patios or retaining walls), and steps.

Decks fit best into informal landscaping styles; paved terraces or patios are more appropriate for formal landscape designs. To save time and money, build decks and patios that fit rather than fight existing slopes. For decks, if you plan several levels instead of one, you'll use fewer materials; for patios, you'll move less soil.

One of the most common ways to create space for a patio on sloping terrain is to carve out a niche for it, then hold back the remaining hillside with a retaining wall—in this case, treated timbers behind I-beams in concrete.

ASSESSING SLOPE SOLUTIONS *(continued)*

Steps, besides allowing access to areas above or below, can act as erosion-controlling bevels. Landings can act as terraces as well. Make garden steps less steep than indoor stairs and as wide as the walk that leads to them. Again, use material that harmonizes.

If you're building your house new, situate the floor levels of your house to adjoin the flat areas outside, if possible. Locate your gardens, service areas, and play areas on the flats and use the rising slopes as gentle walls to enclose these outdoor rooms. Conversely, falling slopes serve as windows to open vistas beyond.

To install a pool, you may have to do some regrading. Use any soil you excavate to fill low spots or to build berms or swales.

Plan driveways and walks to make use of level land or gentle slopes, if possible. Neither should exceed a 10 percent grade. If you let your driveway wind across the contour of a slope, it will slow water runoff and help hold the hillside. Be sure the drive surface slopes for good drainage to prevent ice formation. At the intersection of your drive and the street, control the grade so that you have full vision both ways. Optimally this is the spot for a turnaround, if possible, so you and visitors can avoid backing into traffic.

For fencing, choose an open style, such as split-rail, if your slope is steep. For gently rolling terrain, choose a slightly open fence style, such as one using lattice or louvers; avoid a closed style.

To create a secret nook or cranny, put a bench or arbor at the top or bottom of a hill, perhaps out of sight of the house.

Plantings on slopes

Lawns are fine on slopes, except those too steep for mowing. You can safely mow an incline as long as the ground doesn't rise more than 1 foot for every 3 feet of horizontal slope.

To establish turf on a hillside, use sod. If you can't afford sod and plan to use seed, the grass is more likely to become established if you first divert the surface water at the top of the slope by running a turf gutter—a slight ditch with a lip on the downhill side—across the slope. Then, to further slow water runoff, lay a few strips of sod across the slope at intervals of 4 to 6 feet all the way down.

For extensive slopes, use a process called hydroseeding. Mixes of grass seed or various flowers are combined with fertilizer and a wood fiber to make a spray-on slurry. Transportation departments use this method to plant roadside embankments.

If your slope makes mowing dangerous, plant groundcovers. They're easy and inexpensive to start. If your slope is very steep or long, or your soil is heavy clay that could wash down, seek advice from experts.

Here are some other tips for planting slopes:
• Land too steep for a lawn is good not only for groundcovers, but for trees, shrubs, and wildflowers too. Put birdfeeders and a birdbath on the edge nearest the house for your birdwatching enjoyment.
• Gentle slopes, particularly those facing a house or patio, look great with crocuses or other bulbs, or wildflowers planted among the grass.
• If your landscaping plans require you to regrade, build walls or wells around the roots of choice mature trees to avoid damage.
• For cultivated plants, use beds that follow the contours of the slopes, or create terraces.
• If you have a slope facing south, use it to stretch your growing season. With more sun and natural wind protection, the south-facing slope will warm earlier in the spring, enabling you to grow tender plants, such as dogwoods, where they otherwise might not be hardy. Watch out, though, because that same spring sun will lure some early bloomers into premature growth, and a late frost may also take a toll on plants. Avoid peach, almond, and other early-blooming fruit trees on south-facing slopes. Grow them instead on north-facing slopes, where they will stay safely dormant until spring truly arrives.
• Because cold air collects in low-lying areas, don't plant frost-sensitive fruit trees there.

Gentler slopes such as this one give you an opportunity to capture space for an upper-level lawn, then continue it a few steps below. Terraced areas between the two become ideal showcases for color and texture.

193

CONTROLLING MINOR EROSION

If erosion is a problem on a gentler slope, try one of these four techniques to keep soil from washing away:

• Baffles work well on slight to medium slopes and can vary from small pieces of plastic edging to landscape timbers. Partly buried across the hillside, they slow runoff water, giving it more time to soak into the ground. Use a trowel to install small, lightweight baffles by hand as you plant. For large timbers, dig a slight ditch with a spade and put the soil you remove on the uphill side. Position the baffle before planting.

• Use retaining cloth on slopes where erosion is severe. It can be any porous material—from burlap to the mesh used on steep highway banks. The latter is rather expensive, but topsoil is beyond price. The greenskeeper at a nearby golf course can suggest a source. Avoid using plastic on steep slopes because it prevents rainwater from penetrating soil. Planting will be easier if you soak the ground well, remove unwanted growth, and loosen and smooth the soil before laying the cloth.

• Mulch slows runoff on minor slopes. It also keeps down weeds, and, if organic, adds humus. Spread it thick, at least 4 to 5 inches, and renew organic mulch often. On slight slopes, use mulch alone; on steeper slopes, use mulch with baffles.

• Use stone riprap—made with handpicked rocks or concrete rubble—to cover the steepest area of a hillside or the entire expanse. The rocks act as a permanent mulch and slow water runoff. Plant roots will wind through and under the rocks to further hold soil in place.

Remember, when setting out plants on a slope, always leave water-catching lips on the downhill side to conserve precious water.

Mini baffles—made from pieces of plastic edging cut to lengths of a foot or so—reduce soil erosion. With your trowel, cut into the slope and set the baffles to make a series of small walls and terraces.

To use retaining cloth, prepare and water the soil, then lay and stake the cloth in place. Use scissors to cut holes for plants, then plant with a trowel. Depending on your plant choice, groundcovers fill in within a few years.

Spread a 2-inch layer of mulch between plants to help retain soil as well as soil moisture. A chipped wood or bark mulch won't wash away in heavy rain.

Stone riprap works like a small retaining wall. Dig troughs across the slope and place large stones so they're half buried. Scatter smaller stones, if desired. Pack soil and plants tightly into the spaces between the stones.

GROUNDCOVERS

ALPINE STRAWBERRIES grow easily, producing a sweet and delicious harvest the first year. Spreading by crowns instead of runners, they create a colorful carpet.

PACHYSANDRA includes Allegheny and Japanese spurge, both 8- to 10-inch-tall perennials that thrive in moist soil and like shade. Leaves yellow in full sun. 'Silver Edge' is less vigorous.

ROCKSPRAY COTONEASTER is less than 2 feet tall, features horizontal branches in a pattern resembling fishbones, and has bright red fruit. This sun lover's small, glossy leaves turn red in fall.

VINCA MINOR, or periwinkle, has dark, shiny, evergreen leaves and lavender flowers in midspring. It grows in sun in Zones 4 to 7, in shade in all areas, and in almost any soil.

To control erosion, also try low-growing varieties of shrubs such as juniper, leucothoe, cranberry, and rock rose; vines such as wintercreeper, ivy, honeysuckle, and Virginia creeper; and such groundcovers as bearberry, Carmel creeper, euonymus, and lantana.

195

BUILDING CONTOURS AND BEVELS

To check erosion on an intermediate slope, you can ripple it with contours or terrace it with bevels cut into the hillside and fitted with wood planters. Contours intercept the flow of water and direct it elsewhere. The planters serve as mini retaining walls. Both can add visually to your landscaping plan.

Contour basics

Building contours calls for little more skill than expertise with a shovel, rake, and wheelbarrow. Give thought, however, to where water absorbed by the contours will go. Drain lines must slope away from the house, and codes (as well as courtesy) probably prohibit dumping water onto a neighbor's property.

For the drain lines inside the contours, shown at right, use the perforated version of flexible, corrugated drainage tubing, fitted with a drain sock. At the highest end of the tubing, tie the sock in a knot to keep out dirt, then screw on a louvered end piece (sold for corrugated tubing) to prevent critters from eating through the sock and crawling into the system. (See French drain, page 59.) Plan a drop of at least ½ inch per foot of tubing length.

Bevel basics

Bevels call for very elementary carpentry skills. You construct a series of bottomless boxes, notch them into the hillside, fill them with earth, and plant them with flowers or groundcover.

For the boxes, buy only construction-heart redwood; construction-heart cedar; or ground-contact, pressure-treated common lumber. Anything else will rot away in just a few years. To retard rust, assemble the boxes with galvanized nails, screws, and corner brackets.

Excavate bevels carefully, keeping all cuts straight, both horizontally and vertically. Set soil aside and use it to fill the planters after you've set them in place.

CONTOURS

1 Establish a horizontal reference line with stakes and string. To carry away runoff, the contours must cross the slope at a slight angle. Excavate to 4 inches or so and lay a 2-foot-wide bed of crushed rock or coarse gravel. Scoop out a slight depression in the bed of rock and set in place the perforated corrugated draining tubing with sock.

2 Cover the tubing with more gravel, then mound soil over it to a depth of about 4 inches. Rake the fill to establish a smooth drop down the hillside. Moisten the soil and tamp it well. Tamping greatly lessens the chance that the contour will cave in or lose its shape.

196

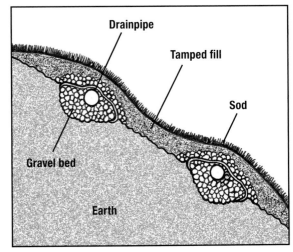

3

Unroll the sod and tack it with stakes on the uphill ends so that it doesn't slide down the slope. Water again. After several rainfalls, remove the stakes.

Drainpipe

Tamped fill

Sod

Gravel bed

Earth

To control erosion, step several contours across a steep slope. Gravel beds and drainage pipe prevent erosion by capturing water and diverting it from its destructive path.

BEVELS

1

Lay out bevels with stakes, string, and a tape measure. Use a spade to cut precise notches. These should be as close to 90 degrees and as nearly level as possible.

2

Build boxes with rot-resistant lumber and galvanized corner braces. Lay plastic to control weeds, then set the boxes in place. Secure them by driving stakes as shown. Hook the stakes over nails to prevent sideward shifts.

3

For drainage, lay about ½ inch of gravel in each box, then fill with soil. Plant with shallow-rooted annuals. Since roots will be above ground level, avoid using perennials; they could suffer winterkill.

BUILDING RETAINING WALLS

Check with your community's building department before setting out to build a retaining wall. Many codes require a permit for any structure that holds back what amounts to thousands of pounds of earth, and most limit the height of an amateur-built retaining wall to 3 feet. If your slope needs a higher wall or requires extensive grading, call in a masonry or landscape contractor—or terrace the slope with two or more lower retaining walls.

Drainage basics

Water is a retaining wall's worst enemy. Without proper drainage, water soon will buckle any structure you put up. Come winter, alternating freeze-and-thaw cycles also can wreak havoc on a retaining wall.

Each of the three walls shown on the following pages uses a different drainage system. For the interlocking version shown at right, perforated corrugated drainpipe was installed in a bed of gravel (see illustration for step 1). Loose-masonry retaining walls (page 200) drain naturally through chinks between the stones. The wood retaining wall (page 201) expels water via weep holes near the base, a solution that works equally well with yet two other materials—concrete or mortared masonry walls.

Material options

The masonry block used in the interlocking wall is but one of many sizes, colors, shapes, and textures available at your local home improvement store. When you do your shopping, be sure to lift each block you're considering, because some of them are deceivingly heavy.

The loose-masonry wall was built with ashlar stone; other, less-regular cuts work equally well, though you might want to tip the wall farther back into the slope for stability. And, for looks, fill gaps between stones with plantings.

For the wood retaining wall, pressure-treated 6×6 pine timbers were used. Avoid railroad ties; these are treated with creosote, which is harmful to some plants and makes the ties messy—and toxic—to work with.

Laying the groundwork

Dig into the hill you want to retain and prepare a base for the wall. The bottom course of blocks should be below ground level. A good guideline is to bury the base row 1 inch below the surface for every 8 inches of height above the ground. To relieve pressure on the wall from behind, install a simple drainage system. At about ground level place a layer of landscaping fabric, followed by some gravel, then a perforated drainpipe, and finally, more gravel. Overlap the whole works with the rest of the fabric. As you proceed with the wall, add fill and compact it with a 4×4 or hand tamper.

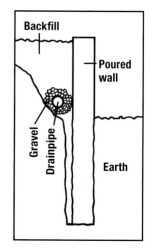

INTERLOCKING-BLOCK WALL

1

The first row of blocks establishes the shape of the project. Therefore it is important to make sure that you have a solid base and that the first row is level. Place stakes at both ends of the wall. Tie a mason's line between them and using a line level, set the line for the top of the first course.

2

If you need to make adjustments to the height of a block, either remove fill below the block or tap it down using a rubber mallet. If a block is loose as you place it, trowel some fill material under and around it to stabilize it. Set each block so that its edge touches the adjacent block. Level the row left to right and front to back.

3

As you finish each row of a wall, backfill behind and between the blocks. Use dirt for backfill for small walls; crushed stone or river rock for walls greater than three rows in height. Compact the backfill using a tamper. Clean the top of each row before you set the next row. Adjust the mason's line height for the top of the next row.

4

Each row will lock to the row beneath it. Some styles of interlocking blocks have a flange on the lower back edge to lock onto the lower row. With flange-type interlocking blocks, you may need to make a correction for a tighter curve. This may require knocking off part or all of the flange with a hammer. But remember that doing so will create a weak link in the wall.

5

Lay subsequent courses carefully, making adjustments so the blocks sit solidly atop other blocks. Be sure to wear gloves and safety goggles as you work. Place the block on a solid support along the score line and hit the unsupported part with firm strokes from a small sledgehammer until the block splits in two.

6

Though not necessary, you may wish to top the wall with capstones. This provides a professional finish and gives you the option of mixing in different material styles and colors to set off the wall. If using a pin-type block, you'll need a cap block for the top row.

BUILDING RETAINING WALLS *(continued)*

LOOSE-MASONRY RETAINING WALL

1 Lay out the wall with stakes and string, then dig a shallow trench, cutting its back side at a slight angle to the slope. For drainage, lay about an inch of gravel in the trench. The wall shown here will turn a corner, but the same techniques apply to straight walls.

2 Lay your longest stones on the bottom; the fewer the joints in the first layer, the easier it is to keep subsequent courses level and straight. Level stones as you lay them, tapping each with the handle end of a sledge. (To prevent possible injury, use your legs, not your back, when lifting heavy stones.)

3 Lay succeeding courses so that each stone bridges a joint below. If you must cut a stone, use a sledge and chisel, as explained on page 343. If a stone wobbles, stabilize it by troweling loose soil underneath.

4 Dig a hole into the slope every 4 to 6 feet and lay a long stone crosswise to the wall. Pressure from earth above these stones will tie the wall to the soil behind it. Finish laying the stones, then backfill as necessary.

1 Cut a beveled trench into the slope, wet the trench, and tamp well. Set the first timber into place and level it. This course will be completely buried in the ground. The wall shown turns a corner; the same techniques apply to a straight wall.

2 Set a second timber on top of the first and bore a hole through the two timbers. (Use a heavy-duty drill with an extended auger bit; small drills burn out when making long holes such as these.) Drive ½-inch-diameter rebar through the holes and into the ground.

3 Continue to place the timbers, staggering joints from one course to the next. Drill holes and use rebar to pin each timber to the one below it on each side of every joint. When needed, cut timbers with a sharp chainsaw, wearing goggles to protect your eyes from flying chips.

4 Backfill as you go, being sure to shovel a 3- to 4-inch layer of gravel against the timbers first, followed by soil. In the course of timbers that's about 1 foot above ground, drill weep holes every 4 feet along the wall's length. (The gravel helps keep these weep holes open.)

BUILDING STRUCTURES OVER SLOPES

Thinking about sinking posts for a fence, deck, gazebo, porch, or other structure? Unless the terrain is absolutely level, you need to locate several points that are, literally, in midair—and sometimes at quite widely varying heights from the ground. How can you determine how high each post should be? And how can you be certain your layout is square?

Neither job is as difficult as you might think. First you establish points where you'll want posts. Then you dig holes and set posts that are taller than they need to be. Finally you cut off the tops of the posts so that all will be at the same level. Some elementary geometry assures that rows of posts will line up precisely at right angles to one another.

3-D layout

To plot a structure that will be built on a slope, you need the same tools required for a level-ground layout plus several stakes that are about 2 feet longer than the elevation at the downhill edge.

Start at the uphill edge. If you're building a deck or other project that will attach to the house, tack strings to its ledger. For a gazebo, shed, or other freestanding structure, drive stakes and tie strings to them, as is done at right.

At the downhill edge, maneuver the taller stakes until they are at perfect right angles to the house or—for a freestanding structure—the string that marks the uphill edge. To be sure the corners are square, use the principle of the 3-4-5 triangle, as explained opposite and on page 65.

After you've found all four corners, double-check that they are square by measuring from each corner to the corner opposite it. If the corners are square, these diagonals will be equal in length. If they are not, go back and check each corner with the 3-4-5 triangle principle until you find the one that's out of square, then readjust the layout.

1 Drive a stake at the starting point, tie a chalkline to it, then extend the line downhill. Have a helper hold a carpenter's square to the starting stake to ensure that the line meets it at a right angle. Tie the chalkline to a taller stake located several feet beyond the spot where your last post will be. Drive this stake into the ground, then adjust the chalkline until the bubble in a line level is centered.

2 Measure from the starting stake to the point where you want the second post, drop a plumb bob from the line at this point, and mark the location with a stake or by spraying an X on the ground with landscaper's paint. Locate and mark other post sites in the line the same way.

3 To site corner posts, use triangulation to square them up. Here the original line was 12 feet (4×3), so measurements were taken 9 feet (3×3) out from the corner. Then the 9-foot tape and another one stretched from the starting stake were maneuvered until the diagonal measured 15 feet (5×3). Their intersection showed exactly where to drive a stake to stretch a line for the second run of posts.

4 After digging holes for posts and adding gravel, set and plumb the posts using a level and side braces, then pour concrete. For more about this, see page 66.

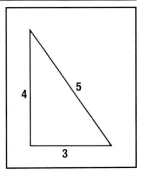

To square a corner, measure 4 feet (or a multiple of 4) in one direction from the corner and 3 feet (or the same multiple of 3) in another direction. Adjust the diagonal between the two until it measures exactly 5 feet (or the same multiple of 5).

5 Level the chalkline at the height at which you want to cut off the posts, then snap it against each one. Draw a line around each post.

6 Use a chainsaw or reciprocating saw to trim posts to the proper height.

GALLERY OF SLOPE IDEAS

Taller plantings nearly hide this stone pathway from view as it wends its way to the house above. Matching stone walls flank the steps, offer seating along the way, and hold the soil in check.

Wooden elements form this backyard stairway: a privacy fence, terraced planting beds, and deep steps, which use matching timbers for the edging and decorative rock for the fill.

Massive, dry-stack stones, laid in a random design, retain a tall terrace and serve as an attractive backdrop for this masonry patio. Gaps in the wall sprout a vertical garden that spreads each year.

A gradually sloping masonry walkway ties into a stairway where the slope becomes steeper. Note how the shingled terraces echo the home's exterior, carrying its architectural flair all the way to the street.

A lawn couldn't begin to compete with the beauty of this entry slope. Its stone-slab steps take the visitor on a curving adventure past rugged rock terraces filled with grasses, shrubs, and flowering plants.

9

PRIVACY AND SECURITY

The greater your measure of seclusion, the more personal and individual your environment becomes. A well-designed combination of privacy plantings and subtle fencing cloak your outdoor rooms exactly as solid walls and window coverings bring privacy and seclusion to your indoor spaces. Outdoor living, no matter how innocent, is limited by your exposure to the eyes of neighbors and passersby. Outside, as well as indoors, it's nice to be able to see the world without the world looking back.

A front courtyard provides an inviting entry while it enhances curb appeal. As a private terrace positioned between the home's dining room and kitchen, it serves many occasions, from morning coffee to formal gatherings.

A low brick wall topped with a picket fence ties the outdoor room to the rest of the house. It also provides seclusion without blocking views of the neighborhood.

An arbor over a graceful gate mirrors the shape of the home's windows and bolsters the entryway's security.

ASSESSING PRIVACY SOLUTIONS

Traditionally, yards were substitutes for the European public square. People sat outside to be seen and to visit. But as modern traffic changed neighborhoods, and lifestyles became more individual and intense, yards began to change. Most people now have an overdose of public exposure and need areas for retreat, outdoors as well as in.

Don't be afraid to demand and design for privacy. It starts with planning.

A good start

First, figure out where you need privacy and what visual intrusions need blocking. Usually that means the areas of your backyard where you'll relax and entertain. Your property also might dictate the need for blocking views into front or side windows. Or you may want to separate parts of your garden from one another (do this carefully, especially where space is limited, because too much division can cause confusion as well as crowding).

Next choose the method. Privacy most often is obtained with plantings, fences, or screens.

Remember, if your plans will affect your neighbors, talk to them early in the planning stage. For instance, where fences are few, people may need reassurance that your intentions are not unfriendly. The neighbors may be as amenable to the idea as you, and even agree to share the cost.

If a proposed new tree planned to give your patio privacy also will block your uphill neighbor's view, try another solution, such as an overhead arbor.

Before starting to build or plant, know where property lines lie. Check laws and regulations, too, concerning the placement and height of fences, walls, and other permanent structures.

Methods

Whether you choose fences, screens, or plantings to obtain privacy, you'll more than likely want a plant or structure that's just above eye level or taller. Six feet usually is a good height for a privacy fence. If your concern is privacy only when sitting, such as for patio dining, 3- or 4-foot plants or structures

will work. What won't is something just below eye level—5 feet or so—because of its distracting height.

Plantings usually are a cheaper way to obtain privacy than fences or screens. Maintenance depends on the type of project you choose: A clipped hedge is more work than a weathered fence; a painted fence is more work than an informal shrub border.

Shrubs and trees provide a lovely green form of privacy, but fences and screens offer the same advantages if they're covered with vines or used as a backdrop for flowers and other plants.

Plantings

For maximum privacy using plants, you'll usually want to grow a border or hedge of shrubs. If your need for privacy extends into the winter—and chances are it will—you'll want to choose evergreen, rather than deciduous, plants.

Shrub borders can be formal and clipped or informal and mixed. The formal version has the advantage of being narrow but requires trimming, a time-consuming and often-repeated task. And this style usually offers only a foliage background.

Untrimmed shrub borders, on the other hand, can spread to 8 feet or more. They'll need less maintenance and can offer flowers, fruit, and fall color, as well as a variety of forms.

Choose your shrubs carefully, noting the amount of maintenance each one needs. Make sure, too, that the mature size of plants won't overpower your house or landscape. Where space is limited— in a side yard, for example—use narrow, columnar shrubs. When mixing shrubs in a border, select no more than three compatible species, with at least two or three of each type.

Don't limit yourself to shrubs when seeking privacy. Vines on trellises can give you quick, inexpensive privacy and are especially effective in narrow spaces. Even single trees or shrubs, carefully placed, can solve many privacy problems. Or choose flowers, particularly tall ones or those suited to raised beds. The seasonal privacy they offer may be sufficient for a patio or summer cottage.

A trellis wall and picket fence give this exposed, seaside front yard enough enclosure to make it a private outdoor room that draws guests to sit and enjoy the ocean air.

ASSESSING PRIVACY SOLUTIONS *(continued)*

Fences

Unlike plants, fences give instant privacy, and they can offer great architectural interest. Select from a wide variety of ready-made panels or design your own. When planning a fence, you'll want to keep a number of considerations in mind.

Solid fencing yields the most privacy, but it also cuts off light and breezes. Slightly open fences, such as those with louvers or latticework, can let in the sun and the wind yet still do a fairly good job of screening views into your yard. The slight openness also can provide an inviting transition from street to garden. Some homeowners combine the best of both and erect a fence with a solid bottom and an open top.

To be most neighborly, you'll want to choose a design that looks as good from your neighbors' yards as it does from yours. Keep in mind, too, that if you're enclosing a large area, you might want to incorporate occasional variations in your fence to avoid monotony. And to make a large expanse of fence less imprisoning, add plantings.

Be sure your fence matches the architecture of your house: Red-brick homes go well with redwood or redwood-stained fences; clapboard-sided homes blend well with fences of a similar look. If your fence will run close to or abut your house, consider painting it the same color or a complementary one.

Pay attention, too, to the character of your neighborhood. Whether it's rustic or sophisticated may go a long way toward dictating your own fence style—weathered or painted, open or closed.

Gates

When designing your fence, carefully plan the location and style of gates. Points of access, of course—whether from front yard to backyard or from your yard to a neighbor's—will determine location. The style of gate you choose depends on how much attention you want it to draw. To extend an invitation to passersby, design your gate to contrast with the fencing. Change the spacing or size of the boards, make the gate taller, add color, or cap it with an arch. If privacy is paramount, build a gate that blends with the fencing. Finally consider width. Will a riding lawn mower pass through the gate? How about larger construction equipment or even cars?

Screens

Screens usually are used within the yard rather than as boundary markers. Purchase or build them in various forms, from sections with fencelike appeal to individual panels. As with fences, screens can block views from outside in or from one section of yard to another. But they take less room, allow more feeling of openness, and restrict air movement less than fences. In design they can be taller than fences yet still be lighter in appearance and weight.

SECURITY SOLUTIONS

Most homeowners know that well-placed lights can deter crime. But many don't consider the importance of keeping shrubs and trees well trimmed.

Clip shrubs near windows and doors low to deprive prowlers of cover should they try to enter your home. Locate trees away from the house and remove lower limbs that could serve as a ladder. And avoid screening neighbors' views of your front door and driveway, balancing security and privacy.

Good fences make good neighbors, and in this case a brick wall adds privacy and security where the space between adjoining properties is tight. Slender hornbeam trees heighten the privacy level and soften the wall behind them.

CHOOSING PLANTS FOR PRIVACY

BORDER, HEDGE, AND SCREEN SHRUBS

ARBORVITAE
Thuja spp.
Type: Columnar evergreen
Height: 40–60 feet or more
Zones: 3–8
Soil: Prefers rich and moist
Light: Medium shade to full sun

Comments: Slow-growing arborvitae works well as a formal hedge because it bears clipping well. Unclipped it makes a semiformal hedge, a good screen, or, in clumps, an effective buffer. Use single plants as accents. The foliage is bright to dark green or yellow green in flat sprays. Except for certain cultivars, the yellow turns unattractive in the winter, so be selective. Arborvitae has few problems, but watch for bagworms. Also, be sure it keeps a central leader; prune competing side branches.

BARBERRY
Berberis spp.
Type: Evergreen and deciduous
Height: 2–9 feet
Zones: 4–8
Soil: Average
Light: Prefers sun; tolerates light shade

Comments: Barberry species include a large group of dense, spiny shrubs widely used for barrier or hedge plantings. Most have small bright yellow flowers, either single or in clusters and borne in great profusion. The fruits are small berries—some brilliant red, some purple or black—about ¼ inch long. Many are decorative all winter. Deciduous barberries have deep red fall color.

EUONYMOUS
Euonymous alatus
Type: Deciduous
Height: 10–15 feet
Zones: 4–8
Soil: Well drained
Light: Sun to shade

Comments: Winged euonymous, also known as burning bush, is noted for its brilliant fall color. Plant this slow-growing shrub where its autumn display will be appreciated. Use it as a specimen, as part of a mixed border, or in an informal hedge. It adapts to a wide range of soils but will not tolerate boggy conditions. Prune out damaged or dead branches any time of year. Prune to shape the plant annually, after the second year.

HONEYSUCKLE
Lonicera spp.
Type: Deciduous to semievergreen
Height: 3–15 feet
Zones: 3–10
Soil: Average to dry
Light: Prefers full sun

Comments: Fast-growing and fuss-free honeysuckle has many species and varieties, but only a few are recommended. Tatarian varieties with upright, arching habit and white to pink flowers are considered the best. Many have very fragrant flowers and showy red fruit that attracts birds; most, however, lack autumn color. Use in shrub borders or as single plants. Twining honeysuckle vines are good on arbors. Prune as needed. Some can become rampant in favorable climates.

ROSE
Rosa spp.
Type: Deciduous
Height: 3–15 feet
Zones: 3–10
Soil: Average to rich, well drained
Light: Sun; late-afternoon shade

Comments: The most-used and -loved garden plant in the world, the rose—available in both shrub and vine forms—is ideal for arbors, archways, and informal hedges. Shrub and species roses are hardier, easier to grow, and have far fewer pest problems than the hybrids; more massive climbers need some attention to training on support structures. Many have beautiful autumn color as well as exquisite flowers and fragrance. Orange to red fruits—or hips—are edible and easily made into a drink rich in vitamin C. Shown here is 'Belinda,' a musk rose that flowers repeatedly.

SPIREA
Spiraea spp.
Type: Deciduous
Height: 6–8 feet
Zones: 3–8
Soil: Well drained
Light: Sun

Comments: Vanhoutte spirea, also known as bridalwreath, is a popular, time-tested shrub. It is showy when covered with white blooms from mid- to late spring. Vanhoutte spirea is tough and adaptable. It can be used as an outstanding specimen or in groups for a dramatic hedge. Plant it in a mixed border or as a foundation shrub to bring old-fashioned charm to the landscape.

VIBURNUM
Viburnum spp.
Type: Mostly deciduous
Height: 5–12 feet, a few taller
Zones: 3–9
Soil: Does best in moist, well drained, slightly acid
Light: Prefers sun

Comments: A handsome shrub that is easy to grow, viburnum is an asset in the mixed border, near the foundation, or as a specimen plant. Its year-round interest extends from flat to ball-shape clusters of small flowers in May to good green summer foliage, scarlet fall color, and bunches of red berries that last into the winter. Viburnums provide food and cover for many birds. Flowers are mostly white or cream; fruits are red, yellow, blue, or black. Some can become small trees.

YEW
Taxus spp.
Type: Needled evergreen
Height: 3–20 feet
Zones: 2–7
Soil: Average to below average; well drained with no wet feet
Light: Sun or shade

Comments: For a trouble-free evergreen, the yew is hard to beat. Its dense, dark green, 1-inch needles are complemented by red berries (inedible; some thought to be poisonous) in midsummer to fall. Yews can be found in globe, vase, columnar, pyramidal, or ground-hugging shapes. They provide privacy as clipped or informal hedges or screens, or in mixed borders. Yews grow more slowly than deciduous shrubs. Males produce no berries.

Because the number of shrubs appropriate for borders and screens is almost limitless, consider mixing several different types. Combine one or two of those listed with edibles such as cherry, currant, blueberry, or quince. Add a hardy ornamental that will provide interest for all seasons: dogwood, azalea, or holly. Plant shrubs in a mixed border farther apart than shrubs in a formal hedge to emphasize the individuality of the plants, staggering the plantings. (For more shrub recommendations, see pages 368–377.)

PLANTING HEDGES

The judicious use of hedges marks the perimeter of your property, provides privacy, and even discourages trespassing. Softer and less forbidding than walls and fences, hedges are often more appealing to the eye too. While some homeowners are less than thrilled at the prospect of building a fence, almost no one complains about planting—and living with—a verdant, well-kept hedge.

Experts define a hedge as a linear arrangement of plants spaced closely enough to form a continuous living wall. The focus is on the overall effect rather than on individual plants. Within that simple definition, however, there's a world of variety.

At one end of the spectrum is the formal hedge planted in geometric lines and clipped into smooth, regular forms. At the other end is the more relaxed, informal hedge that's typically planted in curvy lines following natural features or the contours of the land. Often this type of hedge is composed of several different species of plants. When those plants are left to grow in their natural shapes, they can serve double duty as a shrub border as well.

The biggest attraction of a formal hedge is its solid, architectural look. It's an elegant way to set off a yard from the street and separate it from surrounding properties, or to create smaller garden rooms within a property. A carefully shaped, fine-textured hedge of boxwood or yew is a work of craftsmanship that reflects the care and time a gardener has put into cultivating it. Although a sheared hedge takes up more room than a fence, it covers a lot less space than a shrub border, so it's a good choice for small city properties.

Informal hedges, on the other hand, offer your landscape more variety and color. Although they also follow a linear pattern, the lines can expand and wander to the delight of family and onlookers alike.

Design strategies

While hedges make excellent property-line markers, they can play other roles as well. In a larger yard, use a meandering hedge to break up the space or to create a private hideaway or seating area. Or let

A lush hedge of arborvitae serves more than one purpose. It softens the architecture that it flanks and extends the effect of the privacy fence, especially now that it has matured and filled in. What's more, as a living wall, the hedge beautifully links the hardscape with the surroundings.

it replace a portion of the lawn to reduce mowing. Use larger formal hedges for privacy and use smaller versions to create separate garden rooms with different themes. Here are some things to keep in mind:

• **Consider height.** A hedge can be barely knee-high or extend above the eaves of a two-story house. Though a towering screen can be impressive and create total privacy, it may overwhelm a small city lot. Remember that a clipped, formal hedge more than 5 or 6 feet tall will be harder to maintain because you'll have to climb a ladder when you prune.

• **Avoid monotony.** Use a variety of plants. Try alternating gold- and green-needled cultivars of false cypress. Or use rhododendron varieties that bloom at the same time but with different color flowers.

• **Go for the layered look.** Using plants with different heights at maturity will create an interesting tiered effect. For example, dogwood, witch hazel, and redbud could make up the tall backbone of a hedge. Staggered in front of these would be medium-height shrubs, such as lilac and forsythia, followed by lower, spreading shrubs, such as juniper and cotoneaster. You could even continue this layering with groundcovers, perennials, or bulbs in front.

Maintenance tips

Whether you plan a formal hedge or an informal shrub border, timely maintenance will save you work and frustration in the long run. Formal hedges require more care, but they aren't difficult to maintain if you keep a regular schedule.

Before you plant, research the growth habits of the species you want to use. In general conifers don't tolerate heavy renewal pruning. If they become overgrown and you cut them back too much, the centers will be bare, and it's unlikely they'll resprout. However, many deciduous species can be cut back nearly to the ground to stimulate new shoots.

If you plant bare-root whips, cut them back to half their height immediately after planting. This will encourage branching and bushy form. This step is usually unnecessary for container-grown shrubs, which are normally pruned in the nursery for branching. Pyramidal-form evergreen species such as arborvitae should be left to grow to the desired height before shearing the tops.

For a formal hedge, let plants grow until they're a few inches taller and wider than the desired height and spread before shearing. Depending on the species, this may take several seasons. Take off no more than 6 inches in one pruning of deciduous shrubs and 2 to 3 inches of conifers.

In climates with harsh winters, where the ground freezes to a depth of several inches or drying winds occur, it can be hard for evergreens to take up water. Protect them with a screen of burlap or hay bales. Or spray an antidesiccant in late fall to coat the needles and slow down evaporation.

PLANTING A HEDGE

1 Stake out the corners of the area where the hedge will be planted. Connect the stakes with string to form a digging guide to help maintain a uniform width. Dig a trench within the marked area. Excavating a trench instead of individual holes allows you to adjust the position of plants.

2 Level the bottom of the trench but don't loosen the soil (it could cause plants to settle). Set the plants, still in their pots, along the trench to establish the correct spacing.

3 Water plants to make them easier to extract. Ease the plants out, then gently rough up the sides and bottom of each root ball slightly to untangle any roots that encircle it.

4 Transfer plants to the trench. The tops of the root balls should be at, or just slightly above, ground level. Make sure the shrubs are aligned as well as spaced evenly.

5 Fill in the trench with the excavated soil, making sure not to knock plants out of position as you fill. Firm soil gently around the root balls and water well. Add a 2- to 3-inch layer of mulch over the bed and water again.

BUILDING FENCES

Putting up a fence is a satisfying project that doesn't require any special skills or tools, just a good amount of labor. The hardest part is digging the holes; after that, the structure takes shape fairly quickly. Besides a posthole digger, you'll need only the standard stash of carpentry tools.

Before you proceed, check community building and zoning codes. Many specify maximum fence height, distances you can build from property lines and the street, and even the materials you can and can't use.

Designs vary widely, but most fences consist of the same basic elements: A series of 4x4 (or larger) posts sunk into the ground and connected by rails at the top, bottom, and sometimes in the middle as well; and vertical components—either panels or individual pieces—that are connected to the rails to give the fence its character.

Unless you want to build a rock wall, you likely will choose from three materials: wood, metal, or vinyl. Home improvement stores sell prefabricated sections of fencing in many styles and materials, although you may prefer to custom-design your own fence for a one-of-a-kind look.

Once you've settled on a design and established a location, measure and stake out the site. Plot post spacing for the most efficient use of materials. Depending on the product you use, 6- or 7-foot spans usually work well. Avoid setting privacy-fence posts more than 8 feet apart.

If you're building your fence on a slope, plan to step the fence down the hill, setting each section lower than the one preceding it. Only if the slope is slight—and the fence design won't suffer—should you follow the contour.

BUILDING A VINYL FENCE

Vinyl fencing, often assembled from a kit with components (usually PVC), requires slightly different installation schemes than wooden or metal fencing. Follow product instructions from the manufacturer.

The advantages of vinyl parts are many: They won't rot, rust, twist, chip, or fade. Nearly all styles come as kits with precut parts, and most of these kits require you to do some onsite assembly. And although the basic steps for installation are generally the same, each manufacturer has unique installation details to which you'll want to pay special attention. (Note: The kit illustrated here is more complex than most, so if you can install this one, most other designs will be a breeze.)

A few kit manufacturers furnish materials that require PVC cement or other adhesive for the assembly process. If you do any gluing, work with clean parts and avoid breathing the adhesive vapors.

If you need to deal with a slope, some of the vinyl fencing on the market is made with the capacity to be racked to a contour that follows that slope. Others don't offer that option, but you usually can overcome the problem if the slope isn't too great. Simply angle-cut the ends of the rails and lengthen the existing holes in the posts. Be aware, however, that the amount of adjustment you can make is likely to be small and that such modifications may void the manufacturer's warranty.

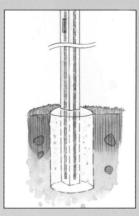

Lay out your fence line according to the manufacturer's instructions and dig all the postholes. Many vinyl fences call for end and gate posts to be strengthened with a concrete core. If your kit requires it too, insert ½-inch rebar down opposite corners of the post and into the bottom of the hole. (You'll pour the concrete later.)

1

Set the first post, bracing it plumb and at the correct height, as shown. Because you can't connect braces to the posts using screws, substitute clamps or wraps of duct tape. Backfill the hole with concrete and let the concrete set up.

2

After the concrete is firmly set, insert the bottom rail in the holes in both the first and second post. It should be alright to set the posts beforehand if spacing is accurate; the rail slides into a slot then retracts part way to extend as needed.

3

Assemble the panel inserts as a single unit. Install the assembled panel in the bottom rail from post to post. Then push the top rail into the hole of the first post; slide it down on top of the entire length of the panel insert and push it into the hole in the second post.

4

If your kit comes with another set of vertical inserts, shove each one into the holes in the top of the middle rail and the bottom of the top rail. Insert the top rail into both posts, then have a helper hold the whole works in place while you set the second post in concrete. Drive a screw from inside the post at an angle into the rail.

5

Continue assembling the fence, section by section, until it is complete. Then mix a batch of concrete to a pourable consistency by adding a little more water than you would for a typical mortar mix. Pour the concrete into the tops of the end and gate posts, if any, to within 6 inches of the tops.

6

Attach caps to the posts using glue or small screws—again, as per the manufacturer's instructions.

BUILDING LATTICEWORK SCREENS

Designs for privacy screens can be as varied as those for fences. A screen, after all, is really just a section of fence. But for a particularly striking effect, consider lacy latticework screens, which provide privacy without blocking balmy breezes. Lattice screens also offer sound support for climbing plants, which increases privacy even more.

Lattice is inexpensive and demands no special expertise to build—you can install it with only simple hand tools and an electric drill/driver.

The term latticework refers to any decorative pattern made with narrow, thin strips of wood (photos on page 221 show four typical patterns). Latticework designed to give privacy has approximately 1½-inch openings; with garden-spaced lattice, the openings are 3 inches or so.

Prefab versus homemade

Most lumberyards and home centers sell 4×8-foot prefabricated lattice panels for a cost that often is less than that for the lath alone. These panels are easy to install because the cutting and nailing already have been done. You have your choice of wooden or vinyl, although the look of wood tends to be more in keeping with most well-designed landscapes.

Inspect prefabricated latticework carefully before you buy, however. Cheaper varieties often are made with lath much thinner than that sold in individual pieces, and the staples holding cheap lattice together may be thin and dislodge easily.

PERMANENT LATTICE SCREEN

1 Set the posts, measure between them, and build a 2×4 frame. Predrill and screw the first of two sets of 1×1-inch stops flush with the outside of the frame.

2 Place the panel against the outside row of stops, then anchor the panel in position by predrilling and screwing the second set of stops to the inside edge of the frame.

REMOVABLE LATTICE SCREEN

1 In this example, the homeowners hung lattice panels from the edges of a pergola to give vertical definition to a seating area. They simply attached chains to the pergola tips.

2 The airy space at the lattice panel bottoms is accentuated by the fact that they float above the ground. For often-windy areas, just anchor the bottoms with matching chains.

3 Two side-by-side 4×8 panels create an open feel yet convert an undefined patio area into a well-defined outdoor room. This design also screens out neighbors and street traffic.

To cut a store-bought panel to fit, place it flat on a sheet of plywood, allowing the excess to extend past the plywood edge. Snap a chalkline and cut off excess with a circular saw set to extend ¼ inch below the lattice.

CHOOSING A FENCE OR SCREEN STYLE

FENCE STYLES

BOARD-ON-BOARD
This simple-but-effective design hides the frame so both sides look good. It creates full or partial privacy, depending on how much you overlap the boards. And it serves as an effective windbreak, provided it's at least 6 feet tall.

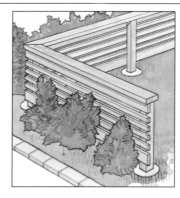

CAPPED POST-AND-RAIL
For a more contemporary look, consider a horizontal-rail design. You sacrifice privacy and wind protection in exchange for simple, modest lines. The varying widths of the rails—1×6s at top and bottom with 1×3s in between—add visual interest, and the 2×8 top cap contributes strength to the structure.

BASKET WEAVE
The weave is made from long, often-pricey boards, which commonly come in ½×6 cedar. Posts are a maximum of 6 to 8 feet apart. The weave adds strength to the fence. It stands up to the elements, softens wind, and blocks sunlight.

LOUVERED
For privacy and security, ideal around a pool or patio, this stylish option filters sunlight without blocking breezes. Louvers control the view, depending on their angle. Use kiln-dried lumber to avoid warping.

PICKET
Equally stylish in a wide variety of landscapes, the picket is also one of the easiest to build. Purchase preassembled fence panels available in a variety of styles, or build the fence of your dreams, cutting and spacing the pickets as you please.

SOLID BOARD
Vertical board fences are probably the most prevalent style of fence you'll find. That's because they go up easily and their design can be varied almost infinitely. Tightly fitted 1×6s or 1×8s give you complete privacy. A solid fence blocks sun but can force wind into downdrafts.

LATTICEWORK STYLES

STANDARD
Thin, crisscrossed wood slats usually form a diagonal pattern. Multifunctional and lightweight, this lattice can be stained, painted, or sealed to resist weather.

GARDEN
Made with wide openings, spaced up to 3 inches, this lattice makes an ideal support for vining and climbing plants. Combined with plants, it forms a dense screen over time.

VINYL
Vinyl lattice comes in a number of colors, and some styles are molded with a woodgrain look-alike pattern. Vinyl lattice isn't as stiff as wood, but it requires little or no maintenance and lasts indefinitely.

OPEN; CEDAR
The toughest lattice is made with cedar 1×2s. It holds heavy vines without sagging and works well for large screens, trellises, and arbors.

JOINERY TECHNIQUES

If you don't like the look of metal rail connectors, attach rails to posts with one of the joints shown here. All work equally well. Choose one based on your tools and skills. To make a lap joint, cut a notch into the post so the rail will be flush (or nearly flush) with the post. For a block joint, screw a short piece of 2x2 to the post, rest the rail on top of it, and screw through the block into the post. For a butt joint, drive screws at an angle through the rail into the post.

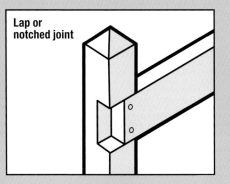

Lap or notched joint

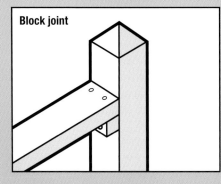

Block joint

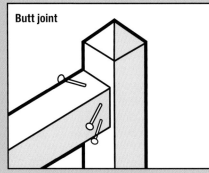

Butt joint

FENCE AND SCREEN PLANTINGS

Just as fences and screens provide the perfect backdrop for plants, the structures need plantings to soften their angular appearance. At the same time, plants, fences, and screens work together to help set the mood for a garden. Roses on a post-and-rail fence sing one song; on a picket fence, a slightly different tune.

Plant pointers

Keep the following in mind when deciding how best to use plants near your fence or screen:

• Your yard will seem larger if you group flowers and shrubs as near to the structure as practical, leaving an open central area. Place tall plants in back and the shortest in front (see chart opposite).

• Shrubs and trees can overpower a fence. Select open and slender varieties for minimum pruning and plant far enough away for uncramped development.

• Vines are especially good on fences and screens. They will often climb wire or trellis unaided. To get some of them to grow up a wood surface, you may need to attach string support.

• Vines can completely cover a chain-link fence, but more elegant structures look better with vines that accent rather than hide them. Also consider the strength of the fence or screen when selecting vines.

• Colors come alive against a fence or screen. Blue delphiniums, lost without a background, stand out when displayed against white.

• Fences and screens can create microclimates, resulting in new growing opportunities. For example, a solid structure protects downwind plants for an area equal to its height. Latticework allows some wind penetration but protects a larger area. Heat is reflected or stored depending on color and material.

Maintenance

Because mowing or hoeing under a fence is difficult, remove all plants and roots before you build. To keep out new roots, bury edging a few inches from the fence. Or place plastic or tar paper covered with gravel under the fence.

A wooden fence, arbor, and gate give a once-exposed front yard a sense of privacy and protection. Roses add beauty; their thorns enhance security.

An open-lattice fence separates garden rooms, forming an entryway to both areas and adding formal structure to them as well. The 7-foot-tall lattice meets up with an arbor and helps hold a fragrant Carolina jessamine vine.

Here's a space-saving gardening secret: Use vertical surfaces, such as fences and walls, as growing space for small trees or large shrubs. The art of espalier is employed to train a flowering almond flat against this fence.

RECOMMENDED PLANTS

Plants with spiky, simple, or striking blooms benefit most from a vertical background to create a fully balanced display.

4 to 5 feet	1½ to 4 feet	2 inches to 1½ feet
Camellia	Bachelor's button	Celosia
Cosmos	Cleome	Daffodil
Delphinium	Columbine	Heather
False cypress	Daphne	Hosta
Hibiscus	Dictamnus	Marigold
Hollyhock	Flax, blue	Nasturtium
Japanese maple	Forsythia, dwarf	Rose, miniature
Liatris	Iris	Salvia
Pieris, Japanese	Leucothoe	Sweet william
Pyracantha	Rose	Tulip
Rose	Snapdragon	

Remember to put the tallest plants nearest the fence, then the midsize varieties, and finally the short plants in front.

Small yards call for creative designs. Here stone steps lead to a secluded lounge area. Built on a slope, the stone platform is only wide enough for a chaise. Planting pockets hold giant bird-of-paradise.

INSTALLING SECURITY LIGHTING

Effective outdoor lighting brings four benefits to a landscaping scheme: It discourages intruders. It prevents accidents. When done creatively it can enhance your landscaping scheme. Perhaps best of all, lighting increases the time you can enjoy your outdoor surroundings.

How much?

The illustration at right identifies points on your property that need illumination for security purposes. In general don't be afraid to install too many lights. Outdoor fixtures aren't terribly expensive, especially if you install them yourself. Operating outdoor lights, however, can be costly, so try to provide separate switching, perhaps with a master switch that controls all. Consider using a few motion-sensor fixtures in key locations; they come on only for a few minutes at a time—when someone appears in the area of their beam. That someone could be you when you need a welcome ray of light, or it could be an unwanted stranger who will be illuminated for everyone to see.

When you shop for outdoor fixtures, you'll find an abundance of choices. Post lights illuminate walks and drives. Step lights prevent stumbles. Floodlights—including the motion-sensor variety—produce powerful beams from their mounts on poles, in trees, under eaves, or high on the sides and back of your house. Inground lights, placed below plants, can erase burglar-friendly shadows.

Installation

Check your community's electrical code before ordering materials for any 120-volt project. The code not only dictates the type of wiring and conduit you use but also tells you how deep to bury it. Most codes also require you to protect outdoor lights and receptacles with a ground fault circuit interrupter (GFCI), a device that senses any shock hazard and shuts down the circuit it controls.

Much simpler to install but less versatile is low-voltage (12-volt) lighting. For more information on this option, see pages 262–267.

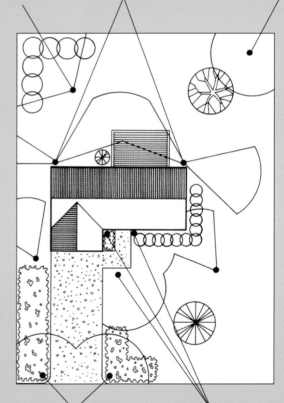

Dark bushes can provide cover for anyone contemplating a raid on your home. Inground lights here wash away the cloaking shadows, as well as play up plantings.

Floodlights at each corner of your home's rear exterior can brighten outdoor living areas and illuminate substantial sections of the remainder of the backyard.

Light far corners of your property with post lights or floods in trees. Aim the lights so that they don't shine into neighbors' yards or windows.

Driveway entrance lights provide a cheerful welcome and supplement street lighting. Be sure to shield fixtures here so that they won't blind approaching drivers.

Front steps, door lock, and house number should be lighted with fixtures on both sides of the door and at any turns in the approach. The extra door fixture serves as a backup in case a bulb burns out.

UNDER-EAVE INSTALLATION

If you have eaves overhanging any exterior doors, it makes sense to install a light above each door, where the fixture will be better protected from the weather than if mounted on a wall. Also you're likely to find it easy to run electrical cable from an attic junction box to the eaves.

Consider installing motion-detector floodlights in these spots. They're inexpensive, and if you wire each one to be controlled by a regular wall switch—although this involves significantly more work—you have the option of being able to turn off the motion-sensing feature if you wish.

1
Before you start cutting, turn off the power. Then draw an outline of the new box on the eaves. (A retrofit box with wings that attach to the eaves works well.) Drill starter holes on your outline, then cut the hole with a jigsaw.

2
Fish the cable from the attic junction box and run it through the new box, securing it with the clamping device that's part of the box. Firmly attach the box to the eaves.

3
Connect the house wiring to the fixture wires, using wire connectors. Then screw the light firmly to the box. Wait until dark to make final adjustments to the lamps.

ADJUSTING A MOTION SENSOR

Do your adjusting at night. Aim the lamps so that they help you but don't bother neighbors or passersby. Then set the time of the lights' duration; many manufacturers offer two, five, or ten minutes. Point the motion sensor toward the area you want to cover and set the range control to the middle position. Walk toward the light to see when it turns on. At the same time, make sure it doesn't come on when you don't want it to—for instance, when you walk by on the sidewalk. Aim the motion sensor or adjust the range control to get it right.

GALLERY OF PRIVACY IDEAS

In a new development, where mature shade trees and privacy hedges are scarce, a vinyl-lattice screen provides instant privacy. The 7-foot-tall fence and attached pergola require little upkeep.

This bird's-eye view of a formal patio shows how the privacy fencing frames the room. French doors open to the driveway and nearby street. Trim evergreens enliven the room and reinforce its formal style.

A bamboo fence and plantings ensure a sense of privacy for a corner of this backyard where an inground spa bubbles invitingly. Bamboo was chosen as a building material for its earthiness and durability.

Evergreens, such as arborvitae, form a lush living fence that stands up to winter winds and summer sun. Arborvitae can be trimmed for a more formal look or left naturally freeform.

Lattice panels form a cozy corner for intimate conversation or peaceful moments of solitude. The structure makes the tiny patio as inviting and comfortable as any roomier space.

A small table and two armchairs plus a planting bed transform a new patio into a quaint sitting area. The fence makes it a sheltered place to escape from the workaday world.

CHAPTER 10

BEYOND THE BASICS

For many people, a yard must offer more than a patio or deck to attract them to the pleasures of outdoor living. Some like to relax in a graceful gazebo or refresh near a still garden pond; others prefer to splash in a swimming pool or let loose in a play area. The options for creating the right outdoor living scheme are limitless. Most importantly, select those features that allow for your favorite activities, while working within the limitations of your site conditions.

This setting didn't come about as a result of piecemeal additions along the way. Instead, an overall plan at the outset pulled together this beautiful, cohesive combination of design elements.

The peaceful mood of this landscaping success originates from just the right proportions of stone walkways, colorful planting areas, and shimmering water.

A custom-designed gazebo a few steps from the house—and an impressive architectural match—serves as one of the focal points of the landscape. The pool's edge was shaped to mirror the angles of the gazebo.

Part of this design's charm can be found in its series of curving lines that flow from one area to another harmoniously.

CREATING THE ULTIMATE GAZEBO

From the footings to the cupola, a gazebo's design and use varies greatly from yard to yard.

Yours could be a Japanese teahouse, a Victorian summer room, or a geodesic dome. It could be round, square, hexagonal, octagonal, or another creative shape. (Octagonals are the most popular; squares, the easiest to build.)

A gazebo can be a rather substantial structure made of timbers or brick—or, more typically, a light and whimsical one, with lattice rails and scrollwork under the eaves. A variety of designs is available in precut kits; for a challenge, design your own. Choose the look that reflects the mood and style of your house and garden as well as the ways you intend to use the structure.

Provide a minimum diameter of 10 feet if you plan to use the gazebo for entertaining. Make the floors and benches nonskidding and quick drying. Pick the floor material that best fits your gazebo's style. Choices include wood, synthetics, gravel, flagstone, tile, concrete, slate, and brick.

Choose a slatted roof to protect from the sun only, or a solid version—with shakes, shingles, tile, thatch, or tin—to protect from rain. Plan walls that are open, screened, or glassed. Include a barbecue, spa, or storage nook, if you wish.

Location

Because a gazebo is such a strong focal point in any setting, its location is as important as its design.

Gazebos ordinarily are set some distance from the house; if you plan to use yours as an outdoor dining room, however, make sure it's near—or easily accessible to—the kitchen. Also consider wind direction, sun and shade patterns, nearness to neighbors, and the views of the garden that each side of the gazebo will frame.

Usually a gazebo is freestanding, but it also can adjoin a patio, deck, or possibly a fence. It doesn't need much planting around it; it's decorative enough in itself. A freestanding gazebo does need to be connected to the house and garden by an easy and inviting path.

Angled post braces, vertical half-walls, a knotty pine ceiling, and an antique candelabrum give this deck-top retreat a lot of charm. It's tucked off one corner so as not to intrude on the overall deck space.

This elaborate Victorian design includes a weather vane on top. Arches on all sides, ornate lattice infill, and a low brick base wall exude character.

Sometimes you choose a gazebo design to blend well with its surroundings. However, in this example, both were created together. A two-tiered cupola and ornate trim are standout features of the gazebo.

231

BUILDING GAZEBOS

To construct a bell-roof, 10-side Victorian gazebo like the one we built, you can: A) Spend several weekends painstakingly computing, cutting, and assembling a hundred or more complicated angle joints; or B) let a manufacturer of prefabricated gazebos do the intricate geometry for you, allowing you to put the whole thing together in just a couple of days. This example follows the second course of action. The gazebo shown was built from a kit.

Kit structures, including different models from one manufacturer, can vary greatly in design, but this example gives you a general idea of the process involved.

This kit consisted of precut deck joists, 10 preassembled deck panels and side frames, 10 precut triangular roof panels, precut rafters, a king post for the point where the roof panels converge, miscellaneous trim pieces, plus all the hardware needed to fasten the components to one another.

Tools? In addition to renting a power posthole auger and a hammer drill, the entire job was done with this basic assortment: a builder's level, tape measure, automotive-type socket wrench set, stepladder, hammer, pliers, a few clamps, cordless drill/driver with bits, and for getting the roof shingled—a staple gun, utility knife, and tin snips.

Foundation work

The project shown has poured individual concrete piers, but many of these kits can be ordered without the wood floor deck and installed on a slab foundation. In areas where the frostline is far below grade, use tube forms and pour deep concrete footings. For smaller structures—or in areas where frost heaving isn't a concern—you can support the deck frame on precast concrete piers that simply rest on compacted soil.

Siting

Before you start building, carefully determine the proper placement and orientation of your gazebo by considering factors such as sun exposure, prevailing winds, and proximity to other structures.

Clean lines and decorative flourishes give this gazebo a custom appearance. Only the homeowners and a few friends know it came from a kit and was completed in just a few days.

1 Instead of guessing about the precise placement of bolts in wet concrete, wait until you have the deck frame assembled and resting on the cured footings. Then drill holes with a rented hammer drill and install wedge-type anchor bolts.

2 After you've secured the bolt, nut, and framing bracket, align the bracket next to the deck joist and drill for a bolt. High-wind sites require additional reinforcement; don't skimp on the hardware.

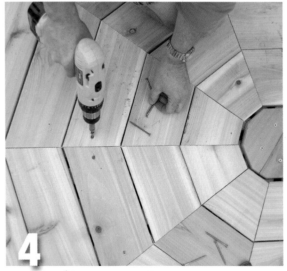

3 For strength and ease of assembly, the kit manufacturer supplied two precut pieces to fill the gap over the center block. Install these before you attach any of the remaining decking so you can carefully lay out the entire floor.

4 The decking pieces that comprise each of the 10 sections of flooring are fastened together (underneath) as a unit. Loose-fit all of the sections until you're satisfied with the spacing, then screw into the underlying joists.

BUILDING GAZEBOS *(continued)*

5

The wall frames are relatively easy to set up but aren't stable until you have several of them fastened together. Recruit a helper to hold the frames steady as you attach them to each other. Don't fasten them to the deck just yet.

6

With all of the wall frames in place, adjust the positioning so you have consistent alignment around the perimeter of the deck. Then drive screws near the lower ends of the posts to secure each section to the floor deck.

7

Confirm that the deck assembly is flat and level. To make minor adjustments, loosen the anchor bolt hardware enough to shim any low corners. These corrections ensure a better fit for the roof.

8

The beauty of building with a kit is that the difficult geometry work is already done for you. Here, the precut rafters make that process simpler, so you can focus on assembly.

9

At this stage, the basic structure is established. The upper wall plates tie the individual frame sections together and provide a platform for attaching the rafters.

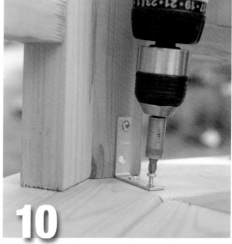

10

At the wall-to-deck connections, add some metal angle brackets to reinforce the structure. Where possible, drive screws into framing—in this case, joists under the decking.

11 Placing the precut roof panels will require a helper. Align as best you can, then secure each panel temporarily with just two nails, partially driven. Nail off when all the panels are fitted.

12 Precut roof fascia boards are part of the kit's trim package. Fit each piece tightly up against the underside of the roof panel, then nail into the upper wall plate around the perimeter.

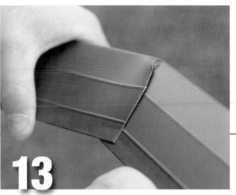

13 Instead of cutting small pieces of metal drip flashing for each facet, extend one long piece around several sections. Just cut the top flange, then fold it to create an overlapping corner.

14 Trimming the roof can follow immediately after the plywood panels are nailed to the rafters. Start by installing the flashing along the lower edge of the roof, using roofing nails.

15 Rather than wrestle with a heavy full roll of roofing felt, simply cut oversize lengths on the ground and bring them up individually to install. Always overlap edges so water runs off properly.

16 For the first few courses of shingles, work from a ladder and cover one section at a time. Use a straightedge and hook-blade utility knife to trim the excess along each ridge.

17 A faceted center block serves as a hub to connect the upper ends of the cupola rafters. Recruit an extra pair of hands to help steady the components as you fasten them together.

18 The fascia boards for the cupola will be well out of reach after the assembly is installed. To avoid having to work on the roof, apply any finishes before you install the cupola.

19 Screw together 10 prefab sections to form the cupola's wall frame, then attach the top plates with screws as shown here. This assembly will serve as the base for the cupola's roof frame.

GALLERY OF GAZEBO IDEAS

This carefully crafted beauty is one of the classiest and most subtle gazebos imaginable. Stone columns support wood beams and a vine-covered metal framework.

Snuggled amid breathtaking greenery, this elegant structure appears as if it grew there along with the plants. Ornate framing details and hardware add flair.

This cozy example has windows all around and a good-size door that can protect the family from insects as well as nippy breezes.

Five steps up from the main deck and perched on its own upper-level platform, this octagonal gazebo supplies a covered sanctuary for dining and entertaining. Its railing adds exactly enough privacy.

A gazebo doesn't have to be big to provide a covered spot where you can sit and enjoy the scenery. A small entry bridge spans the boulder-lined pond, and a platform at left overhangs the water.

CREATING THE ULTIMATE POND

The shimmering surface of the ideal garden pond should reflect peace and tranquillity, as well as the surrounding foliage, flowers, sky, clouds, and sunsets. Sound too visionary? Definitely not, because water features are adaptable to more garden situations than most families realize.

And despite the new realms of plant, fish, and wildlife pleasures offered by these ponds, they need not require a lot of time or money. You can learn enough to begin the venture in just one evening, paging through a catalog. And the typical water garden requires no more work and little more cost than the standard flower border.

By placing their pond and waterfall directly off the deck, the homeowners not only created an ideal scene to enjoy from the deck, but also put the sounds near the house so they can drift through an open window.

Design

To test your pond design ideas, shape a garden hose on your lawn at various locations and in a variety of configurations.

To keep fish, a pond needs to be at least as large as a bathtub; a surface area of 50 or more square feet—a 7-foot square, an 8-foot-diameter circle, or a 5×10-foot rectangle—is best. Smaller ponds get too hot in summer, which can lead to algae problems. A depth of 1½ to 2 feet works for most goldfish. Japanese koi need 3 feet. (Ask a local naturalist for dimensions ideal for your particular climate.)

As you plan your pond, give thought to the possibility of incorporating a waterfall and a stream of some kind into the overall layout.

Depending on the steepness of your terrain, you might be able to build a rather high waterfall and enjoy the wonderful around-the-clock sounds it produces. Or, if you're dealing with a flat area, you can bring in soil and boulders to form your own slope—as tall as you want it.

Streams can take on a variety of lengths and widths, and you can design them so that they meander throughout your property, if you wish. In fact, if you were to build two or more small ponds, a stream could connect them.

Maintenance

Most ponds can be filled with a hose and emptied by siphon or bucket. Where winters are severe, transfer fish and tender plants indoors. In mild climates or with added heat, fish will live under a foot of ice as long as an air hole is kept open. Don't do this by smashing the surface, however; the concussion could damage or kill the fish. A floating deicer will do the job. Wherever ice forms, put a log in the pond in winter to absorb the thrust of the ice.

Every few years, drain and clean your pond in the spring. If algae build up, ask at your pond-supply store for algae-killing chemicals that will not harm fish. Use them and add more plants.

Not all ponds need to be freeform and surrounded by boulders. Rectilinear shapes such as this one blend better with the adjacent architecture of almost any setting. The location of this pond delights folks in both the dining area and the pergola.

239

BUILDING PONDS

Building a pond might seem like a daunting task. There's the digging, of course, and dealing with the liner, pump, filter, and fountain. But in reality, a garden pond isn't much more than a hole filled with water and a few accessories—an undertaking that's not nearly as difficult as it might seem.

Placement tips
• Avoid putting your pond under a large tree; if you do, you'll be cleaning out debris on a regular basis.
• If you're working on a slope, install your pond on level ground at the top of the grade; if placed at the bottom, it will become contaminated from runoff carrying debris, fertilizers, and possibly pesticides.
• A sunny location allows you to enjoy reflections dancing on the water. In addition, many water plants need at least six hours of daily sunlight to bloom.
• Locate smaller ponds next to patios and courtyards close to the house; put larger versions—because they stand out even from a distance—farther away.

The fountain pictured is a bamboo-style model that makes a soft, clacking sound when the receiving rod fills with water and drops into place to discharge its contents.

Pond kits
• A pond kit will give you the basics in one package. Most come with a liner to prevent water leakage, a pump to circulate water, a filter to keep water clear, and the necessary tubing and fittings.
• Kits typically don't include accessories such as a fountain, lights, and statuary.
• You usually have two choices of liners—preformed or flexible. Rugged, preformed liners come in rectangular and freeform shapes that don't require pulling and stretching. They are small and generally have built-in shelves. Flexible liners, such as the one pictured, let you create a custom-shape pond. They require a protective underlayment; either use an extra layer of liner or old carpet, cut to cover the bottom of the excavation, cushioning the liner from potential puncture.

1 Use string and stakes or flour to outline the shape of the pond and a path surrounding it. Excavate for the pond, using a shovel. Most ponds are about 12 to 24 inches deep. Your pond can have a shallow end and a deeper end, if you like. Deeper water is necessary for growing water lilies.

Pumps and filters
• The pond's size will determine how big a pump and filtering system you'll need. Pumps come with waterproof cords that should be connected to a ground-fault-protected outdoor electrical outlet.

Dig out a ledge that's about 4 inches deep and 6 inches wide around the perimeter. Leave a planting bed next to the ledge, then excavate a 4-inch-deep circular path. Cover the bottom of the excavation with underlayment. Grasp the liner into the shape of a bag and lower it into place. Then position the lines for the pump.

Spread out the liner and temporarily anchor the edges with rocks. Fill the liner with water and smooth out wrinkles as the pond fills. Fold over excess portions of the liner, repositioning the rocks as you go. Stop filling the pond before water reaches the outer edge.

Place rocks along the ledge surrounding the pond to hold the liner permanently in place when you completely fill the pond in a later step. Leave about 1 foot of liner beyond the rocks; use a heavy-duty cutting blade to remove excess.

Now finish filling the pond. Add plants. Spread landscape fabric to create a path around the pond and cover it with 2 inches of gravel. Install the pump and filtering system, then set up the fountain. Finish by adding plants and fish.

BUILDING STREAMS

The genius of water is that it always knows where to go—downhill. Harness this law of nature and you can create a stream that meanders down even a modest slope, tumbles over falls, and trickles through turns before it's pumped back to its origin—ready to perform its refreshing journey again for everyone to enjoy.

Any site with a slope of 1 inch per 10 feet will support a stream, but a steeper incline expands the possibilities for building waterfalls. If you need more slope for your stream, you can create it, as long as you don't overdo.

Also consider drainage patterns. A heavy rain can add more water to your stream than your facilities can handle, so you may have to raise the stream's edges with excavated soil and stone to direct rainwater runoff away from the stream.

Remember, too, that your stream can be a source of runoff as well. Power outages that stop the pump—or a breakdown of the pump itself—will cause the stream to overflow at the bottom. If this occurs, you'll be glad you have some type of collection device, such as a dry well, just beyond the low end of the stream.

If the stream is rather shallow, you can expect to need to add water every few weeks—and, in hot weather, weekly.

Professional installation means much of the work will be done for you; regardless, you need to consider several factors. For example, in most areas, building codes for swimming pools also apply to other water features. In addition, be sure you know ahead of time where your utilities are buried. And, finally, decide in advance where you'll want your nighttime lighting so you can install service for it while you're running wiring for the pump.

Building a stream is a major project for most do-it-yourselfers, so consider hiring a pro, at least for parts of the project that may be beyond your abilities. Either way, the basic steps of building a stream are the same.

Complete the process by adding an array of streamside plantings. (Though homeowners often choose simply to shut down the pump until spring arrives, in most climates, the entire stream system can continue to operate through winter. In the northern states, the biggest danger is the formation of large ice chunks, which may need to be broken with a sledgehammer if they block the flow.)

Dig the stream by hand. You must keep the banks of the stream level with each other, but you can vary the width, as well as the number of drop-offs.

2 Line the stream with underlayment or used carpet, topped by a 45-mils rubber liner. (Both have a 20-year lifespan.) To carry water from one end of the stream to the other, bury flexible piping about 8 inches deep along the outside of the bed. Then install the pump.

3 Set the largest rocks in place to sculpt the stream, stabilize its edges, and create falls. If necessary, use expanding foam to seal gaps.

4 Adjust the liner, then cover the entire surface of the streambed with smaller rocks and gravel. In addition to hiding the liner, the rocks and gravel host beneficial bacteria and algae that help keep the water clean.

5 Fill the stream with water and adjust the pump volume. When the water is flowing properly, you can make final adjustments to the falls and ripples.

INSTALLING PUMPS, FOUNTAINS, AND WATERFALLS

Want a pond that stirs silently beneath the surface, with scarcely a ripple above? Prefer a dramatic fountain that arcs a jet of water above your pond or even from a remote location? Or how about a waterfall that burbles down a steep slope into a lily-speckled catch basin below? With a submersible recirculating pump, you can put your pond's water into motion in all of these ways—and more.

A submersible pump pulls in water through a screen that snags leaves and debris, and expels a steady stream through its outlet. To gently move water and keep it from stagnating, set the pump a few inches above the pond bottom (perhaps on a brick or two) and connect it to a source of electricity.

For an in-pond fountain, attach any of several nozzles to the outlet. To pump water from the pond to a waterfall or remote fountain, run flexible vinyl tubing from the outlet to wherever you want the water to go (see illustration below).

To help you choose a pump, your dealer will need to know the height at which you want the water to discharge and the volume of water in your pond.

Safety musts

Check with an electrician or consult your community's electrical codes before bringing power to a submersible pump. This receptacle should be protected by a ground fault circuit interrupter (GFCI); a GFCI shuts down the circuit instantaneously should a potentially dangerous malfunction occur.

Check the code, too, to learn the components required for underground wiring in your area. Most call for underground feeder (UF) cable, rigid conduit, or a combination of both—conduit above ground, UF cable below. Codes also specify how deep cable and conduit must be buried. Neglect these regulations at your peril: Electricity and water can be a lethal combination, especially outdoors.

Check local codes to determine the electrical requirements for a water garden. Most codes require that a pump be plugged into a weatherproof receptacle located within 6 feet of the pump and 18 inches above the ground.

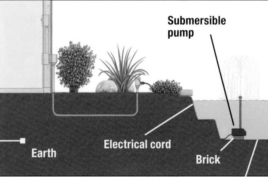

Submersible pump

Electrical cord

Earth

Brick

PVC liner or other material

For a waterfall, run tubing from the submersible pump's outlet to a remote, and higher, site. Use concrete or PVC liner and stones or other material to construct the waterway. Each level of a stair-stepped waterfall should have a vertical drop of 6 to 12 inches.

Submersible pump

Clear vinyl tubing   Earth   PVC liner or other material   Brick   Electrical cord

CREATING WATER GARDENS

Plant your water garden after the weather warms in spring. You can plant in bottom mud, but containers allow flexibility in depth and position and make cleaning easier. Use a mix of garden loam and pea gravel rather than compost, peat moss, or composted manure.

First, add submerged oxygenating plants, such as parrot's feather, waterweed, or underwater grasses. Fill several 5-inch pots or shallow containers with soil, topping off the uppermost inch with sand. Root several oxygenators per pot by pushing them a third of the way into the soil.

Plant only one water lily per 20-inch pot; pygmy varieties need only 8-inch containers. Plant hardy varieties at an angle against the pot side; in harsh climates, store them indoors during cold months.

Plant tropical water lilies only after the nights grow warm. Set each tuber in the center of a pot with the crown at the soil line. Sink pots 6 to 8 inches below the water surface. Treat these plants as annuals and order new roots each year.

Fish facts

Add one fish per 2 square feet of pond surface. You can choose from among many colorful goldfish, such as calicoes, comets, black moors, and fantails. If your pond is large and at least 3 feet deep, you can add Japanese koi.

Do not let the bags the fish come in get hot in the sun. Before freeing fish, float the bags in the pond for a half hour to equalize temperatures.

Feed the fish every one to three days. Remove any leftovers after 5 to 10 minutes. Give high-protein food in the fall and halve feedings from November until March, a natural resting period for the fish.

Welcome any frogs, toads, or turtles that come. You also can buy them and add them to your menagerie. With the fish, they help control insects and algae growth.

WATER GARDEN PLANTS

HOSTAS are fine plants for shady edges. They come in a wide variety of sizes, colors, and foliage patterns. Many have fragrant spikes of flowers as well.

SIBERIAN IRIS are edging plants that produce yellow, white, blue, or purple blooms among 2- to 4-foot-tall swordlike leaves. Grow iris in full sun to partial shade.

SWORD FERN is one of many ferns that thrives on moist banks in full sun to partial shade. This fern is hardy and easy to grow. It spreads by spores or by division.

WATER LILIES come in many colors and sizes. They do best with their roots in containers on the pond floor. Some are fragrant. Most bloom freely all season long.

Floating plants such as water lettuce or water hyacinth need no soil. When these spread too far, scoop out the excess. (No more than half of your pond's surface should be covered by plants.) Other pondside plants include primrose, lily, daylily, forget-me-not, water snowflake, grasses, and reeds.

GALLERY OF POND IDEAS

Boulders, water, and plantings can bring the country to town. Here, a mortared-stone patio forms a perfect viewing platform.

The original shape and condition of this woodland landscape convinced its owners that all it needed to become a magical place was a pair of rock-lined ponds, connected by a perpetual waterfall.

The star of this backyard scene is a waterfall that cascades over the mortared ledge of a rock wall, bounces off large boulders, and splashes into the inviting pond below.

In this pastoral scene, the pond is wide enough and deep enough to require an arched walking bridge to span it and take visitors to mysterious vistas beyond. Water lilies and fish add bright color to the setting.

In this traditional patio, the pond, though small, provides the center of attention. The formal-style inground pond features an edge wide enough for seating.

247

CREATING THE ULTIMATE SWIMMING POOL

A personal swimming pool offers the ultimate in backyard recreation. It's there for you when you want a brisk before-breakfast dip or a few healthful laps at lunchtime—all without requiring a long trip to the local swimming hole.

And for those of us who would be hard-pressed to spend much time at a crowded beach, a home pool allows family swim time, an enjoyment that would go unexperienced otherwise.

There was a time when even baths were public facilities. Now swimming pools have become mostly private. Although the trend started in the Sunbelt, Southerners seldom swim before May or much after September, except in heated pools. Summers in Northern states are also hot, and a swimming pool there can add as much pleasure to outdoor living.

Ideally a pool should be integrated into the landscape. Patios, decks, and nearby plantings should be carefully planned to enhance the scene's beauty and enjoyment, yielding an adjoining space for sunbathing and a shaded area where nonswimmers can relax and avoid splashes. A drinking fountain and access to a bathroom or shower add great convenience.

Many inground pools are designed to be the visual focus from both indoor and outdoor rooms; some are visible through a foyer from the front door, adding to the grandeur of the entryway. Even during winter, these pools can give visual refreshment and reflection.

Some homeowners, however, prefer not to see their pool in the dead of winter; if you are among them, plan your pool's location accordingly. Or use plantings or surrounding materials to make the winter scene as pleasant as possible.

Some pools, especially in yards with overhanging trees, are completely enclosed with screening to keep out insects, falling leaves, and other blowing debris. Screening also cuts down somewhat on the sun's intensity, a benefit in summer. But the water will be colder in spring and fall.

The naturalistic plantings around this rock-edge pool help blend it with the landscape. Groundcovers, low-growing shrubs, and gravel mulch combine in easy-care planting areas.

A tall fence—for privacy and security—provides the backdrop for this attractive pool area. A boulder display, cantilevered fountain shelf, and contemporary pergola make key contributions.

A disappearing-edge pool works well in native environments, on picturesque hillsides, and in small spaces. The pool is painted dark blue to help it disappear even more.

ASSESSING SWIMMING POOL OPTIONS

The addition of a swimming pool to your yard is a big decision. As you begin to read, research, and consider the options, also talk with other homeowners who have pools. Learn all that you can about what kind, shape, and size of pool might be best for you.

A pool can provide years of summer fun, exercise, and relaxation; and, with the right decisions, it will increase dramatically your yard's beauty, value, and use.

If you decide that a pool isn't right for you now but may be in the future, plan your present use of the space for easy changeover: a lawn or flower garden, not a patio or clump of trees. Also remember to leave access for heavy machinery. In areas where swimming pools are the norm, lack of construction access could be a serious drawback to would-be buyers someday.

Pools today can be installed quickly— by professionals, that is. As you research the work required to build a pool, you'll quickly realize that this is not a typical do-it-yourself project.

Safety and cost

A pool can be as safe or as dangerous as the family car, but it isn't as essential. You can postpone building a pool until the children are old enough to ease the worry factor (although at no age should you allow them to swim or play in the pool unsupervised). Begin planning and saving now and you'll enjoy your pool all the more later on.

The cost of the pool itself represents only 50 to 60 percent of the total outlay; the fencing, decking, and surrounding plantings that will transform the pool from the visual appearance of a raw wound to that of a luxurious landscape constitute the remaining expenses.

This cost comes into better perspective, though, if you realize that, when you sell your home, you can largely recover the money spent on a professionally built pool, as long as the pool doesn't exceed 10 percent of your overall property value.

Besides cost, consider the maintenance demands of a pool too. Time spent maintaining water quality and equipment will seem minimal as long as you and your family enjoy the pool. If your leisure interests change, however, maintenance can become a major annoyance.

Site

There isn't a great deal of choice in most yards as to where to put something as big as a swimming pool. But if you do have a choice of sites, consider these points:
• Will the foundation of existing buildings be weakened by the excavation? Will the slope and grade accommodate the pool? Often the grade can be built up around the pool, thus reducing the hole's depth and the cost of carting off soil.
• How about the soil type and the drainage? The soil has to bear the weight of pool materials and water, and it must drain well enough so that the pool won't float out of the ground.
• What about sun and wind patterns? These affect warmth and cleaning. Too much sun could promote algae growth. If possible, the prevailing wind should drive all floating debris toward the skimmers. A strong wind against the flow decreases efficiency. You can build wind baffles and screens, if necessary.
• Do you prefer to swim in the morning or evening, in sun or shade? If possible, site accordingly.
• Will the pool be far enough from trees, flowering shrubs, and hedges to avoid droppings from branches and birds overhead? Don't let the lawn come too close either; otherwise, grass cuttings will blow or be tracked into the water.
• Is there access to electrical and water lines, and proper drainage for overflow? Filters are best kept as near to the deep end of the pool as possible so suction pipes are short.
• How do zoning and fencing regulations affect your plans? Often, self-latching gates are required.
• Finally, for safety's sake, will the pool be visible from the house?

Three fountains flowing from matching stone columns catch your attention at this formal pool. Its unusual shape and modestly sized walking surfaces are examples of good, discreet design.

ASSESSING SWIMMING POOL OPTIONS *(continued)*

Types

Pools are installed either in the ground or above it. Your site selection may determine which is better for you. Aboveground pools may not seem as luxurious as inground pools, but they offer certain advantages:

• They're less expensive. True, they take some landscaping to fit, but an inground pool usually requires more plantings.

• They're not as permanent. If you change your mind, you can move or get rid of an aboveground pool. If you are not so sure that you want a pool, you can afford to try an aboveground model as you make your decision.

• They can be safer because very small children usually are unable to make the climb that would allow them to fall into the water. Some attractive decking and fencing right around the pool can add to its safety as well as to its enjoyment and visual appeal.

Inground pools, on the other hand, should be considered major investments. Planning for them is more important than it is for aboveground pools because they are permanent and prominent.

Shapes and materials

Swimming pools today come in almost any shape, from freeform to kidney, oval, L, or rectangle. Rectangular is the most economical.

Your site selection and choice of pool material may help decide your pool shape. Fiberglass pools—perhaps the least expensive—are limited to preformed shapes. So are vinyl-lined pools. Gunite or concrete pools can be built in any shape and generally are more durable.

Knowing how you'll use the pool will also help determine its shape. Lap pools should be long and narrow; often they are shallow. Diving pools take more room and depth where divers enter the water. Rectangular shapes work best for pools used mainly for recreational games such as water volleyball.

If cardiovascular exercise is your main motivation, consider building a lap pool such as this one.

It blends, rather than dominates, and doesn't need to be as deep as a standard pool.

Trees can provide shade, serve as windbreaks, and frame and soften the scene. To avoid overhang and debris, however, keep a good distance between all trees and the pool. Or screen the pool area.

Pick a pool design that fits both the function and feel of the yard and house. Siting, material, and intended use can influence the design. Simple shapes often work better than fanciful ones.

The necessary fencing and equipment storage area should be designed to fit the scene. The surrounding decking also can add greatly to a pool's look and use. Make room for sitting.

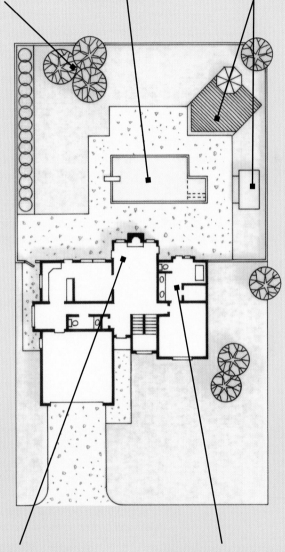

Consider the view from inside the house and during every season of the year. Pools are safer if they're in full view. With proper planning, the scene can be pleasant, even in winter.

Provide access to dressing areas and bathrooms via a water-resistant surface that's also easy on bare feet. Pool use, climate, and ages of swimmers will largely dictate the extras.

ASSESSING SWIMMING POOL OPTIONS *(continued)*

Once you've decided on the site and shape of your pool, carefully consider its size. Some families are happy to have the pool dominate the landscape. They plan the surrounding deck and plantings to eliminate mowing altogether. Others prefer the pool to be secondary in size and importance to other aspects of the garden. Often, however, pool size will be determined by the available space and by budget.

Typically, allow 100 square feet of pool surface for each diver, 24 to 36 square feet for each swimmer, and 10 square feet for each splashing child. If you intend to use your pool for a variety of activities, plan on one that's at least 16×32 feet. In most cases, the smaller the pool, the lower the maintenance costs.

Families may want a shallow section for waders. Underwater benches around the edge of a pool can add to the relaxation and provide footing for babies.

Pool lights

You will want both exterior and underwater lights for your pool to extend the enjoyment and the beauty into warm summer nights. Such lights are good safety and security features too.

Choose both lights and locations to avoid glare in a diver's face or into the house.

Underwater lighting can be regular 120-volt or the lower 12-volt system. The latter is safe, even if it should short, and thus is recommended.

As a general rule, use one lamp for every 24 to 30 linear feet of pool side. In a 16×32-foot pool, for example, you might have three lamps: one on each side and one under the diving board. Put one of the side lights near the ladder or steps.

You also can buy a portable underwater light that is safe, runs on low voltage, and operates on a rechargeable battery. If you have a pool without lighting that's less than 20×30 feet in size, one of these portable lights can yield lovely effects.

Decorative floating lights and candles are striking when people are gathered around but not in a pool.

Other pool components to consider buying are ladders, steps, grab rails, diving and jumping equipment, floating ropes to mark off the deep end, floats for both relaxation and safety, and play equipment for basketball or other games.

Decking

The solid surface surrounding your pool requires both careful planning and its share of costs. It also affects the appeal and enjoyment of your pool.

The width of the solid surface should be a minimum of 3 feet; 6 to 8 feet is much better. More activity will occur around the shallow end of the pool, so if there is to be a wider area of surrounding decking, put it there.

Concrete decking is used most often. It is both practical and economical. Exposed aggregate can add nonskid, nonglare safety and comfort, as well as a richness of color and texture. Both concrete and aggregate can get hot from the searing sun, though; a troweled-on cooling surface that costs more but saves soles is available.

Other pool decking possibilities include modular paving tiles, blocks, bricks, flagstone, and wood.

Wood decking works well where the grade level around a pool changes. Use wood along with concrete for a pleasant contrast.

The material and prominence of the coping that immediately surrounds the pool are largely matters of personal preference. The coping can be a definite, dominating line, or the decking can extend right up to the pool's edge covering it altogether.

Proper drainage of the decking area is vital. Puddles can cause people to slip and fall in summer, and concrete decking to freeze and crack in winter. Runoff of treated water into adjacent planting areas could harm plants.

Pool plantings

Plants near pools should be of the low-care, high-drama variety. For the most part, you should separate plantings somewhat from the pool itself. But placing a few plants so they cast a reflection on the water—such as a raised bed at water's edge—

A fence plus massed plantings are all it takes to create a beautiful oasis for soaking and relaxing.

will relieve the flat surface and increase the effect. Trees and shrubs that are fairly distant from the pool still cast interesting shadows and reflections. If you plant them to the north or west, they'll also reduce chilling breezes without blocking the sun's warmth.

Avoid trees with invasive root systems. Don't plant trees with leaves so tiny that they escape skimmers, nor plants with slippery fruit or small litter; pine needles and bottlebrush stamens clog filters.

Most plants thrive in the increased humidity near a pool, but some are much more sensitive to chemical splashes than others. Fragrance is a valuable plus for poolside flowers, but don't plant bee-favorites nearby. The bees probably would be harmless enough but could cause panic.

Avoid plants that are fussy in any way, that need spraying, or that drop messy leaves, blossoms, or fruits. Among the limited edible choices, bamboo, natal plum, and some herbs are especially good.

Professional help

When building a pool—or even a custom spa—most homeowners work with a pool contractor as well as an architect, landscape architect, or landscape designer. Your hiring decision will depend on your budget, the person's background, and your yard.

Interview and get bids from several pros. Ask to see their previous work and talk with their clients. Make sure that the one you hire has liability insurance and workers' compensation, and check with your own insurance company to see if you need added coverage while work is underway.

Draw up a contract clearly stating who's responsible for zoning compliance and building permits. The contract should include a scale drawing of the location, shape, and dimensions of the pool and its support system. Have an attorney check specifications, such as work to be done, materials to be used, equipment to be installed, and dates to start and finish, as well as the cost of relocating utility lines, clearing access to the site, final grading, and cleanup.

SPAS

If you think your family will ever want a custom-built spa, now's the time to consider when and where you'd want to locate it. Many families prefer to put their spas right next to their pools so that they can jump from one into the other. There are other advantages for this togetherness theory. First of all, if the pool and spa are built into the ground, you'll save money on labor and materials if you install both at the same time. Secondly, this side-by-side arrangement also allows the features to share the same pump and filter.

On the other hand, if you choose a freestanding model, add it whenever and wherever you prefer. You may want it right outside your bedroom, tucked into the corner of your deck, or smack in the middle of your courtyard. But keep in mind that privacy is key to most families' enjoyment of spas, so you might prefer to put your spa in the most secluded spot on your property. This placement, however, does have one big disadvantage: Although a remote spa may be romantic in the summer, the distance between the toasty interior of your home and the spa will feel a lot longer when temperatures drop. One solution to this scenario is to situate your spa just a short dash from a door to your house, then add screening or fencing to create the privacy you want.

When you shop for freestanding spas, be prepared to tell the salesperson the number of people it needs to accommodate, as well as any space limitations you might face. You might be pleasantly surprised by the large number of shapes, sizes, and colors available. Freestanding spas, usually made of fiberglass or vinyl, are the most common and affordable type of spa. They come in a variety of seating configurations, and you can move or remove the complete unit when necessary, even if it's surrounded by a raised deck.

Custom-built spas, usually made of concrete and lined with tile, are often set into the ground to mimic a natural hot spring. This type of unit is generally more expensive than freestanding versions and is less body-conforming than its competitors.

Whichever type you choose, a spa can take the place of a pool if you simply want to relax in water. It won't dominate the landscape, it costs considerably less than a pool, and it's much easier to cover for security purposes. And because a spa's water is heated, it offers you a longer season of use.

EQUIPPING AND MAINTAINING YOUR POOL

Pool water is seldom drained. Rather it's kept clean and healthy by circulation through a system of skimmers, filter, heater (if there is one), lint trap, pump motor, piping, and valves. All of the water in your pool should circulate throughout this system at least once every 8 to 12 hours.

To accomplish this, both the pump and the filter need to be of the proper size for the volume of water in your pool. If oversized, they waste money and electricity; if undersized, they won't do the job and eventually will burn out.

To be safe from puddling and easily accessible for draining, the pump and filter need to be 24 inches above ground level. To save on plumbing and piping costs, place them close to the pool. Include ventilation in any housing that you provide for the equipment.

All pools must have at least one skimmer. More are required for odd-shaped pools than for simple rectangular ones. Maintain the water level at the middle mark of the skimmer.

Filter options
Three types of filters are available, all of which clean by straining the water through a tank containing material that catches dirt and debris.

Diatomaceous earth (DE) filters remove particles as small as a half micron. They require the addition of powder. Cartridge filters remove particles of 20 microns and larger. They must be cleaned or replaced. Sand filters remove particles only as small as 40 microns. Some of the dirt is recycled. To clean these, you must flip a valve to allow water to backwash through the sand and out into a drainage system.

The kind of water you have may dictate your choice of filter. Hard water, for example, often clogs a DE filter.

Hoses are used only on aboveground pools (all inground pools have hard plumbing). These hoses should be changed yearly whether you think they need it or not. Usually people wait until their hose springs a leak. But at that point their pool is half empty, and water is everywhere.

Pool heaters
Three methods are most commonly used for heating pool water: solar heating, conventional heating, and solar covers.

Solar heating requires that the water be circulated through solar-collector panels that face south or just east of south.

A solar heater works only with ample sunshine. If more than half of the days in your area typically are cloudy (check with your local weather bureau), you may need a backup heater. Some systems will switch automatically.

Conventional heaters include gas- and oil-fired heaters and heat pumps.

Solar covers or blankets can raise pool-water temperature by 10 degrees or more, at a fraction of the cost of other heating methods. The covers also lessen the amount of water lost through evaporation. Because they help keep debris out of the pool, they reduce the wear and tear on filters and save on chemicals.

Covers—whether solar or not—can be made to blend in fairly well with pool decor. They also can be installed on tracks for easy removal. Some pool blankets—with properly restrained edges—can support several adults and possibly save a small child from drowning. If a person falls on a free-floating cover, however, the cover could add to the danger of drowning by wrapping around and pulling the person under.

Special chemicals also are available to help cut heating costs. These chemicals increase the surface tension of the water and form a thin, invisible layer that reduces heat loss and evaporation.

Other needs

To keep your pool clean, you will need a net for skimming fallen leaves or dead bugs from the surface.

A must, too, is some type of vacuum cleaner to remove any debris that escapes the filter and settles to the bottom. These vary in price and use from a simple brush and hose attachment for the filter to a separate robot that crawls around the pool bottom.

Winter

Pool winterizing chores vary by climate. Where pool water freezes, lower its level to 2 to 3 inches below the bottom skimmer faceplate in an inground pool. In an aboveground pool, lower the water surface to 24 inches below its usual level.

Clean and treat the water. Drain pipes and place winter plugs in the suction and return fittings. Remove and store ladders, slides, and such. Put an empty barrel in the water to help protect walls against the expansion of freezing.

Covers will prevent evaporation and help keep out dirt and leaves. Water that remains out of sight, however, often is neglected. In the South, pull back the cover at least every month and treat the water as needed.

When removing a cover, take care not to let the accumulated gunk and untreated water that collects on top of the cover get into the pool.

ELECTRICAL NEEDS

A swimming pool requires electricity for the water circulation system, for lighting, and possibly for heating and nearby outdoor power receptacles. For maximum economy and efficiency, consider your electrical needs and wants thoroughly when planning your pool.

Strictly follow code requirements for the wiring and grounding of all equipment associated with a swimming pool as well as the bonding and grounding of all metallic additions. Power outlets must be at least 18 inches above the level of the pool apron and fully protected. The electrical service to the pool must have its own circuit; so must the pump and filter. An electrician or your pool contractor can check your current amperage capacity to ensure that it's adequate for your pump.

POOL CHEMICALS

You can have pool experts come weekly to check and add pool chemicals or you can do it yourself with the aid of a simple test kit.

Chlorine—in the form of powders, tablets, or other stabilized forms—is added to pools on a day-to-day basis to meet regular needs. It's also added at intervals—after heavy rains, for example—in shock form.

Such shock treatments work better if you check and adjust the pH level first. That way, the chlorine immediately attacks and destroys bacteria and algae, and is quickly expended or exhausted in the process.

Shock your water after, not immediately before, swimming. Apply the treatment after heavy rain, extensive use, or whenever the color of the pool water begins to turn green or brown, an indication of algae growth. If the water does not return to its clear, clean color, you may need to add an algaecide.

Milder sanitizing chemicals that take longer to work but have a less irritating effect on the skin and eyes of extra-sensitive people are available.

Also test weekly the balance of the pH levels in the pool. Do this more often in very hot weather or with heavy use. If the reading is below 7.2 or above 7.6, add the needed chemicals.

Total alkalinity in the water is the measure of carbonates and bicarbonates. This measure should range from 60 to 100 ppm for best chlorine effectiveness and scale control, minimum eye and skin irritation, and least corrosion.

GALLERY OF SWIMMING POOL AND SPA IDEAS

When viewed from the opposite end of the pool, this end appears to have a disappearing edge. The waterfall, spa, and adjacent deck create a secluded area for relaxing.

A keyhole-shape spa becomes a decorative addition to a contemporary stone patio. The vine-covered fence and stately magnolia tree provide soft contrast against the cool stone.

Here's proof that your swimming pool doesn't have to look like, well, a swimming pool. In fact this scene seems to be right out of some tropical paradise. The artificial boulder surround and waterfalls are very realistic.

258

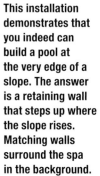

This installation demonstrates that you indeed can build a pool at the very edge of a slope. The answer is a retaining wall that steps up where the slope rises. Matching walls surround the spa in the background.

If you have a big yard, it can accommodate a good-size, kidney-shape pool like this one. There's even space for an extended lounging area that continues the curved lines of the pool.

CREATING THE ULTIMATE LIGHTING SCHEME

When Louis XVI strolled with his courtiers through the gardens of Versailles, thousands of torches lit the way. Today you don't have to be royalty to enjoy the wonder of the garden at night. After sunset, even the most modest of gardens can assume a regal enchantment, thanks to skillfully used lighting.

Most outdoor settings, however, disappear into the dark when the sun goes down. Sometimes they lack even enough lighting to satisfy safety and security requirements.

The benefits of the right decorative lighting scheme are numerous. With today's busy schedules, people do most of their relaxing and entertaining after nightfall. Garden lighting can stretch the hours of outdoor living, as well as the seasons of garden enjoyment. Few activities are more exciting for children or adults than to go out in the first snowfall of the season or to step outdoors after dinner on an unusually warm evening in February.

Lights on and around a deck invite long evenings of pleasant visiting. Path lights in the adjacent landscape make the homeowners and their visitors feel more surefooted and welcome. Various

downlights serve as task lights, making it possible to read, cook, or traverse the deck's multiple levels after sunset.

When done well, garden lighting also creates a living mural beyond your windows, which you can enjoy without venturing outdoors in rain, ice, or cold. Well-placed and carefully chosen fixtures can create dramatic pools of light near plants or structures and direct the patterns of shadows. This same lighting can play up interesting textures and forms—whether of foliage or branches.

New or evolving gardens sometimes benefit the most from lighting. Precisely aimed fixtures can illuminate the garden's outstanding features and cast the rest into darkness.

Even if you cherish the peace darkness brings, you can enjoy the diffused perimeter lighting of garden features. A wide variety of fixtures is available that offer glow without glare.

Best of all, today's low-voltage kits let you install energy-efficient garden lights quickly with minimal expense, no electrician, and complete safety. See the following pages for more on selecting, placing, and installing outdoor lights.

Low-voltage light fixtures along this walkway bestow a warm glow to plantings and invite nighttime strolls. Such subtle and diffused lighting often makes gardens look better than ever while also creating magical moods.

Pole lights, wall-mounted fixtures, spots under the overhangs, and ground-level uplights comprise a well-coordinated scheme designed for safety, security, and mood.

ASSESSING LIGHTING OPTIONS

Study the exciting possibilities for outdoor lights carefully before you buy the first bulb. Decide what effect will add the most enjoyment—both visual and recreational—to each area of your yard.

To begin, go outside at dusk and again after dark with a strong flashlight or a trouble light on a long extension cord. Shine the light in different directions, trying to play up moods rather than simulating daylight.

Lights pointing down give a broad, natural highlight to interesting features of the yard. Upward lighting makes leaves glow. Backlighting accents the drama of a tree or structure, particularly if the lighted object is in front of a plain surface.

Lights diffused with translucent screens shine down subtly from high in a tree or on the side of a house, mimicking moonlight. Lights that graze or wash across an interesting architectural surface, such as a fence or chimney, can be striking.

The height and brightness of a light, as well as the direction of its reflector, will change the effect. Avoid glare in a stroller's eyes or on nearby properties, especially into windows.

Drawing a plan

Once you've developed your lighting ideas, lay tracing paper over your landscape plan and mark which light types you want placed where. Try to visualize the overall look. The goal is to highlight certain use areas and visual elements in the landscape, while at the same time provide a low level of light throughout to give the site warmth and charm.

If your house is in the planning stage, let the electrician who wires the house install major fixtures such as door lights, floodlights, and post lights. These will have bright lights that operate on the same 120-volt system as your house. If your house and yard are established, hire an electrician; tackle simpler 120-volt installations yourself if local code allows; or work with easy-to-install but less versatile 12-volt lighting systems.

Here, three types of lighting—path lights flanking the walkway, accent lights on the edge of the deck, and spots highlighting the fountain—work together to create a beautiful scene.

Wide-spreading lights accent the patio plantings and the rock garden. Illuminating one area or both at the same time shifts the focal point and feel of the garden at night.

Diffused lights wash the fence and hedge to create a soft backdrop for the yard. The lighting visually spreads out rather than closes in the space, yet forms a frame for the setting.

Pole lights around the gazebo and low-level patio lights near the house emit enough illumination for outdoor living without glaring or intruding on the peace of the evening.

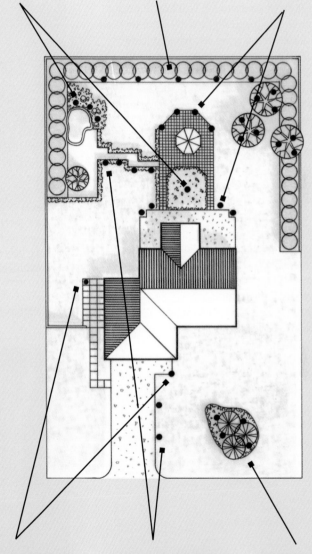

Bright post lights near the entry and the service area enable people to come and go, work on the car, or unload groceries after dusk. Additionally they provide security.

At the front of the house, low-level drive and walk lights extend a sense of welcome or safe return. In back, they connect the patio and rock garden, encouraging evening garden walks.

Lights hung in or directed up into the trees move the eye up from the ground to give that all-important third dimension to the night garden. They highlight patterns and textures.

263

ASSESSING LIGHTING OPTIONS *(continued)*

Put switches indoors if possible. That way, you can enjoy the sight of your garden late into the night or in bad weather, when you really don't want to go outside to turn lights on and off. Also consider whether you want a central switch to command all lights, several switches so you can use them separately, or an automatic timer. If you have a 120-volt system and only one central switch, be prepared for some high electric bills.

Low-voltage highlights

Low-voltage fixtures let you light up the night without burning out the budget—either for installation or operation. Their secret is the transformer or power pack; it reduces to 12 volts the 120-volt current from any grounded outlet.

Few code restrictions apply, so you usually can set up these lamps without an electrician. The wiring is so safe that it need not always be buried, and it doesn't need encasing in conduit.

There are drawbacks. The transformers usually can handle only five or six fixtures, with bulbs no brighter than 75 watts. Also, the longer the run of wire, the dimmer the light.

On the plus side, you'll find an increasing array of affordable fixtures available to complement any style of landscape and house. Quality fixtures, made to weather the elements and last for years, function like jewelry and provide an attractive finishing touch.

FIXTURES

SOLAR LIGHTS are the answer when the feature or pathway you want to illuminate is a long way from an outdoor receptacle. Each fixture has a tiny photovoltaic panel that converts sunlight into electricity during daylight hours, storing power in a small battery until it's needed after dark.

POST LIGHTS extend the effectiveness of fixtures located next to or above your entry by illuminating the important space between the curb and your house. They can be powered by your home's electrical service or by the sun.

WELL LIGHTS are low-profile units that are set in a shallow well below ground level and pointed up to illuminate trees, shrubs, or walls. The well shields the bulb and prevents glare. Some models resemble stones or other objects.

SUBMERGED LIGHTING creates a lovely, luminous addition to a water garden and extends enjoyment of it after sunset. A timer kit allows you to set the time that the lights turn on and off.

GARDEN LIGHTS come in many interesting shapes, from long, sparkling sticks to round stepping-stones that have low-voltage bulbs in grooves around the edges. Some hang on fences or strings like Christmas lights. Others provide safety lighting under deck railings or steps.

PATH LIGHTS direct their beams downward. They come in many styles, such as tulip, bollard, and post lights. Use them wherever you'd like a muted pool of illumination.

MUSHROOM LIGHTS—sometimes with large shades—direct a subtle shine downward on walks, steps, or plants. Shade or height changes alter the width and intensity of the circle of light.

HALOGEN SPOTLIGHT bulbs shine whiter and brighter than ordinary incandescent bulbs. Because they're so efficient, they can be small enough to use in a low-voltage system yet produce as much light as a regular bulb.

SPOTLIGHTS focus intense beams on an object, as well as provide security. Use them in the yard for dramatic effect, illuminating focal points, creating shadows, and lighting large areas from above. For vertical emphasis, install them in the ground and point them skyward. Use these units sparingly, however, because they tend to overwhelm the rest of your yard lights.

ACCENT LIGHTS, available in a variety of shapes, sizes, and brightness, give garden features more prominence at night. Change the direction of the light to create different effects.

INSTALLING LOW-VOLTAGE LIGHTING

It's easy to install a variety of low-voltage lights around the landscape within a couple of hours.

You can buy either the individual elements or a kit that contains the lights, the cable, and a transformer sized correctly for the amount of power the fixtures and cable will draw. (If you buy the parts individually, be sure to add up the total number of watts the bulbs will use, then pick a transformer that will handle at least 50 percent more.) In most cases, a kit is a good choice. The main drawback to this option is that you won't usually be able to expand a kit because of the limitations of its transformer and its lights.

Plan the route of your lights and decide how many you need. To install, mount the transformer near an outlet. Put it as close to the fixtures as possible. If the kit includes a photosensitive control that turns lights on at dusk and off at dawn, be sure to position the sensor so that it's exposed to daylight but not to artificial light at night.

Determine your layout and arrange the lights where they'll go. To insert a fixture into the ground, first try spiking it in. If the ground is hard, slice it with a shovel and then shove the light into the slice. As you install the remaining lights, make sure the last one is within reach of the cable.

Starting at the transformer—and leaving enough extra cable to reach from it to the ground—route the rest of the cable from light to light until you've reached the last fixture.

Most kits come with simple devices that connect each light to the cable. Position the two parts of the connector over the cable, then snap them together on the cable.

4

Dig a shallow trench, lay the cable in the trench, and cover it with soil; top with mulch or sod. Because the cable carries only 12 volts, the wiring isn't dangerous.

5

Strip the ends of the cable wires and connect them to the transformer's terminals. Turn on the system to check if the fixtures are working and casting light the way you want. If not snap them elsewhere on the cable.

If one of the lights doesn't work after you've plugged in the circuit, the pierce-points inside the connector may have missed the wire inside the cable. If so, repair the connection the old-fashioned way: Cut the cable, strip its wires, strip the lamp wires, then make connections with wire nuts. Protect the unions with heat-shrink rubber tubing.

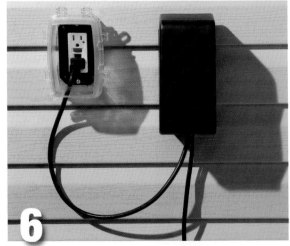

6

Mount the transformer where it's unlikely to be bumped. Plug into a GFCI receptacle that's fitted with a watertight cover. If the receptacle is located in a remote box far from the house, set a small post next to it to hold the transformer.

7

The transformer can be set to turn the lights on when it gets dark. Otherwise, you may choose to program the timer to turn on and off at certain times.

CREATING THE ULTIMATE PLAY AREA

Your yard should be primarily a place for family members of all ages to play and enjoy the outdoors.

The same children who drive you crazy indoors can delight you with their wonder and imaginations outside. Teenagers can spend hours shooting baskets or giggling on a distant private swing. Grown-and-gone young adults will return periodically and want a lively game of volleyball or badminton. Older folks can pitch horseshoes or play shuffleboard, or just enjoy one another's company on a porch swing.

Planning

The ideal play area doesn't develop haphazardly. It's designed and situated so that it directs kid traffic away from a potential danger, such as a busy street, to the desired avenue of escape, such as a treehouse. It's fashioned so that it neither violates nor dominates the rest of the landscape.

The play area should allow room to roam without fear of unplanned encounters with obstacles. That's easy, of course, in a big yard. But even the smallest outdoor space can become an ideal play area with the right planning and equipment. After all, a single swing hung from a tree branch can provide hours of entertainment.

The ideal play area also should offer children and adults special places for private retreats (though, for children, it should be somewhere they can be seen).

Growth and play

Because children grow quickly and adult interests change over time, the best play area relies more on convertible and multifunction uses and fixtures than on permanent, unchangeable installations such as tennis courts.

A good play area can offer something for children in a range of ages or for children of one age for several years. When choosing a play structure, look for one with many possible uses; it will hold children's attention longer. Once swinging is passé, the kids can slide or play house on a platform.

What's a better pastime to bring together parents and kids than a putting green? You can buy special material made for do-it-yourself greens or plant bentgrass and keep it closely mowed.

This playhouse, built amid mature trees, has multiple entries. It's made to be big enough for kids of all ages (even adults) to enjoy it. The area underneath the structure is ideal for a sandbox.

Surrounded by brick terraces, enclosed by a unique metal fence, and approached by a classy series of masonry steps and landings, this rather formal, multipurpose play court satisfies all ages.

269

ASSESSING PLAY AREA OPTIONS

Location of play areas is important. They'll be used more hours of the day and seasons of the year if they have some sun and some shade. A sense of seclusion and some wind protection also add to kids' enjoyment.

Few yards have as much space for play as most families desire, but you can condense the games. An area as small as 20×40 feet can work if you make a point not to plant a tree in the middle. You can set short pieces of tile or pipe in concrete in the ground and take down or put up poles or stakes as needed.

Concentrating plants around the edges of a yard will yield the most open play space. Be sure to surround play areas with expendable plants. If games are frequent and space is at a premium, try putting tender plants in movable containers and planting only the most rugged ones in the ground.

Use tough turfgrass such as tall fescue where the neighborhood kids gather for football or baseball. Around play structures, a soft surface underfoot is best. This can be grass, though it will become spotted from wear and tear, feet will get wet, and mowing will be more difficult. If you use sand or mulches such as pea gravel or tanbark, you may want to lay plastic underneath and spread the mulch thick enough that weeds will not grow through.

As children grow older, you can emphasize to them how their strength and skill have outgrown the yard and strongly suggest that they move on to the nearest park. Or you may turn the tired patch of green into a swimming pool at that time.

Play structures

Design and build your own play structure or assemble one using plans or a kit. When selecting equipment, consider first the ages of your children and what will best help them develop muscular coordination, self-confidence, and creativity.

Locate play structures where they'll be used and where you can keep an eye on the kids often from indoors.

With a basketball court and a swimming pool in your yard, there's no doubt the kids will be drawn outdoors to play.

Locate play areas where kids have lots of open space to run and far enough from the house so you're separated from the noise. Put play structures on a level surface.

Overhanging trees and adventurous children can do one another possible damage. Plan for safety by installing plenty of sturdy railings or downplay the temptation with separation.

Look up and around before you make a final decision. Keep high-flying activities away from power lines, balls away from the street, and tricycle-riding areas away from driveways.

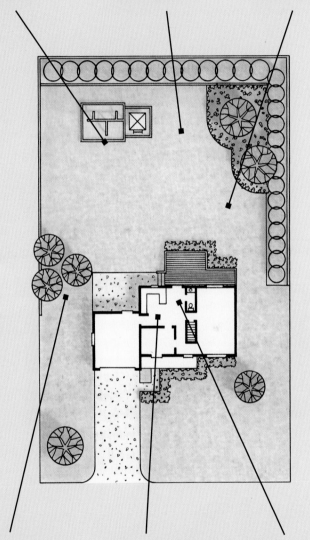

Avoid putting play areas near gardens you want to protect. Any planting behind home plate or first base will be trampled often. Here the gardens are deep in right field.

For peace of mind, position play areas within easy view from indoor rooms (usually the kitchen or family room) where you can watch your children while you work or rest.

Consider easy access between the kids and the bathroom to allow for inevitable emergency runs. Make sure your path to play areas is unimpeded, too, for quick access if needed.

271

ASSESSING PLAY AREA OPTIONS *(continued)*

A green screen of mixed shrubs provides a buffer between the deck and a nearby play structure.

Instead of dominating the yard, the play area fades into the background, yet it is within supervisory view.

eave plenty of room for swing clearance and slide landings. Check equipment often for rough edges, splinters, or protruding pieces that could cut or scratch. All bolts should have smooth heads and covered ends. Firmly anchor the bases in concrete. Ask children to report any damage and involve them in frequent maintenance checks.

Make sure that swings, ladder rungs, and ropes are at usable heights. On many units, you can add additional features as children grow, thus keeping their interest and spreading out your costs.

Equipment that is beyond little ones' capabilities should be safely out of their reach and is better out of their sight.

Sand castles

Sand provides great entertainment for kids of all ages, whether it's in a tractor tire, a sunken pit, or a veritable backyard beach. Provide good drainage under inground boxes by lining the bottom with gravel or flagstones.

A retaining edge can serve as a seat or a drying surface for sand pies—as well as keep the bulk of the sand inside the box. Put the box far enough from the house so that the sand kids carry out of the box on their clothes has a chance to sift off. A cover is nice, especially if cats are around.

Sandboxes, which can occupy unused corners as long as they are in view from the house, are easily converted back to gardens when the time is right.

Private worlds

Hiding places are great for children of all ages. These can be as elaborate as treehouses and playhouses or as simple as a cubby under the deck or on the far side of a sheltering tree. Shrubs and trees, especially those with pendulous or weeping branches, are great for games of hide-and-seek. A pole tepee or a little house covered with beans or flowering vines also can make an inexpensive playhouse.

SAFE DIMENSIONS FOR PLAY EQUIPMENT

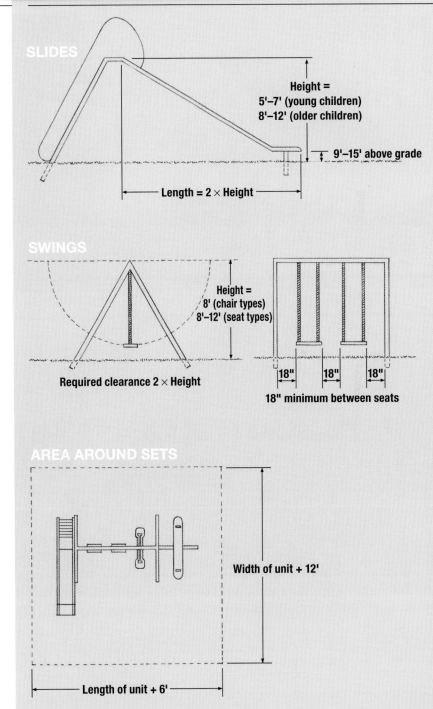

SLIDES

Height =
5'–7' (young children)
8'–12' (older children)

9'–15' above grade

Length = 2 × Height

SWINGS

Height =
8' (chair types)
8'–12' (seat types)

Required clearance 2 × Height

18"   18"   18"

18" minimum between seats

AREA AROUND SETS

Width of unit + 12'

Length of unit + 6'

GALLERY OF PLAY AREA IDEAS

Sturdy beams support this elevated and railed play tower. Ropes hanging above the ladder and swing give a steadying hand to all users.

Three levels are at play here—the floor of the two-story playhouse at right, the elevated platform built around the tree, and ground level. A big plus: There's plenty of room to store toys under both structures.

Tall brick walls and a door define this youngster's private courtyard. A cantilevered slab leads from the house to a sand base, suitable for roughhousing. And the two waterspouts are hard to resist.

There's no end to the fun and exercise kids can get in their multipurpose play area. Large beams, well anchored in the ground, support steps, climbing bars, a roofed lookout, and a slide.

A thick layer of mulch offers soft landings for kids enjoying a play structure. A strong railing around the raised platform provides additional protection.

275

CREATING THE ULTIMATE PORCH OR SCREENED ROOM

Porches are back in style—in a big way. Many new houses come with them, sometimes on the front, sides, and back. And older homes are getting new leases on life as families add porches or convert covered patios to screened-in living space.

Check out porches in your area and browse through some books, magazines, and catalogs for the look you want to achieve. Pay particular attention to the screening itself. (Note that black screening is less noticeable than the other colors.) Then study the characteristics of the various screening materials before you proceed:

• Fiberglass screening is the least expensive and comes in a range of colors. Although it's more forgiving than metal, fiberglass must be anchored tightly or it will sag.

• Aluminum is somewhat more expensive and slightly harder to work with, but it maintains a crisp and taut appearance for years.

• Bronze screening—actually 90 percent copper and 10 percent zinc—is a more practical material for oceanside properties because it stands up to the corrosion that damages aluminum. However bronze material is about triple the cost of aluminum.

• Solar screening—vinyl-coated fiberglass—blocks 50–90 percent of the sun's heat and glare, protecting furniture from fading. However, its tight weave results in poorer visibility. It's twice the price of aluminum.

• Woven vinyl-polyester resin screening, though often difficult to find locally, is seven times stronger than fiberglass, making it quite tear- and hole-resistant. As a result, it's effective in those areas where pets can reach the screening. It's about twice the cost of aluminum.

Translucent glass panels in the roof cap off this bright and airy porch and protect the family from rain except on very windy days. Widespread wall dividers and arching spaces at the top maximize exterior vistas.

Shuttered doors at the end of this enclosed porch serve as a backdrop for a whimsical swinging bed, suspended by chains from the ceiling. This setting qualifies as today's version of the old sleeping porch.

This porch provides an ideal indoor-outdoor room. Its stone fireplace, knotty pine wood, and cozy furnishings invite you to sit, relax, and let problems evaporate.

ASSESSING SCREENED ROOM AND PORCH OPTIONS

A new screened porch blends with the house when painted to match. Paint pros can mix paint to match an old and faded color if necessary.

One of your key decisions is whether you want to attach your new screened room directly to your house or put it somewhere else on your property. Take an inventory of your landscape. Do you have a concrete slab that's in fairly good condition or a remote deck that you'd use much more frequently if it were free of bugs? Is there space near your pool to add an outdoor room? Would your outdoor cooking area benefit from a protected sanctuary next to it? Do you already have an open porch that simply needs to be screened—or partially screened if it's extra large?

Once you've done this inventory and chosen the overall design, spend some time planning the interior features of your project. Do you want an overhead fan, a swing, even a fireplace? Do you plan to use new or existing furniture or install a rainproof seating unit around the perimeter? How about the flooring and ceiling—fancy or rustic, bright-colored or subdued? To jog your creativity, check catalogs, magazines, and books.

Then decide how you want to install the screening. Some builders like to sandwich the screening between pieces of trim or staple it to rectangular frames that are screwed into openings in the porch framing. Others prefer to use a track system—attached to the framing, either inside or out—that holds the screening in place thanks to a special spline–and-roller process that uses a cap piece to cover the edges of the screening.

The family whose project is pictured here chose to enclose an existing back covered patio with materials to match their house. The roof and its supports gave them a head start on the process— no need to pour footings, install posts, or pour a slab—so the rest of the project moved along well.

278

BUILDING SCREENED ROOMS

Fill in the walls with 2×4 framing, including toe plate and top plate. Space the vertical studs to accommodate the width of the screen sections. Install crosspieces between studs at the point where the stub wall ends and the screened sections begin. (You can directly nail or screw through the uprights on every other crosspiece; for the others, use toe nailing.)

Run the wiring for a switch and ceiling fan plus whatever receptacles you might want in the walls. Then cut and install the interior wall surfaces—in this case pine-and-plywood beaded paneling that comes in 4×8 sheets. You will probably need to trim the bottoms of the panels if the floor is uneven.

Cut and install preprimed 4×8 ceiling panels, fastening to the ceiling joists. A rented nail gun and air compressor make this job easier. Don't be concerned about the seams where the end of one panel meets another; you'll cover them later with wood trim.

Connect the wires to the ceiling fan, then hang the fan support column from its base and attach with screws. Nail preprimed trim pieces to the ceiling to cover the panel seams.

BUILDING SCREENED ROOMS (continued)

5

Apply exterior paint to the lap siding; allow it to dry overnight, then add a second coat. Thoroughly coat both the back and front.

6

Nail the pieces of lap siding in place—one at a time—from the bottom up. Mark each piece for a consistent exposure or reveal.

7

As you install the siding, leave the perimeter frame uncovered to accept the grid pieces.

8

Hang the screen door, according to the manufacturer's instructions. (The critical work was done in advance when the carpenter installed and plumbed the door framing.)

9 To install the screening, first screw vinyl grid pieces to the exterior framing around the entire perimeter of each screening opening.

10 Then cover the spline and channel by tapping a cap piece onto the base grid; this cap also locks the screening in place.

11 Stretch the screening across the grids and use a roller to force a spline—and the screening—into a channel in the grid. Trim off excess screening, being careful not to pull it out of its channel.

The finished project adds elegant usefulness to a once sparse patio that was home to mosquitoes. And the new lines flow smoothly into the rest of the house, enhancing the house's size and appearance.

CREATING THE ULTIMATE OUTDOOR KITCHEN OR DINING ROOM

You've probably noticed that no matter where you put the appetizers and beverages inside your house, guests tend to hang out in your kitchen. So why not set up the same appeal outdoors?

The outdoor kitchen is quickly evolving from a simple barbecue area into a full-fledged, hardworking kitchen, complete with appliances, prep space, storage cabinets, and a permanent roof.

If you're thinking of creating your own outdoor cooking paradise, here's a beginning checklist:

- List the activities you want to include. Do you want to concentrate on grilling—or add a range and oven so that you can prepare other dishes? How many cooks will you want to accommodate simultaneously? Will this spot be more a party place than a cook's kitchen? Do you anticipate a lot of sit-down entertaining? Do you want to have a bar somewhere—either nearby or as an integral element of your kitchen? Will you want buffet lines?
- What cooking supplies will you need? Do you want to have spices, cooking oils, pastas, and other ingredients on hand? Do you plan on having an inventory of dishes, glassware, and silverware?
- Determine your other storage needs. List the larger items you'll want on the scene—pots and pans, griddles, small appliances, containers for leftovers, and the like. Then map out the amount of space you'll need in the form of base cabinets, wall cabinets, open shelving, and counter area.
- Evaluate your site options. Is space available just off your indoor kitchen? Can you add a roof there without running into complications? Would an existing patio serve as a potential site? Does the slope of your land add complications? Would a step-down or step-up deck solve your problems?
- Factor in an appropriate dining area. Do you prefer a group of tables under umbrellas? Under a roof?
- Choose weather-resistant building products, such as stainless-steel appliances and stone or similar materials for flooring and countertops.
- Carefully plan your plumbing. If you live in an area where the winters are cold, make sure you'll be able to disconnect and drain the water supply easily.

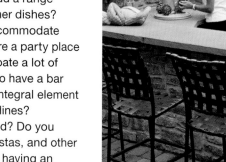

A bold white pergola extends over this upscale cooking area, structurally connecting it with the house. A classic fireplace with a massive chimney surround adds glamor.

In this stone-wall kitchen, the all-weather counter is at bar height to accommodate guests on one side while you prepare refreshments on the other.

This gazebo has about three times the usual space, but it's also outfitted with a wraparound grill kitchen and a spacious dining area—all with a beautiful, open view.

ASSESSING OUTDOOR KITCHEN OPTIONS

Once you've put your plans on paper, the next step is to involve a professional designer who can review your initial thinking with you and recommend improvements. This type of project isn't necessarily cheap—you can easily spend $50,000 on a first-class version—and you don't want to invest money in an effort that may have pitfalls you'll regret a few years down the line. Moreover, the pro might suggest that you proceed in planned stages, so you can pay as you go.

At the least, many homeowners want to start out with a grill, a refrigerator, and a prep sink, then expand from there. But the expansion can't be willy-nilly, so that's why you want to spend time envisioning what might come in the following years.

As you evaluate your cooking equipment, remember that outdoor cooking and dining are usually casual affairs. You may want to plan on simpler cuisine outside and save the more intricate dishes for a controlled indoor setting. This means you may need only a full-size refrigerator, a built-in grill with auxiliary burners, and a sizable island—with standard sink—for preparing and serving food. And if you're setting up a snack center for the kids and their friends, all it really needs are a basic refrigerator, a microwave oven, and a small work counter with a sink for simple food prep and cleanup.

Rotisserie ovens or meat smokers are both naturals for an outdoor kitchen, and you can either install them at the beginning or wait until later.

Although rain is the bane of the outdoor chef, you can protect your outdoor kitchen with an awning and install a permanent roof later on.

One last option: Be aware that permanent installations aren't your only choice. You can buy modular components for an outdoor kitchen—mounted on casters for portability—that let you set things up as needed and roll them into a storage shed when you need the space for another activity.

After you've solidified your initial plan, ask yourself if it reflects a thoughtful commitment to a minimum level of function. If it does, your project is worthwhile. So get started and let the fun begin.

A curving seating area below a gently arcing pergola creates a stylish backdrop for this sitting/dining area. Its hand-built oven is much more appropriate for this look than is a standard grill.

Tucked into a corner of the lot and fenced off for privacy is a gorgeous stone fireplace. Upper shelves and matching counters frame a sink at left and a grill at right.

284

In this example a patio adjoining the house is home to a cooking and dining area only a few steps from the indoor kitchen. The stainless-steel grill is built into a long, low buffet-look cabinet that's topped by an extra-long counter.

BUILDING FIRE PITS

There's something relaxing and mesmerizing about an open fire. It can turn an evening into something special. You have many options to consider—a stone fireplace, a raised or sunken fire pit, a stone-encased oven, or a wide array of portable units on the market.

Before you build or buy anything, check your local codes for any regulations that might affect you. Some authorities want to inspect your site, while others may require you to apply for a recreational burning permit. And in some areas any sort of open fire is illegal—either at all times or when dry-weather burning bans are in effect.

Also be very careful in choosing a site for your pit. Keep it a safe distance from your house, outbuildings, fencing, and any other flammable or heat-sensitive items. And avoid locations that are under or near tree branches.

Many of the more complex fireplaces require an experienced stonemason who specializes in fireplace construction, because a good fireplace needs to draw well and has to be structually sound.

Fortunately, however, most do-it-yourselfers find they are capable of constructing a fire pit, mainly because it doesn't need a chimney or a complicated support system.

If you have a safe site and get the go-ahead from local authorities, here's an attractive yet easy-to-build fire pit that will provide you and your family with many enjoyable experiences.

Lay a perimeter surround, using the same kind of base you installed in the pit and matching the blocks as well as you can. Then gather around and initiate your new outdoor treasure.

Start by finding a flat area at least 10 to 12 feet in diameter. Use a stake, string, and spray paint to draw the perimeter of the pit. Dig out dirt within the marked circle; this pit is 56 inches in diameter and will be 18 inches deep.

2 Fill the pit with 6 inches of gravel; rake it smooth and tamp after each load to ensure a solid base. Then spread a thin layer of coarse sand over the gravel. Tamp the sand as well and make sure the surface is level.

3 To create the fire pit surround, use small, modular retaining-wall units. Use string and spray paint to mark an inner circle—a 38-inch inner diameter, in this case—as a guideline for placing the first layer of retaining wall.

4 Place the first row of retaining-wall units in a complete circle, tamping them into the gravel and sand base with a mallet. Use a level to make sure the units are level from side to side and front to back.

5 Add a second row of retaining wall blocks. Look for interlocking units to simplify this step. Add the top row of coping blocks, using a concrete-compatible construction adhesive to glue these blocks into place.

11

SERVICE AREAS

Like a smash hit at the theater, an enchanting landscape relies as much on what happens behind the scenes as it does on the drama before your eyes. A yard's backstage—its service areas—should organize and hide tools and trash, cars and compost, air-conditioning and other utilities, gardens and potting areas, mowers and miscellaneous items. Keeping necessary elements out of sight but within easy reach goes a long way toward enhancing your landscape's livability. And performing essential chores becomes more satisfying too.

Tucked into the back wall of a garage, this garden galley includes generous storage as well as a potting bench. The cupboards and counter are shielded from rainfall.

The 12-foot-long workbench hosts a variety of tasks, from potting plants to completing carpentry projects. Beneath the counter, there's more space for storage.

A vine-laced trellis screens the work space from nearby patio seating. An overhead beam is part of a pergola that extends from this area down the adjoining walkway.

Brick pavers form a wash-and-wear floor that matches the adjoining walkway and nearby patio.

ASSESSING SERVICE AREA OPTIONS

Tired of backing out the car every time the lawn needs mowing? Making visitors hike from the street because there's no place for them to park on your property? Though not the most glamorous parts of a landscaping scheme, service areas—convenient but inconspicuous—should be intrinsic elements in the master plan for your yard.

The pages that follow shed light on the process of planning and building storage sheds, driveways, and potting areas. Here are some other points to ponder as you plan ways to put your yard at your service.

Paving options

For driveways and other service areas, you'll need sturdy, goodlooking surfaces that require minimal upkeep from year to year. Here are your major service area paving choices:

• Concrete lasts for years with little maintenance. It also offers you many ways to introduce texture, pattern, and color to your landscaping scheme.

• Asphalt costs somewhat less than concrete, but working with large expanses of it requires expertise and equipment beyond the reach of most do-it-yourselfers. The final surface texture of an asphalt installation depends for the most part on the size of the aggregate used by the asphalt supplier. Color usually varies only with age. When first installed, asphalt is a rich black; after a few years it weathers to a medium-to-light gray unless you reseal it with a tar-based coating. Asphalt can be tinted, but you may find the cost of doing that prohibitive.

• Loose fills, including materials such as rock, pebbles, and sand, can be installed with less grading and less subsurface preparation than concrete or asphalt, and they cost less than either. Also, loose fills that have been in place for several years make an excellent base for concrete or asphalt paving. The most economical loose fill to use depends on the materials readily available in your area. Loose fills come in a variety of colors too. The biggest problem with them is that they don't always stay in place. Besides migrating to the lawn when children are around, loose fill can stick to shoes and the treads of tires, wash away during rainstorms, or be shoveled up with snow in winter. Loose fill also is not a good choice for a steep drive.

• Brick makes an elegant surfacing material for service areas. The cost ranges from moderate, if the bricks are set in sand, to very costly, if you decide to first pour a concrete slab, then mortar the bricks to it. Some types of brick can become quite slippery when they're wet; these are not a good choice for steep drives.

Vegetable gardens

Raising even a few juicy tomatoes or crunchy radishes is an enjoyable, delicious, and educational experience for the entire family.

As you plan the crops for a vegetable garden, bear in mind that some plants require more space than others in proportion to their yield. Corn, for instance, though a favorite, produces relatively few ears per square foot of garden. Tomatoes, on the other hand, produce pounds of succulent fruit in only a few square yards of space.

Location is the key to a successful vegetable garden. Vegetables need a lot of sun—at least six hours of full sun per day for warm-season crops such as melons, corn, and tomatoes. Plant tall crops where they will not cast a shadow over smaller plants. Perennials such as asparagus and rhubarb should get a spot that is free of traffic and undisturbed by the plow or tiller.

The quality and nature of the soil also are important to a vegetable garden's success. Most plants do best in slightly acid soil.

Concrete patches separated by strips of turf break up the monotony of one large poured slab and complement the architecture of this house. The same treatment continues as an entry walk.

ASSESSING SERVICE AREA OPTIONS *(continued)*

To test for this and for the soil's fertility, use a soil-testing kit, available from most garden-supply outlets. Your county extension office also can arrange for a test at the nearest soil-testing station. Even the poorest soil is easily improved by adding compost, manure, and other organic matter. See below for more about compost heaps.

Cutting gardens

Tempted to bring the beauty of a flower garden inside? To enjoy your own cut flowers without having to give up the wealth of color outside, plant a cutting garden. For a listing of popular landscape flowers, see pages 387-393.

The best place for a cutting garden is a separate and relatively unseen site set aside specifically for growing indoor bouquets. It could be in a backyard or simply tucked behind a taller flowerbed that's intended for show. If space is tight, or if you simply don't have time to tend two gardens, design a single garden that's so well planned, varied, and abundant that flowers cut from carefully chosen sections won't be missed. Or combine your cutting garden with a vegetable planting area.

Compost heaps

As mentioned earlier, a compost heap provides a thrifty way to organically nourish any type of garden—and lets you recycle leaves, clippings, and food wastes that would otherwise be thrown out.

Think carefully about where to set up your composting area. You'll need a fairly level spot with reasonably good drainage. Avoid placing the heap in a depression, where the compost could become waterlogged during a wet season.

Your location also should be close to a water supply—or at least within reach of a garden hose—so that if the compost becomes too dry, you can easily sprinkle it down.

A shady spot is preferable because too much sun will dry out the pile too frequently. The compost heap also should be close to your garden, accessible to a wheelbarrow, and screened from outdoor living areas.

Although not absolutely necessary, an enclosure around your compost heap makes the pile much easier to build and maintain. An enclosure also helps keep loose materials from blowing around your yard.

The type of bin you build can be simple or elaborate, depending on the construction materials you decide on. Bricks, concrete blocks, wire, snow fencing, and wood all work well. If you use wood, however, bear in mind that the same bacteria that are working in the compost pile also will be trying to break down the wood. Use only cedar, cypress, redwood, or pressure-treated lumber.

Also remember to build your enclosure so that air can get in to nourish the bacteria. Lay concrete blocks so that the holes are horizontal; if you use wood, leave space between the boards.

A common size for a compost bin is 4 feet square by 3 to 4 feet high. A pile less than 3 feet high tends to dry out; one that's taller than 4 feet is difficult to turn. If you need more room, you'll find that two small side-by-side bins are much easier to manage than one large one, especially when it's time to turn the compost.

You needn't worry about adding a floor or cover to the bin. Microbes and earthworms coming up from the soil beneath the pile are necessary players in the process. And if your pile is rained on, the shower will save you the trouble of hosing the pile down.

Camouflage screens

Then there are the uglies—those familiar items you'd rather not have to look at, such as air-conditioning units, utility boxes, trash cans, and recycling bins.

Your first temptation might be to stash the movable items in the garage or a storage shed. But you actually can hide them—as well as the permanent installations—with low-walled structures that may need only two or three sides. Look at the fencing styles on page 220 and adapt your favorite to a customized version for your screen.

You might be able to hear an occasional hum, but you won't have to look at the actual air-conditioning unit thanks to this clever fence that takes a right-angled jog around it. Lush plantings soften the scene.

Fencing and an ornate entry gate screen this potting bench and storage unit located on a patio at the back of the house. This site has the advantage of being next to a water faucet.

Few utilities are as unattractive as a gas meter, especially in cities that don't allow you to paint it to match the house. Here a simple lattice screen and climbing vines help make it disappear into the background.

CREATING THE ULTIMATE STORAGE UNIT

Efficient, goodlooking storage units don't simply happen. In fact planning one is a process that should unfold over a period of time. First you need to inventory the items you want to keep in it. Next list the other jobs your storage unit might do. Then decide where to locate it. Finally come up with a design that will harmonize with your house and overall landscaping scheme.

Taking stock

Bicycles, trash cans, garden tools, recycling bins, patio furniture, the lawn mower, barbecue equipment, sports gear, ladders—along with all of the other candidates for shelter in a storage unit—could (and sometimes do) fill a two-car garage. As you list the things you'd like to get out from underfoot, note the dimensions of each and add them together to get the approximate number of cubic feet your structure should contain.

Realize, too, that space alone is not enough. Organization is at least as important: Gardening, outdoor cooking, and entertaining go more smoothly when the items you need are properly stored so that they're ready when you are.

Perhaps when your inventory is complete, you'll find out that you don't need a full-blown storage unit at all. If so, look for tuck-away spaces under decks or benches or in handy corners.

Think multipurpose

The best storage units do a lot more than simply hold things. They also solve other problems, such as creating privacy or providing a protected place to nurture seedlings. The examples shown at right and on the opposite page are five cases in point.

Your shed can be freestanding or attached to a house, garage, carport, or other outbuilding. It should be sited and styled so that it's not only convenient and accessible but also compatible with its surroundings. Keep the structure in scale with your house and yard, and develop a design that complements rather than competes with the architectural styling of your home.

If space and money permit, consider building a multipurpose building that can store your garden tools and equipment, house a small potting table, and leave enough room for a greenhouse extension to kick-start the planting season.

These side-by-side bins show an efficient and effective method of composting. The compost is started in one bin and the nearly finished product is moved to the other bin.

Opting for a ready-made shed from your local home center? You'll need to decide where to put it. One of the less conspicuous locations is the space directly behind your garage—where you can stash those endless items that crowd your cars.

One of the favored places to hide the garbage and recycling bins is behind the house or garage. But an enclosure such as this one is large enough to accommodate several containers plus a few toys, and it looks good too.

Tired of looking at your rolled-up garden hose? Design and build your own screen or copy this one. The bottom portion is a typical section of railing with turned balusters, and the top is latticework.

BUILDING SHEDS

Storage or garden sheds can be found in a variety of styles and sizes, from a pre-assembled structure brought to your home, a store-bought kit meant for do-it-yourself assembly, or one built from the ground up to match an existing home or site.

The basic materials used to construct the cedar shed shown include:

Floor assembly: 2×6 pressure-treated joists form a frame that's topped with a ¾-inch pressure-treated plywood floor 70 inches wide by 90 inches long.

Wall assemblies: 2×4 spruce/fir framing; studs are notched to accept horizontal let-in braces cut from 1-inch-thick (5/4) cedar decking. Stud spacing can vary from the standard 16 or 24 inches on center; this example uses 22½-inch spacing to accommodate the width of 1×12 cedar boards (actual width: 11¼ inches).

Siding: 1×12 cedar boards, oriented vertically with approximately ⅛-inch gap between boards and capped with 2-inch-wide cedar battens cut from 1× cedar stock. Cedar is installed with the rough face out.

Windows: 20×25-inch barn sash with pine frames, trimmed to fit into frames made of cedar decking.

Door: divided-lite French-style, exterior-grade, with a frame of Douglas fir.

Roof assembly: The roof features a 5:12 pitch (rise to run) and is framed with fir 2×4 stock for the rafters and collar ties, a 2×6 fir ridge beam, and two 4×4 cedar beams that rest on the side wall plates. Roof sheathing is ⅝-inch exterior-grade plywood and is covered with 30-lb. builder's felt and shingled with three-tab asphalt shingles.

A cedar garden shed, although built from scratch, features a relatively simple design and basic construction techniques, which put it within reach of most handy homeowners. The vertical board-and-batten siding mimics the look of a rustic barn and adds character you won't find in a generic building kit.

1

The floor deck establishes the footprint for the shed. Use 16d galvanized nails to secure the cross joists to the rim joists, and reinforce the connections with metal joist hangers. Align the plywood flooring to square up the assembly, then attach it with 2-inch decking screws. Make sure the frame lies flat before attaching the plywood.

2

For efficiency and consistent dimensions, clamp the wall studs together and gang-cut the notches for the crossbraces. Set the blade depth to 1 inch, then guide the saw with a square to make the two outside cuts. Make a series of closely spaced freehand cuts, then knock the waste free with a hammer and clear the remnants with a chisel or rasp.

3

This design doesn't offer the advantage of squaring up the wall frame with large sheets of plywood sheathing, so set the frame on a flat surface and measure the diagonals, adjusting until they're identical. Start to nail the crossbraces in place by using one nail, partially driven, at each stud until all the braces are fitted. Check for square, then nail.

4

Carefully align the 1×12 siding and fasten it to the wall plates and horizontal braces, using screws or nails only in the center of the board. This will help prevent splitting as the board width shrinks and swells in response to humidity changes. Allow a ¾-inch extension at the bottom to cover the plywood floor edge and 3½ inches at the top for the cedar 4×4 beams along the sidewalls.

5

For the gable (end) walls, mark the roof angle (22.5 degrees for a 5:12 slope) onto the siding and use a portable circular saw and guide to cut it to the correct length and angle. Be sure to allow height for the base of the roof assembly. After cutting, attach a narrow cedar trim board along the upper (angled) edge to keep boards aligned.

6

Narrow (2-inch) battens cover the gaps between the 1×12 siding boards and are secured to the horizontal braces and/or wall studs. Install the battens before the wide planks have a chance to start cupping up at the edges and drive nails or screws into the gap between planks. If you pin the edges of the 1×12s, they are more likely to split from normal seasonal movement.

BUILDING SHEDS *continued*

7 After carefully positioning the two 4×4 roof beams and connecting them with 2×4 collar ties (the horizontal framing members shown), set the ridge beam in place and attach the rafters with screws. Rafter spacing should correspond to the stud spacing on the sidewalls, and the cedar siding will require notches for the rafters.

8 Drive nails or screws every 8 inches to attach the plywood roof sheathing to the rafters. Note that the upper edge of the sheathing is held back to create an air gap at the ridge. A flexible continuous vent will be installed later, when the roof is shingled. It takes more time, but you can also stick-build the roof in place, atop the shed walls.

9 After setting concrete piers at the site and leveling the floor assembly on them, set the rear gable wall and a sidewall together at a corner. Use clamps and a helper to steady the walls, then drive large screws to secure the bottom plates to the floor deck. Then install the remaining sidewall.

10 With the front end of the structure still open, set support blocks onto the sidewall top plates and fit the roof assembly in place. You'll need to recruit friends or neighbors to lift it into place. Align the assembly so the rafters will nest into notches in the cedar siding, then remove the support blocks and lower the roof in place. Attach with screws, then install the front gable wall.

11 Cover the wall corners with trim similar to the battens. These corner pieces should cover any gaps in the siding where the walls meet. Cut one of each pair ⅞-inch narrower to allow for the thickness of the mating piece when installed as shown.

12 After fitting and attaching all the trim on the corners and walls, do the same for the roof. Use cedar boards for the fascia and cut them wide enough to cover the angled ends of the rafters. For a better fit, bevel the top edge of the fascia to match the angle of the roof slope.

13 Farm-supply stores and building centers often sell small wood windows called barn sash. Trim, square, and fit the sashes with cedar frames, then insert them into the wall openings. Fasten with a few screws so the window can be removed for repairs if necessary.

14 Leave the sill plate on the front gable wall intact across the door opening to keep the assembly more stable during handling. When you're ready to install the door, cut the plate out with a handsaw. If possible, find a pre-hung entry door—it will be easier to install.

299

CREATING THE ULTIMATE POTTING AREA

Your potting area could range from a small bench tucked in the back of your garage all the way to a 16×20-foot structure in the backyard that serves many purposes, including garden shed, workshop, potting center, and greenhouse.

Whether you build a modest outdoor potting bench or opt for an elaborate building of some kind, take a walk through your property and evaluate locations. If possible, favor a northern site, leaving the areas with southern exposure for outdoor-living pursuits. This suggestion is especially applicable if you're constructing a building that includes a greenhouse, because putting it on the north edge of your lot allows you to control what's to the south of it. And if you plan to spend a lot of time in the building, orienting it toward the sun will keep your spirits up because people have the same preference for sunny interior spaces that they do for sunny yards.

Think, too, about a water source—that is, if you plan to have a sink in your bench or shed. Perhaps the cost to run lines to a rather remote part of your lot might convince you to locate nearer the house. On the other hand you might consider the convenience of a permanent, freezeproof water service well worth the expense.

Finally, whether you're aiming for a building or a bench, make a list of its essential features. Start with plenty of storage—for bags of various soils, fertilizers, and additives; for materials to be recycled or tossed; for extra pots; and for your army of tools.

If a building, will you want many windows—and if so, where? How about access doors—where and how many?

If a bench, will you want some type of overhead protection from sun and storms, a simple surround to give it character and define the area, and maybe some cabinet doors to keep out critters? If so, perhaps you really want a hybrid—something that's fancier and larger than a bench but less elaborate than a building. The examples pictured might strike your fancy.

This lattice shed makes the potting area a distinct feature of the yard, and its open design provides plenty of daylight for the gardener. Ample shelves offer space for gardening supplies and tools.

Put a simple potting bench against the back wall of your house or garage, then spruce it up with four corner beams, some square-woven lattice in one wall, and a mini pergola above. Paint and enjoy.

BUILDING POTTING BENCHES

ny avid gardener knows the value of a good potting bench. It provides a generous surface to work on and plenty of storage for organizing tools and materials. This version sports a lower shelf that houses as many as four containers of potting soil for various plant requirements and has another shelf for storing small items. Also, there's an easy-to-clean laminate countertop that extends past the base at each end so that you can sweep dirt and debris straight into a waste bin. It's designed as a companion to the cedar garden shed on pages 296–299, but can be built for any setting.

PARTS/MATERIALS:

Legs (6): 1½×3½×36-inch (fir or cedar)
Stretchers (6): 1½×3×66-inch (fir or cedar)
End rails (6): 1½×3×22-inch (fir or cedar)
Shelves (2): ¾×20×70-inch (pine or fir plywood)
Top (1): 25×72-inch prefabricated laminate countertop with integral backsplash
Hardware: Deck screws (1⅝- and 2½-inch); angle brackets (6); ¾-inch #8 screws; wood glue

Organized storage helps you make the most of a potting bench's potential. On the lower shelf, 6-gallon galvanized pails store potting soil and amendments. For the upper shelf, shallow trays or bins (in this case, restaurant-style cutlery bins), provide a home for small tools, gloves, and other small garden-related items.

1 After cutting all the parts to size, find a flat, open area such as a patio or driveway to start assembling the base frame. Fit the stretchers into one set of legs (three front or three rear); check alignment with a square, then apply glue and drive 2½-inch deck screws to secure. Repeat for other leg assembly.

2 Three rails on each end of the bench connect the front and rear leg assemblies. Apply glue and clamp in place as shown, then check alignment with a square. Secure with deck screws. Attach all six end rails to the same leg assembly (either front or rear), then turn it so the outer edges of the legs rest flat on the ground.

3 The large one-piece plywood shelves are notched at their centers and ends to fit around the frame legs. This means you can't maneuver them in place after the base frame is closed up, so install them before you connect the remaining leg assembly. For now, use a few 1⅝-inch screws to fasten only to the stretchers, not the end rails.

4 With the partially completed bench base still turned on its face, position the remaining leg assembly in place for a test fit. After you've checked that everything lines up, remove to apply glue at joints, then re-fit the frame and secure with deck screws.

5 Stand the bench base frame upright, recheck alignment, then drive screws to attach the shelves to the stretchers and end rails. With that done, you can install the top, which attaches with screws and metal angle brackets like the ones shown.

A prefabricated laminate countertop provides a stable and easy-to-clean work surface. An overhang of several inches at each end allows direct sweeping of soil and debris into an adjacent waste bin.

CREATING THE ULTIMATE AREA FOR VEHICLES

At most homes, the driveway and perhaps an additional parking area are already well-ensconced parts of the landscape. Removing them and paving a different route from street to garage are expensive and often impossible propositions. None of this is to say, however, that you can't add to your driveway, resurface it with a more pleasing material, or reshape its edges.

The site plan opposite identifies the main points to consider when thinking about driveway and parking area changes. Use these to prepare a traffic report about the situation at your house and as a source of ideas for improvements that might be needed.

Improving an existing drive

Start with the width of your drive. Builders typically stick to absolute minimums of 6 to 8 feet rather than the recommended 10 to 12 feet. If your drive doesn't measure up, you needn't widen it along the entire length, only at the points at which people will be getting out of their vehicles.

Also there's no rule that says you must match the driveway's current surface when you widen it. Instead why not add a distinctive walk area to one or both sides of your driveway?

Next, consider surfacing your entire driveway with a different material, especially if your drive is due for a resurfacing anyway. Loose fill could give way to concrete, perhaps tinted to pick up a hue from your home's exterior or textured to improve traction.

A small touch makes a big difference. Complementary materials, such as asphalt, brick, and pavers, work together to create a driveway design that adds to the overall aesthetic appeal of the landscape.

Screen parking areas with low fences and plants. For security reasons don't obscure them, and leave a clear line of sight from the car to the door you will enter at night.

A different surface material can give a driveway a whole new look. Consider surfaces that will better relate the drive to your home, or use the same material that covers a backyard patio.

Let your overall landscaping style determine the shape of a drive and connecting paths. Use curved edges with a loose, informal scheme; straight lines for a symmetrical, formal look.

Tired of playing musical cars? Provide extra parking for visitors and deliveries. Make auxiliary parking easily accessible but take care that it doesn't overpower your home and yard.

Drive and parking areas should be 10 to 12 feet wide so that drivers and passengers step out onto pavement, not grass or groundcover. If the drive also serves as a walkway, add another 2 feet to it.

If extra off-street parking is sited here, instead of alongside the garage, the space also can serve as a turnaround. Again, screen cars with plants or fencing.

305

GALLERY OF DRIVEWAY AND PARKING AREA OPTIONS

The connector between driveway and house is often as important as the driveway itself. Here a wide walk, surrounded with colorful planting areas, curves its way to the porch, then branches onward.

Rather than the typical, continuous, asphalt driveway, consider adopting this design. It not only looks great, but the masonry keeps the edges of the asphalt from crumbling.

This concrete-and-grass grid is an excellent design choice for the contemporary house adjoining it. The sections of concrete are sized as if they're individual parking spots.

Because this garage is at basement level, its siding matches the entry steps rather than the house proper. An overhead deck takes advantage of the flat roof.

A painstakingly laid cobblestone driveway adds formality to this home. Note how much more interesting the front facade is with its continuously flowing line of trellis work.

MAINTAINING YOUR LANDSCAPE

You've designed your landscape; you've built and planted it. Now it's time to take care of your creation. Fortunately, with careful planning, you can shape a landscape that matches your ability and desire to maintain it.

For the most part, you can schedule and pace the work to fit your lifestyle. And, if nothing else, this outdoor work gives you a great excuse for skipping other work that isn't nearly as pleasant.

Keeping up your landscape involves time, hard work, and expense. But it's all worthwhile when you enjoy the routine tasks involved and savor the multifaceted rewards of your efforts.

Minimize the demands of your landscape by planting easy-care shrubs and trees wherever possible. They will enhance the value of your property as well as its beauty.

Trees add value to your property as well as shade, color, and seasonal interest. In addition to regular watering if rainfall is inadequate, young trees need only occasional pruning to remove damaged or dead wood.

Lawn maintenance takes more time than any other landscape chore. Trade areas of lawn for planting areas, and mulch around and between plants to minimize upkeep.

OUTDOOR TASKS MONTH BY MONTH

COLD-WINTER CLIMATES

Month	Tasks
January–February	Enjoy indoor gardening and rest. Read nursery catalogs. Order seeds and plants. Start slow growers such as geranium, delphinium, and pansy indoors. Check tubers of stored dahlias; if too dry, sprinkle with water. Inspect all stored bulbs, corms, and tubers, and cut off any decayed parts. Sweep snow off evergreens before it has a chance to break branches. Use deicing salt sparingly.
March	Begin pruning roses and fruit; feed all. Prune early-flowering shrubs only after bloom. Plant bare-root woody plants. Spray fruit trees with dormant oil when temperature exceeds 40 degrees and before they leaf out. Remove rose cones when forsythia blooms; remove mounded soil gradually. Gradually remove mulch blanket that covered plants over winter. Plant grass and hardy annuals outdoors. Check structures for damage.
April	Clean up. Spread compost around trees and shrubs. Pull mulch back from the crowns of perennials. Begin transplanting indoor seedlings outside; harden them off first with several short days outdoors. Watch seedlings carefully for wilting; protect from wind. Start mowing when grass reaches 2½ inches. Spread preemergence herbicide to control crabgrass. Divide late-blooming perennials.
May	Plant tender bulbs. Water new trees and shrubs deeply. Sprinkle seedbeds to keep surface soil moist. Check the date of your area's last expected frost; begin planting tender plants, seeds, and bulbs accordingly. Remove deadheads from spring bulbs; let foliage die down naturally. Stake plants early.
June	Water as needed. Feed roses. Remove spent roses by cutting back to a five-leaflet leaf. Spread and deepen mulch. Sweep decks and patios often. Check container plants daily for moisture. Pinch back chrysanthemums, petunia, and most annuals for low, bushy growth. Break pine candles in half; prune other evergreens back to desired size. Trim clipped deciduous hedges before growth hardens.
July	Divide iris if overcrowded. Dig with fork. Trim decayed or corky ends; trim foliage to fan shape. Replant with rhizome near or on the surface and roots well buried. Bury sections of branches of low-growing shrubs and vines so that they can form roots for new plants. Harvest bush fruits daily. Check pool every few days and after every rain for chemical balance. Set mower blade higher in dry weather.
August	Move chrysanthemum plants to center stage as they begin to flower. Shear deadheads and feed annuals. Feed roses before midmonth so that you won't encourage late, winter-tender growth. Potted trees and shrubs can be planted anytime, but the longer they settle before winter, the better.
September	This is the best time for seeding or repairing lawns. Combine post- and preemergence herbicides. Plant trees and shrubs in mild climates. Divide early-blooming perennials. Take cuttings for winter houseplants. Gather and compost all fallen fruits and nuts. Plant daffodils. Check structures for damage; make repairs. Bring in houseplants before frost. Have covers ready to protect tender blooms from early frost.
October	Dig and store tender bulbs. Rake leaves; compost or use as mulch. Bag some leaves for insulation around foundations. Plant spring bulbs. Add a pinch of bonemeal to every hole. Prepare pools and ponds for winter by lowering water level, adding floating logs, and covering. Mulch perennials.
November–December	Water plants well before a freeze. Mulch to prevent freezing and thawing. Mound soil around the bases of roses, even under cones. Clean and oil tools. Feed birds and provide water. Spray evergreens, Christmas trees, and treasured plants with antitranspirant spray. Add wood ashes to the compost pile.

WARM-WINTER CLIMATES

Month	Tasks
January–February	Place catalog orders. Prune roses and fruit trees; move woody plants while dormant. Seed cool-season annuals such as sweet alyssum, stock, sweet pea, and larkspur outdoors; set out seedlings of pansy, petunia, snapdragon, and calendula. Spray full-strength dormant oil on fruit and deciduous trees; use half-strength spray on broadleaf evergreens. Prepare lawn furniture and tools by cleaning and repairing them.
March	Plant tender bulbs and annuals outdoors when trees leaf out. Pick old blooms; feed blooming plants. Divide fall-blooming perennials. Plant seeds of astilbe, delphinium, hollyhock, and other biennials or perennials indoors. Feed lawn; mow grass when it's above 2½ inches. Check structures for damage.
April	Plant rest of tender plants after danger of frost passes. Feed lawn; aerate it anytime. Pinch chrysanthemums until midsummer to keep bushy. Also pinch most annuals. Finish feeding or give booster to all plants. Spread mulch. Prune spring-flowering shrubs after bloom. Shorten pine candles; prune other evergreens just before growth starts. Remove diseased plants. Thin crowded fruit.
May	Sow seed, lay sod, or plant plugs of warm-season grasses now through summer. Keep watered until settled. Plant heat-resistant annuals such as vinca, portulaca, celosia, and cosmos; use impatiens and coleus for shady spots. Start oleander from cuttings of mature wood. Stake large plants.
June	Prune and thin spring-blooming shrubs. Transplant when rainy season starts. Watch for insects; wash or pick them off plants before they can multiply. Use fungicide where diseases usually are a problem, especially on roses. Expose graft junctions of roses. Mow lawn as needed; dethatch now for fast recovery; treat for chinch bugs. Continue to water plants as needed, especially newly set trees and shrubs.
July	Water and work outdoors in early morning or evening. Check pool chemicals every few days and after every rain. Sweep deck and patio often. Check evergreens for spider mite and bagworm. For spider mites, spray with miticide twice at two-week intervals. Plant evergreens toward end of summer.
August	Layer or take cuttings from plants during rainy season. Feed roses again. Renew mulches. Start pansies and other cool-season annuals indoors for transplanting outside after summer heat. Move chrysanthemums into empty spots for fall bloom. Now through late fall cut back selectively the new buds along the branch sides of firs and spruces. Give a last trim to deciduous hedges; trim evergreen hedges.
September	Plant sweet pea in deeply worked soil in a sunny spot. Sow in a trench 4 inches deep. Cover with 2 inches of soil. As plants grow, mound soil around roots and train tops to climb a fence. Sow winter-blooming plants in Sunbelt. Plant new trees and shrubs and spring bulbs. Make major lawn repairs; feed and lime old lawns.
October	Plant anemone and ranunculus tubers with the claws down. Plant biennials and spring-flowering bulbs. Gather and compost or bag leaves. Wrap young trees. Protect trunks from rabbits, using loose wire wraps. Pull mulch back about 4 inches from trunks to discourage mice. Continue to mow grass until it goes dormant (stops growing over winter). Prepare pools and ponds for winter.
November–December	Mulch perennials for winter. Use herbicide for winter weeds when lawn is dormant. Update your landscape plan for any needed changes. Check structures for damage again. Clean and oil tools. Dig and store tender bulbs before frost. Keep camellias moist to prevent bud drop. Be ready with frost protection to save plants of borderline hardiness. Water plants well and mulch before freeze.

MAINTAINING LAWNS

To seed a bare spot, loosen soil 4 to 6 inches deep, then add humus and fertilizer. Rake it smooth. Spread seed, tamp it down, and keep the soil moist with frequent sprinklings several times a day.

Spread lawn fertilizer in spring and fall. A handheld spreader works well for small areas. For larger yards, rent or buy a push spreader. Spread half the fertilizer while walking in one direction, the other half in a second pass at right angles. Or use soluble food and a hose sprayer.

The secret to a successful lawn is constant and consistent care. If you make the work a pleasant habit instead of a dreaded chore, the right work will be done easily at the right time.

Watering

Water deeply and thoroughly, 1 inch a week, or not at all. Dig down to be sure that you are soaking 6 to 12 inches of soil. Sandy soils need less water more often. The more humus you have in your soil, the more it will soak up and retain water. A bluish tint, loss of resiliency so footprints show, and slower growth all indicate thirst. But even when grasses are allowed to go dormant for a whole summer, they usually green up quickly once rains return.

Feeding

Proper applications of fertilizer make grass plants strong and healthy so that they can withstand drought and traffic and crowd out weeds. In the spring, use a fertilizer with a 2:1:1 ratio of nitrogen to phosphorous and potash. In fall, use a fertilizer with a 1:2:2 ratio for healthy root growth during winter.

If the thatch in your lawn becomes too thick to let water and new growth through, cut through it using a core aerator. Overseed the lawn after aerating.

Apply about 4 pounds per 1,000 square feet. Slow-release fertilizer is the best form.

Weed and pest control

Thriving grass is the best control for weeds and pests. If problems do appear, begin treatment immediately. Check with your extension office for advice on effective and safe solutions.

Leveling

Level your lawn wherever freezing and thawing, mole activity, or planting changes such as tree removal leave you with humps or dips that interfere with mowing.

Raise low spots by spreading a weedless mix of soil or sand and peat right on top of the grass, but no more than ¼ inch at a time. Smooth the soil, then repeat twice a year until level. For deeper hollows, slice and roll back the existing sod. Fill the depression with clean, rich soil. Smooth and tamp it firmly, then spread the sod back in place. Topdress with ¼ inch of soil or peat; water deeply.

Remove humps by taking out wedges of turf 6 inches deep. Repeat at 10-inch intervals over the entire mound. Soak, roll, and repeat spring and fall until the hump disappears.

Bare spots

Reseed bare spots in early fall or spring. At other times, use sod or plugs.

To seed, prepare the soil by raking away debris and getting rid of weeds. If you use an herbicide, wait as directed before proceeding. Loosen the soil, then add humus and a light application of balanced fertilizer. Rake the soil smooth, spread good seed, tamp down, and keep the soil moist until the seed germinates.

MOWING YOUR GRASS

Mowing is a critical part of lawn care and yard neatness. Match your schedule to the growth rate of your grass: perhaps every 5 days in a wet season, every 10 to 14 days during dry times.

Cut grass to the ideal height specified for the kind. For bluegrasses, ryegrasses, and fescues, that's usually about 2 inches during active growth, 3 inches otherwise. Mow bent-, bermuda-, and zoysiagrasses as low as ¾ to 1¼ inches. Mow tall fescues, st. augustinegrass, and bahiagrass higher, from 3 to 3½ inches.

Get a mower you can push, turn, and change blade heights on easily. Sharpen blades monthly, more often if you hit stones or sticks. Dull blades wound and tear grass.

As long as you mow often enough, clippings can stay on the lawn. Short pieces will settle among new growth, decompose quickly, and add nutrients and humus to the soil.

Edging and trimming are easy with mowing strips and power equipment. Be careful not to damage tree bark.

Mow the grass diagonally, alternating directions with each swath. This prevents a striped look and ensures that grass blades are cut more sharply and evenly. Cut higher in a dry summer to conserve water and crowd out crabgrass. In the shade, cut grass higher or less often.

Because grass naturally grows green on top and turns brown near its base, try to mow it often enough that you cut only the top one-third of the blades. This encourages low, thick, green growth and also discourages weeds.

MINIMIZING LAWN MAINTENANCE

A lawn, the most prevalent part of many yards, also is the part that takes the most work. Lighten your lawn maintenance load by taking steps to make mowing easier and reduce the amount of grass you need to mow.

Making mowing easier

To reduce the effort required by mowing, try some of the following:

• Plant trees in groups, in swaths of mulch or groundcover, or in gardens. A lawn dotted with trees is a challenge to mow. Trees are safer anyway if you can avoid mowing near them.

• As trees grow taller, prune their lower limbs. Continue to do this until the canopy of leaves is high enough for you to walk and mow under it comfortably. Such pruning also lets more light hit your lawn and allows gentle breezes to reach you on your patio.

• Install mowing strips: bands of concrete, brick, or other material on which the mower wheel can travel. These edges speed mowing and reduce trimming chores. They also can serve as attractive outlines in your landscape. Crucial to an effective mowing strip is that it be placed low to the

ground. If you have a sprinkler, locate heads in the center of these bands to put them out of your and the mower's way.

• Design your areas of lawn so that you can easily move the mower from one area to another. In reducing the size of the lawn with other plantings, avoid leaving islands of grass.

• Do lawn chores as needed: Cut the grass before it needs raking, feed it before it needs reseeding, and treat pests and diseases before they do extensive damage. A lovely lawn is easily maintained if you take the work in stride. Fall behind and the problems can overwhelm you.

Lawn alternatives

Lawns began as status symbols for pastoral people who could finally afford to have a bit of pasture without any animals on it. The whole concept has since gotten so out of hand that Americans now use more fuel and fertilizer on their lawns than some countries spend for their entire agricultural economies.

You can reduce your lawn to a manageable size in several ways. Concentrate first on areas where the grass is unsightly or does not grow well anyway and replace it with easy-to-grow groundcovers, such as creeping thyme, ajuga, or Irish moss.

Groundcovers

While mulches are attractive enough, groundcovers make absolutely lovely carpets of various colors and textures with seasonal changes of bloom, fruit, or foliage color.

For best results, use plants that do well in your climate. Set cuttings or divisions in mulch. The closer you set the plants, the sooner they will cover the area. With plants 6 inches apart, 100 will cover 25 square feet. Do a section at a time and divide the plants as they multiply.

Pull weeds by hand until the groundcover fills the area. After that, the bed will be self-sustaining. For an extra season of bloom, plant spring bulbs among ivy or pachysandra.

A yard that consists of terraced planting areas filled with low-maintenance groundcovers and shrubs entails more work up front to install and help establish, but in the long run it requires less upkeep than typical turf.

Trees and shrubs

Plant trees and shrubs, too, to take up lawn space. Set them among the mulch and they will grow faster. Plant groundcovers or shade-loving hostas or flowers under large trees; plant sun lovers under smaller trees until they cast more shade.

Mulches

Removing unwanted sod and spreading a mulch—shredded bark or leaves, straw, or grass clippings, for example—in its place cuts your maintenance chores right away. It also conditions the soil for future plantings. Keep the mulch neat and safe with edging.

Put mulch where you're thinking of later adding a walk or patio so that you can test the location. If you change your mind, it costs very little to restore the lawn and move the mulch.

To eliminate unwanted lawn without tilling, spread overlapping newspapers over the area, then top these with a 3-inch-deep layer of grass clippings, chopped leaves, or layers of chopped compost. The turf will decompose within a few months.

Plant through these layers right away by digging the holes needed for trees or shrubs as usual. Plant smaller plants right on top of the newspapers; just place enough potting soil around the roots or over the seeds to cover. The roots will grow right through the paper (roots can split a rock), but weeds will not have the light they need to push up from underneath.

Consider using plastic under more costly mulches such as stone or bark to keep weeds from pushing through the shallow layer you're likely to use. Don't lay plastic, though, if you plan to put a lot of plants in the area; you'll tire of cutting through the plastic.

Many mulches are available free. Ask your neighbors to save leaves and grass clippings. As new laws banish these products from landfills, people will be happy for someone to take them for free. Many utilities will dump truckloads of wood chips. Other byproducts may be available in your area too.

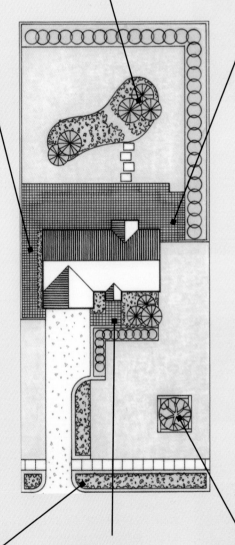

Narrow side yards and strips near house or walk are hard to mow. These areas often are in shadow so grass does not grow well. Paving or mulch here is neater and easier to maintain.

This island of flowers and small trees reduces mowing and adds interest and shade to the backyard. Plan a smaller area if you need open space for games.

Surfaces and structures such as patios, walkways, and decks give a high return in outdoor living space while reducing the time you have to spend mowing, watering, and fertilizing the lawn.

Strips of grass between the curb and sidewalk are difficult to keep looking good. Groundcovers give the areas color, texture, and bloom. Put paving stones where needed for foot traffic.

Pave and plant the entryway so that you don't have to mow sparse grass right up to the door. Paving keeps feet dry; plants along the walk give visitors a warmer welcome.

Place mulch and edging around trees to avoid ducking under branches as you mow. Trimming too close to trees and damaging their bark often leads to delayed growth or even death.

CHOOSING LOW-MAINTENANCE LAWN ALTERNATIVES

BLUE STAR CREEPER

Isotoma fluviatilus
Height: 4–6 inches
Zones: 7–8
Soil: Rich, moist
Light: Sun to partial shade

Comments: Named for its tiny light blue flowers that appear in spring and summer, this semievergreen ground-hugger may lose some leaves in cold winters. Plant it around stepping stones, along paths, in rock gardens, or in rock walls where it will get full sun most of the day and some afternoon shade. Water plants regularly, keeping the soil moist but not wet, to help them become established during the first season. Water weekly during dry periods. Trim plants if they creep too far over a path.

CHAMOMILE

Chamaemelum nobile
Height: 3–10 inches
Zones: 3–10
Soil: Average to below average
Light: Prefers full sun; will tolerate partial shade

Comments: The fragrant, ferny foliage of chamomile is delightful near walks, where footsteps send up clouds of scent. You also can mow it as a lawn substitute, forcing plants to form a tight carpet. Chamomile spreads fast, but sections may die of unknown reason. Fill from surrounding area. Start from seed, or from cuttings or divisions set 6 to 12 inches apart. Chamomile has small daisylike flowers in summer. It survives drought well. Can be used for teas.

LAMIUM

Lamium maculatum
Height: 9–12 inches
Zones: 4–9
Soil: Any moist garden soil
Light: Full to partial shade

Comments: This easy, fast-growing, vigorous plant, with types that include spotted dead nettle and yellow archangel, can be set a little farther apart than most groundcovers. Its crinkled leaves are variously colored and marked with silver and green. Flowers come in white, pink, lavender, yellow, and purplish red. Lamium can get weedy or take over; contain it with edgings. The common name of dead nettle refers to the fact that this plant does not sting like a true nettle.

MOSS: IRISH, SCOTCH

Sagina subulata; Arenaria spp.
Height: 2–4 inches
Zones: 4–10
Soil: Prefers moist, rich
Light: Full sun in cool areas, afternoon shade elsewhere

Comments: The many species covered by these common names are not true moss but flowering plants that include pearlwort and sandwort. Irish moss is usually dark green; Scotch moss is golden green. Both form low tufts of dense, linear foliage with white flowers in spring. They work well between stepping-stones and among rocks. Fallen leaves from deciduous trees should be removed; rake only after a hard freeze.

PACHYSANDRA

Pachysandra terminalis
Height: 10–12 inches
Zones: 5–9
Soil: Moist, well drained, acid
Light: Shade

Comments: Also known as Japanese spurge, this low-maintenance plant spreads slowly by underground stems called rhizomes. It features short spikes of white flowers followed by red berries. Space plants about 10 inches apart. This slow grower takes about three years to form a mat and fill an area. Allegheny spurge (*Pachysandra procumbens*), a similar plant, is more evergreen and native to the eastern United States.

SPEEDWELL

Veronica spp.
Height: 6–36 inches
Zones: 4–9
Soil: Tolerates many
Light: Full sun in North, some shade in South

Comments: Speedwells—often referred to as creeping, rock, or woolly—have dark green foliage with mostly blue, some pink or white, flowers. Bloom time ranges from late spring to September. Short varieties grow well between paving stones. Speedwell makes a good, easy edging plant, spreading to 2 feet wide. Withstands considerable foot traffic.

THYME

Thymus spp.
Height: 2–15 inches
Zones: 3–10
Soil: Poor
Light: Sun; light summer shade in South

Comments: Creeping thyme has tiny dark green leaves and a wonderful fragrance. It has clusters of red, pink, white, or purple flowers in summer. Woolly thyme has gray foliage and fewer flowers but creates a more undulating and lower mat; it's perhaps the best thyme for use as a groundcover. Because crushing releases fragrance, both work well between stepping-stones or under a garden seat.

WILDFLOWER AND NATURAL GRASS MIX

Variety of species
Height: To 5–6 feet by fall
Zones: 3–10
Soil: Mixes available for any
Light: Mixes available for sun or shade

Comments: Grown from seed mixes, an ever-changing tapestry of meadow or woodland blooms can be delightful in the right place. But there's been much controversy about these natural lawn replacements; they are too untidy for most front yards, and neighbors sometimes complain. Meadows, however, work well at the outer edges of larger lawns and on steep slopes. Use mixes of native seed. Let annuals reseed to continue. Mow once in the fall.

In the South, try fragrant star (or confederate) jasmine, lantana, or liriope. West Coast favorites include ice plant, gazania, cape marigold (or African daisy), and Carmel creeper. For most of the country, anemone, artemisia, astilbe, lily-of-the-valley, goutweed, perennial geranium, hosta, and vinca are good under trees. Keep mints and moneywort confined, or they can take over. Good groundcovers for sun include bellflower, candytuft, ajuga, crown vetch, ivy geranium, mahonia, creeping phlox, pinks, sedum, snow-in-summer, thrift or armeria, and woolly yarrow. For winter interest, plant bearberry, Japanese holly, wintergreen, box huckleberry, or Oregon boxwood.

INSTALLING IRRIGATION SYSTEMS

Tired of dragging hoses around your yard, returning from vacation to a parched lawn, or waking up to a marsh because you forgot to turn off the sprinkler the previous night? Go underground with a subterranean irrigation system that gives your landscape exactly the amount of water it needs, when it needs it.

Inground irrigation networks fall into two categories: drip systems and sprinklers. Drip irrigation carries water directly to trees, shrubs, and groundcovers, bringing them a slow, steady trickle that sinks deep into the soil. Sprinklers toss water into the air, treating vegetation to a gentle shower. Drip systems are best for deep-rooted plants. Lawns require sprinklers. Your landscape might benefit from a combination of the two.

Planning

Inground irrigation systems are more affordable than ever thanks to easily assembled components that let you do most or all of the installation work yourself. Planning the job can be tricky, however, so consult with a sprinkler-parts dealer to determine the layout and equipment that will work best for you.

The dealer will need a detailed site plan that identifies all plant materials, soil conditions, and the like, along with the water pressure at your house in gallons per hour. This can be measured with a simple gauge that screws onto an outside hose cock. (The local supplier may be willing to lend you a pressure gauge for a few days.)

Pressure is important because the flow rate from all the heads in a system must total a maximum of 75 percent of available pressure; 60 percent is better. Need more heads than that? Break your system into separate circuits, as does the site plan, opposite. Turn on each circuit at a different time of day.

Manual sprinkler controls are inexpensive but require that you do the turning on and turning off. More costly controls consist of servomotors activated by programmable timers. These provide automatic, worry-free sprinkling.

1 After you and a dealer have worked out a plan and you've bought the parts you need, familiarize yourself with those parts. The system begins with a loop of PVC pipe, shown at upper right, and an antisiphon valve, shown at upper left and on page 321. This prevents water in the sprinkler system, which could be contaminated with lawn chemicals, from being sucked back into your home's water supply.

2 Dig 6- to 10-inch-deep trenches with a spade or trenching machine. Plan to bury all but the tops of sprinkler heads. Flexible plastic tubing is impervious to freezing and needn't be sunk below the frost line. Pressure causes heads to pop up when the water is turned on.

3

Fittings clamp onto the plastic pipe wherever you need an outlet; then you punch a hole in the pipe by screwing this special tool into the fitting.

4

Start your system by clamping a hose bibb to a short piece of tubing. The bibb, located between the antisiphon and control valves, provides a connection for flushing out the system.

The first step in planning an irrigation system is to check your home's water pressure, as explained opposite. This determines how many sprinkler heads can operate at the same time.

Next determine where you want heads. Here there are separate circuits for the right side and rear. The total flow rate of each circuit is limited to 75 percent of a home's water pressure.

Make runs as straight as possible, avoiding layouts where piping doubles back. For 100 percent coverage, space heads so that spray from each will nearly touch neighboring heads.

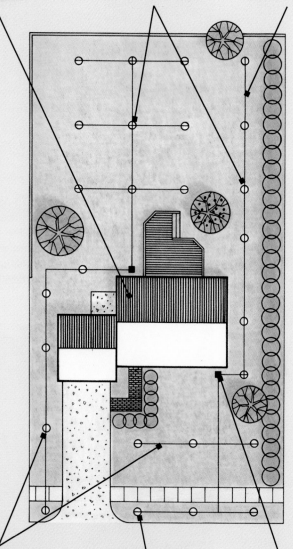

This plan also provides separate circuits for the front and left side, a total of four. Plan your layout so that you don't have to tunnel under a driveway or other large paved area.

At borders, choose heads that will conserve water by keeping if off a street, walk, drive, or neighbor's property. Some heads rotate, some spray a gentle mist, others bubble water.

Each circuit has a control valve. Two valves will go here, one for the front yard, one for the side. The plan calls for two more valves at the rear. Each valve can be wired to its own timer.

319

INSTALLING IRRIGATION SYSTEMS *(continued)*

5

Now install a control valve for each sprinkler circuit. This one is activated by a low-voltage solenoid that will be wired to a timer inside the garage. You also can buy manual control valves. Situate control valves so their cover boxes will be flush with the ground.

6

Lay tubing in trenches and piece together. T-, elbow, and four-way fittings enable a circuit to branch out in one or several directions. Simply force each fitting into the plastic tubing, then tighten hose clamps with a screwdriver. For gentle curves, bend the tubing.

7

Attach clamps, puncture the tubing, and screw in sprinkler heads. Cut green risers to the right height. Lawn heads should be above ground level yet low enough so that a mower can pass over them without nicking. Shrub heads should rise above foliage.

8

After all heads are in place, but before connecting to the house, attach a hose to the hose bibb and flush out the system. This also is a good time, before trenches are filled in, to check that each head provides good coverage.

9 Drill a hole through the foundation or siding and connect PVC pipe to your home's water supply. You'll probably want to hire a plumber for this step. Caulk around the hole into the house. Connect antisiphon valve to water supply, then to irrigation system.

10 Use crimp connectors to wire each control valve to the antisiphon valve. Run wires from the antisiphon valve to the spot you've chosen for the timer that will operate the circuit. Low-voltage wires can be buried along with the tubing or in shallow trenches of their own.

11 Sprinkler timers resemble automatic setback thermostats. You program the times you want the system to turn on and off. Watering in the early morning gives plantings a good start on the day.

12 Drop cover boxes over each control valve, fill the trenches with earth, tamp, and replace sod. Some sprinkler heads are adjustable so that you can fine tune the system.

MAINTAINING PLANTS

Giving your plants the care they need to flourish and contribute to the landscape entails basic tasks, including feeding, watering, mulching, and pruning. Practiced regularly, these tasks minimize the need to spend time on other chores, such as weeding, dealing with pests and diseases, and replacing spent plants.

Feeding

Your landscape's success lies, in large part, in the soil. When it comes to nourishing plants, your first step should be in building fertile, healthy soil. Even gardens with good soil benefit from regular additions of organic amendments, including compost, chopped leaves, grass clippings, and rotted manure, to improve the soil's fertility as well as its ability to hold and drain moisture. In addition, you'll find an array of plant foods and ways to apply them in any garden or lawn situation. Seek detailed advice at a local nursery or garden center.

Watering

The best way to water plants is whatever works well for you and your garden. Water conservation is important in any garden and essential in arid regions where drought occurs regularly and water restrictions apply. Deciding how and when to water is part of the art of gardening; it depends on the plant, its stage of growth, and the time of year.

Mulching

You and your plants will enjoy the benefits of mulching as it controls weeds, conserves soil moisture, protects plants from extreme temperatures, and adds a finishing touch. Plan to mulch in spring and then again in late fall.

Pruning

Most trees and shrubs benefit from occasional pruning. Make this your goal: Prune to improve or maintain plant health and vigor while retaining the plant's natural shape.

Fertilize as needed, depending on your soil and your plants. Don't feed too late in summer or when soil is too dry. When possible, cultivate fertilizer into the soil where soil moisture can activate its benefits.

Prune branches that cross, crowd, are damaged, or form too narrow an angle with the trunk. Cuts will heal more quickly and surely if you cut just beyond the branch collar, usually a series of ridges, instead of absolutely flush.

Water long and often. Some gardeners prefer to use root feeders, fitted with fertilizer cartridges, so both water and food can penetrate deep into the soil. However, deep feeding, though helpful, isn't always essential.

Nothing cuts work and promotes growth as well as mulch because it conserves moisture and controls weeds. Organic mulches decompose eventually and become humus in the soil. Replenish them as needed.

MAINTAINING CONCRETE, MASONRY SURFACES

Concrete and masonry promise permanence, but even the best-built walls, patios, walkways, steps, and driveways require attention from time to time. Fortunately most repairs can be accomplished in an hour or two with no special skills and just a few hand tools.

Before you set out to make concrete and masonry repairs, try to diagnose what caused the damage. Water, especially ice, is usually the culprit. Frost in the ground causes heaving and settlement; water coursing down a wall or standing in low spots on a patio can leach away mortar and concrete, seep into joints, and wreck masonry units. The tactics shown at right and opposite cure minor concrete and masonry ailments. If the deterioration is chronic or extensive, you may need to solve an underlying drainage problem first.

Patching concrete

Repairing concrete is a lot like dentistry: You clean the cavity, then fill it. To fill shallow cracks and chips, use a commercial latex, vinyl, or epoxy patching compound mixed according to the manufacturer's instructions. Patching compounds hold better than conventional cement-and-sand mixtures and require you to do less preparatory work to the old surface.

For deeper cavities, apply patching compound in several thin layers. Or use a conventional cement-and-sand mixture, making sure to apply a bonding agent (available at building centers) first. If you use concrete to fill a deep cavity, undercut the edges around the perimeter of the damaged area so that the crack or hole is somewhat wider at the bottom than at the surface. After you pack in the new concrete, the existing concrete helps hold it in place.

Tools

For most concrete and masonry repairs, you'll need a 2-pound sledge, brick chisel, trowel, wire brush, and a bucket. When you chip away old material, protect your eyes with safety glasses. When removing stains, wear waterproof gloves.

To remove stains from concrete, sprinkle on a mixture of pumice and rottenstone or an industrial abrasive. Dip a wire brush in water and scrub vigorously. Then use a high-pressure sprayer.

To replace a crumbling brick or stone, break away the mortar around it with a sledge and chisel, then smash the brick or stone and remove the pieces. Butter a new unit with mortar and slide it into place.

To repair cracks in concrete, undercut the edges with a chisel and vacuum out all debris.

Then either mix your own compound or buy a premixed one and fill the crack as shown.

To patch the edge of a crumbling step, first chip away all loose concrete, then secure a retaining board with a heavy object as shown. Moisten the concrete, and apply the patching compound.

To repair spalled concrete, first chip away all loose concrete with a chisel. Moisten the area well (don't let water stand, though), then apply a commercial patching compound. Let patch dry.

To level sunken paver blocks, bricks, or stones, lift them, then prop with a piece of 2x4. Fill underneath with equal parts sand, sifted earth, and cement. Tamp, if possible, or overfill to compensate for settling.

MAINTAINING WOOD SURFACES

Rot is wood's worst enemy, so closely scrutinize decks, sheds, fences, and other wooden structures every spring and fall, paying special attention to wood at or near ground level or anywhere else moisture might collect. If you detect any signs of rot (poke with a screwdriver if you're not sure), take immediate steps to remedy the problem before it gets worse.

Catch rot early and you may be able to arrest it by saturating the area with wood preservative. For more severe damage, you'll need to cut away the affected element and replace it. Use only redwood, cedar, or pressure-treated lumber for repairs.

During your semiannual inspection, also keep an eye out for decking boards, railings, or other items that might be pulling loose. These pose a safety hazard and should be hammered or screwed back in place right away.

Termites

Termites fall into two groups: Subterranean ones eat wood but live underground, usually commuting back and forth via mud shelter tubes; nonsubterranean types live in the wood itself.

Nonsubterranean wood-boring insects—which include powder post beetles and carpenter ants as well as several termite species—dig across the grain of the wood and sometimes break through the surface, leaving telltale piles of sawdust pellets. Subterranean termites bore along the grain of the wood and often leave nothing but a shell behind.

If you suspect termites, call a licensed exterminator. To eliminate subterranean termites, exterminators inject chemicals into the soil. For nonsubterranean termites, extermination consists of boring holes into the wood and injecting a liquid or powdered chemical.

Clean your deck regularly. Sweep the surface once a week to minimize the amount of dirt and debris **that collects in cracks. Also scrub the deck with warm water and detergent once a month.**

When pressure-treated decking is cut off at the ends, some of the exposed wood isn't protected by the chemicals forced into the lumber. That's why it's important to saturate the end grains with two or three coats of sealer.

It doesn't take long for dirt, leaves, and other debris to collect in the cracks between decking boards. This gunk soon collects moisture, which rots the board edges. Regularly remove the debris manually or with a pressure sprayer.

This photo shows old warped boards that weren't treated with preservatives through the years. The two in the middle need to be replaced. The others might be salvageable if sanded heavily. Then the entire deck needs to be sealed.

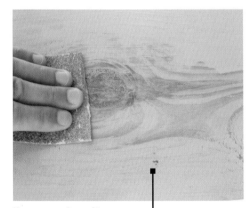

Heavy sap deposits can bleed right through most stains. The cure: Sand the area, seal it with a nonbleed finish such as shellac or marine varnish, then restain. To remove mildew, scrub the area with a solution of water and household bleach, or use a commercial mildewcide.

Pull popped nails, then drill pilot holes and drive galvanized screws adjacent to the old nail holes. Seal the holes with caulk. Reinforce a weakening structural member with galvanized L-, angle, or T- brackets. Again use only galvanized screws.

Cut rotted boards back to sound wood. Plan cuts so they will expose framing to which you can nail or screw a new piece of lumber. In this situation, caulking where the wood abuts concrete could prevent rotting in the future. Secure the new piece with galvanized nails or screws.

13

CONSTRUCTION AND PLANTING BASICS

How long a nail do you need? What are the correct proportions for mixing concrete or mortar? When's the best time to start a lawn? Tackle any of the projects covered earlier in this book and you may puzzle over questions such as these. For answers, turn to the pages that follow. Here you'll find a concise compendium of information about hardware and fasteners, wood, concrete, masonry, wiring, and plants.

HARDWARE AND FASTENERS

The hardware and fasteners you choose for a building project are as important as the lumber and other materials they join. This page gives you a look at nails, the fasteners you'll use most often.

The right nail

The photo below right depicts a dozen nail types, each engineered for a specific purpose. Starting from the top:

1 Double-headed nails, also known as scaffold nails, are good choices for temporary nailing jobs, such as building forms or attaching braces to a post. The second head makes the nail easy to pull when you no longer need it.

2 Masonry nails are specially hardened to penetrate concrete or mortar.

3 Spiral and ring-shanked nails provide more holding power in wood. Spiral nails are threaded, somewhat like screws, and twist into materials; ring-shanked nails have ridges that grab the wood.

4 Corrugated fasteners, or wiggly nails, are used mainly to strengthen already-fastened joints. You also can use them alone for light-duty jobs such as building frames for screens.

5 Brads are miniature finishing nails, good for small molding and more delicate jobs.

6 Finishing and casing nails have small heads that are easily countersunk (set below the surface).

7 Roofing nails have wide, thin heads to hold down shingles and roofing paper.

8 Box and common nails are similar, but common nails have a thicker shank; this increases holding power but can cause splits in some boards.

Nail sizes

To determine the size nail you should use, multiply the thickness of the material you'll be nailing through by three. A ¾-inch-thick board, for example, calls for a 2¼-inch nail.

Nail coatings

All nails used for outdoor construction should be rust-resistant so that they won't discolor the wood. Stainless-steel and aluminum nails ensure resistance to rust, but both are expensive, and aluminum nails bend easily and shouldn't be used with pressure-treated lumber. For economical rust protection, choose hot-dipped galvanized steel nails.

One other coating deserves mention. Cement-coated nails have an adhesive film that bonds to wood fibers under the heat and friction of driving. They are typically used for framing walls and other structural assemblies.

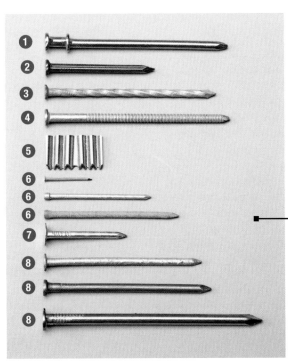

Here are the profiles of the nails most commonly used in outdoor construction projects. To learn what each nail does best, check the text at left. Nails longer than 4 inches (20d) are called spikes.

HARDWARE AND FASTENERS *(continued)*

For the few seconds it takes to drive them, nails do a remarkable holding job. But at critical junctures you'll surely want the strength and neatness of screws and bolts.

The photo below shows the two broad types of screws available: wood screws ❶ and metal screws ❷. Metal screws have a flat, broad head and a shank that's threaded from head to tip, making them ideal for securing thin materials such as sheet metal and plastic. For wood-to-wood joints, use flathead, ovalhead, or roundhead wood screws. You can drive flathead screws flush with the surface. Ovalhead screws add a decorative accent. Roundhead screws handle more utilitarian tasks. When required, use a flat washer with a roundhead screw, trim washers with flat- and ovalhead screws ❸.

Sizing up screws

As with nails, the right size screw for the job should go about two-thirds of its length into the member you're fastening to. When ordering wood screws, specify the length (from ¼ to 5 inches), gauge or shank diameter (No. 0, which is about ¹⁄₁₆ inch, to No. 24, about ⅜ inch), head type (flat, round, pan, and others), and material (stainless or galvanized steel for outdoor projects). The larger a screw's gauge, the greater its holding power.

Turn to lag screws ❹, often called lag bolts, for heavy framing jobs. To order these, specify diameter (from ¼ to 1 inch) and length (from 1 to 16 inches).

Machine bolts (such as the hex-head bolt ❺ shown) and carriage bolts ❻ handle all kinds of heavy fastening jobs, and are paired with a matching threaded nut. You need two wrenches to tighten a machine bolt and one for a carriage bolt.

When ordering bolts, specify the diameter, length, and type (machine or carriage). To determine the correct length, add about ¾ inch to the combined thicknesses of the materials to be joined. Carriage bolts have diameters ranging from ¼ to ¾ inch and lengths from ¾ to 20 inches; machine bolts have diameters of ¼ to 1 inch and lengths of ½ to 30 inches.

A lag shield anchor ❼ or plastic expansion anchor ❽ enables you to drive a screw into masonry or mortar joints. You drill a hole, insert the anchor, then turn a screw into it. As the screw cuts its threads, it expands the soft lead fitting snugly against the sides of the hole.

Screws thread into wood or other materials. Bolts go all the way through and are secured by nuts. Tighten screws with a straight or phillips screwdriver, or, in the case of lag screws, a wrench. Washers prevent the screwhead from marring the surface of the material. Use anchors when fastening to concrete or masonry.

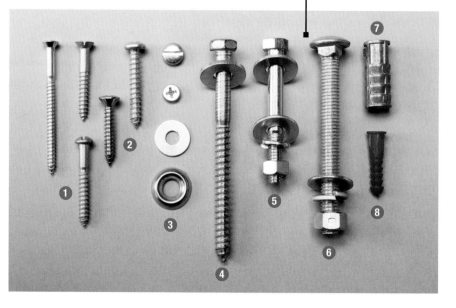

Plates and hangers

Want to beef up an otherwise weak wood joint? Reach for one of the devices shown at right. Mending plates reinforce end-to-end butt joints. Corner braces strengthen right-angle joints by attaching to edge surfaces. Flat corner irons do the same thing but attach to the faces of the materials. T-plates handle end-to-edge joints.

Framing fasteners, such as the joist hanger shown in the photo below, solve tricky framing problems. Other fasteners include saddle brackets for beam-on-beam or joist-on-beam applications, post caps for securing beams to the tops of posts, rafter brackets, angle brackets, seismic ties, and stair cleats. As with nails, screws, and bolts, all plates and hangers for outdoor use should be made of galvanized steel or other rustproof material.

Gate hardware

If your construction project will include a gate, you have some additional choices to make. The photo at lower right shows just a few of the hinges, latches, handles, and springs available at home centers.

Brick hinges install in mortar between bricks. You chip out old mortar, fit the support into the recess, then force a light concrete or mortar mix around it.

Screw hinges thread into holes in a post. Decorative hinges typically attach to the post and gate with lag screws. T-hinges reinforce the gate by covering its corner joints, always the weak spots in any gate. Use these for large garden gates, garage and barn doors, and any other application that calls for a sturdy, functional hinge.

Besides hinges, a gate requires a latch and some sort of handle. A self-closing latch automatically engages hardware on the post when the gate swings shut, protecting the gate and hinges from damage caused by strong gusts of wind.

You can make a wood handle with scraps left over from building the gate. Or fit the gate with a store-bought metal handle. Whether or not your gate has a latch, a spring can keep it closed. Simply mount it and adjust for fast or slow closure.

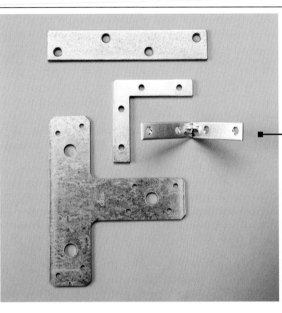

These are only a few of the specialized plates you can find in the hardware sections of home centers. From top to bottom: Mending plate, flat corner iron, corner brace, and T-plate.

If your plans call for a gate, door, or other moving element, you have an equally wide selection of hinges, latches, handles, and other hardware to choose from. Let appearance and function guide you.

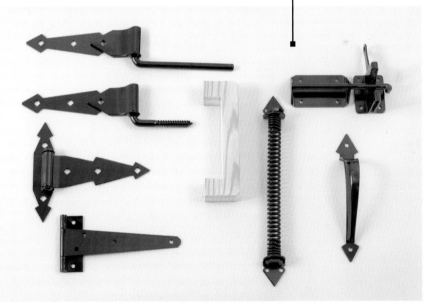

WOOD

Because all successful outdoor woodworking or carpentry projects start with the right tools and materials, look first at these prerequisites. Then, on pages 334–337, we show you some basic techniques for working with wood.

Choosing tools

Though not exhaustive, the photos on the opposite page depict many of the tools required for landscape construction with wood.

When selecting tools, keep in mind that good craftsmanship begins with quality tools. If, like most homeowners, you already have a few tools lying around, take a critical look at them before beginning a project. Toss out any that are bent or broken—and stay away from the bargain bins when you are shopping for replacements.

Instead, if at all possible, spend more money and invest in top-of-the-line professional-quality tools. Sturdily built to exacting standards, these tools will endure years of hard use. Some companies even offer lifetime guarantees.

Choosing lumber

Any lumber you select for outdoor projects must be naturally or chemically rot-resistant. Pages 180–181 present the pros, cons, and relative costs of five popular choices: redwood, cedar, cypress, synthetic, and pressured-treated lumber.

Once you've decided what type of wood you want for your project, consider which grade of wood will work best for the project's various components. In general, think in terms of two overall classifications: select and common. Quality grades run in descending order and should be used for different purposes. Consider pressure-treated wood, for example: Grade No. 1 is used for railings and benches; Grade No. 2 or better is used for decking. Additionally, kiln-dried wood is more dimensionally-stable than air-dried wood. Look for a KDAT stamp to ensure the wood you are using is kiln dried.

Bear in mind that most pieces of lumber have a set of nominal dimensions (what you order—for example,

2×4) and a set of actual dimensions (the size after the lumber is milled and dried—for example, 1½×3½). To learn about nominal and actual dimensions of various size members, consult the chart on page 335.

Ordering lumber

Before you set out for the home center or lumberyard, draw up a list detailing exactly what wood you'll need. To order, state the grade, species, quantity, thickness, width, and length—in that order. Example: construction-heart redwood, 40 pieces, 2×6 inches, 10 feet long.

Do everything you can to get a firsthand look at what you're buying. Most lumber retailers allow you to go into the yard and hand-select your choices. Reject any boards that have serious defects. Realize, though, that few boards are absolutely perfect and that minor problems can be trimmed off when you cut the lumber or straightened out when you nail it in place.

Choosing plywood

Use only exterior-grade or marine-grade plywood for outdoor projects; moisture quickly dissolves the glues in plywood. If a project is made from plywood that will be continually in contact with the ground, use only pressure-treated material. Ask your home center for PT plywood rated for "ground contact—0.40 pcf." Grade CDX is a thrifty choice for concrete forms, rough screening, and temporary walks.

Storing lumber

Before your lumber is delivered, give thought to where you want to put it. You may choose to stack it in the garage or near the project site. Use blocks to keep it off the floor or ground, and cover it to protect against moisture and intense direct sunlight. If you won't be using it for a while, separate layers with crosspieces to allow air circulation. Store sheet goods flat. Lumber is not dimensionally stable; fastening only restricts some of the movement, which—if excessive—will cause cracking, warping, and such. Finishing to reduce moisture exchange is equally critical to prevent excess movement.

CARPENTRY TOOLS

You may already own many of the carpentry tools you'll need for outdoor projects. While most corded tools are double-insulated to prevent electric shock, you might prefer to use a cordless electrical drill or jigsaw, for instance, for more freedom of movement.

1   Circular saw
2   Cordless drill
3   Jigsaw
4   Power drill
5   Miter box and backsaw
6   Keyhole saw
7   Adjustable wrench
8   Locking pliers
9   C-clamp
10 Utility knife
11 Handsaw
12 Framing square
13 Angle square
14 Combination square
15 Carpenter's level
16 Coping saw
17 25-foot, 1-inch-wide
    tape measure
18 Drywall saw
19 Rasp
20 Wood file
21 Chalkline
22 T-bevel
23 Hammer
24 Nail set
25 Plumb bob
26 Phillips-tip screwdriver
27 Straight-tip screwdriver
28 Awl
29 Wood chisel
30 Block plane

WOOD *(continued)*

All carpentry projects follow essentially the same steps. You begin with good measurements. After that, you cut pieces to size, then nail, screw, or bolt them together. Finally, when working outdoors, you often protect everything with a preservative. Here we take you through these processes.

Measuring basics

Whether you're building a 50-room mansion or a doghouse, there's no such measurement as "about." Measurements should be as precise as possible.

Be sure, too, that your measurements take into account the narrow opening the saw will leave in its wake—called the kerf. If you're making just one cut, allow for the kerf by identifying the scrap side of the cutoff line with an X. This tells you which side to cut from. For multiple cuts along a board or on sheet goods, allow for the kerf between the cutoff lines.

With few exceptions (such as large timbers, posts, and fence slats), commonly available lumber is completely milled (S4S) on both faces and edges. If it's out of square, it's because of movement after milling, usually due to further drying. Most outdoor projects don't require the precision of true edges.

Cutting basics

The vast majority of the cuts you'll be making fall into two categories: crosscuts across the grain and rip cuts parallel with the grain.

Crosscut boards with either a hand- or power saw. Start cuts by carefully positioning the blade so that its kerf will be on the scrap side. With a handsaw, place the blade at a 45-degree angle to the work and, using the knuckle of your thumb as a guide, pull the saw back toward you; with a power saw, squeeze the trigger and let the blade get up to speed before easing it into the wood. Keep a firm but not clenched grip on the saw handle, and don't force the cut.

For rip cuts, a power saw works best. To ensure that you'll get a straight edge along the entire length of the cut, clamp a straight board or straightedge parallel to the cut line and guide the saw along it.

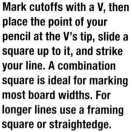

Mark cutoffs with a V, then place the point of your pencil at the V's tip, slide a square up to it, and strike your line. A combination square is ideal for marking most board widths. For longer lines use a framing square or straightedge.

When you near the end of a crosscut, support the scrap side with slight upward pressure from your free hand. This keeps the piece from snapping off and splintering. Position your fingers well away from the saw blade.

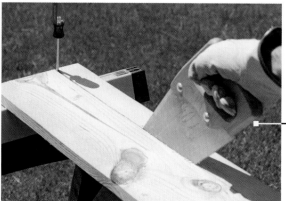

Saw blades tend to bind in longer rip cuts. If this happens, widen the kerf by wedging a nail or screwdriver into it. Be sure, too, that you are using a saw with a tooth grind designed for rip cuts.

LUMBER SELECTOR

Type		Nominal Size	Actual Size	Common Uses
Strips	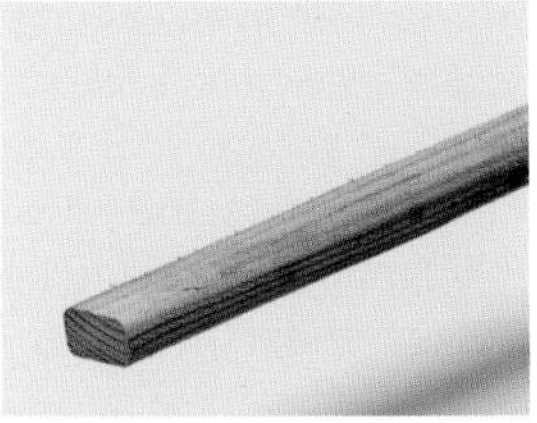	1×2 1×3	$\frac{3}{4}×1\frac{1}{2}$ $\frac{3}{4}×2\frac{1}{2}$	Trim, spacers, shims, bridging, stakes, shallow forms, battens, screen frames, edging, latticework, and trellises. Strips are inexpensive and versatile building materials.
Finish Lumber (Boards)		1×4 1×6 1×8 1×10 1×12	$\frac{3}{4}×3\frac{1}{2}$ $\frac{3}{4}×5\frac{1}{2}$ $\frac{3}{4}×7\frac{1}{2}$ $\frac{3}{4}×9\frac{1}{4}$ $\frac{3}{4}×11\frac{1}{4}$	Sheathing, siding and soffits, subflooring and flooring, decking, fencing, edging, walks, trim, planters, benches, storage sheds, and forms. Besides the ordinary board shown here, finish lumber also includes lumber with tongue-and-groove or shiplap edges.
Framing Lumber		2×2 2×3 2×4 2×6 2×8 2×10 2×12	$1\frac{1}{2}×1\frac{1}{2}$ $1\frac{1}{2}×2\frac{1}{2}$ $1\frac{1}{2}×3\frac{1}{2}$ $1\frac{1}{2}×5\frac{1}{2}$ $1\frac{1}{2}×7\frac{1}{4}$ $1\frac{1}{2}×9\frac{1}{4}$ $1\frac{1}{2}×11\frac{1}{4}$	Structural framing, stakes, decking, structural finishing, forming, fencing, walks, benches, screeds, and stair components. Framing lumber provides structural support and a nailing base for finish lumber and trim.
Posts		4×4 6×6	$3\frac{1}{2}×3\frac{1}{2}$ $5\frac{1}{2}×5\frac{1}{2}$	Heavy-duty structural framing, support columns, fence posts, deck posts, retaining walls, and edging for patios and walks. You also can buy round posts in several diameters.
Timbers		Rough-sawn; sizes vary	Actual sizes vary slightly up or down from nominal sizes.	Heavy-duty structural framing, support columns, retaining walls, and steps. Timbers are a good building material for architectural and decorative interest. Maneuvering hefty landscape timbers is a two-person job.

WOOD *(continued)*

Fell a tree and its wood stops growing. But this organic building material has an afterlife of sorts because humidity changes cause the wood fibers to expand and shrink with the seasons—a process that can play havoc with weak joints in outdoor projects. To minimize twisting, racking, warping, and splitting, use nails, screws, or bolts at all critical structural points.

Nailing basics

Bend a few nails or split a perfectly good piece of wood and you'll soon discover that no one is born with an innate knack for pounding nails. Actually you don't pound a nail at all; you drive it with a few well-directed blows. As with golf or tennis, learning to direct those blows means you must perfect your swing.

Grasp the hammer at the end of its handle, not up around the neck. Start the nail with a gentle tap, then lift the hammer in a gentle arc. Now, keeping your wrist stiff, drop the hammer squarely onto the nail. With practice you'll find yourself driving nails smoothly, without straining (or maiming) your arm, wrist, or hand.

Your last blow should push the head of a common nail flush with the surface of the wood; drive the heads of finishing or casing nails below the surface with a nail set.

For maximum holding power in rough projects, use nails about an inch longer than the combined thicknesses of the pieces you're fastening. Drive the nails, then turn the members over and clinch (bend) the exposed portions of the nails in the direction of the grain so that they're nearly flush with the surface. For showier projects, or when you can't get at the backs of the materials, drive pairs of nails at opposing angles. For help in selecting nails, see page 329.

Drilling basics

The electric drill/driver has made all hand-powered boring tools obsolete. With a complement of bits, you can make holes in just about anything and use the drill to drive screws as well. Here are some tips for using this jack-of-all-trades drill/driver:

• To prevent the drill bit from skating away from the point where you want a hole, make a shallow pilot hole first with an awl or the tip of a nail. Grip the drill/driver with both hands and center the bit in the hole, then apply firm pressure and begin drilling. If you have a variable-speed model, bring it up to full power gradually.

• To assure that a hole will be perpendicular, hold a combination square against the wood and align the drill/driver with the square's blade.

• When you want to drill one or more holes to a certain depth, wrap masking or electrical tape around the drill bit so that the tape will touch the surface of the wood at the depth you want. Drill with gentle pressure, then carefully back the bit out as soon as the tape hits the surface.

• To keep wood chips from clogging the bit and causing it to bind when you're drilling deep holes, feed the bit into the wood slowly, and back the bit out of the hole frequently with the drill/driver's motor still running.

Screw basics

The threads along the shank of a screw grip the fibers of the wood being joined and pull them together with tremendous pressure. Here's how to get good results with these super fasteners:

• First drill pilot holes. Screws driven in directly can split all but the softest of woods. Make the holes slightly smaller than the screw's diameter.

• Select the correct screwdriver for the screw you're driving. It should fill the recess completely.

• Turning a lot of screws—or even just a few—by hand can tire you. To reduce fatigue and speed the operation, drive the screws with your drill/driver and a screwdriver bit.

• Faced with a hole that's a little too big for the screw you're driving? Glue a toothpick or sliver of wood into the hole. Tightening the screw forces the filler material against the wall of the hole, holding the screw tight.

Bolting basics

Nails and screws depend on friction between the fastener and the wood to do their jobs. Not so with bolts. When you tighten a nut on a bolt, you're mechanically clamping adjoining members together, creating the strongest joint of all. Here are ways to get the best out of bolts:

• Tighten an adjustable wrench snugly onto the work. Otherwise, it could slip and strip a nut or bolt head.

• Adjustable-end wrenches can handle most bolting jobs, but a set of automotive socket wrenches speeds the work and helps you out in tight corners. Socket-wrench sets typically include a crank-style handle for speedy tightening and a reversible ratchet that lets you move the handle back and forth without removing the socket from the work.

• Never force a wrench by tapping its handle with a hammer. And don't slip a pipe over a wrench handle to gain leverage; you could snap the wrench or the fastener it's tightening.

Finishing basics

Most exterior lumber, including redwood, cedar, cypress, and pressure-treated wood, stands up to weather and lasts longer, when finished with periodic applications of preservative, stain, or paint. This is especially true in extreme climates, where sun, rain, ice, snow, and wind take a toll on wood eventually. Synthetic lumbers, on the other hand, don't need added preservatives.

Apply clear preservative immediately to maintain the original appearance of redwood, cedar, and cypress. Or, wait and let the wood weather before sealing it. Staining preservatives can give pressure-treated lumber the color of redwood or cedar.

Apply the finish with a brush, roller, or an inexpensive pressure sprayer, depending on the product and the manufacturer's recommended tools and techniques. If you spray, wear a mask, gloves, and eye protection.

To make sure the hammer strikes the nail, not your fingers, keep your eye on the nail and let the weight of the hammer's head do the driving. Blunt the point of a nail that will be driven near the end of a board to reduce the chance of splitting.

A spade bit can splinter wood when it exits through the back. To prevent this, drill until just the tip of the bit penetrates. Then carefully back out the bit and finish drilling from the other side.

To bolt two pieces of wood together, slip a flat washer onto the bolt, then slide the bolt through the hole. Put another flat washer, then a lock washer, over the opposite end of the bolt; follow the washers with a nut. Tighten with two wrenches.

CONCRETE AND MASONRY

Everyone calls it cement, but you can't build much of anything with plain Portland cement. Mix it with other materials, though, and cement becomes the key ingredient in the magic muds known as concrete and mortar.

On these two pages you'll find a review of some of the tools you'll need when you do concrete and masonry work.

Concrete tools

As you decide which of the tools shown on the opposite page you will need for your project, bear in mind that you can either buy or rent most of them. If you buy, purchase only good-quality tools.

To aid in mixing and transporting masonry materials and concrete, lay your hands on a sturdy contractor-quality wheelbarrow—the kind with a 3-cubic-foot or larger tray and one or two pneumatic rubber tires. Also handy, but not essential, are a mortar box and mortar hoe for mixing ingredients.

To prepare sites and move concrete and mortar ingredients, you must have either a round-bladed shovel or a couple of specialists: a spade for squaring up excavation edges and a square-bladed shovel for moving sand and wet concrete.

For placing concrete, you'll need a tamper, a wooden float, a screed (not shown), and a darby or bull float. Screeds, used to level wet concrete flush with forms, often are nothing more than straight lengths of 2x4. Use the darby, bull float, or a small hand float to smooth screeded concrete and push larger stones below the surface. You can make a screed from scrap lumber, if you like.

To finish, use a steel trowel to further smooth and compact the concrete, an inexpensive edger to round off and strengthen the edges of concrete slabs, and a jointer to put grooves in slabs to control cracking. If you plan to cut control joints after the concrete hardens, fit a circular saw with a masonry blade for the jointing work.

Masonry tools

If you're working with mortar, you can dispense with the tools needed for finishing concrete, but you'll need several others. To cut bricks, blocks, and stones, buy or rent a bricklayer's hammer, a brick set or masonry chisel, and a 2-pound sledgehammer (often called a baby sledge or mash hammer).

And when building concrete or masonry walls, lay your hands on line blocks, a modular spacing rule, and a plumb bob.

For placing mortar use a well-balanced, pointed brick trowel. Use a pointing trowel or a caulking trowel to force mortar into joints being repaired. A jointer or joint groover helps you finish mortar joints.

Because dried concrete and mortar are almost impossible to remove, wash and dry tools—and your boots—thoroughly after use. Follow the drying with a light coat of oil on all metal parts.

Mixed in the right proportions, coarse aggregate (gravel or crushed rock), sand, cement, and water turn into concrete, a pliable material that soon hardens into a stonelike mass. Mortar—made from sand, cement, lime, and water—bonds bricks, blocks, and stones.

Coarse aggregate

Sand

Cement

Water

MASONRY TOOLS

Besides specialized concrete and masonry tools, you'll need carpentry tools—such as a claw hammer, handsaw or circular saw, levels, chalk box, mason's line, and framing square—for building forms and batter boards.

1 Mortar box and mortar hoe
2 Bricklayer's hammer
3 Tamper
4 Round-bladed shovel
5 Narrow spade
6 Level
7 Tape measure
8 Mason's line
9 Chalkline
10 Edger
11 Jointer (groover)
12 Darby (magnesium)
13 Baby sledge
14 Bull float (magnesium)
15 Wood float
16 Concave jointer
17 Masonry blade
18 Pointing trowel
19 Framing square
20 Line level
21 Line blocks
22 Plumb bob
23 Modular spacing rule
24 Wheelbarrow
25 Hand brush
26 Masonry chisel

CONCRETE AND MASONRY *(continued)*

Working with concrete is a six-step process: You prepare the site, build forms, place the mix, strike it off, float and trowel the surface, then help it cure. Here's what each of these steps entails.

Preparing the site

If at all possible, place your slab on undisturbed soil. If you must pour on top of recently filled soil, as would be the case around a new foundation, pack the soil by watering it for several days and allowing it time to settle.

Lay out the site with strings and stakes or batter boards, as explained on pages 64–65. Then excavate to a depth equal to the thickness of the slab you've decided on, plus 2 to 3 inches for a sand or gravel drainage bed, minus 1 inch so that the slab's surface will be above ground level. Make the excavation about 3 inches larger all around to provide room for forms.

Building forms

Because slabs generally run about 4 inches thick, 2×4s that are smooth and straight make ideal forming material. Securely anchor the form boards with foot-long stakes (1×4 lumber works well) every 3 to 4 feet. Attach the stakes to the form boards with double-headed nails, which are easy to pull later. Or nail through the form boards and into the stakes using regular-headed nails. Hammer the stakes' tops so that they are level with the top of the form or cut them at that level so that you can drag a screed across the form.

For proper drainage, forms should slope at least ¼ inch per foot. To establish the proper slope, measure down from both ends of a level string stretched from the top end of the slab (perhaps at the house or garage) to the point where the slab will end. For a 20-foot slab, for example, the downhill edge should be 5 inches lower than the uphill edge.

Shape curves with 3½-inch-wide strips of ¼-inch-thick hardboard or plywood. With plywood, cut the strips perpendicular to the grain so that they're easier to bend. For a snug fit, tack one end in place, driving two 4d nails through the thin form member into a stake. Then spring the board into the desired shape, cut it to length, and nail it to a second stake.

To control cracking, prop up ½-inch-thick expansion strips wherever the new concrete will abut old concrete. (See pages 148-149 for details on tooling control joints into poured concrete.)

Mixing or ordering concrete

Compute how much concrete you'll need by multiplying the form's width and length; for circles or cylindrical forms, multiply the square of the radius by 3.14. After you know how many square feet you'll have, consult the Concrete Estimator on the opposite page. To ensure that you won't run short, increase your estimate by 10 percent.

When buying concrete, you have three options. For small jobs, such as setting a few fence posts, buy premixed concrete. Premixed bags include cement, sand, and aggregate. You simply add water. Each sack yields from ⅓ to ⅔ cubic foot of concrete, depending on its size.

For jobs that require a half cubic yard or more of concrete, buy the cement, sand, and aggregate separately and mix them yourself, or order ready-mix concrete. (Some concrete haulers may require a minimum order; check first.) Mixing it yourself—using 10 shovelfuls of portland cement, 22 shovelfuls

Use 2×4s for forming material when making slabs. Drive pointed, wooden stakes into the ground every 3 to 4 feet. Nail or screw the stakes to the forms.

For curves, substitute 3½-inch-wide strips of ¼-inch hardboard or plywood for the 2×4s. Tack one end to a stake, spring the form into a curve, cut it to length, and nail it to stake.

of sand, and 30 shovelfuls of aggregate for each cubic yard—lets you make a small batch at a time. This allows you to place and finish one section before repeating the process.

If time and energy mean more to you than cost, order ready-mix concrete. You'll get a more reliable mix and also avoid hauling and mixing messes.

Pouring and finishing concrete

Spread sand or gravel in the form, then lay reinforcing mesh of a gauge appropriate to the job. Next pour wet concrete into the form, spreading it with a garden rake. Use the rake's tines to pull the mesh midway into the slab's thickness.

Level the surface by screeding it with a 2×4 laid across the slab, from one side of the form to the other. Move the screed back and forth in a sawing motion and draw it horizontally across the unleveled concrete, as shown on page 147.

Smooth the concrete with a darby or bull float. Then, when water no longer rises to the surface, run an edger between the slab and the form. After that, use a jointer and a straight board to hand-tool shallow control joints (every 8 feet or so in a patio; every 4 feet or so in a walk). Finish with a wood or steel trowel, or give the surface a special texture (see pages 82–83).

Keep concrete wet during the first week after you pour. One way to do this is with a hose or lawn sprinkler. You also can retard evaporation by covering the slab with plastic sheets.

CONCRETE ESTIMATOR
In cubic feet and (cubic yards)

Thickness	Surface Area of Job in Square Feet				
	20	50	100	200	500
4 inches	6.7 (.2)	16.7 (.6)	33.3 (1.2)	66.7 (2.5)	166.7 (6.2)
6 inches	10 (.4)	25 (.9)	50 (1.9)	100 (3.7)	250 (9.3)
8 inches	13.3 (.5)	33.3 (1.3)	66.6 (2.5)	133.3 (5.9)	333.3 (12.5)

CONCRETE MIXING PROPORTIONS

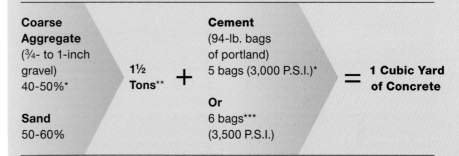

Coarse Aggregate
(¾- to 1-inch gravel)
40-50%*

Sand
50-60%

1½ Tons**

+

Cement
(94-lb. bags of portland)
5 bags (3,000 P.S.I.)*

Or

6 bags***
(3,500 P.S.I.)

= **1 Cubic Yard of Concrete**

* The more cement and aggregate, the stronger the mix.

** These ingredients can be purchased separately in the proportions described here or together in a mixture commonly known as con-mix.

*** For projects requiring extra lateral strength, such as a driveway.

1) Mix dry ingredients.
2) Add water; stir until it's the consistency of mud; smack concrete with back of shovel; chop with shovel to create groove 2 inches deep. 3) For indistinct groove, add water. 4) If groove maintains shape, it's OK. 5) If groove caves in, add sand, gravel, cement.

CONCRETE AND MASONRY *(continued)*

STONES

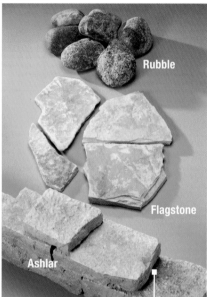

Rubble

Flagstone

Ashlar

Stone is classified according to how it's cut. Rubble is uncut and highly irregular. Flagstones—typically sandstone, limestone, or quartzite—are big, flat rocks. Ashlar consists of squared but still irregular shapes.

BRICKS (NOMINAL SIZES)

Modular
4"W×1-2⅔"H×8"L

Roman
4"W×2"H×12"L

Normal
4"W×1-2⅔"H×12"L

Engineer king
3⅜"W×3³⁄₁₆"H×10"L

Patio
4"W×1-3"H×8"L

Bricks and stones come in myriad sizes. To estimate how many you will need, figure the area of your project in square feet. A masonry dealer can tell you how many bricks or stones of a given size will cover 1 square foot.

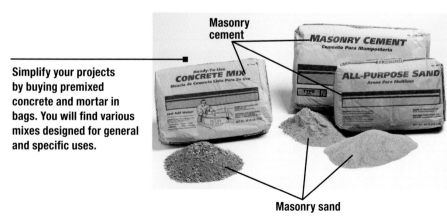

Masonry cement

MASONRY CEMENT
Cemento Para Mampostería

Ready-To-Use
CONCRETE MIX
Mezcla de Concreto Lista Para Su Uso

ALL-PURPOSE SAND
Arena Para Multiuso

Masonry sand

Simplify your projects by buying premixed concrete and mortar in bags. You will find various mixes designed for general and specific uses.

Easy to work with and nearly indestructible, stones, bricks, and blocks make sense for a wide range of outdoor building projects. First take a look at your choices in masonry units; then you'll learn how to put them together.

Options

Masonry work can be accomplished with any number of different building materials.

Stones fall into the three broad categories illustrated at far left. Rubble stones interlock like three-dimensional jigsaw puzzles. Because they're irregular, rubble stones work well for walls but not for horizontal surfaces such as patios and walks.

With flagstones, it's the other way around. These come in irregular shapes or precut squares and rectangles that are more or less uniform in thickness. Use flagstones for walks, steps, and patios, and anywhere else you want a durable, dressy surface.

Ashlar or dimensioned stone is cut on all sides, making it easy to stack. You still have to do some final cutting and fitting, though.

Bricks vary in color, texture, and dimensions. Modular bricks are sized to conform to modules of 4 inches, which makes it easy to estimate how many you will need. Nonmodular bricks do not conform to the 4-inch standard.

When a dealer tells you the dimensions of a brick, he is talking about its nominal size, which is the brick's actual size, plus a normal mortar joint of ⅜ to ½ inch on the bottom and at one end.

For outdoor projects that must withstand moisture and freeze-and-thaw cycles, ask for SW (severe weathering) bricks. If temperatures in your area are moderate year-round, you can get by with MW (moderate weathering) bricks. Use NW (no weathering) bricks only for interior projects such as fireplaces.

Concrete blocks are cast from a stiff concrete mix into hundreds of different sizes and shapes. A typical block has a nominal size of 8×8×16 inches and weighs 40 to 50 pounds.

To cut a stone, score all around the desired break line. Lay the stone across a support, tap the unsupported part. Wear goggles when doing this.

To cut a brick, score around it. Set the brick on sand, hold a brick set with its bevel away from the side of the finished cut, and rap sharply.

Concrete blocks come in two grades— N, designed for outdoor freezing, and S, for use above grade and where the blocks won't be directly exposed to weather.

Masonry veneers of brick, terra-cotta, slate, and stone offer a way to put an attractive face on otherwise plain materials, such as concrete. Terra-cotta quarry tiles are made in many colors and shapes. They measure ⅜ inch or ½ inch thick. Slate tiles also come in several colors and in uniform thicknesses ranging from ¼ inch to 1 inch. Flagstones aren't uniformly thick, which means you must lay them on sand or in a thick mortar bed.

Dry vs. wet setting

Once you've settled on the sort of masonry units you'd like for your project, you need to decide what to put between them. Here your choices are two: Dry-set the units without mortar or wet-set the units using mortar to bond them.

To dry-set a patio or other surface, you simply excavate, lay down a bed of sand, set the masonry on this bed, then sweep more sand into the joints. You also can lay a stone retaining wall without mortar.

Dry-setting masonry is the easier way to go, but mortaring isn't as difficult as you might imagine, once you get the hang of it.

Mixing mortar

How you go about preparing the mortar for a job depends on the project's size. For small jobs and repairs, buy premixed mortar that already contains sand. For larger ventures you'll save money by purchasing the special sand and masonry cement separately and mixing them yourself.

To mix mortar, carefully measure three parts masonry sand and one part cement into a sturdy wheelbarrow or mortar box. Spread half of the sand first, then the cement, then the rest of the sand. Use a hoe to thoroughly mix the dry materials.

After you've completely blended the sand and cement, make a depression in the center of the dry mix, pour a small amount of water into it, then fold

the mix into the water with a hoe or trowel. Add more water until your mix has the right adhesiveness. (To check this, pick up a small amount of it with your trowel, stick it to the trowel with an upward jerk, then turn the trowel upside down. If the mortar sticks, it's ready to use.) Be sure to take your time. Generally you'll need about 2½ gallons of water for each bag of cement, but this can vary, depending on the moisture content of the sand. Don't run water from a hose into the mix; you might drown the mortar.

Working with mortar

Lay mortared masonry paving units on top of only sound, clean concrete. If you have to pour a concrete slab first, follow the steps explained on pages 146–147, skipping any steps after the screeding.

Wet the surface just before troweling on an even ¼- to 1-inch layer of mortar. Use a thinner layer for even-surface paving units such as brick, a thicker one for irregular stones. Screed this to a uniform depth with a piece of 2×4, then place the paving units on the mortar, leveling each one as you position it. Let the mortar holding the masonry set and cure for a day or two before you fill the joints between them with more mortar.

343

WIRING

If you've successfully pulled off a few indoor wiring projects, the principles you learned there can help you do the same outside. Exterior electrical equipment differs slightly, however, and you must take a few additional precautions to protect wiring against moisture.

Read these two pages for details on the tools and components you'll need. Pages 346–347 discuss the techniques you'll need to master.

(Caution: If this is your first time to work with electricity, outdoors is not the place to start. For this reason, any discussion of basic procedures such as making connections and hooking up receptacles and switches has been omitted.)

Cable

In planning an underground installation, first find out whether local codes permit plastic-clad underground feeder (UF) cable, or whether they require that you run standard thermoplastic insulated wires (TW) through rigid conduit. If you're permitted to use cable, you'll still have to protect it with conduit in aboveground situations. Your local authorities will tell you how deeply you must bury cables and conduit.

When you buy fittings make sure they're the weathertight type designed for outdoor use. Exterior components look much like the ones used inside, but they're heftier and have gaskets, waterproof covers, and rubber-sealed connections.

Also, because the potential for serious shock is much greater outdoors, you must protect all exterior receptacles with ground fault circuit interrupters (GFCIs). These devices, which can be installed in your home's service panel or in lieu of a standard receptacle, instantly shut off power should a malfunction occur.

Tools

You may not need all the items pictured opposite, and you may already have quite a few of them, but here is an explanation of what each does.

Long-nose and lineman's pliers are musts. The first help you curl wires into the loops needed for many electrical connections. Lineman's pliers handle heavier cutting and twisting jobs. Side-cutting pliers are handy for snipping wires in tight places.

A utility knife slices through anything that calls for a cutting edge. A multipurpose combination tool cuts and strips wires, sizes and cuts off screws, crimps connectors, and more. If your wiring is protected by cartridge-type fuses, a plastic fuse puller lets you remove them without danger of electrical shock.

Several types of testers are available. The continuity type has a small battery and bulb for testing switches, sockets, and fuses with the power off. A neon tester, on the other hand, lights up only when current is flowing. It tells you whether an outlet is live and hooked up properly.

You'll need one of each of these or you can invest in an inexpensive voltage tester instead. If you'll be installing a number of new receptacles, you also might want a receptacle analyzer.

With an electric drill, a spade bit, and a bit extension, you can bore holes for wiring in just about anything, even through the side of your house.

Most of the gear shown here packs easily into a tool tote. Electrical work keeps you on the move, and you'll appreciate the convenience of having everything you might need in one open carrier.

Low-voltage wiring

If you don't relish the arduous job of burying 120-volt wiring underground, consider a low-voltage lighting system instead. These step down house current to a 6- or 12-volt trickle, which means you can safely string fixtures like most Christmas tree lights. Simply plug a transformer into a standard 120-volt receptacle and run lightweight cable to the fixtures.

WIRING TOOLS

Armed with these tools, you can do just about any electrical job, indoors or out. If you'll have a lot of digging to do, you might also want to rent a gasoline-engine trenching machine. Even for short runs, you can count on a hard day of excavating by hand.

1 Lineman's pliers
2 Combination stripper
3 Long-nose pliers
4 Side-cutting pliers
5 Continuity tester
6 Rotary screwdriver
7 Electrician's screwdrivers
8 Neon voltage tester
9 Multilevel tester
10 Utility knife
11 Voltage tester
12 Receptacle analyzer
13 Wire-fishing drill bit
14 Conduit bender
15 Armored-cable cutter
16 Analog meter (above);
    digital meter (below)
17 Hacksaw
18 Flat pry bar
19 Two-part circuit finder
20 Drywall saw
21 Voltage detector
22 Fuse puller
23 Fish tape
24 Electric drill/driver;
    spade bit
25 Tubing cutter

WIRING *(continued)*

To complete an outdoor electrical installation, you first have to decide where the power is going to come from. Next you dig a trench from that point to the site or sites where you would like lights or receptacles. Then you lay conduit, cable, or a combination of the two and make the final connections.

Tapping power

If there's an exterior receptacle nearby, you're in luck. Simply dig a trench to the receptacle and hook up to it as shown at upper right.

If there's no convenient source of power outside, look around your basement for a junction box or run a new circuit from the service panel. This requires boring a hole through the wall, as is illustrated at lower right.

In some localities you can run sheathed cable through the wall to a new box outside; in others, you're required to use conduit or armored cable. Find out what codes permit. In most cases it's best to install a junction box back-to-back with the exterior box, then connect the two with conduit or cable.

A third option is to take power from an exterior light fixture, illustrated opposite. This is probably the least desirable way to go because you have to run conduit up to the eaves and your new outlet will be live only when the light switch is turned on.

In the trenches

Once you know where power is going to come from, it's time to plan an itinerary for the trench or trenches you will need. Route these well away from water, gas, electric, telephone, sewer, and sprinkler lines. For conduit be sure to keep the trenches as straight as possible; sheathed cable can easily snake around obstructions.

After you've laid out a trench, strip away sod and set it aside on plastic sheeting. Keep the sod slightly damp. For electrical metal tubing (EMT) and UF cable, you'll need a trench that is about 8 inches

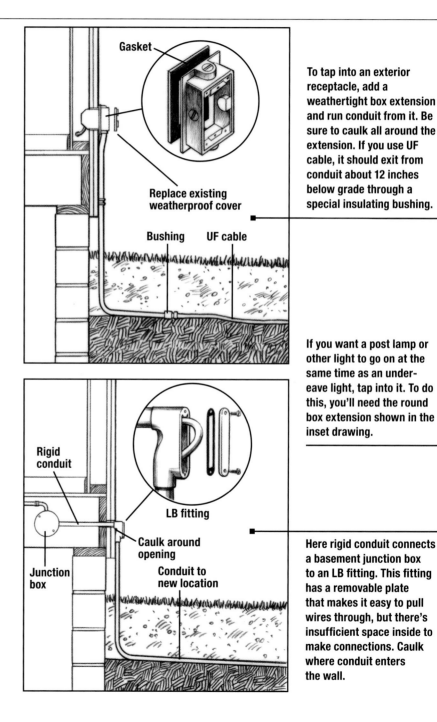

Gasket

Replace existing weatherproof cover

Bushing   UF cable

To tap into an exterior receptacle, add a weathertight box extension and run conduit from it. Be sure to caulk all around the extension. If you use UF cable, it should exit from conduit about 12 inches below grade through a special insulating bushing.

If you want a post lamp or other light to go on at the same time as an under-eave light, tap into it. To do this, you'll need the round box extension shown in the inset drawing.

Rigid conduit

LB fitting

Junction box

Caulk around opening

Conduit to new location

Here rigid conduit connects a basement junction box to an LB fitting. This fitting has a removable plate that makes it easy to pull wires through, but there's insufficient space inside to make connections. Caulk where conduit enters the wall.

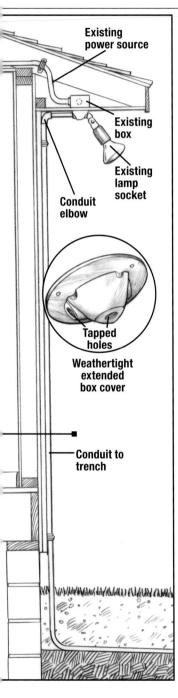

Existing power source

Existing box

Existing lamp socket

Conduit elbow

Tapped holes

Weathertight extended box cover

Conduit to trench

wide by 1 foot deep; rigid metal conduit requires one that is 4 inches wide by 6 inches deep. (Be sure to check local codes.) To avoid tearing up a sidewalk, dig to one side of it, then resume on the other. After you've finished digging, flatten one end of a piece of conduit, lay it in the trench, and drive it through the ground under the walk. After it emerges on the other side, cut off the flat end. You also can rent an auger.

Bending conduit

Metal conduit comes in 10-foot sections: typically, ½, ¾, or 1 inch in diameter. To work with conduit, first shape it with a bender, then cut it to length. Always bend the conduit before cutting it, because each bend shortens the total run by a few inches.

If this is your first time to work with conduit, buy an extra length or two and experiment until you get the knack of bending the tubing in gentle arcs, avoiding crimps that might impede the pulling of wires.

To bend conduit, slip the conduit into a bender, with its handle pointing up and away from you. Then, with one foot on the conduit, pull the handle slowly and steadily toward you. Make a bend gradually, with a steady pull along its radius. Pull too sharply at any point and you'll crimp the tubing. When the handle reaches a 45-degree angle with the ground, you've completed a 90-degree bend.

EMT conduit bends easily. Bending rigid tubing requires more muscle—for simple runs consider substituting elbow connectors for bends. Codes forbid a total of more than 360 degrees in bends along any run. This limits you to four 90-degree quarter-bends, three if you have offsets (which you'll need for a box that's mounted on a wall).

Cutting and connecting

Cut conduit with a hacksaw or, better yet, an inexpensive tubing cutter like the one shown on page 345. Clamp the cutter onto the conduit, rotate a few times, tighten the handle, then rotate some more. A folding reamer blade on the cutter lets you remove

sharp burrs that could chew up wiring insulation. Stick the point into the cut tubing end and rotate the cutter.

Join conduit sections end to end with waterproof couplings. At boxes, use special connectors. Some of these connectors include offsets, which can save a lot of bending.

Connect conduit carefully. Pulling wires through conduit can subject components to stress, and good grounding depends on secure metal-to-metal connections.

Pulling wires

Now comes the time when you learn why codes are so specific about bends, crimps, and burrs in tubing. As you pull wires through your conduit, you'll quickly notice that any hangups can lacerate insulation or even make the task impossible.

For a relatively straight run, you can probably push the wires from one box to another. If you can't push the wires, you'll need a fish tape and a helper. Snake the tape through the conduit, then hook the tape and wires together.

Next begin pulling with gentle pressure. As the wires work past bends, expect to exert more muscle. Have your helper gently feed wires into the conduit. With a lot of wires or a long pull, lubricate the wires with talcum powder or pulling grease (available from electrical suppliers).

Leave 6 to 8 inches of extra wire at each box, and never splice wires inside conduit. They must run continuously from box to box.

Aboveground receptacle

When installing a freestanding exterior receptacle that rises out of the ground on a conduit stalk, be sure to firmly root the stalk in concrete below. First cut the bottom out of a large coffee can and slip it over the conduit. Then plumb the stalk and brace it with guy wires. Next fill the can with concrete. Bevel the top so water will run off. Extend the stalk 20 to 24 inches above ground so that no one will trip over it.

347

PLANTS

Essential to all landscapes, of course, are plants. These two pages show some of the tools you'll need when working with plants and offer a brief discussion about improving your soil. On the pages ahead, you'll find details on choosing and starting plants and starting a lawn. The information on climate zones should guide you in selecting plants. And for specific plant recommendations, see pages 358–393, plus the charts throughout the book.

Tools

Having the right yard tool at hand can make all the difference in how, when, or whether a job gets done, and in how much you enjoy or resent it.

Your tool choices depend largely on the size and makeup of your yard, as well as your temperament and the time you have for yardwork.

Most garden work can be done with a hoe and a trowel. But a power shredder, edger, composter, and bicycle-tire cart add greatly to the ease and satisfaction for some people.

Examine tools before you buy. If a handle is too long, short, or heavy for you, try another. Check connections. The best spades, forks, and shovels have a metal shank extending up the handle for additional strength. Trowels are more durable when they have wooden handles driven into a metal shank.

Wheelbarrows and carts come in many materials and sizes: small enough to go down the cellar steps or big enough for six bags of leaves.

Choose hoses for weight, length, durability, and ease of repair. Consider soaker hoses, mist nozzles, and sprinklers according to your yard's needs. Hose attachments for fertilizers and sprayers have finally reached the no-plug stage and work well.

Tool care

With care, well-made tools will last for years. Here are some maintenance hints:
- Clean tools after each use with a paint stick or steel brush to keep soil from encrusting.
- Wipe wooden handles with linseed oil. Paint them a bright color if you tend to lose tools.
- Sharpen tools for efficiency and safety. Follow manual instructions. Use a file to sharpen the inside edge of your hoe.
- Check and tighten bolts and screws regularly.
- Wind hoses when not in use. Excessive sun shortens their life. Drain well before winter.
- Remove grass clippings, dirt, and grease from your mower and sharpen as needed. Before winter, run mowers until gasoline is used. Drain the crankcase. Clean the oil filter. Add clean oil.
- Sharpen the blades of shears, mowers, spades, and hoes before storing for winter. Apply oil, floor wax, petroleum jelly, or lard.
- Wash and dry sprayers thoroughly after each use. Oil the plunger rod and leather plunger often.
- Have a storage area handy to the garden.
- Store all sprays, dusts, and poisons out of the reach of children and pets.

Soil improvements

There are three main types of soil, one of which is best for growing plants. Loam—the ideal soil— molds into a loose mound when squeezed lightly. Squeezed harder, however, it crumbles. Soil high in clay forms a tight, sticky mass if squeezed when wet. Sandy soil feels grainy and crumbles when wet.

If your yard's soil is clayey or sandy, turn it to a depth of at least 1 foot wherever you want to garden and add humus in the form of compost, peat, grass clippings, shredded leaves, or any other organic matter. If you religiously use all organic material produced in the garden and house as mulch or compost, you'll soon have a wonderfully friable, workable soil that smells of life.

Also important are a soil's acidity and its levels of certain nutrients. To judge your soil, buy and use a soil test kit or have your soil tested. The test will tell you exactly what your soil needs. Check with your county extension office for more details.

LANDSCAPING TOOLS

Here are most of the basic tools you'll use in the garden and landscape. You may prefer to rent rather than store a spreader. Chances are you'll also need a lawn mower, perhaps an edger, and garden hoses. The final choices depend largely on the jobs you'll be doing most often and the tools that you prefer.

1 *Hand pruners*
2 *Compound-action loppers*
3 *Hedge shears*
4 *Spading fork*
5 *Hand cultivator*
6 *Bow saw*
7 *Field hoe*
8 *Leaf rake*
9 *Garden (iron) rake*
10 *Garden trowel*
11 *Forged garden spade*
12 *Narrow spade*
13 *Auger-type hole digger*
14 *Clamshell-type digger*
15 *Round-bladed shovel*
16 *Hand tamper*
17 *Finishing trowel*
18 *Retractable pruning saw*
19 *Fertilizer spreader*
20 *One-piece pruning saw*

PLANTS *(continued)*

To begin creating the green part of your landscape, buy plants from a reputable local or mail-order nursery, or start them yourself. The decision depends mainly on the size of plants you want to start with.

Nursery plants

Bare-root stock, the most economical nursery plants, must be purchased and planted while dormant, usually in late winter or early spring. With cold storage, some nurseries can extend that dormancy for several weeks into the spring. Swelling of buds and suppleness of branches indicate life. Place roots and as much of the rest of the plant as possible in water for several hours to overnight, then plant.

Mail-order stock may arrive at the beginning of a week of rain. If you can't plant soon, heel in the plants by placing them slantwise in a shallow trench and covering the roots with soil. As soon as possible, move the plants to their permanent homes.

When selecting container plants, pick ones with good foliage color. If the choice is between present blooms and basic shape, choose the best branch structure—you'll get more blooms in the long run.

Balled-and-burlapped or potted trees and shrubs can be planted any time of the year, but spring and early fall are the best times. The worst is late fall before a hard winter or in a hot summer without proper follow-up care.

Consider both heirloom and new varieties of plants. The tried-and-true and the latest developments have much to offer, especially in terms of disease resistance, hardiness, color, and form. A dwarf-variety or variegated shrub might be just right for your yard.

Planting

For years, the rule was that it was better to dig a $5 hole for a $1 plant than vice versa. It still is necessary to dig a generous hole so that the roots will have plenty of room, but it's no longer advisable to fill it with such good soil amendments that the roots will never push outward.

Dig your hole 2 feet wider than the root ball. It need be no deeper. If roots have become tangled within a pot, pull some of them apart. Fill the hole with good soil; replace subsoil or clay with topsoil.

Remove any labels, instruction tags, or strings that encircle branches so that they won't restrain or become embedded in the growth.

Whenever you plant anything, water well, as much to settle as to moisten the soil. Then mulch the soil surface and leave a surrounding doughnut-shape ridge—a foot or so from a tree trunk, several inches from the crown of a perennial flower—to hold in waterings or rain. Prune only to remove any broken or crowding branches.

Very large trees should be planted by an expert who has the special equipment needed. This equipment also will require a certain amount of space, so plant your big trees before you put in surrounding plantings.

There are several ways to support newly planted trees. One is to drive three stakes a few feet from the trunk (as shown). Then loop three web straps around the tree above the first branch and attach each strap to its stake with wire or cord.

1 For a potted or bare-root tree, dig a hole large enough to spread the roots without crowding. Place the tree at the same depth at which it was planted before, as indicated by the darker area of the trunk. Stake on the windward side.

1a Make comparable preparations for planting a balled-and-burlapped tree, starting with planting a roomy hole. You can cut away the excess burlap and leave the remainder to rot away, but remove any plastic, wire, or cords.

2 Shovel in the loose soil from the excavation, breaking up any clods you find. When the hole is half full, tamp down the dirt with your foot, then finish filling the hole. Tamp the soil a second time to get rid of air pockets so the soil will be in direct contact with the roots.

3 Build a ridge around the perimeter of the hole to serve as a reservoir, then give the entire area a good soaking. Your intent is to soak the root ball and surrounding soil with water. Then add a 3- to 4-inch layer of mulch to retain the moisture and discourage weeds. Add more water.

PLANTS *(continued)*

Starting plants

For starts of shrubs, perennials, or groundcovers, consider seeking divisions from friends' plants. Or try planting one section of your yard this year—say, with a groundcover—then letting the plants multiply there until you have enough to start another section.

Shrubs are best divided in early spring, when they're still dormant. For late-blooming perennials such as phlox and chrysanthemum, divide just as shoots are coming up. Divide after flowers fade for early bloomers such as iris or peonies.

For some plants—including Japanese iris, rhubarb, and the offshoots of a lilac bush—simply cut a chunk of branch and root from the edge of the clump with a spade. You won't disturb the rest of the plant at all.

Many clumps, such as those of ajuga, can be carefully dug with a spading fork and divided by pulling the crowns apart. Others, such as ferns, may have such entangled roots that you'll have to pry the clumps into sections with two spading forks or cut them apart with a sharp knife. Replant each section in good soil with ample room for the plant's natural spread. Water well.

Seeds

Seeds are the most inexpensive way to start many plants, but they take the longest and may not always be true to color. Annuals and herbs are often started from seed planted indoors in late winter or outdoors as soon as cold weather is past. Most seed packets give the best time to plant and instructions as to depth and distance apart.

Indoors, plant in a sterile medium such as purchased soilless potting mix in a seed-starting tray, cell pack, or other container that has drainage holes. Pack and moisten the medium. Scatter the seeds and press them into the substance. Tiny seeds need no covering; larger ones can be planted as deep as their greatest width.

Set the container in a warm, sunny place or under a grow-light. Supply bottom heat using a horticultural heating mat or a waterproof heating pad. Low heat speeds germination. Cover the container with a loose sheet of plastic. Keep the medium moist until they germinate. Most seeds do not need light at this point.

Packets or catalogs also may tell you when to expect germination, which can vary from two days to a few weeks, depending on the kind of seed. (Some tree seeds take several seasons.)

As soon as the first sprouts begin to emerge, move the container to a bright, cool place and take off the plastic. Keep the medium moist but avoid overwatering. Feed and transplant when the second set of leaves appears.

Harden off the seedlings before transplanting them outdoors. To do this, keep them slightly on the dry side, but don't let them wilt. Place the containers outdoors for a few hours each day until they are used to the sun and wind. If the weather is harsh the first few days after transplanting, put milk jugs or other protection around the seedlings.

If you plant your seeds outdoors, you'll have less control over seedling growth but more space. Prepare the soil. Water it well. Plant seeds, cover them a bit more deeply than indoors, and keep the soil moist until seedlings appear.

The main drawback to seeding outdoors is that you must be familiar enough with the seedling to know whether it is a desirable plant or a weed coming up. Seed packets, planting in rows, and time will help you tell for sure.

Thin and transplant seedlings as needed, and pinch most annuals to encourage bushiness.

PLANTING ANNUALS

1 For bedding plants you want the soil to be loose to a depth of at least 8 to 10 inches, so get to work with your spading fork or, for a large area, use a powered garden tiller. After the soil is good and loose, you're ready for the next stage—adding amendments. Spread on top of the soil your favorite plant food, whether it's compost or composted manure, then mix it in thoroughly.

2 Spread out a 2- to 3-inch layer of mulch. Buy it at your local garden or home center. Or find local sources of free mulch, such as wood chips, shredded bark or leaves, straw, or herbicide-free lawn clippings. (The mulch will condition the soil and retain moisture.) Then temporarily arrange the plants on top of the mulch.

3 When you're ready to do the actual planting, use a trowel—or your hands if the soil is loose enough—to form holes that are a bit larger than the plants' root balls. Then place each plant in its hole at the same level as it was in the container from which it came. Fill around the plant, press the soil down firmly, and scrape the mulch away from the plant base about 4 inches all around.

PLANTING PERENNIALS

1 The best time of year to plant perennials is midspring. If you happen to pick a hot day, plant early in the morning or late in the day to avoid subjecting the transplants to heat stress. Before you dig holes, know the plants' widths at maturity so that you can space them properly. Then plant them as shown.

2 Don't be concerned if your newly planted perennial bed appears too sparse—as if the plants are too far apart. And resist the temptation to move them closer together; if you do, you'll most likely find yourself having to thin and divide them the following year.

3 A year later, the faster-growing perennials will have filled their spaces, and the slower, longer-living species will still have some maturing to do. But you can see where there is room to walk and room to grow now.

PLANTS *(continued)*

Since a good lawn will last for generations, it's vital to plant it carefully. (And after you get it started, it's just as vital to give it continuously good care.)

Grading the lawn

Before starting, make sure the lawn area is as level as possible and drains properly. For good drainage, slope the lawn gently away from your house. Consider groundcovers or a retaining wall for severe grades (see Chapter 8). Mowing steep slopes is difficult and can be dangerous.

Whenever building or drastically changing grades, remove the topsoil first, then respread it over the leveled surface. You can do small jobs yourself with a spade and rake or an old tire pulled by a rope. Hire a tractor for big jobs.

Improving the soil

Also before starting, test your soil with a simple test kit or contact your county extension agent and follow instructions. Most grasses thrive at a neutral or slightly acid pH of 6 to 7. Add lime as needed to improve the structure and provide the best environment (less acid, better chemical balance) for beneficial bacteria and earthworms.

Adding organic matter, such as moist peat or weed-free compost, and additional topsoil, if needed, will increase growth and decrease maintenance. Also broadcast a complete fertilizer (10-10-10, for example) using 10 to 20 pounds per 1,000 square feet, depending on the fertility of the soil. Till or spade 6 inches deep, making the soil pebbly but not powdery. Remove any rocks or debris and rake smooth, leaving shallow crevices to catch grass seeds.

Choosing the seed

Choose from new, improved grasses according to how much sun your lawn will get and how you will use the yard. In the Southern states, warm-season grasses grow most from March through August. They turn brown after frost. Overseed with a winter grass in the fall to keep weeds out and to extend and intensify the lawn's green color.

After your soil is ready for grass seed, use a mechanical spreader, a shoulder planter, or hand broadcasting to apply half of the seed while walking back and forth one way. Then spread the rest going in a perpendicular direction over the same area.

When sodding, prepare the soil well as for seeding. Lay the sod within a few hours after delivery. Stagger the end seams. Roll and water. Mound soil around exposed edges. Keep the area well watered until new growth starts.

Plugging is a convenient and economical method to repair or establish a lawn with warm-season grasses. Most Southern lawns are started this way. The runners spread above ground to fill in quickly, crowding out weeds.

354

Planting sprigs (or stolons) is another way to start a new lawn. Again, prepare the soil well. Bury the sprigs with only the top nodes above ground. Space most 12 inches apart, zoysiagrass 6 inches. Mulch will help. Keep the area watered.

Bahiagrass is the only Southern grass often started from seed and thus is less expensive. It also is less elegant but takes less care. St. augustinegrass makes a thick turf and is beautiful as long as it is protected from its several and serious enemies.

Bermudagrass is used on Southern golf courses and athletic fields. 'Meyer' zoysiagrass will thrive farther north than any other Southern grass. 'Cashmere' zoysiagrass has finer texture, grows faster, and tolerates shade better.

In the northern two-thirds of the country, use mixtures of cool-season grasses. These grasses flourish in spring and fall but turn brown in the dead of winter and during summer drought.

Most sunny cool-season lawns use largely bluegrasses. New varieties such as 'Bonnieblue,' 'Eclipse,' and 'Sydsport' have superior color, density, and are heat and drought tolerant.

Fescues are the best for shade and for play areas that get rough treatment. New ryegrasses are especially good for establishing a lawn fast.

When buying grass seed, always check the label for percentage of germination, varieties included, and percent of inert ingredients. Better seed is worth the price; cheap seed is no bargain if you have to redo all the work or settle for an inferior lawn.

When to start

The ideal time for planting seed is early September, with very early spring second best. Sow the amount listed in the package directions (too much seed can cause the tiny grass plants to choke out one another). Then walk backward and rake lightly so that the seed is covered with no more than ½ inch of soil.

You can plant sod, sprigs, and plugs almost anytime, though spring or fall is preferred. When you choose sod, look for well-rooted, moist rolls that are uniformly green and not yellowing.

Roll the area after planting seed or sod, then, if seeding, cover with mulch to conserve moisture. If you rent a drum roller with a surface of mesh fabric, you can roll the ground and apply a thin mulch of peat moss at the same time. Or spread straw about ½ inch thick—so that you can see soil through it—after you've rolled the area. If you use burlap to retain moisture, remove it as soon as germination begins. A mesh material that allows grass to grow through is available though more expensive. Save it for steep slopes or difficult spots.

Watering and mowing

The main cause of new lawn failures is lack of moisture. Water newly planted lawns with a fine mist from two to several times a day for the first week; the next week, water at least once a day. Water less frequently but more deeply as grass grows.

Weeds also may germinate, but your new grass soon will crowd them out. Keep traffic off the lawn until it is well established.

Mow the grass with sharp blades set at about 1½ inches when the new growth is 2 inches tall. Once hot weather arrives, set the blade to 2½ inches.

355

USDA PLANT HARDINESS ZONE MAP

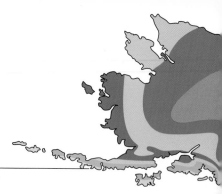

One key to successful landscaping is planting the right plant in the right place. This map of climate zones helps you select plants for your garden that will survive a typical winter in your region. The United States Department of Agriculture (USDA) developed the map, basing the zones on the lowest recorded temperatures across North America. Zone 1 is the coldest area, and Zone 11 is the warmest.

Find and keep in mind your zone number when choosing any plant for your landscape. In this and other garden books, catalogs, and plant labels, zones of hardiness are given for many plants.

Plants are classified by the coldest temperature and zone they can endure. Plants rated for a range of hardiness zones can usually survive winter in the coldest zone as well as tolerate the summer heat of the warmest one.

Microclimates

This zone map and others are general guides. Most yards have several microclimates determined by exposure, wind, elevation, and surroundings. In the warmer microclimates of your yard, you may be able to grow a few plants from the next warmer zone. Or you may find that most of your yard requires extra hardiness and you'd be wiser to choose from the next colder zone.

In yards near water or in cities surrounded by concrete, tender plants may escape damage while the same plants a few miles away suffer winterkill.

Here are some factors to consider when choosing plants and deciding where they might grow best.
• Southern and western sides of houses and other structures are sunnier and warmer than northern or eastern exposures.
• Southern and eastern exposures usually are protected from chilling winter winds.
• Strong winds can damage plants by either drying the soil or knocking over fragile growth.
• Cold air sweeps down hills and rests in low areas of neighborhoods.
• Your microclimates will change as your trees grow larger or when you add a fence or deck.

HAWAII

AUSTRALIA

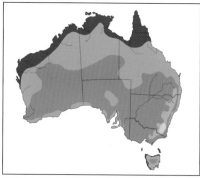

Range of Average Annual Minimum Temperatures for Each Zone

Zone 1: Below -50 F (below -45.6 C)
Zone 2: -50 to -40 F (-45.5 to -40 C)
Zone 3: -40 to -30 F (-39.9 to -34.5 C)
Zone 4: -30 to -20 F (-34.4 to -28.9 C)
Zone 5: -20 to -10 F (-28.8 to -23.4 C)
Zone 6: -10 to 0 F (-23.3 to -17.8 C)
Zone 7: 0 to 10 F (-17.7 to -12.3 C)
Zone 8: 10 to 20 F (-12.2 to -6.7 C)
Zone 9: 20 to 30 F (-6.6 to -1.2 C)
Zone 10: 30 to 40 F (-1.1 to 4.4 C)
Zone 11: Above 40 F (above 4.5 C)

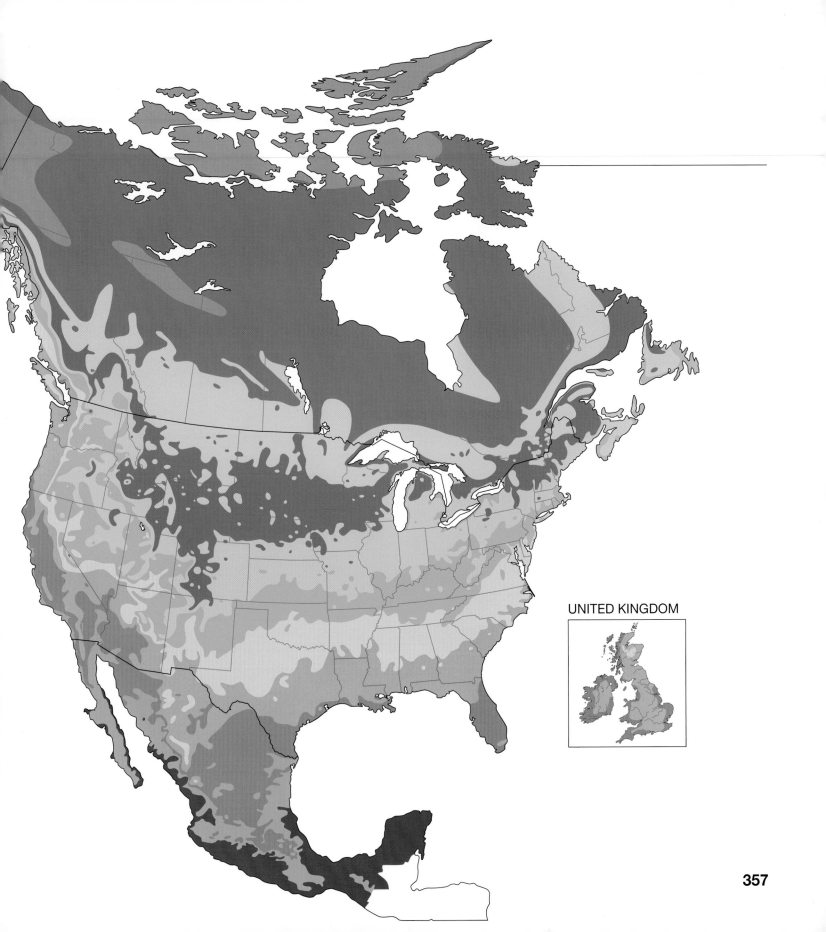

UNITED KINGDOM

357

14

RECOMMENDED PLANTS

After completing your general plans, you are ready for the fun of picking particular plants. To help you begin, this chapter describes many popular trees, shrubs, vines, groundcovers, and flowers. While making your decisions, keep in mind that your selections will satisfy you more if they serve several purposes and offer interest for several seasons. Remember, too, that the botanical world is vast and that there are many fine plants beyond those listed in this review.

DECIDUOUS TREES

SMALL *(up to 30 feet tall)*

Crabapple *(Malus spp. and hybrids)*

Many flowering crabapple varieties and cultivars make excellent small to medium landscaping trees that provide year-round interest. Crabapples prefer acid soil, but plant them where dropping fruit won't create cleanup chores. Select disease-resistant varieties. 15–25 feet; Zones 3–8.

Fringe Tree, White

(Chionanthus virginicus)

This slow-growing native tree has fleecy white flowers in early June and bright yellow fall color. The foliage is bold and similar to magnolias. The vase-shape crown is wider than it is tall. Leaves and flowers come late; blooms are aromatic and long lasting. Good near patios, fringe tree can be trained as a shrub or tree. 20–30 feet; Zones 5–8.

Dogwood, Flowering; Kousa

(Cornus florida, C. kousa)

Dogwoods are among the choicest trees for interest all year. They like light shade and acid soil. In fall, leaves turn deep burgandy; crimson berries attract birds. 15–30 feet; Zones 4–9.

Fruit Trees (stone) *(Prunus spp.)*

Peach, cherry, plum, apricot, and others in this group offer fine edible landscaping; highly ornamental fruitless varieties also are available. All are covered with blooms before leaves show in spring. Some have interesting shapes or bark and good fall color. 20–25 feet; Zones 4–10.

Franklin Tree *(Franklinia alatamaha)*

Rare and lovely, franklin tree is a slow grower that prefers sheltered valleys and partial shade. Camellia-like flowers, 3 inches across, open singly over many weeks. Leaves turn crimson in autumn. Franklin tree likes rich, acid soil. It's sometimes hard to grow and can die suddenly. 20–30 feet; Zones 6–8.

Hawthorn *(Crataegus spp.)*

Tough, thorny hawthorn has delicate clusters of white or pink flowers in spring, glossy green foliage, orange to red fall color, and scarlet or yellow fruits. Hawthorn tolerates clipping, salt, pollution, and other adverse conditions but can get fire blight. 15–30 feet; Zones 5–9.

DECIDUOUS TREES *(continued)*

Hazelnut *(Corylus avellana)*
Easy to grow, European filbert or hazelnut works well near a patio or entry, or as a screen or accent. It adapts well to many soils but needs full sun. Two or more are required to bear nuts, but you can plant them in clumps or as a hedge. Catkins bloom on winter branches, dark green leaves are woolly underneath, and nuts come in frilly green clusters. 6–25 feet; Zones 4–8.

Lilac, Japanese Tree
(Syringa reticulata)
A true tree, this lilac has a spreading umbrella form, cherrylike bark, a fragrance similar to privet, and large trusses of white flowers in mid-June. It is attractive, disease free, and drought resistant. 20–30 feet; Zones 5–8.

Magnolia, Merrill; Saucer; Star
(Magnolia ×loebneri 'Merrill,' M. ×soulangeana, M. stellata)
These trees have large, striking flowers of pink and white, and bloom when young. Velvety buds, pods with red seeds, and multitrunked habit all add interest. Magnolias like full sun or light shade, and rich, acid soil with plenty of root room. Late frosts can damage flowers. 15–30 feet; Zones 5–10.

Maple, Amur *(Acer tataricum ginnala)*
Usually multitrunked, this maple has fragrant, nonshowy flowers, bright red winged seeds in summer, and brilliant fall foliage. Its leaves are oval or globe shape. This tree withstands cold and wind better than does Japanese maple. 15–20 feet; Zones 5–10.

Maple, Japanese *(Acer palmatum)*
Japanese maple is a fine accent tree with dense burgundy to green leaves, scarlet autumn color, and horizontal gray branches. Japanese maple likes slightly acid soil and some protection from wind. It produces its best color when grown in sun to part shade. 15–25 feet; Zones 6–9.

Redbud *(Cercis* spp.)
Redbud is prized for its purple spring blooms, heart-shape leaves, yellow autumn color, multiple trunks, and rounded habit. Good in woodlands or shrub borders or as an accent plant, redbud tolerates shade and many soils. Unfortunately, it is susceptible to wilt and borer. 25–30 feet; Zones 4–8.

Serviceberry (Amelanchier canadensis)

Also called shadblow, serviceberry has white flowers that briefly cover its branches early in spring; its fall color ranges from beautiful yellow to red. Edible maroon and purple berries attract birds. This tree gives light to medium shade and does best in acid soil and natural settings. Serviceberry doesn't tolerate pollution well. 6–20 feet; Zones 4–5.

Silverbell, Carolina (Halesia tetraptera)

This small tree, also called snowdrop tree, has bell-shape white flowers in May. An open grower—sometimes multitrunked—it is fine for light shade and screening; it also combines well with evergreen backgrounds or underplantings of azaleas or rhododendrons. Its leaves turn yellow in fall. Carolina silverbell likes moist, acid soil and has no pest problems. 25–30 feet; Zones 5–10.

Stewartia, Japanese
(Stewartia pseudocamellia)

This all-season performer begins its show in winter with silky brown buds. In summer, camellia-like white blossoms open from pearl-like buds. You might grow this tree for its fall color—turning from apple green to reddish-purple—alone. Plant it under power lines as a streetside tree or in shrub borders or lawns. 30 feet; Zones 5–7.

TREES FOR SPECIAL INTEREST

Spring Flowering
Butternut
Cherry, sargent
Crabapple
Dogwood
Fruit trees
Hawthorn
Magnolia
Mountain ash
Pear, bradford
Redbud
Serviceberry

Fast Growing, Temporary
Acacia
Alder
Catalpa
Chinese tallow tree
Elm, Siberian
Empress tree
Gum
Locust, black
Mimosa
Poplar
Willow

Summer Flowering
Catalpa
Chestnut, Chinese
Crape myrtle
Dogwood, Japanese
Franklin tree
Fringe tree
Goldenchain tree
Goldenraintree
Jacaranda
Linden
Mimosa
Smoketree
Sourwood
Tulip tree
Yellowwood

Fragrant
Acacia
Arborvitae
Bayberry
Cedar
Crabapple
Fringe tree
Fruit trees
Gum
Hemlock
Katsura tree
Linden, littleleaf
Locust, black
Magnolia
Maple, amur
Mimosa
Pine
Russian olive
Silverbell
Sourwood
Viburnum
Yellowwood

For Winter Interest
Alder
Amur cork
Birch
Crabapple
Crape myrtle
Dogwood
Ginkgo
Holly
Katsura tree
Magnolia
Poplar
Oak
Sweet gum
Tulip tree
Tupelo, black
Willow
Yellowwood

Fruiting
Chinese jujube
Crabapple
Fruits, stone
Pecan
Persimmon
Prunus species
Serviceberry

Avoid Near Street, Drive, Pipes
Black locust
Box elder
Catalpa
Hawthorn
Mountain ash
Poplar
Willow

DECIDUOUS TREES *(continued)*

Smoketree *(Cotinus obovatus)*
Smoketree makes a fine tree or shrub because it is fast growing and easy to move. Flowers followed by fruit panicles are lovely all summer; autumn colors are brilliant. 'Purpurea' has purple foliage. For best effect, plant smoketree where the sun will shine through it. 15–20 feet; Zones 5–9.

Sourwood *(Oxydendrurn aboreum)*
Also known as sorrel tree or lily-of-the-valley tree, sourwood is superior for landscaping. Its laurellike leaves are lustrous, dense, and leathery. They turn deep red in late August and remain so until mid-October. Blooms in mid-July are pendulous clusters of white. Sourwood does best in full sun and moist, acid soil. 25–30 feet; Zones 5–9.

Birch, River; European White *(Betula nigra, B. pendula)*
River birch has peeling bark with layers of gray and reddish brown. It likes wet soil but resists borers. European white (or weeping) birch is not as hardy. It has delicate foliage and paper-white bark for a dramatic effect. It's often short lived and prone to borer attack. 40–50 feet; Zones 2–9.

Cherry, Sargent *(Prunus sargentii)*
This, the largest and hardiest of the Asian cherries, bears masses of pearly pink flowers. Dark green, shiny leaves turn red-bronze in fall. The tree's bark is attractive, dark, and lustrous. Good dense shade and specimen tree. Columnar varieties available. 50–75 feet; Zones 5–9.

MEDIUM *(30 to 50 feet tall)*

Amur Cork Tree
(Phellodendron amurense)
This fast grower gives light, open shade beneath low, spreading branches. Do not crowd. Compound leaves turn yellow in autumn and drop quickly. Male plants have clusters of black berries. Cork-like ridged bark gives winter interest. Tolerates drought and pollution. 30–40 feet; Zones 4–9.

Hornbeam *(Carpinus spp.)*
The adaptable European hornbeam is good as a street tree or in paved areas. American (blue beech) and Japanese hornbeam are smaller. All are slow growers with fluted gray bark and elmlike foliage that turns yellow to orange-red in fall. They bear interesting clusters of nutlike fruit and are pest free. 30–60 feet; Zones 4–8.

Horsechestnut, Red

(Aesculus ×carnea)

This buckeye relative has upright conical clusters of red to pink flowers in May, five-finger leaves, and a dense mushroom form. It can become slightly untidy and grows slowly. Prone to leaf scorch in hot winds, it does best where summers are cool and moist. No notable fall color. 30–40 feet; Zones 4–8.

Linden *(Tilia cordata, T ×euchlora)*

With its dense pyramid of heart-shape dark green leaves, linden makes a good street, lawn, or shade tree. Bees will buzz around the tiny clusters of fragrant, early-summer flowers. Linden withstands adverse city conditions, heat, and drought, and yields fast, hardy growth. 'Greenspire' and 'Redmond' are choice cultivars. 35–70 feet; Zones 4–9.

Mountain Ash, European

(Sorbus aucuparia)

This fine, upright tree is prized for its white clusters of spring flowers, striking red-orange berries that attract birds, and smooth gray bark. Lustrous foliage turns orange and scarlet in the fall. Mostly problem-free, this tree doesn't tolerate city pollution well. 25–50 feet; Zones 5–9.

Pear, Bradford

(Pyrus calleryana 'Bradford')

This formal-looking, upright, pyramidal tree is covered with white flowers in spring, bears no fruit, and produces brilliant crimson-red fall foliage. Thornless and fire blight resistant, it is a good, undemanding street or specimen tree. Prune this tree only when it is damaged by ice. 25–35 feet; Zones 5–9.

Sassafras *(Sassafras albidum)*

Sassafras has short, stout, contorted branches that produce an open shape and dappled shade. Its bark is corky and dark red. Lustrous leaves—irregularly shaped like mittens with one, two, or no thumbs—turn orange to scarlet in fall. Sassafras will grow in poor soil, but its long taproot can cause transplant problems. 30–60 feet; Zones 5–9.

Yellowwood *(Cladrastis kentukea)*

A broad, slow-growing tree with rounded crown; good in a grouping or as a specimen. Smooth gray bark provides winter interest. White, fragrant flowers in early June. Crotches can be brittle; to keep the tree from bleeding, prune only in summer. 30–35 feet; Zones 4–9.

DECIDUOUS TREES *(continued)*

LARGE *(50 to 120 feet tall)*

Ash *(Fraxinus* spp.)

Fast growing and adaptable, ash likes full sun and has good yellow to purple fall color. Grass grows well under this tree. Some ash trees can get too large for small yards. Insects can be a problem for this tree. New cultivars such as 'Marshall's Seedless' and 'Autumn Purple' are worth trying. 30–90 feet; Zones 2–9.

Chestnut *(Castanea* spp.)

The Chinese chestnut and the newer disease-resistant forms of the American chestnut make majestic, spreading trees. Plant two or more for pollination. Chestnut does best on a north-facing slope in fertile, slightly acid soil. Mulch to keep soil moist. Train to central leader. 40–100 feet; Zones 5–9.

Beech *(Fagus* spp.)

Beeches are magnificent trees for forest or park. If you have one, treasure it for its smooth silvery gray bark and golden-bronze autumn color. Some have bronze leaves all year. Beech is too slow growing to figure in landscaping plans for decades to come, and only moss will grow beneath it. 50–100 feet; Zones 5–10.

Gingko *(Ginkgo biloba)*

Also called maidenhair tree, ginkgo has unique fan-shape leaves that turn golden yellow in fall. Its open habit and stiffly diagonal, uplifted branches provide filtered shade. Easy to care for, ginkgo is one of the best street trees. Ginkgo needs sun for best results. 50–80 feet; Zones 5–10.

Birch, Paper *(Betula papyrifera)*

Also called canoe birch, this native of Canada and Alaska has bright yellow autumn color. Bark is reddish brown on younger branches; later it turns chalky white and peels. Usually planted in clumps, birch does best in ample sun and well-drained, sandy, moist, acid soil. Borers can be a problem. 40–70 feet; Zones 2–8.

Hickory *(Carya* spp.)

Bitternut, shagbark, pecan, and pignut hickories are prized for their lovely yellow autumn color, general sturdiness and stateliness, and shaggy bark. They make fine shade or specimen trees. Large, slow growing, and late to leaf out in the spring, they have long taproots that make transplanting difficult; buy hickory from a nursery. 60–120 feet; Zones 4–9.

Honeylocust, Thornless
(Gleditsia triacanthos var. *inermis)*
Honeylocust's delicate leaflets give light shade and need little raking. Honeylocust adapts to seashore or difficult conditions but has some pest problems, especially in warmer climates. To avoid thorns and seedpods, choose the improved cultivars. 30–60 feet; Zones 5–9.

Katsura Tree *(Cercidiphyllum japonicum)*
This tree gives medium to dense shade with open foliage that allows good air circulation. Fine-textured heart-shape leaves turn yellow to scarlet. It resists diseases and insects and can have multiple trunks. Kept to one trunk, it will be a slim oval while young, then spread at maturity. 40–60 feet; Zones 5–9.

Larch, Golden; Japanese
(Pseudolarix amabilis; Larix kaempferi)
This unique tree has cones and feathery, needlelike foliage that turns golden yellow in autumn, then falls. It is a large, broadly pyramidal tree that grows easily but needs plenty of room. Slow growing, it likes acid soil and needs some wind protection. 50–120 feet; Zones 6–8.

Maple, Norway *(Acer platanoides)*
This tough, versatile tree has improved cultivars such as 'Emerald Queen,' 'Summer Shade,' and the red-leaved 'Crimson King.' It gives dense shade, has bright yellow autumn color, and grows quickly. Spreading roots make growing grass underneath it difficult. 40–70 feet; Zones 4–9.

Maple, Red; Sugar
(Acer rubrum, A. saccharum)
Fast-growing red or swamp maple has tiny, red blooms in early spring and brilliant red leaves in early fall. The cultivars 'Bowhall' and 'Scanlon' are narrow. 'Red Sunset' and 'October Glory' are most colorful. The slow-growing sugar, hard, or syrup maple of New England does poorly in city conditions. 50–100 feet; Zones 3–7.

Oak *(Quercus* spp.)
Oaks are among the most useful native trees and are preferred for landscaping where room permits. Cherish any you have. Long lived, they are fast growing where soil suits them, giving medium to dense shade. Plant them where acorns will be no trouble. Consider red, pin, or scarlet oak varieties. Plant evergreen cork, holly, live, and laurel oaks in warm climates. 30–100 feet; Zones 4–9.

DECIDUOUS TREES (continued)

EVERGREEN TREES

NEEDLED

Sweet Gum (Liquidambar styraciflua)
Named for its fragrant, sticky sap, sweet gum has star-shape, glossy leaves that turn yellow to scarlet to purple in fall. Given room, it develops unmatched Christmas-tree elegance. Ball-shape fruit gives winter interest. Sweet gum needs full sun and likes acid soil. It takes time to settle in, then is trouble free and fast growing. 60–120 feet; Zones 5–10.

Arborvitae (Thuja spp.)
This stately, reliable tree has flat sprays of scalelike foliage. Slow growing, it is excellent for natural or clipped hedges, screens, columnar accents, or windbreaks. It tolerates wet soils unless winds are high. Plant in sun to part shade; train to a central stem. Choose improved cultivars such as 'Nigra' or 'Hetz Wintergreen.' 40–60 feet; Zones 3–8.

Tulip Tree (Liriodendron tulipifera)
Beloved for its pyramidal form, squarish leaves, tuliplike flowers, and yellow autumn color, tulip tree has green, yellow, and orange flowers that hide among the leaves but are striking when viewed from above. Tulip tree can have weak wood, and its roots can become invasive. 60–100 feet; Zones 5–9.

Cedar, Deodar; Atlas
(Cedrus deodara, C. libani atlantica)
True cedars are fairly rare, but they make excellent specimen or skyline trees where hardy and given enough room. Cedars grow at a slow to moderate rate. Upright cones on upper sides of branches grow 4 inches long. The bluish needles are borne in starlike clusters in a picturesque, open pattern. 'Glauca' is the bluest. 40–70 feet; Zones 6–10.

Walnut (Juglans spp.)
Black walnut, English or Persian walnut, butternut, and heartnut are stately trees, even in winter. Walnuts leaf out late and drop their leaves early. They can inhibit some plants beneath their spread. Good for shade and screening. Walnuts need space and are self-pollinating (although having two trees spurs a better harvest). 20–80 feet; Zones 3–9.

Douglas Fir (Pseudotsuga menziesii)
More beautiful and dependable than spruce or true fir, quick-growing douglas fir has soft, spiraling, bluish green needles. New spring growth is an attractive apple green. Foliage is fragrant. Pendulous cones are 2 to 4 inches long. Dwarf varieties of douglas fir make good hedges. 80–100 feet; Zones 5–9.

Fir *(Abies* spp.)

Good specimen trees, firs may lose their lower branches as they age. Two-inch, bristly needles are dark bluish green on top, silvery gray beneath. Firs do best in cool climates, full sun, and rich soil. White fir withstands city conditions, heat, and drought. 55–80 feet; Zones 4–8.

Spruce *(Picea* spp.)

Spruces have short, squarish needles and hanging cones. Cultivars come in shades of white, red, and blue. Spruces are moderate to fast growing and often overgrow their location. For small yards, choose smaller cultivars. Spruces do best in cooler climates. 50–100 feet; Zones 2–9.

Hemlock, Canadian *(Tsuga* spp.)

With nodding top and drooping branches, hemlock exhibits a special grace. Use it as a background plant, among pines in a grove, or as a clipped hedge. Hemlock likes deep, moist loam and takes light shade. Do not plant it near the house. Usually problem free, it does need water in dry periods. Prune to make it dense. 50–80 feet; Zones 4–8.

BROADLEAVED

Holly *(Ilex* spp.)

Many hollies make handsome shrubs or even trees, especially in warmer climates. In colder areas they may shed their leaves in winter yet survive. Hollies like acid soil and nearly full sun; most need male and female trees to produce berries. Hollies have some insect problems. 20–70 feet ; Zones 6–10.

Pine *(Pinus* spp.)

Pines vary widely and fill many landscaping needs, from windbreaks and tall hedges to shade and specimen trees. Eastern white pine is one of the hardiest and most graceful. Austrian pine is stiffer and more rugged. Scotch pine, with its horizontal spreading branches and red bark, often gets an interesting, contorted shape as it ages. Lacebark pine has multiple trunks. 30–100 feet; Zones 3–9.

Magnolia, Southern
(Magnolia grandiflora)

Also called bull bay, southern magnolia has large, lustrous, dark green leaves with brownish undersides and huge, waxy white blooms from May to August. Most are dense and heavy looking; 'Glen St. Mary' is smaller, about 20 feet. 60–75 feet; Zones 7–9.

DECIDUOUS SHRUBS

SMALL *(up to 5 feet tall)*

Azalea
(Rhododendron spp. and hybrids)
Dwarf and Exbury hybrids offer spring blooms as well as good fall color. Locate plants where they'll receive filtered light and wind protection. Acid soil and excellent drainage are crucial. 3–4 feet; Zones 5–8.

Cotoneaster, Cranberry
(Cotoneaster apiculatus)
Cranberry cotoneaster works well as a groundcover, at the front of a shrub border, or to hold banks. It has small and shiny leaves, subtle flowers, red berries, and spreading wishbone-pattern branches. Cotoneaster likes sun. It has red fall color in the North and is evergreen in the South. 2–4 feet; Zones 5–8.

Barberry *(Berberis spp.)*
Barberry, with thick, thorny growth, makes a good hedge and barrier plant. Flowers are small; fruit and foliage vary in color according to variety. Easy to grow, barberry likes full sun and will attract birds. 3–5 feet; Zones 4–8.

Currant or Gooseberry
(Ribes spp.)
These fruits are useful for edible landscaping in foundation plantings or under spreading trees. Some gooseberry bushes will cascade over walls or banks. Others are thorny and make effective barrier plants. Both kinds do well in large containers for patios. 3–5 feet; Zones 3–8.

Cinquefoil, Bush *(Potentilla fruticosa)*
Bush (shrubby) cinquefoil stays dainty and is choice for small gardens, borders, or mass plantings. It has soft, needlelike foliage and flowers like buttercups that begin to bloom in May and continue all summer. Easy to grow and to transplant, it needs full sun. 1–4 feet; Zones 2–9.

Daphne, February *(Daphne mezereum)*
February daphne is an upright shrub that produces small, lilac or rosy purple, fragrant flowers. Hardiness varies with species; some types demand limestone soil. February daphne prefers sun or partial shade; its berries, which are toxic, turn red in summer. 3–5 feet; Zones 5–8.

Forsythia, Arnold Dwarf

(Forsythia ×intermedia 'Arnold Dwarf')
This variety and the even shorter Bronx Greenstem grow with typical arching branches that root at the soil line. Small, greenish yellow flowers in early spring aren't quite as showy as on taller kinds. This forsythia has vigorous, dense foliage; it likes sun or part shade. 2–4 feet; Zones 5–8.

Quince, Flowering

(Chaenomeles speciosa)
Flowering quince is widely planted for its bright, often orange, flowers in early spring. Available cultivars range from white to dark red. These shrubs are dense and thorny and make good hedge, border, or barrier plants. Fruits are edible in jams. 2–6 feet; Zones 3–9.

Forsythia, Korean White

(Abeliophyllum distichum)
Not a true forsythia, this shrub has flowers of similar shape and bloom time as yellow-flowered forsythia, but they're white and very fragrant. It has arching stems, is easy to grow, and likes full sun. In northern climates, plant in a protected place to ensure flower bud hardiness. 3–5 feet; Zones 5–8.

MEDIUM *(5 to 10 feet tall)*

Azalea *(Rhododendron spp.)*

Among the most loved flowering shrubs, hardy deciduous azaleas vary in form and color. They are useful in beds, as foundation plants, as accents, or below spreading trees. Some are fragrant. All need good humidity, full sun or partial shade, and moist, acid soil. 4–10 feet; Zones 4–10.

Kerria *(Kerria japonica)*

Also known as globeflower, kerria is a good foundation or border shrub. Its green twigs are attractive in winter; golden yellow flowers appear in midspring. Double varieties bloom longer. Several cultivars include variegated leaves. Kerria likes shade and needs pruning to remove dead wood. 4–8 feet; Zones 5–8.

Blueberry *(Vaccinium spp.)*

Blueberry works well as an interest plant, groundcover, or screen, or in a hedge, border, or container. Foliage is bronze in spring and glossy green all summer. Delicious berries follow clusters of pinkish white flowers. It likes full sun but tolerates part shade in hot areas; needs acid soil. 1–18 feet; Zones 3–9.

DECIDUOUS SHRUBS (continued)

Chokeberry (Aronia spp.)

A dependable native shrub, chokeberry has dense flower clusters of white with pinkish tints in May, followed by bright red fruits, too sour even for birds, that are colorful all fall and winter. Leaves turn red in fall. It does best in full sun in borders. 6–10 feet; Zones 6–8.

Clethra (Clethra alnifolia)

Also called summersweet, clethra is a native that thrives along the seashore and in damp places. It makes a good border plant because of its fragrant white spikes in summer and its yellow to orange fall color. Clethra likes part shade or sun in moist, acid soil. 3–8 feet; Zones 4–9.

Dogwood, Red-Osier; Tatarian (Cornus stolonifera, C. alba)

In winter, dogwoods are standouts, with their red wood contrasting with the snow below. Their flowers and fruits are not showy, but their foliage turns dark red in the fall. Dogwoods like moist soil and are good in borders, near foundations, and beside water. 7–10 feet; Zones 3–9.

SHRUBS FOR SPECIAL INTEREST

For Quick Screens
Beautybush
Elaeagnus
Euonymus
Forsythia
Honeysuckle
Mockorange
Privet
Viburnum, arrowwood
Viburnum, nannyberry
Viburnum, siebold

With Toxic Parts
Apple: seeds
Azalea: all parts
Black locust: seeds, sprouts, foliage
Cherry: seeds
Chokecherry: leaves, stems, bark, seeds
Daphne: berries, leaves
Goldenchain: seeds, pods
Holly: berries
Hydrangea: leaves, buds
Jasmine: berries
Magnolia: flower
Oleander: bark, leaves
Peach: leaves, seeds
Privet: leaves, seeds
Wisteria: pods, seeds
Yew: all parts

Spring Flowering
Azalea, Korean
Barberry
Bayberry
Cinquefoil
Forsythia
Fruit, dwarf
Honeysuckle
Kerria
Lilac
Pieris, Japanese
Pussy willow
Rhododendron
Spirea
Viburnum
Witch hazel

Fragrant
Apple
Azalea hybrids
Bayberry
Boxwood
Butterfly bush
Citrus
Clethra
Daphne
Honeysuckle
Jasmine
Lilac
Magnolia
Mockorange
Pineapple Guava
Plum, natal
Privet
Rhododendron hybrids
Rose
Viburnum, Korean spice
Witch hazel

Summer Flowering
Arrowwood
Azalea, flame
Butterfly bush
Crape myrtle
Hydrangea, peegee
Leucothoe
Mockorange
Mountain laurel
Privet
Rose
Rose of sharon
Spirea, 'Anthony Waterer'
Stewartia

Fruiting
Almond
Apple
Apricot
Blueberry
Cherry, oriental bush
Cherry, Surinam
Citrus, dwarf
Currant
Gooseberry
Nectarine
Peach
Pear
Pineapple guava
Plum, bush
Plum, natal
Pomegranate
Quince

Elderberry, American
(Sambucus canadensis)

Also called sweet elderberry, this shrub has clusters of white, fragrant flowers and edible purple-black berries. Elderberry is fine for borders, screens, or hedges. It needs sun and moist, fertile soil. 6–10 feet; Zones 3–9.

Honeysuckle *(Lonicera spp.)*

Tatarian and winter honeysuckles are best used for mass effect in borders and screens, and where their fragrance and berry-eating bird visitors can be enjoyed. Easy to grow, these vigorous bushes need sun and well-drained soil. 6–12 feet; Zones 3–9.

Forsythia *(Forsythia spp.)*

Loved for its bright, early-spring flowers of yellow, forsythia has good foliage and is an easy, adaptable shrub. It spreads by underground stems and may outgrow small spaces. Get improved cultivars such as 'Meadowlark' or 'Ottawa' for sure bloom in the North. Forsythia needs full sun. Prune right after flowering. 8–10 feet; Zones 5–8.

Lilac *(Syringa spp.)*

Hundreds of lilac types enchant gardeners yearly with their plumes of fragrant springtime flowers. Choose types with varied bloom times to stretch the season by weeks. Give full sun and well-drained, slightly acid soil. 3–20 feet; Zones 2–9.

Fruit, Dwarf (stone) *(Prunus spp.)*

Bush forms of plum and cherry are lovely in hedgerows, as flowering accents in foundation plantings, or near patios. Genetic dwarf plants of almond, apple, apricot, cherry, nectarine, peach, pear, and plum have many uses: as informal hedges, in foundation plantings, as interest plants in shrub borders, and especially in containers. 4-10 feet; Zones 3–9.

Mockorange *(Philadelphus coronarius)*

Mockorange is prized in mass plantings because of its fragrant white flowers that come at spring's end, when few other shrubs are in bloom. This shrub is easy to grow in full sun or light shade. 'Minnesota Snowflake' is very hardy, with 2-inch double flowers. 'Belle Etoile' has pinkish blush flowers. The variety 'Virginal' has semidouble blooms throughout the summer. 4–12 feet; Zones 4–8.

DECIDUOUS SHRUBS *(continued)*

Privet *(Ligustrum* spp.)
Popular for clipped hedges, privet is vigorous and usually problem free, and withstands adverse conditions. It has glossy foliage, white flower clusters, and black berries. In the South, it is evergreen. It will grow in some shade. 9–15 feet; Zones 4–9.

Rose *(Rosa* spp.)
Now the official U.S. flower, the rose in many varieties is a true and hardy shrub. Meadow rose has red twigs for winter interest. Rugosa roses have hips that can be used in drinks and jellies. Roses make good barrier, accent, and border plants. Landscape roses are easy to grow, are disease resistant, and usually bloom from early summer to fall. 3–15 feet; Zones 3–10.

Spirea *(Spiraea* spp.)
Also called bridal wreath, spirea offers fountains of white spring flowers and ease of growth. Now many improved varieties bloom in white to red from April to August. 'Goldflame' has pink flowers and golden foliage; 'Plena' has double flowers. Spirea likes sun but will tolerate partial shade. 1–12 feet; Zones 5–9.

LARGE *(more than 10 feet tall)*

Butterfly Bush *(Buddleia* spp.)
Alternate-leaf 'Sungold' and orange-eye versions of this plant have long spikes of fragrant flowers in white, pink, red, purple, blue, or pale yellow on arching branches. Some bloom in early summer; the orange-eye blooms summer to fall. Blooms attract butterflies. In the North, this plant may die to the ground, but it will grow back and bloom by summer. 6–15 feet; Zones 5–9.

Crape Myrtle *(Lagerstroemia indica)*
These useful, vase-shape, quick-growing large shrubs (or small trees) bloom all summer long in the South. Crape myrtle makes a good accent shrub. New varieties are hardy as far north as Washington, D.C., and can withstand temperatures to –23°F. In bad winters, crape myrtle may die to the ground, but it will grow back from its roots. 10–30 feet; Zones 7–10.

Hydrangea, Peegee
(Hydrangea paniculata 'Grandiflora')
Peegee hydrangea is a big, rather coarse shrub with large clusters of summer flowers that turn pink or purplish as they dry, often keeping the bush attractive even after its leaves have fallen. Use in borders. 25–30 feet; Zones 4–8.

Pussy Willow *(Salix discolor)*

Pussy or goat willow grows quickly and roots easily in water from spring-blooming twigs, but it is coarse and can be pest ridden. Use sparsely in screens or border. 10–25 feet; Zones 2–8.

Viburnum *(Viburnum spp.)*

Viburnums are a group that includes dozens of medium-size shrubs and small trees that are among the finest landscaping plants. Pink buds open to showy white flowers, many of them fragrant in spring. Lush summer foliage turns red in autumn, and clusters of black or red berries attract birds. Most are hardy and easy to grow. Viburnums prefer sun and moist, slightly acid soil; some will tolerate salt spray. 5–30 feet; Zones 3–9.

Witch Hazel *(Hamamelis spp.)*

Witch hazel blooms in fall or late winter—even in snow—with small, inconspicuous to moderately showy, fragrant, ribbonlike flowers of yellow to copper. Witch hazel has good yellow autumn foliage. Mostly native, these shrubs like full or partial sun and rich, moist soil. 5–30 feet; Zones 5–8.

SHRUBS AND TREES BY SHAPE

Shrubs with Arching Branches
Beautybush
Butterfly bush
Daphne, lilac
Deutzia, slender
Forsythia
Spirea

Spreading Shrubs
Cotoneaster, spreading
Crabapple, sargent
Ninebark, dwarf
Quince, Japanese
Sumac, staghorn
Viburnum, fragrant

Columnar Trees
Arborvitae
Ginkgo, sentry
Hornbeam, 'Columnaris'
Hornbeam, 'Fastigiata'
Juniper, blue columnar
Maple, crimson sentry
Maple, red 'Bowhill'
Maple, red 'Scanlon'
Poplar, lombardy
Red cedar, pyramidal
Tulip tree, 'Fastigiata'

Erect Shrubs
Cranberry, highbush
Dogwood, red-osier
Hibiscus
Lilac, common
Mockorange, lemoine

Weeping Trees
Apricot, weeping
Ash, weeping European
Beech, weeping
Birch, slender European
Birch, young's weeping
Boree, weeping
Cedar, deodar
Cherry, weeping
Crabapple, pink weeping
Hemlock, 'Pendula'
Hornbeam, weeping European
Linden, pendant silver
Pines (several varieties)
Spruce, brewer
Spruce, koster's weeping blue
Willow (several varieties)

Rounded Shrubs
Hydrangea
Kerria
Lilac, Persian
Quince, flowering
Weigela
Witch hazel

Pyramid-Shape Trees
Beech
Birch
Black gum
Cedar
Hemlock
Holly
Larch
Linden
Magnolia
Oak, pin
Pine
Sourwood
Spruce
Sweet gum

Trees with Horizontal Branches
Chestnut, Chinese
Dogwood
Fir
Hawthorn
Mimosa
Oak (notably white and live oak)
Pine, red
Pine, Scotch
Redbud
Spruce

BROADLEAVED EVERGREEN SHRUBS

SMALL *(can be kept under 5 feet tall)*

Azalea *(Rhododendron spp.)*

Dense and often spreading, evergreen azaleas have trusses of flowers in many colors that stand proudly above the foliage midspring to early summer. Some varieties lose their leaves in harsh winters. Azaleas tolerate partial shade and like well-drained, acid soil. 3–6 feet; Zones 4–8.

Heather *(Calluna spp.)*

Small leaves and clusters of tiny midsummer flowers in white, pink, or purple are heather's trademarks. Use this plant in borders or rock gardens. Needs acid soil and full or part sun. 2–30 inches; Zones 4–7.

Boxwood, Littleleaf
(Buxus microphylla)

A Japanese evergreen with small, glossy leaves and a spreading habit, littleleaf boxwood is prized for clipped or natural hedges and foundation plantings. 'Green Beauty' and 'Wintergreen' retain green color all winter. Some turn yellowish, especially in cold winters. Boxwood likes mulch over its shallow roots and full or part sun. 2–5 feet; Zones 4–9.

Leucothoe *(Leucothoe spp.)*

Coast and drooping leucothoe have sprays of fragrant bell-shape white blooms in spring and glossy leaves that are deep green in summer and bronze in winter. Branches arch gracefully for covering banks or the leggy feet of other shrubs. Good in borders or near foundations. Likes acid soil and shade. 3–6 feet; Zones 5–9.

Daphne *(Daphne spp.)*

Several evergreen or semievergreen daphnes make excellent foundation plantings. They have clusters of long-lasting, fragrant spring flowers. Some are low enough for rock gardens. Burkwood has whitish flowers and red berries. The upright winter daphne is an evergreen in Zone 8 and warmer climates. Water daphnes sparingly. Some like alkaline soil. 3–5 feet; Zones 5–10.

Oregon Grapeholly
(Mahonia aquifolium)

Also called holly grape or Oregon grape, this shrub has hardy, attractive leaves that turn bronze in winter, clusters of bright yellow flowers in spring, and bluish black, grapelike berries in summer. Good as a barrier, foundation, or border plant, Oregon grapeholly likes acid soil and partial shade and needs protection from heat and drying. 3–6 feet; Zones 5–8.

MEDIUM TO LARGE *(taller than 5 feet)*

Andromeda *(Pieris spp.)*
Beautiful and dependable, andromeda, or pieris, should be used more often in landscapes. Its flowers bloom with fragrant upright or pendulous spires of white to pinkish bells in early spring. It likes wind protection and part shade. 2–9 feet; Zones 4–8.

Camellia *(Camellia spp.)*
Slow growing and dependable, camellias produce exquisite flowers and dark, lustrous foliage. They thrive in temperate, humid areas and as far north as Philadelphia in sheltered spots or containers. By choosing for a succession of bloom times, you can have flowers from late fall into spring. Camellias need shade and acid soil. 6–25 feet; Zones 7–9.

Euonymus, Burning Bush *(Euonymus europaeus, E. alatus)*
Also called spindle tree, this hardy evergreen euonymus is a cousin of the deciduous burning bush. Spindle tree is good in hedges or borders, or as a barrier. Burning bush provides spectacular fall color. Both tolerate many soils and city conditions and like sun or shade. 6–20 feet; Zones 3–7.

Firethorn *(Pyracantha spp.)*
Firethorn produces clusters of white flowers in spring that give way to showy orange to scarlet berries. Plants grow quickly and are excellent for espaliers or hedges, or as specimen, barrier, or border plants. Firethorn will tolerate dry soil but needs sun for berry production. 6–15 feet; Zones 7–10.

Holly *(Ilex spp.)*
Evergreen holly is useful for accent, barrier, foundation, hedge, and border plantings. Some low, compact varieties are good for edging and hedges. Leaves are glossy and leathery, but flowers are inconspicuous. Berries on female plants are showy. Evergreen hollies are easy, but slow, to grow. Keep them moist. 3–20 feet; Zones 5–9.

Mountain Laurel *(Kalmia latifolia)*
Mountain laurel—one of the most beautiful shrubs—is ideal for foundations, as an accent plant, or in woodland settings. Its great masses of delicate blooms range from deep pink to white. Lovely with dogwoods and rhododendrons, it needs acid soil and prefers partial shade. 3–10 feet; Zones 5–8.

NEEDLED EVERGREEN SHRUBS

Arborvitae, American
(Thuja occidentalis)

A slow-growing, compact, columnar shrub or tree, American arborvitae has green or blue-green, scalelike, fan-shape foliage. Use it as a foundation, hedge, or accent plant. It likes rich, moist, well-drained soil and a cool climate. Prune in early spring. 7–20 feet; Zones 3–8.

Japanese Plum Yew
(Cephalotaxus harringtonia)

Japanese plum yew is similar to true yews but less dense. It usually is multistemmed and wide spreading. ('Fastigiata' is columnar with dark green, 1½-inch needles and 1-inch, purple-green fruits.) Use this in a hedge or as a screen. It needs moist, acid soil. Shear it in spring before growth starts. 20–30 feet; Zones 6–8.

Cypress, False
(Chamaecyparis spp.)

This evergreen has deep green, scalelike, fanned foliage and reddish brown shredding bark, making it a fine accent plant. Be sure to get dwarf cultivars: 'Nana Gracilis,' 'Golden Mop.' Basic species will grow too large in foundation plantings. False cypress likes sun, humidity, and moist, neutral to acid soil. It needs protection from wind. 4–100 feet; Zones 4–8.

Juniper *(Juniperus spp.)*

Creeping cedars and junipers that carry the names dwarf common, Hollywood, pfitzer, and shore all have dense, broad, spreading foliage in many hues (depending on variety), blue berries, and wood that smells like cedar. Well-chosen cultivars make fine groundcovers or foundation plants. Shore juniper withstands salt spray. All like sun and dry, sandy soil. 1–20 feet; Zones 3–9.

Japanese Cedar
(Cryptomeria japonica)

Japanese cedar has reddish brown bark, bluish green needles that pick up a bronze tinge in winter, and a broad, pyramid shape. Use it along foundations or in patio tubs. Japanese cedar likes moist soil and is pest free, but it doesn't tolerate drought very well. 3 feet; Zones 5–9.

Leyland Cypress
(×Cupressocyparis leylandii)

A cross between nootka false cypress and Monterey cypress, this narrow, columnar evergreen has scalelike, gray-green to pale green foliage. It grows fast—3 to 5 feet a year—but is easily sheared to any size for hedges and screens. Prune in early spring. It tolerates many soils and climates. 40–50 feet; Zones 5–10.

VINES

PERENNIAL

Pine, dwarf varieties *(Pinus* spp.)
Bristlecone pine, dwarf white pine, and mugo or mountain pine are slow-growing, dense shrubs with bright or dark blue-green needles, 1 to 4 inches long. Use dwarf pines as specimen, border, or foundation plants, and in rock gardens or containers. Pines need full or part sun. They are subject to scale. For thicker bushier form, prune candles in spring. 4–20 feet; Zones 3–9.

Spruce, Dwarf Alberta
(Picea glauca 'Conica')
A dense, pyramidal evergreen with a single trunk and tufted, ½-inch light green needles, dwarf white spruce grows slowly. Use it as an accent or dense hedge with low-growing shrubs, or in rock or formal gardens. It likes sandy soil and a cold climate. 6–8 feet; Zones 2–6.

Yew *(Taxus* spp.)
The darkest, richest green of all the evergreens, yew has soft, flat needles. Female plants have red berries. Many shapes and sizes fill a large range of garden uses: along foundations, in hedges, or as group plantings. Canada yew, the hardiest, is a good groundcover. Japanese yew does well in sun, shade, and most soils, as long as drainage is good. It prefers moist, sandy loam. 3–20 feet; Zones 2–7.

Actinidia *(Actinidia* spp.)
This group includes kiwi, Chinese gooseberry, and some 40 species of twining, woody vines. Grown mostly for its handsome foliage, actinidia has small, fragrant white flowers in spring. It is trouble free and vigorous, and it creates an attractive pattern on a wall, fence, or arbor. The right varieties in the right light and climate produce delicious fruits that keep well. 40 feet; Zones 5–10; deciduous.

Bittersweet *(Celastrus* spp.)
Hardy and twining, thorny bittersweet is good for screening, on banks, or as a barrier. It has inconspicuous flowers, leaves that turn yellow in fall, and red fall berries in orange capsules. It grows in ordinary soil and will tolerate shade, but it fruits best in sun (male and female required). Do not plant on trees. 30 feet; Zones 4–8; deciduous.

Bougainvillea *(Bougainvillea* hybrids)
This thorny twiner grows best in the deep South—in full sun in cooler areas and in afternoon shade in hottest climates. (In the North, grow it as a houseplant.) Bougainvillea has flower clusters with showy bracts in red, pink, orange, and purple. Limit its water (it can withstand drought) but feed well. Frost will damage it. 6–30 feet; Zones 9–10; evergreen.

VINES *(continued)*

Carolina Jessamine
(Gelsemium sempervirens)
A twining vine, carolina jessamine is good on a fence, trellis, mailbox, or lamppost, or used as a groundcover. It has fragrant yellow flowers and long, glossy leaves. A double-flowered form is available. It needs fertile soil and sun or light shade. 10–20 feet; Zones 7–9; evergreen.

Clematis *(Clematis spp. and hybrids)*
Among the showiest of all vines, clematis sports single or semidouble white, blue, pink, red, or purple flowers in early summer. A dainty plant, clematis works best as an accent or as a frame for an entrance. All clematis climb by twisting leaf stalks. They do best with their flowers in sun and their roots in shade. Do not plant too shallow or allow to dry out for long. 5–30 feet; Zones 4–9; deciduous.

Grape *(Vitis spp.)*
Hardy, dependable vines for fruit, screening, or shade, grapes climb by clinging tendrils. Vigorous, they need pruning yearly (or more often), and are excellent as covers on arbors or small structures, or espaliered against a wall. Some can be trained as small weeping trees. Flowers are fragrant but not showy. 50–100 feet; Zones 4–10; deciduous.

Honeysuckle *(Lonicera spp.)*
A good climber, honeysuckle has trumpet-shape, fragrant flowers in many colors and over much of the summer; red or black berries appear in the fall. Honeysuckle also is good as a groundcover on banks and is ideal for quick screening. Vigorous, almost rampant in some climates, honeysuckle can die to the ground in severe cold but is semievergreen in the South. It tolerates drought and sun to dense shade. 12–50 feet; Zones 3–10; deciduous.

Ivy, Boston *(Parthenocissus tricuspidata)*
Carefree Boston ivy will quickly cover a building facade with no support. Its large, waxy green leaves turn bright red in fall and provide shelter for birds (dark blue berries provide food). In winter it creates a dense pattern of gray on walls. It grows in full sun to partial shade. 60 feet; Zones 5–9; deciduous.

Ivy: English, Algerian
(Hedera helix, H. canariensis)
Both ivies are fast growing vines that cling by their rootlets to walls and stone. They also will quickly cover wire fences and can be used as groundcovers. Both have variegated varieties. These ivies do best in rich, moist soil on north or east walls. Both tolerate shade; Algerian ivy (Zones 8–10) can take more sun than English ivy (Zones 4–9). 50–90 feet; both are evergreen.

Jasmine *(Jasminum spp.)*
Winter jasmine is the hardiest jasmine, growing as far north as Boston. Common white and Japanese jasmine thrive farther south. All grow as shrubs with some support. Flowers are dainty and fragrant. Jasmine likes sun and moist or wet soil. 10–30 feet; Zones 5–9; semi-evergreen.

Passionflower *(Passiflora caerulea)*
The hardiest passionflower survives as far north as Iowa, dying back in winter but returning from roots. Others are more tropical. All have exquisite flowers of white, blue, or red. Use on sunny fences and arbors. 20 feet; Zones 7–10; evergreen until frost kills top growth.

Rose *(Rosa spp. and hybrids)*
Climbing and rambler roses offer fragrant flowers in many colors. Good for borders or arbors, or lovely above gates. All need support, pruning, six hours of sun daily, shelter from north winds, and fertile, well-drained soil. 15–20 feet; Zones 4–10; deciduous.

VINES FOR SPECIAL INTEREST

Rapid Growing
Actinidia, bower
Bittersweet
Cathedral bells
Chinese gooseberry
Clematis
Dutchman's pipe
Five-leaf akebia
Grape
Honeysuckle
Hop vine
Ivy, Boston
Ivy, English
Trumpet creeper
Virginia creeper
Wisteria

For Use as a Groundcover
Akebia
Bittersweet
Euonymus, running
Hop vine
Honeysuckle
Ivy, Boston
Ivy, English

For Showy Flowers
Cathedral bells
Clematis
Honeysuckle
Hydrangea, climbing
Jasmine
Mandevilla
Passionflower
Plumbago
Silver fleece vine
Wisteria

For City Conditions
Bean, scarlet runner
Cathedral bells
Cypress vine
Hop vine
Ivy, Boston
Ivy, English
Silver lace vine
Wisteria

For Interesting Fruits
Beans, white and scarlet runner
Bitter melon
Bittersweet
Clematis (most species)
Euonymus, running
Grape
Hop vine
Kiwi
Magnolia vine
Rose, climbing varieties
Virginia creeper
Wintercreeper

Fragrant
Clematis, sweet autumn
Honeysuckle
Jasmine
Kiwi
Madeira vine
Moonflower
Passionflower
Rose
Wisteria

VINES *(continued)*

Virginia Creeper
(Parthenocissus quinquefolia)

Virginia creeper climbs by clinging with disklike ends on aerial rootlets. Self-supporting, it can hang like a lacy curtain from a screened porch, covering but not damaging. Then, in winter, it will drop its foliage to let sunshine in. Five-finger, whorled leaves turn dark red in fall; flowers are inconspicuous. Birds love its blue autumn berries. It grows rapidly in sun or light shade. 50 feet; Zones 4–9; deciduous.

Wisteria *(Wisteria spp.)*

Vigorous wisteria has superb panicles of fragrant white, rose, or lavender blooms in spring. Its twisting trunks provide winter interest. Wisteria is slow to establish; grafted plants bloom sooner. It likes fertile soil and full sun to partial shade; prune to keep in bounds. Provide strong support. 30–40 feet; Zones 4–9; deciduous.

ANNUAL

Balloon Vine
(Cardiospermum halicacabum)

Balloon vine has inconspicuous flowers, feathery foliage, and balloon-shape seedpods; it is a perennial in the South. 10 feet; sun.

Balsam Pear *(Momordica charantia)*

Balsam pear's small yellow flowers bear gourdlike fruits that turn yellow and open to expose large, bright red seeds. Rapid growing, it covers a porch quickly but can become weedy. 8–30 feet; sun.

Black-Eyed Susan Vine
(Thunbergia alata)

Yellow or orange daisylike flowers— some with dark throats—bloom all summer. This vine needs a long season. 6–10 feet; sun or shade.

Canary-Bird Flower
(Tropaeolum peregrinum)

Canary-bird flower, also known as canary creeper, has 1-inch, yellow, feathery flowers in summer. It thrives in poor soil, needs moisture and shade, and prefers cool nights. 6–10 feet; shade.

Cardinal Climber *(Ipomoea ×multifida)*

Cardinal climber has 2-inch, crimson, tubular flowers all summer; its foliage is deeply cut. It twines and likes sandy soil. Good with blue morning glory. 10–20 feet; sun or shade.

Dutchman's Pipe
(Aristolochia macrophylla)

The huge leaves of dutchman's pipe are unequaled for cooling shade or dense screens. This vine needs space to avoid crowding other plants. Pipelike flowers blend a rare shade of mahogany and white but are not showy. Soak seeds in warm water 48 hours before planting. 30 feet; sun or shade.

Cathedral Bells *(Cobaea scandens)*

Also called cup-and-saucer vine, cathedral bells has large, deep bluish purple or creamy white flowers for six months, from spring into summer. A Southern favorite, it grows rapidly and clings by tendrils. It's slow to germinate, so start it eight weeks early indoors. A native of Mexico, it likes heat. 10–20 feet; sun.

Moonflower *(Ipomoea alba)*

This rapid grower is ideal for screening. It has large, heart-shape leaves and deep-throated, large, fragrant white flowers that open at dusk. A native of Florida swamps, moonflower likes a warm climate and poor soil. 15 feet; sun.

Cypress Vine *(Ipomoea quamoclit)*

Cypress vine produces white, red, or pink flowers all summer; its foliage is ferny. It grows wild in the South and starts easily from seed or cuttings. 10–20 feet; sun or part shade.

Morning Glory *(Ipomoea purpurea)*

Morning glory's flowers open at dawn, then close when the sun gets too hot. Good on fences, porches, and lampposts, it thrives in almost any soil in sun. 8–10 feet; sun.

GROUNDCOVERS

African Daisy (Osteospermum ecklonis)

African daisy produces carpets of 3-inch pink or lilac-fading-to-white blooms from November to March, sporadic blooms the rest of the year. Excellent for covering slopes, it's used mostly on the West Coast. It will survive on one or two waterings a year. Mow or cut back every year or two in spring. 1–3 feet; Zones 9–10; sun.

Bearberry, Common (Arctostaphylos uva-ursi)

Common bearberry has tiny, evergreen, trailing leaves and red autumn berries. This groundcover is good on banks, in poor or acid soils, and on seashores. It's vigorous and trouble free. 6–8 inches; Zones 2–8; part shade or sun.

Ajuga (Ajuga reptans)

Also called bugleweed or carpet bugle, ajuga is one of the best groundcovers. It has dark green foliage rosettes with bronze, purple, or rainbow overtones; variegated types have white edges and purple centers. Colors intensify in fall. Blue flower spikes bloom in spring. Good for edgings, ajuga spreads quickly but is not rampant. 3–6 inches; Zones 3–10; sun or light shade.

Bellflower (Campanula spp.)

Also called campanula or harebell, bellflower is low and trailing. It has neat foliage and a profusion of blue to purple upright bells or star-shape cups, mainly in late spring or early summer. Bellflower is adaptable for small areas in moist soil. 6–10 inches; Zones 3–10; sun or light shade.

Artemisia Silver Mound
(Artemisia schmidtiana)

This plant's silvery leaves have woolly texture, are aromatic when crushed, and form attractive mounds. Its yellow flowers aren't showy. An excellent accent plant, artemisia tolerates heat and drought but not dampness. 6 inches–2 feet; Zones 3–9; sun.

Bishop's Weed
(Aegopodium podagraria 'Goutweed')

This groundcover has gray-green, compound leaves with white edges. White flowers resemble wild carrot; remove them to control spreading and prevent plants from becoming rampant. Excellent for problem areas and for edgings where it can be controlled. 6–12 inches; Zones 3–10; sun or shade.

Candytuft *(Iberis sempervirens)*

Candytuft's evergreen foliage is attractive all year. Masses of white, 2-inch-tall flower spikes cover the top in spring. Improved varieties bloom at intervals all season. Candytuft is excellent for edging or covering small spaces; it tolerates salt and seashore conditions. 10–12 inches; Zones 3–8; sun or light shade.

Corsican Mint *(Mentha requienii)*

Corsican (or creeping) mint makes a fragrant, green carpet. In spring it produces small, pale lavender blooms. Its shallow roots need constant moisture. It will take some traffic and is good as a container or bonsai ground cover. 1–2 inches; Zones 6–10; sun or light shade.

Carmel Creeper

(Ceanothus griseus)

This California coast native has dark green, glossy, round leaves and violet-blue spring flowers. It tolerates salt spray and strong winds. Needs extremely well-drained soil; it may develop root rot with too much water. 11–24 feet; Zones 7–10; sun.

Cotoneaster *(Cotoneaster* spp.)

The shiny green leaves of rockspray, cranberry, and bearberry cotoneaster spread 4 to 15 feet in a fishbone pattern. White or pinkish summer blooms yield to red berries and leaves in fall. Cotoneaster is ideal for larger spaces or steep slopes. *C. dammeri* is evergreen. 6–36 inches; Zones 5–10; sun or light shade.

Chamomile *(Chamaemelum nobile)*

English (or Roman) chamomile is a fragrant herb with fernlike foliage and small, daisylike flowers in summer. Place it where it will be brushed or crushed so that it releases its fragrance. Can be a lawn substitute. 3–10 inches; Zones 3–10; sun or light shade.

Fern (many genera)

The fern family includes hundreds of hardy and adaptable plants that offer a light, airy, and cooling look. Their textures contrast well with bolder foliage. Charming in woodlands or shady areas, most ferns die back in winter. Shown here is Japanese Painted Fern *(Athyrium nipponicum* 'Pictum'). 6–36 inches; Zones 2–10; shade.

GROUNDCOVERS *(continued)*

Forget-Me-Not

(Myosotis scorpioides and *M. sylvatica)*

M. scorpioides is a perennial; *M. sylvatica* self-sows. Both have pale blue flowers with pink, yellow, or white centers in spring and summer. Persistent but not invasive. Forget-me-not needs moisture; good along stream banks or with tulips. 2–18 inches; Zones 4–10; partial shade.

Germander *(Teucrium chamaedrys)*

This plant has dark green, ¾-inch leaves, with lavender flower spikes in spring. Evergreen in milder zones, germander is ideal for poor soils and hot locations; it makes a good edging or low formal hedge. Bees love its blooms. 8–18 inches; Zones 5–10; sun.

Ginger, Wild *(Asarum* spp.)

Also called snakeroot, these woodland plants have large, heart-shape leaves. Red-purple flowers hide at the base of the leaves in spring. Cool weather tints the leaves purple. Some varieties are evergreen. 6–10 inches; Zones 4–10; sun or shade.

GROUNDCOVERS FOR SPECIAL INTEREST

Quick Spreading
African daisy
Ajuga
Bearberry
Bellflower
Carmel creeper
Crown vetch
Ivy, Algerian
Lamium
Mondo grass
Moneywort
Sedum
Snow-in-summer
Verbena

For Showy Flowers
African daisy
Agapanthus
Ajuga
Astilbe
Bellflower
Bougainvillea
Bush cinquefoil
Candytuft
Carmel creeper
Cinquefoil
Crown vetch
Daylily
Deutzia
Forget-me-not
Gazania
Geranium
Heath
Heather
Hosta
Lantana, trailing
Lily-of-the-valley
Phlox, creeping
Pink, moss or
   maiden
St. johnswort
Snow-in-summer
Speedwell
Spirea
Verbena

Edible
Chamomile
Cranberry
Mint
Natal plum, dwarf
Rosemary, dwarf
Strawberry
Thyme
Violet

Potential Weeds
Bishop's weed
Buttercup, creeping
Crown vetch
Evening primrose
Honeysuckle, hall's
Ivy, ground
Knotweed
Matrimony vine
Mint
Moneywort
Moss, Irish
Ribbon grass
St. johnswort

Juniper (*Juniperus* spp.)

This low-growing evergreen group includes plants with many textures and subtle hues; most are good on banks and slopes. Junipers are slow to grow but will deter traffic when established. 4–48 inches; Zones 2–10; sun or light shade.

Moneywort (*Lysimachia nummularia*)

Also called creeping jennie, moneywort has bright yellow buttercup flowers in spring—some continuing all summer. A moisture lover, it grows anywhere and is especially good around rocks and pools. It can be rampant and will bear some traffic. 2–6 inches; Zones 2–10; sun or shade.

Lily-of-the-Valley (*Convallaria majalis*)

Familiar because of its light green basal leaves and nodding stalks of delicate, fragrant, bell-shape flowers in spring, lily-of-the-valley tolerates wet or dry soil. 6–12 inches; Zones 3–9; sun to dense shade.

Moss, Irish (*Selaginella involens*)

Similar to scotch moss, this tufted groundcover's needlelike leaves form an evergreen matting. White flowers appear in spring. Irish moss is good between stepping-stones, in rock gardens, and under ferns. 'Aurea' has golden leaves. Can become a weed. 1–2 inches; Zones 4–10; sun or light shade.

Mahonia, Creeping (*Mahonia repens*)

Creeping mahonia has hollylike leaflets that are bluish green on top and powdery underneath; often they turn deep red in fall and winter. It has fragrant yellow spring flowers and will deter traffic. Protect this groundcover from wind. Its roots stop erosion and the plant resists drought. 2–4 inches; Zones 5–10; sun or shade.

Pachysandra (*Pachysandra* spp.)

Also called Japanese spurge, pachysandra has whorls of spoon-shape leaves toothed on their outer edges; some have leaves that are mottled or edged in white. Evergreen in mild areas, pachysandra quickly forms a dense carpet; it is excellent under trees or shrubs, or as an edging along shady walks. 8–10 inches; Zones 4–8; part sun or shade.

GROUNDCOVERS *(continued)*

Sedum *(Sedum* spp.)
Also called stonecrop, these succulents have many forms, sizes, and colors. Their flowers are yellow, white, or pink to rose. Sedums prefer poor soil and some drought, and can spread to cover an acre, but they won't stand traffic. 2–10 inches; Zones 3–10; sun.

Sweet Woodruff *(Galium odoratum)*
Sweet woodruff's dark green, sandpapery, edible leaflets are like spokes on square stems. Tiny white flowers in clusters bloom in early summer. Grow sweet woodruff beneath rhododendrons and high-branched conifer trees. 6–12 inches; Zones 4–10; light shade.

Snow-in-Summer
(Cerastium tomentosum)
Snow-in-summer has tiny silver leaves that form a low mat and send up an abundance of delicate white flowers in late spring. Good for rock gardens or edgings, or among bulbs. Does well in desert, coastal, or mountain areas. 3–6 inches; Zones 2–10; sun.

Thyme *(Thymus* spp.)
Creeping, woolly, lemon, and many additional thyme varieties vary from a matlike growth to small shrubs, all with tiny, dark green leaves and aromatic red, pink, white, or purple summer flowers. Thyme makes a good lawn substitute for limited-traffic areas. 2–15 inches; Zones 3–10; sun.

Strawberry *(Fragaria* spp.)
Alpine strawberry and some ornamental varieties have attractive foliage, white flowers in spring, and fruits both edible and decorative. Tolerant and adaptable, strawberry will stand a little foot traffic and light shade. 6–12 inches; Zones 3–10; sun.

Vinca *(Vinca minor)*
Also called periwinkle or myrtle, vinca has dark, glossy, evergreen leaves and lovely lavender spring flowers. Grow under trees or shrubs, or among bulbs. 10–12 inches; Zones 4–9; shade.

FLOWERS

PERENNIAL

Anchusa *(Anchusa azurea)*
Also called summer forget-me-not, anchusa is covered in summer with intense, true blue flowers. Anchusa grows easily from seed or divisions and has lance-shape basal leaves. 3–4 feet; Zones 4–8; sun.

Bee Balm *(Monarda didyma)*
Bee balm has unusual round clusters of flowers in red, pink, white, or lavender that attract bees and butterflies. An aromatic herb, it spreads aggressively. Good for naturalizing in woodland settings or bog gardens. 2–3 feet; Zones 4–9; sun or light shade.

Aster, Hardy *(Aster spp.)*
Also called michaelmas daisy, hardy aster produces flowers of blue, purple, or pink in late summer and fall. It combines well with lily, kniphofia, and chrysanthemum. Good as a cut flower, it has small, green leaves and needs support. 3–4 feet; Zones 4–9; sun.

Bleeding Heart *(Dicentra spectabilis)*
Bleeding heart is a favorite for its reliability and heart-shape spring flowers. Its foliage turns yellow and disappears by midsummer.
Dutchman's breeches, of the same genus, likes more shade and has ferny foliage. 1–2 feet; Zones 4–9; sun or shade.

Astilbe *(Astilbe ×arendsii)*
Also called false spirea, astilbe has feathery flower heads from June through August, seedheads that provide winter interest, fernlike mounds of foliage, and shallow roots. 15–30 inches; Zones 4–8; shade.

Butterfly Weed *(Asclepias tuberosa)*
A form of milkweed, this handsome native plant is covered with bright orange flowers, which butterflies love, all summer long. Attractive ornamental pods follow the flowers. Butterfly weed stands drought well. Striking with daylily and red hot poker, it is slow to emerge in spring, so mark your planting spot. 2–3 feet; Zones 4–9; sun.

FLOWERS *(continued)*

Chrysanthemum
(Chrysanthemum grandiflorum)

Mums, the glory of the fall garden, come in many forms and rich autumn colors plus lavender. Gray-green foliage is attractive all year. Mums can be moved even when in full bloom. 1–4 feet; Zones 4–10; sun.

Flax *(Linum* spp.)

Flax has delicate flowers in golden yellow or sky blue for weeks in early summer. Excellent when planted alongside Iceland poppy and columbine, flax has attractive, feathery foliage all season. 1–2 feet; Zones 5–8; sun.

Daylily *(Hemerocallis* hybrids)

Daylilies are the glory of the midsummer garden. Each lilylike bloom lasts only a day, but every plant can have dozens of blooms. Plants have attractive, grasslike foliage and combine well with speedwell, liatris, and butterfly weed. 1½–4 feet; Zones 3–9; sun or shade.

Hosta *(Hosta* spp.)

Also called plantain lily or funkia, hosta is prized for its foliage, which varies in color, variegation, texture, and edging. Some also have lovely fragrant flower spikes in summer to early fall. Easy to grow, hosta is excellent as a groundcover or garden accent. 1–3 feet; Zones 4–9; shade.

Delphinium
(Delphinium spp. and hybrids)

Delphinium has few rivals for color and form. Spikes of white, pink, or marvelous blues bloom in early summer, then rebloom in fall. Palm-shape gray-green leaves are nice all season. 2½–6 feet; Zones 2–7; sun.

Loosestrife *(Lythrum salicaria)*

Loosestrife, with its slender spires of pink purple flowers from June to September, is excellent for the back of a border. 1½–4 feet; Zones 4–9; sun.

Peony (*Paeonia* spp.)

Peony is a favorite for its large, fragrant spring flowers. It is long-lived and easy to grow. New cultivars have stronger stems. Place in front of shrubs or use as a border or low hedge. 2–4 feet; Zones 3–9; sun.

Speedwell (*Veronica* spp.)

Also called veronica, speedwell has lovely spikes of blue or white flowers—perfect for a rock garden or border—from June to September. Its foliage is dark green. 6–36 inches; Zones 4–9; sun.

BIENNIAL

Phlox (*Phlox* spp.)

Different varieties of phlox can produce everything from creeping splashes of spring color to tall clusters that give mass and substance from June to early September. Phlox's ferny or lance-shape foliage is handsome all season. 6–48 inches; Zones 3–9; sun.

Canterbury Bells (*Campanula medium*)

Biennial bellflowers have cuplike blooms in white, pink, blue, or purple. Sow seed in June. 1½–4 feet; Zones 4–9; sun.

Shasta Daisy

(*Chrysanthemum* ×*superbum Leucanthemum* ×*superbum*)

Shasta daisy is a classic of simple beauty either in the garden or as a cut flower. If you select several varieties, you can get single and double blooms all summer. Basal foliage is dark green. Plants may die out and need replacing every few years. 1–4 feet; Zones 5–10; sun.

Forget-Me-Not, Alpine

(*Myosotis alpestris*)

Along with a few perennials, the myosotis genus includes this blue-flowered biennial star of the spring garden. It's excellent mixed with spring bulbs or naturalized in a woodland. Sow seed in July or August. 8–24 inches; Zones 3–8; part shade.

FLOWERS *(continued)*

ANNUAL

Foxglove *(Digitalis purpurea)*
The first spiked flower of spring, foxglove produces thimble-shape blossoms in a wide range of soft colors. It has bold basal foliage. Sow seed in June. 2½–5 feet; Zones 4–9; sun.

Ageratum *(Ageratum houstonianum)*
Ageratum's fluffy blue, pink, or white flowers make it good for edgings, border fronts, or containers. 4–10 inches; sun.

Hollyhock *(Alcea rosea)*
Hollyhock produces towers of white, pink, yellow, red, or purple flowers; its foliage can be coarse. Once established, hollyhock self-sows. 3–8 feet; Zones 3–9; sun.

Alyssum, Sweet *(Lobularia maritima)*
Sweet alyssum has low mats of fragrant, delicate flowers in white, rose, lavender, or purple. For continual bloom, shear. Will self-sow. 3–6 inches; sun or part shade.

Sweet William *(Dianthus barbatus)*
Sweet william's lovely, spicy-smelling floret clusters of rich reds, pinks, and white are excellent for the front to middle of flower borders, for cut flowers, in rock gardens, or naturalized at the edge of woodlands. Sow seed in June. Sweet william self-sows once started. 6–24 inches; Zones 4–8; sun.

Bachelor's Button *(Centaurea cyanus)*
Also called cornflower, this annual has gray-green foliage and round flowers in white, pink, blue (which is loveliest), or purple. Repeat sowing for continuous bloom. Bachelor's button likes cool weather. 1–3 feet; sun or part shade.

Begonia, Wax
(Begonia semperflorens-cultorum)
Reliable for nonstop flowers, the neat, compact wax begonia works well as an edging plant or in containers. 6–12 inches; sun or shade.

Coleus *(Solenostemon scutellaroides)*
Coleus is grown for its variety of foliage colors and shapes. Mass in beds or use as an edging or container plant. 8–18 inches; shade.

Calendula *(Calendula officinalis)*
Calendula likes cool weather. Its bright yellow and orange double daisies serve well as cut flowers. Plant in fall or late winter for early bloom. 10–20 inches; sun.

Geranium *(Pelargonium spp.)*
Geranium is one of the most popular and reliable bedding and pot plants. It produces season-long blooms in reds, pinks, and white. 6–24 inches; sun.

Celosia *(Celosia spp.)*
Also called cockscomb, celosia produces two flower types—plumed and crested—that come in a wide range of warm colors. Celosia is ideal for edgings or borders, as a fresh or dried flower, or in containers. It likes heat and has a long season of bloom. 6–30 inches; sun.

Impatiens *(Impatiens walleriana)*
Also called busy lizzy and patience plant, impatiens is a favorite for shady spots. It's neat, has a long season of bloom, and is good in containers. 8–30 inches; shade.

FLOWERS *(continued)*

Marigold *(Tagetes* spp.)
Many forms of marigold exist; all have the colors of sunshine. They're dependable, have one of the longest seasons of bloom, and make long-lasting cut flowers. Marigolds are good for edgings and borders, and in containers. 6–48 inches; sun.

Salvia *(Salvia splendens)*
Salvia now comes in white, pink, rose, and a fine purple. It's easy to grow and likes hot weather. Use it in beds, edgings, mass plantings, or containers. 1–3 feet; sun.

Pansy *(Viola ×wittrockiana)*
Pansies are delightful in earliest spring when their painted faces defy the cold. They bloom until fall, come in many colors, and are perfect for edgings, for rock and wall gardens, in containers, and among spring bulbs. Keep flowers picked. Sow seed in August outdoors or in January inside. 6–8 inches; shade.

Snapdragon *(Antirrhinum majus)*
Snapdragon produces spikes of uniquely shaped florets in every color but green and blue and in many sizes. Snapdragon likes cool weather and occasionally survives the winter. 6–36 inches; sun.

Petunia *(Petunia ×hybrida)*
Long-blooming petunias come in many colors and are excellent for bedding and edging, and in containers. 10–18 inches; sun.

Zinnia *(Zinnia* spp.)
Zinnia is loved for its durability and speed of growth. Choose from a wide range of heights, colors, and forms, from button size to 7 inches across. Zinnias thrive on heat and like arid climates. 6–36 inches; sun.

BULB

Daffodil (*Narcissus* spp.)
Daffodil and jonquil produce delightful spring flowers; some are fragrant. Plant them in front of shrubs or as a border, or naturalize among ivy or vinca. Plants will last for years. 6–20 inches; Zones 3–8; sun or light shade.

Lily (*Lilium* spp.)
Aristocratic lilies are easy to grow. Some are fragrant; others are not. Plant in clumps for best effect. 2–4 feet; Zones 4–8; sun.

Hyacinth (*Hyacinthus orientalis*)
Perfumed florets of pink, white, or blue bedeck this flower. Use hyacinth in the fronts or corners of borders, or in containers. Replace hyacinth bulbs every three to five years. 9–12 inches; Zones 4–8; sun.

Minor Spring Bulbs
These include anemone, crocus, fritillary, snowdrop, and winter aconite. Plant in gardens or in the grass. Naturalize grape hyacinth and scilla. 3–36 inches; Zones 3–8; sun.

Iris (*Iris* spp.)
Easy to grow and quick to multiply, irises range from early-blooming tiny bulbs to late-spring regal beauties. 6–50 inches; Zones 3–8; sun or light shade.

Tender Bulbs
These include caladium, canna, dahlia, gladiolus, tuberous begonia, agapanthus, and others. These need to be lifted before frost and stored inside. 1–6 feet; Zones 3–10; sun or light shade.

INDEX

Note: **Boldfaced** numbers indicate building project instructions. *Italicized* numbers indicate photographs or illustrations.

INDEX *(continued)*

INDEX (continued)

INDEX *(continued)*

INDEX (continued)

METRIC CONVERSIONS

U.S. UNITS TO METRIC EQUIVALENTS			METRIC EQUIVALENTS TO U.S. UNITS		
To Convert From	Multiply by	To Get	To Convert From	Multiply by	To Get
Inches	25.4	Millimeters	Millimeters	0.0394	Inches
Inches	2.54	Centimeters	Centimeters	0.3937	Inches
Feet	30.48	Centimeters	Centimeters	0.0328	Feet
Feet	0.3048	Meters	Meters	3.2808	Feet
Yards	0.9144	Meters	Meters	1.0936	Yards
Square inches	6.4516	Square centimeters	Square centimeters	0.1550	Square inches
Square feet	0.0929	Square meters	Square meters	10.764	Square feet
Square yards	0.8361	Square meters	Square meters	1.1960	Square yards
Acres	0.4047	Hectares	Hectares	2.4711	Acres
Cubic inches	16.387	Cubic centimeters	Cubic centimeters	0.0610	Cubic inches
Cubic feet	0.0283	Cubic meters	Cubic meters	35.315	Cubic feet
Cubic feet	28.316	Liters	Liters	0.0353	Cubic feet
Cubic yards	0.7646	Cubic meters	Cubic meters	1.308	Cubic yards
Cubic yards	764.55	Liters	Liters	0.0013	Cubic yards

To convert from degrees Fahrenheit (F) to degrees Celsius (C), first subtract 32, then multiply by 5/9.

To convert from degrees Celsius to degrees Fahrenheit, multiply by 9/5, then add 32.

This book is printed on acid-free paper.

Copyright © 2007 by Meredith Corporation, Des Moines, Iowa. Second Edition. All rights reserved.

Published by Houghton Mifflin Harcourt Publishing Company

Published simultaneously in Canada

For information about permission to reproduce selections from this book, write to trade.permissions@hmhco.com or to Permissions, Houghton Mifflin Harcourt Publishing Company, 3 Park Avenue, 19th Floor, New York, New York 10016.

www.hmhco.com

Library of Congress Control Number: 2006930216

ISBN: 978-0-696-23082-0

Printed in China

SCP 20 19 18 17 16 15 14 13 12

4500698131

Publisher: Natalie Chapman
Associate Publisher: Jessica Goodman
Executive Editor: Anne Ficklen

Step-by-Step Landscaping
Senior Editor and Group Manager: Michael McKinley
Contributing Project Editor: Kate Carter Frederick
Contributing Writers: David Haupert, Bill LaHay
Contributing Designer: Shelton Design Studios, Inc.
Contributing Project Builder: Tim Arends; Nonesuch Design Works, Inc.
Copy Chief: Terri Fredrickson
Publishing Operations Manager: Karen Schirm
Senior Editor, Asset & Information Management: Phillip Morgan
Edit and Design Production Coordinator: Mary Lee Gavin
Editorial Assistant: Kathleen Stevens
Book Production Managers: Pam Kvitne, Marjorie J. Schenkelberg, Rick von Holdt, Mark Weaver
Contributing Copy Editor: Nancy W. Ginzel
Contributing Proofreaders: Pegi Bevins, Fern Marshall Bradley, Sara Henderson
Contributing Illustrator: Abramowitz Creative Studios
Contributing Indexer: Ellen Davenport Sherron
Contributing Photo Researcher: Susan Ferguson
Other Contributors: Janet Anderson

Contributing Photographers:
David Cavagnaro: 118-4, 365TL
John Glover/Garden Picture Library: 368CR
Bill Johnson: 369CL, 380BL
judywhite/gardenphotos.com: 377CL
Rosemary Kautzky: 118-5, 361BR, 383TR, 384BL
Jerry Pavia: 213-4, 376BR, 377TL, 378TL, 383CL, 385BL
Graham Rice/gardenphotos.com: 360CL
Susan Roth: 364BR, 367BR
Pam Spaulding/Positive Images: 359TR
Joseph G. Strauch, Jr.: 370CL, 376TR
Beigette Thomas/Garden Picture Library: 359BR
Michael Thompson: 212-4, 360TL, 364TL, 364TR, 369TL, 374CR, 382TR
Mark Turner: 362CR, 364CL, 384CL
Justyn Willsmore: 362BL, 363CR
David Winger: 363TR

Contributing Cover Photographer: Jon Jensen